# Money and Banking:

*An Introduction to Analysis and Policy*

# Money and Banking:

*An Introduction to Analysis and Policy*

John G. Ranlett
*Sacramento State College*
*Sacramento, California*

John Wiley and Sons, Inc.,　New York • London • Sydney

To all my family,
especially Dad and Pomma

# *Preface*

This book is intended primarily as a text for the undergraduate course in money and banking. Its emphasis is upon analysis and policy; the operational and managerial aspects of banking and finance are described only insofar as they seem to have significant implications for analysis and policy.

The greatest attention is paid to the "what is" of our present-day monetary system. The history, the "what was," is presented only as it sheds helpful light on understanding present monetary arrangements. Finally, my views of "what ought to be" are offered after certain present-day problems are discussed.

It should not be inferred from the above that monetary history is ignored completely. It is not. An understanding of the operation and significance of the gold standard, for example, is vital to appreciate fully the international payments system of today. Similarly, a knowledge of the national banking system and its weaknesses is useful in understanding the development of the Federal Reserve System. But these discussions of banking history are not ends in themselves. They serve to introduce and tie together the strands of the analysis, and to sharpen the understanding of the present monetary system.

The organization of the book lends itself to one- or two-semester use. If used for a two-semester course, supplementary readings add useful material and viewpoints which had to be bypassed or abbreviated in the writing of the text. For a one-semester course, the chapters most readily omitted are Chapter 10 (Financial Intermediaries), Chapter 14 (National Income and Income Accounting),

Chapter 17 (The Theory of the Rate of Interest), and perhaps Chapters 19–21, which constitute Part V, International Financial Arrangements. For a two-semester course, all chapters can be covered at a leisurely pace with considerable time for discussing outside materials.

Undoubtedly a book reflects the viewpoint of the author. It is my conviction that the appropriate goal of the money and banking course is an understanding and appreciation of monetary policy. But to achieve this end, a good grasp of monetary theory is necessary. This book contains somewhat more theoretical material than the usual money and banking book, but it is my belief that the average student can understand the basic theoretical principles involved. Monetary policy, as well as fiscal and debt policies, since they are closely, perhaps inextricably, tied to monetary policy, are analyzed in terms of which variables can be manipulated and how this manipulation can be expected to achieve some given policy. Indeed, the relationship between theory and policy is presented exactly as the relationship between means and ends: theory provides the means and policy outlines the ends.

The germ of the idea for this book was formed when I taught at Whitman College, and various drafts and revisions were tried out on my students at Sacramento State College. My thanks to my colleagues at these two schools for their help and encouragement: to David Stevens at Whitman College, and to Steve Polkinghorn, Marc Tool, Max Fieser, and William Hickman at Sacramento State. They all contributed to the end product by encouraging me, by reading and criticizing various stages of the manuscript, or by the classroom testing of it in their sections of the money and banking course.

My thanks also to Dr. Gerald Pollack, International Economist for the Joint Economic Committee, for helpful discussion and fresh insight into international financial problems. I must also mention my debt to my former teachers, to Edwin C. Robbins, my first money and banking teacher; to Paul B. Simpson, who first interested me in economic analysis; to H. Tom Koplin, whose unpublished work forms the framework for the chapter on interest rate theory; and to Robert Campbell, a fine teacher, good friend, and fishing companion. The manuscript also has benefited from criticism from a number of unknown reviewers, whose comments have substantially improved the final version. To all these people my thanks; I accept responsibility for all shortcomings. And finally my thanks to Mrs. Wini Farmer and Mrs. Carol Brainard, who took my scribbled notes and put them into manuscript form.

John G. Ranlett

November, 1964

Sacramento, California

# Contents

# PART I

# MONEY AND MONETARY SYSTEMS

# CHAPTER *1*

# *An Introduction to Money*

Why study money? Just what is money? What gives money its importance?

Before answering these questions, a few words are in order about the plan of this book. The study consists of three major topics: (1) money and the banking system; (2) monetary theory; and (3) monetary and fiscal policy. The first of these topics, money and the banking system, deals with questions such as what money is, where it comes from, and how its quantity may be regulated. Thus, the first task is to define money, learn something of the composition of America's money supply, and see how the various elements in the money and banking system intermesh to provide the money supply.

After learning how the institutions of the money and banking system—the money-using public, the commercial banks, and the Federal Reserve System—determine, through their interaction, the composition and size of the money supply, we shall undertake a study of monetary theory. That is, we shall try to find out how money exerts its influence on the broad economic questions of the level of employment, level of prices, and economic growth and stability. Like all social or physical theories, monetary theory will be abstract in the sense that not every possible factor will be considered. But hopefully those factors singled out for study are the more relevant variables, for once a body of theory is established, we can then proceed to a discussion of policy.

But though questions of policy are deferred until late in the study, they are hardly of trivial significance. Indeed, the area of policy is

3

the ultimate goal to which this study leads.   However, to understand policy it becomes necessary to acquire a thorough comprehension of the operations of the money and banking system, and also to grasp the significance of money as outlined in monetary theory.   For professional economists, for business and community leaders, or simply to be informed citizens, a knowledge of policy is of vital importance. To this end this study is directed.

## MONEY: DEFINITION AND KINDS
## IN THE UNITED STATES TODAY

How do we define money?   What are the various kinds of money in circulation in the United States today?   Before we answer these questions, let us review briefly why money is important, why it has been said that money is one of mankind's most significant inventions. Money serves as a medium of exchange, facilitating trade and acting as the unit of account for making economic calculations.   Money is especially important in modern times because of the difficulty that would be encountered in carrying out exchange by means of barter.

The primary function of money is to permit the process of exchange, the exchange of goods and services among the individuals of a society. Conceivably, exchange can take place without money.   But in modern economic society this process becomes extremely complicated.   In the typical situation of a person in the United States, the consumption of the individual requires literally the services of millions of other persons.   An individual cannot possibly arrange barter.   For him to carry on transactions through barter, he would have to find another party who needs the goods and services he offers and who in exchange offers goods and services he needs.   Obstacles to finding such a necessary party would mean that in any given period very little trading would occur.   Thus, the principal need for money is to enable exchange.   Money is not desired for its own sake but rather for what it can purchase.

Another problem with barter is that there is no common unit in which prices are expressed.   Rather, trade in a barter system requires that everyone know the price of every good in terms of every other good.   Once money is introduced into the system, however, one has only to know the prices of goods in terms of the monetary unit.

Money, then, has one immediate and obvious function: it serves as a medium of exchange and as a unit of account; that is, money provides the common denominator in which prices may be expressed.

There are additional properties of money or functions of money; these we shall take up shortly. But with these brief observations on why money is important to our economic organization let us proceed to a definition of money.

### The Definition of Money

*Money is anything that is spendable and defined in the unit of account.*[1] The terms of this definition may very likely need some explanation. By *spendable* we mean that money is generally acceptable, that it can be exchanged for goods and services. In this sense, money functions as a medium of exchange. The term *unit of account* refers to the unit in which assets and liabilities are valued and exchanges are reckoned. In the United States, for instance, the unit of account is the dollar.

Later we shall take a closer look into these principal functions of money and the two concepts just introduced; namely, that money does serve as a medium of exchange and that it also serves as a unit of account. For the moment, however, let us scrutinize the kinds of money found in the United States today.

### Kinds of Money in the United States

Precisely what constitutes the money supply in the United States today? To answer the question of what composes our money supply, we need only to determine if something is (a) defined in terms of the dollar, the unit of account, and (b) if it can be spent directly. On this basis today's money supply consists of the currency and coins supplied by the United States Treasury and the Federal Reserve Banks and of demand deposits—deposits subject to check—held at commercial banks.

As Table 1-1 indicates, on June 30, 1964, the public's supply of

---

[1] Other authors have defined money in a slightly different fashion. For example, A. G. Hart defines money as follows: "Money is property with which the owner can pay off a definite amount of debt with certainty and without delay." *Money, Debt and Economic Activity* (Englewood Cliffs: Prentice-Hall, 1953), p. 3. Similarly, we find in Steiner, Shapiro, and Solomon the following definition: "Money, therefore, may be defined as anything which has a fixed and unvarying price in terms of the unit of account and is generally accepted within a given society in payment of debt or for goods and services rendered." *Money and Banking*, 4th ed. (New York: Henry Holt Co., 1958), p. 10. The crucial aspect is, of course, that money is spendable.

money amounted to some $153 billion, with demand deposits total-
ing $119.8 billion and currency and coin totaling $33.2 billion.  On
this date the Treasury and Federal Reserve Banks had outstanding
coins and currency amounting to $37.7 billion, with banks holding
some $4.5 billion of it as vault cash.  As shown in Table 1-1, coins
outstanding amounted to $3.2 billion and currency to $34.5 billion.
The currency was primarily Federal Reserve Notes, $32.3 billion
with only $2.2 billion of Treasury currency outstanding.

TABLE 1-1  Money Supply of the Public in Millions of Dollars—
June 30, 1964

| | |
|---|---:|
| Demand deposits[a] | 119,800 |
| Currency and coin | |
|    Federal Reserve notes | 32,338 |
|    Treasury currency | 2,191 |
|    Coin | 3,205 |
| | 157,534 |
| Less currency and coin held by banks | 4,534 |
| Total public money supply | 153,000 |

[a] Demand deposits other than interbank and U. S. Government,
less cash items in process of collection.
*Source: Federal Reserve Bulletin*, August, 1964.

Demand deposits constitute the biggest portion of our money
supply, almost 80 per cent, but well over 80 per cent of the dollar value
of all transactions are settled by check.  Thus it is apparent that
demand deposits are clearly the most important part of the money
supply.

The student may very likely think at first that checks, rather than
the bank deposits, are the money in question.  But since it is ownership of the bank deposit that the payee is really accepting in payment,
it is better to classify the demand deposit than the check as money.[2]

---

[2] There are times when the checks themselves may be considered money, but the
circumstances under which this takes place are of only negligible importance.
Ordinarily a check is simply a written order to a bank by a person having a demand
deposit in that bank to reduce the payer's account and to make payment to the
payee.  There do arise occasions, however, when the receiver of a check will
endorse it to a third party.  Thus, a check drawn by A payable to B will be
endorsed by B payable to C, etc.  When a check is endorsed to another party
other than a bank, it takes on a monetary significance all of its own—the check has
become money.

Having classified demand deposits as money,[3] we may find it difficult to determine exactly what money is. Certainly we know what coins and currency are—we can see them and handle them. But what about demand deposits, the bulk of the money supply? The puzzling thing here, at least initially puzzling to most students, is that demand deposits have no physical existence. Demand deposits are simply numbers on the ledger cards of banks, "dots" on a magnetic tape, etc., and nothing more. In modern economic life money has assumed a very abstract form. Certainly currency and coin could be abolished, with only minor adjustment difficulties, but to do away with demand deposits would require considerable adjustment and economic effort.[4]

## THE NATURE AND FUNCTIONS OF MONEY

In the modern complex world money performs, as we have noted, two vital functions. To repeat, money provides (1) a medium of exchange and (2) a unit of account. Additional functions of money may be considered as derivable from or subsidiary to the primary functions. Let us take these up in order.

### Medium of Exchange

The most obvious fact that makes money important is the difficulty of carrying on economic activity by barter. Consider, for example, a college professor. This individual has only his teaching service to offer in exchange for the multiplicity of goods and services necessary to maintain his well-being. His consumption habits necessitate the services of literally thousands, perhaps millions, of individuals. He cannot possibly arrange barter. To do so would require that a tailor, for instance, or some member of the tailor's family, desire the pro-

---

[3] Recall the definition of money: anything spendable and defined in the unit of account. The question now arises, are demand deposits spendable? The answer here is easy. While there may be times when checks lose some degree of acceptability, such as when one's identity is unknown to the receiver of the check, only automatic coin-vending machines really refuse a check.

[4] If currency and coin were to be done away with, legal tender would have to be redefined to include demand deposits. Legal tender privileges are usually determined by statute as to what forms of money must be accepted by creditors in settlement of debt. The creditor does not have to accept legal tender if it is offered to discharge a debt, but if he refuses it he may not take the debtor into court to force payment of other than legal tender. Presently in the United States all currency and coins are legal tender, but demand deposits are not. Since bank deposits can be converted into currency at will, the question of legal tender is of little significance.

fessor's teaching services in exchange for clothing; that the shoemaker need his services and vice versa; and similarly for all the other goods and services necessary for the professor's well-being. Such barter arrangements are essentially impossible to arrange. Money is necessary to carry on exchange. Thus, instead of exchanging goods or services for other goods or services, with the attendant difficulties of finding someone who has what one wants and who also needs what one has to offer, we exchange goods or services for money which may then be readily exchanged for the goods and services we need.

The use of money as a medium of exchange has two immediate consequences. First, it makes possible the determination of the terms of trade—prices—and so allows for division of labor and, consequently, for specialization and greater efficiency in production. Secondly, it also allows for an extension of the marketing process over time. In the first instance money functions as a unit of account; in the second money serves as a store of value.

### The Unit of Account

Since every economic unit is both a buyer and a seller, its decisions to buy or sell are strongly influenced by the prices of the things it can buy or sell. The mere existence of a price system enables one to compare choices in terms of the common denominator of money. Without the price system, goods and services would have to be expressed in terms of *every other* available goods and services. If there were only 1,000 goods and services to be compared, there would be 499,500 different exchange ratios. But by allowing the price of one good, money, to be unity, the number of prices or exchange ratios needed is reduced to 999.

Subject to certain constraints, the price of some product will roughly equal its cost of production. The cost of production consists of the cost of the resources used to produce it. And the price of resources entering into production will equal the value of their productive contributions. Thus, in general, the closer each consumer and each producer comes to equating marginal utilities of goods or marginal substitutabilities of production in each unit of expenditure or production, the more efficient is the economic process. Money is essential to this process in a noncentralized, unplanned, and individualistic society. Thus, by the use of money, the economy achieves greater efficiency in production and consumption through the price system by allowing for specialization and division of labor.

Prices lead producers to provide the items consumers want and also cause the buyer to economize on the use of scarce resources. That is, resources are scarce relative to the uses to which they could be put, and are therefore channeled into those uses that yield the highest utility relative to their price, or the greatest revenue relative to their cost. Through the operation of the price system, the individual decisions of millions of people are organized without any central authority or control.

How specialization is encouraged by the use of money was made clear earlier. The professor, instead of exchanging his services for the various items he needs, exchanges his services for money income. This money income he then exchanges for the goods and services he desires. Thus the individual economic unit, whether a person or company, is able to specialize in the activity most advantageous to it, exchanging its own services for money, with which it can then acquire whatever goods and services it might need.

It seems natural for the modern mind to think of money as inherently involving the unit of account. Nevertheless, there is a distinction between money as a medium of exchange and money as the unit of account. The two concepts, abstractly at least, are distinct, since the circulating media may be of diverse forms worth so much in terms of the unit of account but not directly representing the unit of account. For example, the Hudson's Bay Company found that in the nineteenth century a fictitious currency was being developed in its trading activities. The unit was a "skin" but no particular skin. It was equal to about half a dollar. A beaver skin was worth ten such imaginary skins, a fine silver fox pelt three hundred skins, a muskrat pelt a tenth of a skin, and so forth. Here the unit of account and the circulating media were, in fact, two different items or concepts. Quite often in primitive societies it has been found that some standard of reckoning was used, even though actual exchanges were more in the nature of barter. It is a simple matter, however, to keep the two functions of money separate. As a medium of exchange money functions as something real—a coin, a piece of currency, a credit entry in a bank account; but as a unit of account, money functions as an abstract measure of value—the dollar, the pound sterling, etc.

In our modern society the abstract unit of account is the price of a unit of the concrete medium of exchange. That is, we make our calculations in terms of the dollars we actually use in making exchanges, and differentiation between the two major functions of money becomes of small import.

## Money as a Store of Value

As mentioned earlier, money is generalized purchasing power.   Thus an individual owning money may do with it as he pleases—spend it or hold it.   The presence of money makes it possible for each buyer and seller to look around to find the best seller and buyer with whom to do business.   In consequence, each buyer needs to hold some kind of general purchasing power and be prepared to buy immediately when the best buy appears.   Similarly every seller finds it desirable to hold an inventory of goods while seeking out the best market; faced with an irregular flow of sales such a seller needs some store of value for subsisting and making payments during the time necessary to dispose of his goods.   The result of this extension of the marketing process over time is that money as a medium of exchange has also the useful property of being a *store of value*, that is, generalized purchasing power.

However, since economic activity takes place under conditions of change and uncertainty, the money owned by an individual may change in value over time.   And since the price of money is fixed, is unity, what must be happening is that the prices of the other goods for which money is exchanged are changing.   Thus in an inflationary period, since a "dollar is a dollar," the prices of other goods rise and so any given dollar commands fewer goods and services.   That is, the purchasing power of the dollar falls and so the value of money declines. During a period of price deflation the opposite occurs.

## Liquidity

We shall find that one of the most important properties of money is its liquidity.   What do we mean by liquidity?   What do we mean when we say that money is the most liquid of all assets?   We mean that the price of money is fixed and that money can be readily exchanged for desired goods and services.   In fact, it is upon this notion of liquidity that our definition of money hinges.

Liquidity is simply the ability of an asset to be converted into spendable form promptly without any risk of loss to its holder.   Several elements or conditions are involved in this property of liquidity. First of all, in order to be liquid the asset must be readily marketable or transferable.   Second, it must be stable in price.

Money is fixed in price.   Hence, it has the desired property of being an asset possessing the necessary stability of price.   Similarly, money is certainly marketable or transferable because it actually functions as the medium of exchange. In other words, money is spendable; it is transferable. Money has many competitors as a store of value. These competitors are many and of diverse form. Some of them have their value fixed in terms of money. They include such things as Series E Savings Bonds and savings accounts in commercial banks. What is to be noted here is that although these types of assets may be easily converted to money, they cannot be spent directly until this conversion is carried out. Consequently, they are not as liquid as money that can be directly spent.

Other types of assets also serve as stores of value. For example, common stock listed upon the major stock exchanges are stores of value. These common stocks are marketable; they can be sold promptly. This type of asset, common stock, however, is not fixed in terms of value. Its price stability is considerably less than that of money. Common stock may appreciate in price, but it also may have depreciated in price at the time the holder is forced to liquidate it. If this is the case, these assets do not possess the liquidity of money which does not involve risk of loss to the holder. A dollar is still a dollar.

Essentially limitless numbers of assets serve as stores of value. These rank downward from the most liquid of all assets, money, to the most illiquid, whatever it might be. Assets that do serve as stores of value and possess liquidity to an extent approximating that of money— ranging down from money—include such things as savings accounts, savings bonds, cash value of insurance policies, short-term government bills, common stock, bonds, and real estate. The important aspect of all these different types of assets is that each has its own degree of liquidity. They range from extremely liquid near moneys—items such as savings accounts and short-term government bills, which are convertible into money at short notice and have very little risk—to the most illiquid type of asset—let us say real estate for which a certain price is required and for which considerable time might be necessary in order to obtain that price. In any event, all these assets are of such form that they must first be converted into a spendable form. Thus, they are not money but range from near moneys to anything but near moneys.

## SUMMARY AND HISTORICAL NOTE

Money is anything spendable defined in the unit of account. Thus, for us, money is anything directly spendable and defined in terms of dollars—our money consists of currency and coins and bank deposits subject to check.   Of these forms of money, demand deposits are by far the most important.

Money performs certain valuable functions.   It serves first of all as a medium of exchange.   This is the most important function of money. It is the function that makes money important to the economic system and gives money its value.   But money also serves as a measuring rod. It enables us to compare choices so that the economic system may allocate resources more efficiently.   Because of this property we have a more effectively functioning economy.   Goods and services are allocated on the basis of a pricing system.   The various goods and services to be produced, the persons for whom they are to be produced, and the quantities that are to be produced are determined by the price mechanism.   This pricing mechanism is dependent on the measuring rod or unit of account.   Money also functions as a store of value.   In this sense it is an extension of the medium of exchange function.   By serving as a store of value the marketing function is extended over time. A person is able to hold purchasing power and to bargain more effectively: to hold his goods, let us say, until he can get a good price for them or to hold money until the best buy comes along.   The upshot of these functions is that in a highly complex economic setting, such as we have today, money becomes an indispensable tool for mankind.   It is indeed true that money may well be said to be one of mankind's most important inventions.

It may be of interest to note that the use of money may have occurred in many societies prior to the division of labor and exchange of goods. Although this view counters the usual treatment given to money by economists since Adam Smith, that money was invented because of the need for a medium of exchange, anthropological studies seem to bear it out.   Thus, before the exchange of economic goods, there were social situations of other types which encouraged the use of a media much like money.   Religious ceremonies, marks of distinction, gifts, etc., seem to have suggested the designation of some item as a money.   Sometimes the items so selected had some intrinsic value for decorative or consumption purposes, but often they did not.   The stone money of the Yap Islands, the whale teeth in Fiji, were used in ways having little to do with material existence, at least at the beginning.   Thus, it is not the economic man but more probably the ambitious man who was the creator of money.   Most likely money had its origins in social purposes—holiday festivities, worshipping services, gifts, etc.   For a fascinating account of the various items that served as money in various primitive societies, the student would do well to start with the Einzig[5] work mentioned in the references.

## REVIEW QUESTIONS

1. "In a modern economy, money is indispensable." Explain.
2. What are some of the difficulties of bartering?
3. What is the difference between the value of money and the price of money?
4. Is money a satisfactory store of value?
5. Distinguish money from the functions that money performs.
6. How does money contribute to economic efficiency?
7. What is liquidity? Why is money the most liquid asset?
8. Using the current *Federal Reserve Bulletin*, determine the present money supply.
9. What are demand deposits? Why are they money?
10. Discuss some optional definitions of money.

## SUGGESTED REFERENCES

Chandler, Lester V., *The Economics of Money and Banking*, 3rd ed. (New York: Harper & Bros., 1959). Chapter 1 gives good treatment on the functions of money.

Day, A. C. L., and S. T. Beza, *Money and Income* (New York: Oxford University Press, 1960). Chapters 1 and 2.

Einzig, Paul, *Primitive Money* (London: Eyre & Spottiswoode, 1947). Excellent treatment of primitive money and of monetary evolution.

*Federal Reserve Bulletin.* A monthly publication with valuable analyses of monetary problems and a primary source of statistical data.

Halm, George N., *Economics of Money and Banking*, rev. ed. (Homewood: Irwin Co., 1961). Chapter 1 on the nature of money.

Ritter, Lawrence, *Money and Economic Activity*, 2nd edition (Boston: Houghton Mifflin, 1961). A very good selection of readings on various aspects of money and banking.

Robertson, Dennis H., *Money* (London: Nisbet, 1948). Chapter 1.

---

[5] Paul Einzig, *Primitive Money* (London: Eyre and Spottiswoode, 1947).

CHAPTER *2*

# *Monetary Systems*

Monetary standards fall into two general classifications: the commodity standard and the credit standard. The "gold standard" is an example of a commodity standard. There is a subtle distinction to be noted between a commodity standard and a credit standard, and it should be noted well. The commodity standard used as money has a monetary value equal to its value in use for nonmonetary purposes; in the credit standard the money's commodity value is nil, it has value only as a money. Thus, the gold standard, a particular commodity standard, assures its adherents that something of intrinsic value is backing their money system.

In this chapter we shall contrast the views of the commodity standard and the credit standard. We shall also supply an introduction to the evolution of the present-day monetary system in the United States. Only in a remote way is the United States linked at all today to a commodity standard—gold. Rather, all its circulating money is credit money.

What do we mean by the term "monetary standard"? The concept of monetary standard refers simply to the nature and conditions of the issue of the *standard money* of a monetary system.[1] Standard money

---

[1] Some authorities define monetary standard somewhat as follows: the monetary standard of a country is the whole set of laws and practices by which the quantity of money in the system is controlled. Thus, a monetary standard includes not only the selection of a unit of account but also the arrangements necessary for the issue of government paper money, coins, bank notes if any, rules regarding the buying and selling of precious metals, and regulations concerning the expansion and

is that money in which the monetary authority may ultimately discharge its own obligations. Thus, if a nation should adopt the gold standard, it is simply making its paper money and bank deposits convertible either into gold coin or into a fixed amount of gold bullion. In similar fashion, a country on an inconvertible paper standard is making its paper moneys convertible one into another; these moneys are not themselves convertible into gold.

Now let us turn to a consideration of the principal classes of monetary standards.

## THE COMMODITY STANDARD

A commodity standard is a monetary system in which the unit of account is defined in terms of some specific commodity or groups of commodities. At least in recent years, the commodities chosen most frequently have been gold, silver, or both.[2] In the past, a whole host of other commodities have served as principal standards. These have included slaves, oxen, elephants, stones, feathers, salt, and many others.[3]

Whereas it is often assumed that the most generally exchanged economic good came to be the medium of exchange and to be accepted as the monetary standard, this explanation is difficult to reconcile with many of the money types known to monetary history. Although objects have served as a standard of value or unit of account in order to measure wealth and prestige, many of these same objects can scarcely have served as a medium of exchange. Witness, for example, the elephants used as money in Cambodia or the use of human skulls in

---

contraction of demand deposits. Such a definition is, at best, awkward, since it says that every change in the monetary system changes the monetary standard. See, for example, Raymond P. Kent, *Money and Banking*, 4th ed. (New York: Holt, Rinehart, and Winston, 1961), p. 19.

[2] Although metals have recently been the commodities selected oftenest there is no compelling reason for their selection. Whatever commodity is chosen it must possess at least the following qualities: it must be reasonably durable, so that some storage is possible; relatively stable in value in respect to other goods; have relatively high exchange value with respect to its size so that transportability is assured; and finally, it must be available in fairly uniform and convenient units. From these considerations it is evident that many commodities in addition to gold and silver possess the above attributes, for example, wheat, corn, coal, sugar, petroleum, etc. It may be argued, in fact, that a composite "market basket" of the above and similar commodities would make a much better standard than gold does.

[3] See Paul Einzig's *Primitive Money* referred to earlier for an interesting survey of such standards.

Borneo.   The possession of elephants could easily be used to compare individual wealth.   Similarly, the possession of skulls assured a degree of prestige.   But the skulls did not circulate.   Rather pigs and palm nuts acted as the medium of exchange, but were evaluated in terms of skulls, the unit of account.

Indeed, the evidence suggests that barter was not the principal factor in the evolution of money.   The objects commonly exchanged in barter did not develop into money, and the more important objects used as money seldom appeared in the ordinary, everyday process of barter.   Money apparently entered the economic system from the outside.   The items used as money originally were adjuncts in religious ceremonies and other legal or social activities.   Money seemed to symbolize power and status long before it meant good living and comfort.

Although early money was often a useful object, the movement has been from a more useful object to a less useful and more ornamental object.   In terms of the commodity standard this makes sense.   For example, if the commodity were a useful, consumable item, say grain, in time of famine it would be consumed even though it was the standard money.   This, obviously, is undesirable since the means of exchange is being used up.   As noted earlier, moreover, the money material should have a stable value.   Because items that are necessities usually have an inelastic demand, their value is subject to greater change than are the values of luxury goods, which are generally elastic in demand.   Thus, the luxury good, the ornamental object, tends to have a more stable value.   The use of gold and silver as monetary standards necessarily follows, since these are two of the world's most ornamental and decorative metals.

As we have seen, a commodity standard is a monetary system in which the value of the monetary unit is kept equal to the value of some specified amount of some commodity or group of commodities.   That is, the unit of account is defined in terms of so much of the commodity.   Originally "pound sterling" meant a given weight of a particular item, silver.   This was true commodity money since it could be used as money or as a commodity.   In this sense commodity money is sometimes called "asset" money.   It is a true *physical asset* which has two uses: as a commodity, and as money.   The value of the commodity as money must equal the value of the commodity in its nonmonetary uses.

From these considerations the necessary conditions for a commodity standard are evident.   First, the unit of account must be defined in terms of the commodity; and second, there must be a free market for the commodity chosen as the standard so that its value both as money and in its nonmoney use remains the same.   The identity of value in the two uses is the essential feature of asset money.

But even under a commodity standard not all money is asset money. Many times the physical asset is held in storage while a paper certificate convertible into the commodity circulates in its place.   These paper certificates are "debt" money or "credit" money, since debt and credit are the same thing seen from different vantage points.   Thus, silver certificates, for example, are debt money; they are circulating receipts for silver held in storage.   It is just one step further for debt money to exist simply as promises to pay, such as Federal Reserve notes, but only to pay in *some kind* of money and not in a specific commodity.

For a long period of time debt money retained a link to the past through legal and other connections with some commodity base.   In other words, the circulating paper media—debt money—was a promise to pay in some sort of asset money; to pay in terms of the commodity base.   But today this connection has become remote.   Debt money generally stands alone with little pretense of commodity backing.[4] The outstanding example of debt money today, at least the most abundant, is checkbook money—demand deposits.

This evolution from commodity money—asset money—to credit (debt) money is important on several counts which, for two reasons, concern the limitation on the quantity of money.   First, the quantity of physical assets, and thus asset money, is subject to physical limitation.   Second, the amount of commodity money may be altered because of changes in the supply and demand conditions of the commodity.

In the first instance, although there is a physical limit to the amount of asset money that may exist at any given time, there is no such limit to the amount of debt money that may be in existence.   And in all communities, the quantity of money must somehow be limited if the money is to maintain its value.   Since there are no natural limitations to the issue of debt (credit) money, the exercise of restraint by the issuing authority is required.   Many times this restraint has been lacking.   Witness, for example, the hyperinflations in Germany after the First World War and in China after the Second World War. Thus, in modern society the quantity of credit money must be limited by law and regulation.

On the second point, the volume of asset money may be influenced by supply and demand factors.   This volume may be limited by costs of production, as in the case of grain or gold, or by scarcity in nature, as is the case of the Yap Islander's rocks.   The difference between scarcity

---

[4] This, of course, to the utter dismay of the advocates of the gold standard.

and cost of production is only one of degree. When money can be produced, the cost of production—the supply side—naturally influences the value of money. Contrarywise, the use of a commodity as money influences its value as money. On the supply side increasing costs exist because of the limited availability of, say, quality gold ores. On the other hand, an increase in the demand for a commodity brought about by using it for monetary purposes must raise its value. If, say, in a community which does not use money, five cows exchange for one bride, then in a similar community using cows for money we can be sure that fewer than five cows will exchange for one bride. The use of cows as money has raised the value of cows—through an increase in demand for cows as money—relative to brides. Similarly, if an ounce of gold has the same value as a pair of shoes when gold is not monetized, the ounce will buy more than one pair of shoes if gold becomes monetized.

The drift from a commodity standard to a credit standard has been a gradual development over many years. It has had an important consequence, however, in the area of monetary management. From an automatic, market-regulated commodity standard, we have reached the point at which the management of the quantity of the money supply has become one of modern government's most important tasks.

Let us turn now to a consideration of the most famous commodity standard, the gold standard.

## THE GOLD STANDARD

The gold standard is the best known commodity standard. An understanding of its working and its advantages and disadvantages will also serve to illustrate the same for commodity standards generally.

The principal characteristics of the gold standard are these: (1) The unit of account is defined in terms of gold. For example, the United States dollar is said to be equal to $15\frac{5}{21}$ grains of gold nine-tenths fine; there are 480 grains to an ounce, hence, one ounce of gold equals $35. (2) There must be a free market for gold. This means the Treasury must stand ready to buy or sell unlimited amounts of gold at the rate determined by the definition of the unit of account. (3) For a full gold standard the public must also have the right to import or export the metal freely.

Given the above provisions, several variants of a gold standard are possible. We shall briefly mention two of them: the gold-coin standard and gold-bullion standard.

Gold coin was the official monetary standard for the United States from 1900 to 1933, although the United States was *de facto* on such a standard since 1879.   Under a gold-coin standard, currency is freely convertible with gold in quantities as small as the smallest gold coin available.   Not only do gold coins circulate, but also other types of money such as silver coins, token coins of base metals, paper money of various kinds, and bank demand deposits.   In this situation the gold coins are the *standard money*, or the money of ultimate redemption in which all the other money forms are redeemable.   Since these other moneys are payable in gold coin they are credit (debt) money.

The gold-bullion standard is similar to the gold-coin standard. There is one notable difference, however.   Instead of having free convertibility of currency into gold in any quantity, under the gold-bullion standard currency is convertible into gold only in large amounts, and there may also be qualifications as to who may possess the gold. For example, perhaps gold might be obtainable only in bars worth $14,000 each, and only the central bank or licensed individuals might hold it.   In 1934 the United States went on a "modified" gold-bullion standard.

### The Gold Standard, Pro and Con

It is possible to sum up the claimed advantages of the gold standard in terms of three criteria: (1) confidence in it by the public; (2) automaticity of its operation, and (3) stability in the price level.   Let us examine the arguments pro and con for each of these alleged advantages.

### Confidence

The reason that a gold standard promotes public confidence in a monetary system is the belief that gold is almost universally desired because of its intrinsic value.   Gold is valuable for purposes other than for monetary use, which is not so of irredeemable paper money.   This argument is true as far as it goes.   The question is, just how far does it go?   Gold undoubtedly has nonmonetary uses.   It can be used for decorative purposes, jewelry and the like, and it can be used for dental work.   What more?   Not much.   The fact must be faced that gold is principally valuable because it does have monetary use, not the other way round.   For if the gold now held as monetary reserves were ever released for industrial use, the price of gold would inevitably fall.

It is also argued that a gold standard increases confidence because the total amount of money of all kinds—coins and paper money redeemable in gold—is limited by the total amount of gold available for monetary purposes.   In other words, since the issuers of paper money that is redeemable in gold must be always concerned about the possibility of claims for redemption, this is an automatic curb on the possibility of overissue of paper money.   Thus, the people are confident not only of the gold coins but of the redeemable paper money as well, considering it as equivalent to gold itself.

But it is exactly this aspect of the gold standard which has led critics to label it as a "fair-weather" standard.   If people have confidence it works fine, but let some doubts arise as to the redeemability of the paper money in gold and trouble starts.   Runs on banks ensue.   Even though a country may have substantial gold reserves they may not be distributed in the best fashion.   Those who have gold hoard it and those who have paper currency clamor at the banks for its redemption in gold.   In order to protect the dwindling gold reserves the monetary authorities "suspend" the gold standard.   Seemingly the gold standard acts in a reverse fashion.   When confidence is not needed, it is there.   But in times of economic crisis suspension of the standard is accepted as the way out.   Thus, when gold should instill confidence in the standard, in times of crisis, this is exactly the time that the people fear the suspension of the standard and lose their confidence in it.

There is another argument which perhaps needs mentioning in favor of the gold standard as it relates to confidence.   It is related to the notion that the size of the gold stock limits the total amount of money which may be issued.   In this particular view, since an issuer of paper money must stand ready to redeem it in gold, this requirement acts as a brake on reckless government expenditures financed by credit money. Hence, if the government expenditures must be increased, the government must also increase its tax revenues.   For if it simply covers its expenditures by creating credit money, either printing its own or borrowing from commercial banks, people would soon lose confidence in credit money.   They would present it for redemption in gold, and the subsequent loss of its gold reserves would of necessity force the government to learn to live within its means.   This seems to be a compelling argument for the gold standard.   But suppose we examine it, granting for the moment the assumption that the amount of gold effectively limits the total volume of all money.   Governments, like individual people, have emergencies to face, often at inconvenient times.   Limiting expenditures to the available gold reserves is to tie the hands of the government in financing a war, supplying foreign aid to strengthen one's allies, or attempting to carry out counter-cyclical policy to keep a recession from developing into a major depression. Thus, it may be argued that sound financial policy for government cannot be tied to an arbitrary automatic mechanism.

## *Automaticity of Operation*

Under the gold standard it is a simple matter to make the monetary system operate automatically.   The only thing necessary is to set forth the gold reserve requirements and stick to them.   Thus, for whatever non-gold money that may circulate—paper money, coins, or demand deposits—gold reserves in some designated fixed proportion must be kept.[5]   In this situation whenever the gold reserves increase, more money must be forthcoming.   Contrarywise, when gold reserves fall the money supply must contract.   The expansion and contraction of the gold reserve can be due to a number of factors: gold may be imported or exported; there may be new production of gold or gold may be hoarded in greater amounts; changed quantities of gold may be used for industrial purposes, etc.   Whatever the reason, the supply of gold available for monetary purposes determines the amount of money that may be created.   The quantity of money is automatically adjusted as the gold reserve changes.   There is no authority or agency tinkering with the nation's money supply trying to determine if the supply is appropriate or if it should be expanded or contracted.

The absence of monetary tinkering is the heart of the matter. Advocates of the gold standard fear the confusion and possible disaster that may result from inept management of the money supply if the gold standard is ignored.   They believe that it is better to tie the expansion and contraction of the money supply to the available gold reserves than to delegate such power to a few men.   But this view is open to criticism on several grounds.   In the first place, even in countries presumably on the gold standard the monetary systems have been managed, at least since the First World War.   Countries gaining gold as well as those losing gold found it necessary to short circuit the automatic working of the gold standard to prevent disastrous inflation on the one hand, and equally disastrous deflation and unemployment, on the other.   Management of the monetary systems was necessary.

Furthermore, and more fundamental, there is nothing to guarantee

---

[5] For a truly automatic system the gold reserve ratio must be fixed, and it must be both a minimum and maximum reserve-ratio requirement.   That is, regardless of whether it is a fractional reserve or 100 per cent reserve ratio, for every dollar of gold in the monetary-gold reserve there must be issued against it the legal maximum of credit money.   Thus, if the gold-reserve ratio is 50 per cent, for each $1 of gold reserve there *must* be issued $2 of credit money; and as the gold reserve changes the amount of credit money fluctuates in the same direction.   It is not permitted to have excess uncommitted gold reserves.

that the changes in the money supply produced by the automatic working of the gold standard are the changes needed by the economy.
That is, there is no neat relationship between the amount of money the
economy *needs* and the amount of money its gold reserves make available.   For example, the supply of gold reserves can increase because less
gold is hoarded, less gold is used in industry, or more new gold is being
produced from mines.   But just because more gold reserves are
available does not mean that there is need for more money.   The result
can be an undesirable rise in the general price level.   Or if the monetary
gold reserve should decline through increased hoarding of gold, greater
industrial use of gold, the export of gold, or because no new gold is
being produced, then the money supply must fall.   But again, none of
these is necessarily linked to a lesser need for money.   This could
cause deflation and unemployment.

As desirable as it may seem to have a monetary system which functions automatically, the rule of a fixed reserve ratio of gold to the money
supply probably was never completely realized in any of the leading
gold-standard countries.   There were always exceptions and deviations
in practice.   But in the final analysis, why should an economy be subjected to an automatic standard, especially gold?   To do so means
that the money supply varies directly with the monetary gold reserves,
and the factors that affect the size of the gold stock oftener than not are
unrelated to the nation's capacity to produce and consume.   It is these
latter considerations which should govern the size of the money
supply, not the amount of gold in the country.

### Stability of Prices

The last of the three principal virtues claimed for the gold standard is
stability in the price level.   We should perhaps qualify this statement
to some extent.   Most gold-standard advocates do not claim that
prices are absolutely stable, but rather that in the long run the gold
standard will provide greater stability than any other standard.   However, an examination of the price levels during the period 1900–1933
when the United States was officially "on" gold reveals marked fluctuations.   The argument for price stability under a gold standard consequently cannot be argued in terms of absolutes.   The argument is
simply that *greater* stability develops under a gold standard than could
be achieved under any other monetary standard.

The basis for the argument for stability of prices is based on the
stability of the world's monetary gold stock.   Since the amount of
gold available for monetary purposes is relatively stable, a price system

whose monetary unit is defined in gold should also be a stable one. It is true, of course, that the aggregate supply of gold is fairly stable. All the current gold stock is from past production and one year's output adds very little to the total stock. Indeed, the year of the greatest output of gold added only about 5 per cent to the previously existing gold stock. The average yearly increment to the total gold stock is around 2 per cent. The preceding remarks which apply to the world monetary gold stock and to total global production seem to prove the existence of a stable monetary gold stock. But does the conclusion of stable prices necessarily follow?

The argument encountered oftenest in support of the gold standard as a price stabilizer is this: The output of gold and the price level tend to move in opposite directions. As prices move up gold production becomes less profitable and output is restricted because the costs of producing the gold rise, whereas the price at which gold may be sold is fixed—in the United States the price since 1933 has been fixed at $35 an ounce. In a situation where the price level is falling the opposite conditions emerge. The price at which the gold may be sold is fixed, say $35 an ounce, but the costs of producing the gold are declining. Hence, output of gold is stimulated as profits increase. Presumably the situation is automatically self-correcting in a gold-standard country. If prices start to fall the gold supply, and thus the money supply, increases to halt the decline in prices. In the contrary situation, the reduction in gold output as prices rise restricts the money supply, and the price rise ceases. The question is, how effective is this mechanism?

Due to several shortcomings, the foregoing analysis fails to prevent price-level fluctuations. First of all, since the gold stock is an inheritance from earlier years and current changes affect the total stock only slightly, the money supply may change only in small degree. Second, it takes time to produce gold. If prices are falling it may take considerable time and equipment to obtain and process the poorer quality ores which are now profitable. Thus, the price adjustment is delayed. Similarly, after having incurred fixed costs in driving shafts, etc., if the price level rises making it less profitable to produce gold, gold production may nevertheless continue for as long as the variable costs of production are recovered—and perhaps some of the fixed charges, as well. Thus, the money supply continues to increase even though the price level is rising.

Even granting the conditions of an inverse relation between gold production and the price level, of a stable volume of monetary gold, and of a year's output adding only a small amount to the total, the price stability thesis can still be challenged. Thus, an *individual* country's monetary gold stock is not necessarily stable.   Gold may be flowing into or out of the country, thus changing the gold stock and money supply, while contrary changes are going on elsewhere.   And all the while the world's total monetary gold stock is stable in size.   In fact, under the workings of the classical gold standard, inflation and deflation respectively were the necessary companions to a favorable or unfavorable balance of trade.   Thus, the presence of external trade almost guarantees price instability under the gold-standard mechanism.

## Conclusion

The gold standard is pretty much a thing of the past.   Gold's present role is to serve as an international means of payment and store of value. The transfer of gold is the balancing item to settle accounts in international trade.   Although few countries today allow international gold movements to dictate their internal monetary affairs, the loss of gold may be used to strengthen the public appeal of anti-inflation measures. A case in point is the present gold outflow from the United States which began in 1958.

Whatever vitality the gold standard had derived principally from people's faith that gold had some intrinsic value, that it *was* money. Indeed, as one writer put it, this faith amounted to a "monetary religion."   But today the faith is gone, and there remain no useful ends to be served by a return to gold.   Nevertheless, there are those who advocate a return to the gold standard alleging that ". . . gold is the sole prophylactic against the plague of fiat moneys. . . ."[6]   It is essentially the gold standardist's view that to use any standard other than gold is to cheat, to deceive, and to destroy freedom—and that it will lead ultimately to complete moral degradation.

## THE CREDIT STANDARD

The entire supply of money in circulation in the United States today is credit money.   In practice, the United States is on a credit standard, the definition of the dollar in terms of gold notwithstanding.   The present United States monetary standard is sometimes termed a "modified" gold-bullion standard.   It might equally well be called a "modified" paper standard.   For domestic or internal purposes the

---

[6] This phrase was used by the late J. M. Keynes in describing gold-standard advocates.   John Maynard Keynes, *A Treatise on Money*, Vol. II (New York: Harcourt, Brace and Co., 1930), pp. 290–291.

monetary standard is an inconvertible paper standard; money is not redeemable in gold and gold may not be freely bought and sold by individuals.   On the other hand, for external purposes, the United States is on a gold standard since the dollar is defined in terms of gold and the Treasury freely buys from and sells gold to foreign governments and central banks at $35 an ounce.   Dollars are thus redeemable in gold if presented by foreign monetary authorities, but not if presented domestically.

Perhaps the best way of looking at the credit standard is to contrast it with the commodity standard, and to note that a credit standard is in fact a noncommodity standard.   Inconvertible paper is the principal type of noncommodity standard, though token coins may also circulate.   Recall the conditions for a commodity standard: the unit of account is defined in terms of the commodity, circulating credit moneys are redeemable in the commodity, and the value of the commodity as money and for industrial purposes is kept the same by freedom in buying and selling the commodity.   In contrast to this, a credit standard has the following characteristics: the unit of account is not defined in terms of a commodity, the commodity value of the circulating media is practically nil, and the purchasing power of the monetary unit is not kept at par with any commodity.[7]

Although inconvertible paper standards are now the rule rather than the exception, this has not always been the case.   From about the 1870s to the outbreak of the First World War gold ruled supreme.   To be sure, even prior to 1914 there were occasions when nations would go "off" gold and adopt a paper standard.   But these occasions arose during times of war or other economic disturbance, and the paper standard was considered as only a substitute, a temporary expedient, for gold. As soon as more normal times prevailed, the monetary systems would return to the gold standard.   According to the thinking of the period, only a second-class nation would consider any monetary standard other than a gold standard.

But as we have observed, crises did arise and the gold standard was suspended.   Over the years there arose a growing criticism of the gold standard and an increasing movement toward inconvertible paper standards.   Today gold retains monetary significance only in the area

---

[7] Often governments are reluctant to acknowledge that their monetary systems are, in fact, of the fiat or credit type.   The term "fiat" means by decree; so in a fiat standard the government simply designates what the money is.   In the United States, even though we define the dollar in terms of gold, our money is not redeemable in gold; hence we are on a credit standard and the government has decreed what our money is to be.

of international financial settlement. For internal money arrangements, the inconvertible paper standard has proved superior to the gold standard.

The advocates of an inconvertible paper standard state their case as follows: the factors that really dictate how much money a country needs are such things as business activity, the level of employment, the state of development of banking, and other similar activities. These factors are not directly connected with the volume of gold reserves. If the amount of money the gold reserve makes available is insufficient to utilize productive resources fully, the monetary standard should be changed.

The credit-standard school further argues that deliberate monetary management is in order, rather than leaving the system to the automatic workings of the gold standard. Its adherents argue that the money supply should be manipulated according to the needs of changing business and economic activity, not left to changes in the nation's monetary gold reserve. They thus believe the management of the money supply should be delegated to the central bank or some board or agency, charging it with the duty of controlling the money supply to promote economic advancement.

The criticisms of an inconvertible paper standard are the advantages claimed for the gold standard. The two principal criticisms, at least those most often emphasized, are: (1) the danger of overissue; and (2) confusion in international financial transactions. Let us take up the second criticism first.

If two countries are both on the gold standard their two monetary units are directly linked. Since each unit of account is defined in gold, it consequently is a simple matter to determine the exchange rate of one monetary unit for the other. But when the units of account are not defined in gold, the exchange rate may fluctuate over a wide range. This possibility of fluctuation is not necessarily harmful to international trade. In actual practice, however, fluctuating exchange rates may well be a deterrent to international trade.

The principal concern, however, is over the possible excessive issue of paper money. Certainly the overissue of paper money can lead to rising prices and the misallocation of resources, which may work hardships just as severe as those resulting from an inadequate money supply. The gold standard has built-in limits as to the maximum amount of money which may be built on any given gold base; the inconvertible paper standard may have no such upper limit. The overissue of paper money is a real possibility—it has happened on numerous occasions, not only in other countries but in the United States as well. It is interesting to note, however, that in many cases when an inconvertible paper standard was adopted and difficulties ensued, the paper standard was adopted because some type of emergency had previously forced the suspension of the gold standard.

Although the managers of an inconvertible paper standard usually try to control the issuance of money to achieve some goal, such as price-level stability or full employment, the actual achievement of such an objective may be politically difficult to attain. For example, if expenditures of the government exceed its receipts it may become tempting to print new money to cover the difference, instead of raising the tax rate or levying new taxes. The latter type of action is generally quite distasteful to lawmakers—especially in election years.

Although there is always the possibility of overissue of money under an inconvertible paper standard, there are no inherently compelling reasons why an ably managed fiat standard cannot provide all the advantages claimed for the gold standard—except, obviously, the fact that the fiat standard is managed and not automatic—with none of the disadvantages. Certainly since the 1920s the inconvertible paper standard has come to be accepted as the best type of monetary standard for a nation's internal monetary affairs. The paper standards have shown that a country can get along quite well internally without linking its money supply to gold or providing for the redeemability of its money into gold. Similarly, reasonable price stability can be attained under managed inconvertible paper standards. And finally, and probably most important, the inconvertible paper standards have shown that they retain the people's confidence even though not redeemable in gold. On the other hand, in the area of international monetary affairs the paper standards have not proved as successful as the gold standard. It is in this area of international financial transactions that gold retains an advantage, and still serves as a means of international payment.

## BIMETALLISM

There have been instances when a country has simultaneously defined its unit of account in terms of two metals. The classic example of this is found in the history of the United States' monetary experience. The Coinage Act of 1792 defined the dollar in terms of either gold or silver. Since both commodities were metal, the term "bimetallic standard" followed. The rationale for this bimetallic standard in the early days of the United States was a pragmatic one: the United States did not have sufficient gold stock to enable it to go onto a gold standard, even though this was the first choice of Alexander Hamilton, the Secretary of Treasury at the time. Thus, the Coinage Act of 1792 defined a dollar as being equal to 24.75 grains of gold and also equal to 371.25 grains of silver. Given these weights of gold and silver it followed that the ratio of silver to gold was 15 to 1. This meant that 15 ounces of silver would have the same value as one ounce of gold.

The requirements for a bimetallic standard are essentially those for the monometallic gold standard. We have, however, the added requirements that silver must also be redeemable, and that there must exist a free market to buy, sell, import, and export it, just as in the case of gold. In effect, going on a bimetallic standard means simultaneously being on a gold standard and a silver standard. Even though the United States adopted a bimetallic standard simply because there was a shortage of gold, which would not permit the establishment of a gold standard, there are some supposed advantages to a bimetallic standard.

Presumably, under a bimetallic standard, the value of money is likely to be more stable than under either a gold or silver standard alone. The reasoning behind this point of view is that the value of the bimetallic standard will be based on the value of the two metals together, and that fluctuations in the supply and demand conditions for the two will tend to average out. Thus, if gold were to rise in value, the bimetallic standard would vary less than a pure gold standard; similarly, if silver were to rise in value, the bimetallic standard would be more stable than a silver standard alone. But despite these so-called advantages, there are some very real disadvantages associated with the bimetallic standards. Instead of functioning as a double standard—simultaneously a gold standard and a silver standard—it tends, in effect, to break down down into either a *de facto* gold standard or a *de facto* silver standard.

When a monetary authority defines the standard currency to be the specific weights of two metals it is necessarily establishing a mint ratio of exchange between them. There is no way to escape this development if a nation adopts bimetallism. But there is a hazard in the mint ratio accompanying a bimetallic standard. Specifically, the mint ratio of exchange often leads to a breakdown of the bimetallic standard into a monometallic standard. This breakdown occurs unless the mint ratio happens to coincide with the ratio of exchange between the metals in the market. The market ratio is whatever all buyers and sellers of the metals, other than the Treasury, determine it to be. If the mint ratio and the market ratio differ, the bimetallic standard becomes, in fact, a monometallic standard.

Because of the difficulty of maintaining a mint ratio equal to the market ratio, it has frequently proven difficult to sustain a bimetallic standard. This was precisely what occurred in the United States. Even though the Treasury may initially adopt a mint ratio that is the same as the ratio prevailing in the market, there is no guarantee that the market ratio of exchange will not change. For example, there might be new discoveries affecting the supply of either the gold or the silver. Or changes may occur in the demand for these metals either because of changes in tastes and preferences, or because of technological changes in the industrial uses to which they may be put.

Whatever causes the ratios to diverge, the market ratio is assumed to be the correct one, reflecting as it does the decision of so many different buyers and sellers. It is the Treasury, not the free market place, that is overvaluing one metal and undervaluing the other. The consequence of such a difference between the free-market ratio and the mint ratio is that the undervalued metal tends to disappear from circulation. The nation though still legally on a bimetallic standard is *de facto* on a monometallic standard, the particular metal being, of course, the overvalued metal. This principle, that only one metal tends to remain in circulation, is known as Gresham's Law, often stated as: "Cheap money drives out dear money," or "Bad money drives out good money."

### Gresham's Law and United States Currency Experience: Early Period

The Coinage Act of 1792 put the relative values of gold and silver at a ratio of 15 to 1. At the time this was close to the existing market ratio of the two metals. Soon, however, silver began to depreciate in terms of gold. An increase in the production of silver, that is, an increase in supply given the demand for silver, led to a lowering of its value. Also, in 1803 the French Government established a bimetallic standard, exchanging silver to gold at a ratio of 15½ to 1 for French coinage. As a result of these factors, the Act of 1792 establishing the ratio of 15 to 1 for the United States gave silver a higher coinage value relative to gold than it had either in the world market or at the mints of foreign countries. The result of this situation was that Americans receiving payments from abroad preferred the foreign silver to the foreign gold, since any given sum in silver could be recoined into more dollars than could the equivalent sum of gold. In similar fashion, foreigners receiving payments from the United States preferred to receive their payments in American gold.   As a result gold flowed out of the country and silver flowed in.   In time the legal-tender currency was composed almost entirely of silver coin.   The gold coin that did circulate did so at a premium.

The explanation is quite simple.   On a bimetallic standard both gold coins and silver coins are full-bodied.   Since the gold coins contain more metal than their face value, they actually disappear from circulation.   They are melted down into bullion or are exported.   This is simply the application of Gresham's Law.   For example, suppose that the mint ratio were 15 to 1 and the market ratio something approximating 16 to 1.   Under these circumstances, an ounce of gold will command 16 ounces of silver in the market.   But only 15 ounces of the silver are necessary to purchase another ounce of gold at the mint.   This ounce can now be used to purchase another 16 ounces of silver in the market.   If this goes on for long, clearly the mint will continue to receive silver but it will very soon run out of gold.   In the United States this is exactly what happened from 1803 to 1834.   Silver drove gold out of circulation because gold was more valuable as a metal than it was as coin or money.   Let us now try to apply the principle of Gresham's Law to a brief survey of the currency history of the United States.

A more proper statement of Gresham's Law is: "A commodity that has value in monetary and nonmonetary use will tend to move to that use in which its value is the higher."   That is, the use that has the higher value, whether as money or as a commodity, will tend to attract that particular metal.   This, of course, is a basic principle of economics, that any commodity tends to migrate into the use in which it has the highest value.

Under the provisions of the Coinage Act of 1792, gold or silver bullion could be brought to the mint in unlimited quantities by any person to be coined without charge into legal-tender money.   However, in the establishment of this mint ratio of 15 to 1 an unfortunate error was made.   Although the ratio of 15 to 1 was approximately correct in 1792, as time passed this ratio represented an overvaluing of silver as compared to the price of silver in the market, and this discrepancy was increased still further by the end of the century.   Under an effectively operating bimetallic standard, a process of arbitrage tends to shift the overvalued metal (silver) from the market into monetary use and to shift the undervalued metal (gold) out of its money use into the commodity market.   This transfer of one metal out of and another metal into monetary use tends to continue until such time as the market values equal the mint ratio.   For this type of process to work out, the flow of overvalued metal into money use and the flow of undervalued metal out of money use must be of sufficient magnitude to dominate the supply and demand conditions for the two metals in the market.   But at the turn of the nineteenth century this condition was not met.   The United States was then too small and too weak to have any kind of significant effect in bringing about a conformance of the market ratio to the legal ratio.

The difficulties of an inappropriate mint ratio were further compounded when the French set theirs at 15½ to 1.   This ratio was considerably closer to the market ratio than was that of the United States.   At that time the monetary influence of France was considerably greater than the monetary influence of the United States.   The French ratio served to strengthen the market ratio and to offset any tendency for the latter to conform to the American ratio.   The result was to confirm and perpetuate the difference between the United States legal mint ratio and the market ratio of gold to silver.

Since the United States' official mint ratio overvalued silver and undervalued gold, the market value of gold exceeded its monetary value; thus, very little gold was brought to the mint to be coined.   On the other hand, silver was used as money since its monetary value exceeded its market value.   Yet surprisingly, at the same time new silver dollars tended gradually to disappear from circulation—surprisingly, because we have just argued that silver would tend to replace gold and be the only circulating medium.   This is easily explained. These silver dollars of United States coinage were accepted in the Caribbean area and the West Indies as being the equivalent to Spanish and Mexican silver dollars.   But the Spanish and Mexican dollars were actually slightly heavier than the United States dollars.   Consequently, the shiny American dollars tended to be sent to the West Indies, to be exchanged for the heavier Spanish and Mexican dollars, whose silver was shipped back to the United States to be recoined into American money.   The process repeated itself.   The newly minted money was sent to the West Indies, while Spanish and Mexican dollars and bullion were brought back to be recoined.   This tendency of United States dollars to disappear from circulation led President Jefferson in 1806 to order the mint to stop the coining of silver dollars.

The situation continued until 1834.   Up to that year, though legally on a bimetallic standard, the United States was really on a *de facto* silver standard, but the items which circulated did not include the United States silver dollar.   United States fractional coins circulated as did lightweight foreign coins, with the balance of the circulating media composed of bank notes which were often of questionable value.

### Gresham's Law and United States Currency Experience: Post-1834

In an effort to correct this situation Congress in 1834 changed the mint ratio between the two metals. To get rid of the *de facto* monometallic silver standard, the ratio was changed from 15 to 1 to 16 to 1. The effect of this change, however, was to reverse the previous pattern which had overvalued silver. Now gold was overvalued. This result was inevitable because the ratio in France was still 15½ to 1 which conformed closely to the market ratio.

Suppose we consider this in a slightly different fashion. Given the new mint ratio of 16 to 1, silver was worth $1.292 per ounce at the mint whereas gold was worth $20.67 per ounce. Anyone could take silver to the Treasury and receive $1.29 an ounce for it. But in the open market silver was worth considerably more than $1.29 an ounce. Instead of taking their silver bullion to the mint, owners of silver took it to the open market. Silver dollars, being full-bodied coins, were melted down and disappeared from circulation. Indeed, so few were minted in the period subsequent to 1834 that, in the year 1873, the United States eliminated the silver dollar from the list of coins to be minted.

Instead of resulting in a true bimetallic standard, this change to a ratio of 16 to 1 established a *de facto* gold standard. Silver was undervalued. It was not brought to the mint to be coined; even if it had been the coins would have promptly been withdrawn from use as money. Gold, which was the overvalued metal now, was brought in for minting. However, it is impossible to coin the necessary small change from gold. Pennies, dimes, and quarters, for example, cannot practically be made out of gold. If the Treasury had undertaken to coin full-weight fractional silver coins on its own initiative, it would have incurred a continual monetary loss. On the other hand, the Treasury did not wish to issue lightweight silver coins, not wanting to be accused of currency debasement. Finally, a law was passed in 1853 which authorized the issue of lightweight coins.

The effect of this law was twofold. First, the government began to issue small coins because it could do so without financial loss. Second, the coins, being light weight, remained in circulation since they were more valuable to the country as money than as a commodity. Finally, twenty years later, the Coinage Act of 1873 included the gold dollar as legal money while dropping the silver dollar from the mint list. At the time, omission of the silver dollar seemed relatively unimportant, for silver was not then in circulation and silver dollars had not been minted in any quantity for years.

But in this same year of 1873, the Comstock Lode was opened in Nevada. With the vast outpouring of silver metal from the western United States the supply of silver increased so much relative to the demand for it that the value of silver began to decline. Indeed, by 1874 the market price of silver had fallen to $1.24 per ounce. If the silver miners had been able to sell their silver to the mint for $1.29 per ounce they would have stood to have made a handsome profit. But to their utter consternation and dismay they discovered that the silver dollar had been struck from the mint list in 1873.

As the market ratio between gold and silver began to change, the silver mining interests quickly realized that the elimination of the silver dollar from the list of coins to be minted had cost them a sure market which would have prevented a fall in the price of their product. Immediately they attacked the law claiming that it had been conceived in wickedness and enacted in stealth, and demanded its repeal. The silver bloc's demand for the repeal of the law was echoed by the debtor classes, especially farmers who were conscious of the burden of the falling prices on their own production and who wanted the cheaper money they believed silver would provide. Thus, the Coinage Act of 1873, which closed the mint to silver, came to be known as "The Crime of '73." If this crime had not been committed, the nation would indeed have been placed upon a silver standard instead of a bimetallic standard. Gold would have again been undervalued at the mint, and gold coins would again have disappeared from circulation.

The way things turned out, the United States stayed on what amounted to a gold standard until 1900, when the Gold Standard Act of 1900 officially placed it on gold. One should not believe, however, that, subsequent to 1873, the silver supporters gave up—quite the contrary. From 1873 onward, United States history records almost continual efforts by the so-called "silver bloc" to do something for silver.

It is interesting to note that from 1861 to 1879 the United States was, in fact, on neither a gold, silver, nor bimetallic standard, but rather on a fiat standard. This fiat standard resulted from the monetary disturbances touched off by the Civil War. On December 30, 1861, the banks stopped the redemption of both their own and the Treasury's paper currency issues. The Treasury suspended gold redemption the following day. From this time on, gold was not available from either the Treasury or banks in exchange for paper currency. This effectively put the nation on an inconvertible paper or fiat monetary standard.

To help finance the Civil War, Congress in 1862 passed the Legal Tender Act. This Act provided for the issue of some $150 million dollars of United States Notes which were called "Greenbacks." The issue of additional amounts was approved in later years. A final total of $450 million dollars was ultimately authorized by Congress and almost as much was issued by the Treasury.   But almost immediately after issue these Greenbacks began to depreciate in terms of gold. They depreciated to such an extent that, even though in 1853 the Treasury had begun the minting of lightweight silver coins, it was profitable by early 1862 for people to begin to withdraw even this subsidiary silver coinage from circulation.   The value of the metal even in these lightweight coins tended to exceed their value in monetary use.

After the end of the war the question arose as to when the paper currency in circulation might become redeemable in specie.   Even though redemption in specie technically meant redemption in gold or silver it was really redemption in gold, since full-weight silver coins had not circulated in the United States to any significant extent for more than thirty years.   There was, moreover, no real question in anyone's mind as to the desirability of resuming specie redemption.   The basic questions simply were, when to resume, and whether to resume before or after the amount of Greenbacks in circulation had been reduced. What actually happened was that the outstanding amount of Greenbacks was reduced from approximately $450 million to slightly less than $350 million dollar's worth and then in 1875 the Specie Resumption Act was passed.   This Act provided for the redemption of Greenbacks in gold on or after January 1, 1879.   By the end of 1878 the Treasury's depleted gold reserve had been built up to almost $150 million dollars.   As this gold build up occurred and with the redemption date approaching, Greenbacks began to appreciate in value in terms of gold and reached par in the New York Gold Market in December, 1878.

After 1879 the United States was effectively on a *de facto* gold standard.   This was the result of the Specie Resumption Act of 1875, together with the Coinage Act of 1873—the latter, of course, eliminating the silver dollar from the mint list.   It is therefore safe to say that from 1879 onward, the United States was on a gold standard lasting until 1933, although the official phase did not set in until the turn of the century when the Gold Standard Act became the law of the land.

## TYPES OF MONEY

What are the various classifications or types of money?   Into which classifications does our own money supply fall?   As might be expected, the classifications parallel the two principal monetary standards, the commodity standard and the credit standard.   The classifications into which money falls are full-bodied money, representative full-bodied money, and various credit moneys. The following breakdown may be useful.

The first item in Table 2-1 is *full-bodied* money. This kind of money exists when a monetary system is based on a commodity standard. Thus, full-bodied money is money whose value as a commodity in other than monetary use is as great as its value as money. The gold coins of a nation on a gold-coin standard are full-bodied money. The value of the gold as money or for industrial use is kept the same by a free market in the buying and selling of gold at the established mint price.

**TABLE 2-1**  Classifications of Money[a]

---

1. Full-bodied money
2. Representative full-bodied money
3. Government-issued credit money
    a) Token coins
    b) Representative token coins
    c) Promissory notes and fiat money
4. Nongovernment-issued credit money
    a) Promissory notes of central banks
    b) Promissory notes of commercial banks
    c) Demand deposits

---

[a] Adapted from L. V. Chandler, *The Economics of Money and Banking*, 3rd ed. (New York: Harper and Bros., 1959), p. 16.

*Representative full-bodied* money is simply paper money "representing" full-bodied money. It represents a claim to the full-bodied money. The obvious difference between full-bodied money and representative full-bodied money is that the former's money value and commodity value are equal, whereas the commodity value of the latter is nil. The gold certificates that circulated in the United States prior to 1933 were representative full-bodied money.

The remainder of the money listed in Table 2-1 is *credit* money. It will be recalled that under a credit standard the unit of account stands alone, that it is not defined in terms of a commodity. Thus, credit moneys are promises to pay, but not in any specified commodity; their commodity value is negligible because their value derives from their use as money. As shown in Table 2-1, credit money may be issued by governments or by private institutions.

The first *government-issued credit* money shown in Table 2-1 are token coins. A token coin is a coin whose monetary value is considerably greater than the market value of the commodities of which it is made. All circulating coins in the United States today except silver dollars—all half-dollars, quarters, dimes, nickels, and pennies, are token coins: their value as money exceeds the market value of their metallic content.[8] Token coins literally developed to provide the community with its necessary "small change." Full-bodied coins would have to be so small as to be inconvenient for small transactions. Paper money would also quickly wear out with the frequent exchange.

In order to maintain acceptability of these coins at their face value the government issuer must: (1) limit the coinage of token coins—the amount of coinage is adjusted to the needs for token coins, the small change of the economy; (2) make the token coins redeemable into other forms of money; (3) grant the token coins legal-tender privileges. Through the use of these devices token coins circulate with a monetary value considerably in excess of their commodity value.

Representative token money is similar to representative full-bodied money, in that it is redeemable in the token coins it represents. But since the token coins are not full-bodied, the commodity value of the coins or their bullion equivalent is below their monetary value. In the United States the silver certificate is the best example of representative token money, although at present the market or commodity value of the silver represented by the silver certificate equals its monetary value.

The circulating paper money issued by governments may be of two types, promissory notes or fiat money. The distinction between the two is this: a promissory note carries a promise to redeem the note on demand in some other type of money, while the fiat money bears no such promise of redemption—it is simply money by decree. In the United States this distinction is of no significance. Our circulating currency carry such inscriptions as "redeemable in lawful money," but since they are not redeemable in a commodity but in other "lawful money" this means that our promissory notes are really fiat money. The only promissory note issued by the United States government still circulating is the United States Note—the Greenback of the Civil War fame.

---

[8] Presently the market price of silver is approximately equal to the monetary value of $1.29 an ounce. Thus, the silver content of silver dollars equals their market value. The other coins are light weight with a silver content less than their monetary value. The present high market price of silver is a rather recent development; from 1874 until 1962 the market price of silver metal was below the monetary value of $1.29 an ounce.

It may perhaps come as a surprise to some readers to learn that Federal Reserve notes are not issued by the United States government, or that the Federal Reserve System is not a government agency. This happens to be the case, however. Federal Reserve notes are issued by the Federal Reserve Banks which are private, nongovernment, but federally chartered institutions, as we shall see when we study the Federal Reserve System in a later chapter.

The last item in Table 2-1 is *non-government-issued credit* money. Although the table lists promissory notes of both private commercial banks and central banks, the private bank notes no longer circulate in the United States, though at one time they formed the bulk of the money supply. Demand deposits, as we have seen, constitute the major portion of the money supply.

In the United States the Federal Reserve System acts as the central bank. It issues paper currency, Federal Reserve notes, which are credit money. These Federal Reserve notes constitute the largest portion of the currency supply. They are backed by noncirculating gold certificates and United States government bonds or rediscounted commercial paper. They are not, however, redeemable in gold.

At one time commercial banks issued bank notes; this no longer is the case. Although a few such bank notes still circulate, they are retired from circulation whenever spotted. Prior to the Civil War both state-chartered and federally chartered private commercial banks issued bank notes. National bank notes, the notes of federally chartered banks, constituted a major portion of our currency from about 1864, when the bank notes of state-chartered banks were eliminated from circulation by a punitive tax, until 1935. Since 1935 these national bank notes have been in the process of being retired. The only currency presently issued is that of either the Treasury or the Federal Reserve Banks.

The final item in the table is demand deposits, or checking-account deposits. These deposits are a liability incurred by a bank from the receipt of a consideration from its customers. These liabilities are debts which must be paid by the bank as the creditor orders in his check.

Contributing to the widespread use of demand deposits are certain advantages. These include: (1) easy transportability regardless of amount or distance involved; (2) less risk from loss or theft than other moneys; (3) the order to pay, the check, can be made out for the exact amount involved thus doing away with the need for making change; (4) the endorsed check serves as a convenient receipt. There are disadvantages, but the chief one of sometimes having an unknown person's check refused can be overcome by the use of traveler's checks, cashier's checks, etc.

The factors that underlie the expansion and contraction of these demand deposits will engage our attention later.    Although the process of deposit creation and extinction is relatively simple, the consequences of these actions are extremely important and pervasive.

Let us summarize the composition of the United States money supply in the light of Table 2-1.    The information presented in Table 2-1, may be broken down to show the type of money and its issuer, as is done in Table 2-2.

TABLE 2-2   The Money Supply of the Public, by Type and Issuer, in Millions of Dollars—June 30, 1964

| Form | Issuer | Type | Amount |
|------|--------|------|--------|
| Demand Deposits[a] | Commercial Bank | Promissory | 119,800 |
| Silver Dollars | Treasury | Token | 482 |
| Other silver coins | Treasury | Token | 1,987 |
| Minor coins | Treasury | Token | 736 |
| Silver certificates | Treasury | Rep. Token | 1,708 |
| United States Notes | Treasury | Promissory | 321 |
| Federal Reserve Notes | Federal Reserve | Promissory | 32,338 |
| In process of retirement | | | |
| National Bank Notes[b] | Commercial Bank | Promissory | |
| Federal Reserve Bank[b] Notes | Federal Reserve | Promissory | 162 |
| Gold Certificates | Treasury | Rep. full bodied | |
| Less coin and currency in banks | | | 4,534 |
| Total Public Money Supply | | | 153,000[c] |

[a] Demand deposits other than interbank and U. S. Government, less cash items in process of collection.
[b] Federal Reserve Bank notes and national bank notes are now a Treasury liability.
[c] May not add to total due to rounding.
*Source: Federal Reserve Bulletin*, August, 1964.

From Table 2-2 several facts stand out.    First, the entire money supply of the United States is credit money.    Full-bodied coins do not appear in the list.    Though gold certificates are shown in the table, these are pre-1933 certificates which cannot legally circulate.    As they appear they are withdrawn from circulation.    The bulk of those outstanding are probably held by collectors or have been lost or destroyed.

The second thing we note is that the Treasury's role is to provide the monetary system with the necessary small change.  And finally, as we learned earlier, demand deposits are the principal component of the money stock.

## SUMMARY

In this chapter we have investigated the two principal types of monetary standards, the commodity standard and the credit standard. Historically the movement has been from a commodity standard, usually gold, to a credit standard, usually an inconvertible paper standard.  The principal advantages claimed for commodity standards are these: presumably they promote confidence in the monetary system, they are automatic in operation, and they promote price-level stability.  However, these same advantages may accrue to inconvertible paper standards, without the disadvantage of an insufficient money supply if the monetary gold stock is small.  There is the danger of overissue with a credit standard, whereas the gold standard has built-in limits.  As far as actual practice goes, most nations have adopted an inconvertible paper standard for internal monetary affairs while using gold in the international financial area.

We learned also that the United States has had a number of monetary standards at different times during its history.  Initially the United States was on a bimetallic standard, defining the dollar in terms of gold or silver.  The practical difficulties of such a bimetallic standard forced the United States first onto a *de facto* silver standard, and then later onto a *de facto* gold standard although legally, during both these periods, the nation's monetary standard was bimetallic.  These movements to monometallic standards are explained by Gresham's Law, which simply says that the overvalued metal will circulate as money while the undervalued metal will move into its more valuable commodity uses.

When the United States money stock is broken down by type, it becomes evident that all our money is credit money and that we are on an inconvertible paper standard for internal arrangements, the definition of the dollar in terms of gold notwithstanding.  For international purposes we are on a modified gold-bullion standard.

## REVIEW QUESTIONS

1. What is a commodity standard?  Give an example.
2. Distinguish between "asset" money and "debt" money.

3. Explain the principal advantages claimed for the gold standard.
4. What are the disadvantages of the gold standard?
5. What are the principal advantages of a fiat standard.
6. Explain the disadvantages of a fiat monetary standard.
7. Why may it be said that all our money is debt?
8. Since all money is debt, does it follow that all debt is money?
9. Are we today on a gold standard (the dollar is defined in terms of gold) or on a paper standard?   Explain.
10. What are the supposed advantages of a bimetallic standard?   Evaluate the bimetallic standard in terms of theory and in practice.
11. What is Gresham's Law?   How does it help us to understand the history of United States monetary standards.

## SUGGESTED REFERENCES

Chandler, L. V., *The Economics of Money and Banking*, 3rd ed. (New York: Harper and Brothers, 1959).   Chapters 3 and 5.

Einzig, Paul, *Primitive Money* (London: Eyre and Spottiswoode, 1947), Book III, Parts 2 and 3.

Gayer, A. D., C. L. Harriss, and M. H. Spencer, *Basic Economics* (Englewood Cliffs, N.J., Prentice-Hall, 1951).   For an entertaining account of our currency's irredemability, see reading 65, "A Dollar Is a Dollar Is a Dollar."

Steiner, W., E. Shapiro, and E. Solomon, *Money and Banking*, 4th ed. (New York: Henry Holt and Co., 1958).   Chapters 2 and 3.

CHAPTER *3*

# *The Money and Banking System:*
# *Introduction*

The term "commercial bank" refers to those banks that maintain checking accounts, or, more properly, demand deposits, for the public. We have seen that the major portion of the money supply in the United States is in the form of these demand deposits. Because of this fact, we shall begin our study of the behavior of the money supply with the commercial banks. The commercial bank system is composed of 13,669 individual banks, of which somewhat less than half, 6,180, are members of the Federal Reserve System.[1] Slightly more than one-third (4,702) of all banks are national banks with federally granted charters; the remainder are state-chartered institutions. Although member banks of the Federal Reserve System constitute less than half the total number of banks they are the more important ones, holding more than 85 per cent of all bank deposits.

The history of commercial banking in the United States is an interesting subject, but space does not permit its intensive study in this book. What we shall do is to take the present-day commercial banking system, together with the Federal Reserve System, the Treasury, and the money using public, and see how these interact to produce changes in the money supply. The simplest way to understand the interrelationships among these sectors is to examine the balance sheets of each one; that is, the commercial banks, the Federal Reserve Banks, the Treasury, and the public. As we have just seen,

---

[1] These figures are as of June 30, 1964. *Source: Federal Reserve Bulletin*, August, 1964.

all our money is credit money, and since credit is the opposite side of debt, our money is debt, somebody's liability. Thus, to study our monetary system, we shall look at the principal assets and liabilities appearing on the balance sheets of the monetary system—the commercial banks, Federal Reserve, and Treasury—and the money-using public. Someone's liability is someone else's asset, and some of these liabilities, when owned by the public, constitute the money supply. A word of caution is necessary: though all our money is debt, the contrary is not true; all debt is not money. Now let us turn to the balance sheets, and the principal assets and liabilities they contain.

## THE BALANCE SHEET OF THE COMMERCIAL BANKS

The principal assets of a commercial bank include its holdings of coins and currency, that is, vault cash. Also among the assets are government securities of various types, including obligations of the United States government and of state and local governmental units, loans and discounts, and the bank's reserve balance at the Federal Reserve.[2] These are the *principal*, but by no means *all* of the assets which actually appear on a bank's balance sheet. Obvious exclusions are, for example, the bank's buildings and equipment and balances held at other banks.

The principal commercial bank liabilities are demand deposits and time deposits. Again, these are the *principal* liability items. There are some that we are neglecting; for example, the capital account. But the assets and liabilities that we are singling out for consideration are the ones that exert the greatest effect on the money supply.

### Vault Cash

The holdings of currency and coin in a bank's vault are called vault cash. Since this vault cash is issued by the Treasury and Federal Reserve Banks it is their liability and the commercial bank's assets. Because the holding of assets in this form, vault cash, foregoes the earning of interest, a bank will attempt to keep its holdings of currency and coin as small as possible. In the course of any given banking day the bank will have to stand ready to provide its customers with currency and coin should they desire it. But at the same time the bank is providing some customers with currency, other customers are deposit-

---

[2] Since the deposits of member banks constitute better than 85 per cent of all bank deposits, little is lost and our analysis is simplified by assuming that all commercial banks are members of the Federal Reserve System and so carry reserve balances at their district Federal Reserve Bank.

ing currency and coin with the bank.    Thus, holdings of coin and currency can be kept to a necessary minimum.    For the banking system as a whole, vault cash runs less than 3 per cent of the deposit liabilities and is an even smaller percentage of total bank assets.

## Government Securities

The commercial banks hold many government securities.    They own not only those issued by the United States Treasury, but also bonds issued by state and local government units.    For our purpose the obligations issued by the United States Treasury are the most important, yet it must be recognized that the obligations of other political subdivisions are also held.    Unless specifically noted the term "government" shall refer to the Federal government.

The United States government obligations are of several kinds: Treasury bills are obligations maturing in three months; Treasury certificates of indebtedness are obligations maturing within one year; Treasury notes are obligations maturing between one and five years; and Treasury bonds are obligations issued in maturities longer than five years.    The banks hold the above in differing quantities, but until there is compelling reason to differentiate among them we shall simply refer to them as "bonds."    Table 3-1 shows commercial bank holdings of government obligations and other investments.

**TABLE 3-1**    Commercial Bank Investments (millions of dollars)— December 20, 1963

| | | |
|---|---|---|
| U. S. Government | | 63,196 |
| Bills | 11,059 | |
| Certificates | 1,658 | |
| Notes | 22,415 | |
| Bonds | 28,065 | |
| State and Local Political Subdivisions | | 29,786 |
| Other Securities | | 5,173 |
| Total Investments | | 98,155 |

*Source: Federal Reserve Bulletin, August, 1964.*

## Loans and Discounts

For all practical purposes loans and discounts may be considered the same thing.    As we all know, a loan is an interest earning asset for the lender.    The borrower agrees to repay the principal sum together with interest at stated periods in time. A discount is simply a loan with the interest taken out in advance. For example, $500 at 6 per cent for one year means the borrower actually receives $470 ($500 less $30 interest in advance) and repays $500. The true interest is not 6 per cent but nearer 6.4 per cent. What is important for our purposes is that the bank has accepted someone's IOU.

Loans may be classified according to a number of criteria: by maturity, i.e., short term, long term; by borrower or use, i.e., business, farm, individual, etc. At one time commercial banks felt that the only proper type of loan was for short-term productive purposes, such as carrying a crop through harvest, carrying an inventory, etc. These loans were self-liquidating, since as soon as the crop, etc., was sold, the

**TABLE 3-2**  Loans of Commercial Banks (millions of dollars)— December 20, 1963

| Type of Loan: | Amount |
| --- | --- |
| Commercial and industrial | 52,947 |
| Agricultural | 7,470 |
| For carrying securities | 7,862 |
| To financial institutions | 13,084 |
| Real estate | 39,056 |
| Individuals | 34,550 |
| Other | 4,034 |
| Total Loans | 159,003 |

*Source: Federal Reserve Bulletin*, August, 1964.

loan could be repaid. Since the loans arose through the course of normal business activity the volume of such loans would be directly tied to business needs. There could be no disruption of economic activity due to excessive credit because the only legitimate purposes for lending were "productive" ones. This school of thought had many aliases such as "commercial-banking principle," "real-bills doctrine," "commercial-loan theory," etc. Today much of what this doctrine preached has gone by the boards. Commercial banks do make long-term commitments to both governmental units and private individuals, they do loan for real-estate purposes, and they have considerable consumer credit outstanding. The commercial bank today has been aptly described as a "department store" for credit.

Table 3-2 categorizes the loans of commercial banks as of December 20, 1963.

## Commercial Bank Reserves

Most of the reserves of the commercial bank system are in the form of deposits with the Federal Reserve.  We say most reserves, since only member banks are subject to compulsory reserve requirements. Nonmember banks are required to maintain reserves as stipulated in the banking laws of the state granting the bank its charter.  The commonest form for these nonmember bank reserves is as vault cash or deposits with other commercial banks.

Until 1959 member banks could satisfy the reserve requirements only by maintaining deposits at the Federal Reserve equal to some stipulated fraction of their net demand deposits.[3]  Since November 23, 1960 vault cash may be counted as satisfying some of the reserve requirements.

The terms "country" bank, "central reserve city" bank, and "reserve city" bank are carryovers from the National Bank System. Prior to the establishment of the Federal Reserve System in 1913 the predecessor National Bank System classified banks into these three categories.  "Central reserve city" banks, banks in New York, Chicago, and St. Louis, had to maintain all their reserves as vault cash equal to 25 per cent of their note and deposit liabilities.  "Reserve city" banks in 47 other leading financial centers had to keep reserves equal to 25 per cent of their monetary liabilities, but only one half of this (12½ per cent) had to be held as vault cash while the remainder could be deposits with central reserve city banks.  The last class of banks, the "country" banks, were required to maintain reserves equal to 15 per cent of their monetary liabilities, but of this amount only two fifths (6 per cent of liabilities) had to be kept as vault cash while the remainder could be held as deposits with reserve city or central reserve city banks.

With the establishment of the Federal Reserve System the reserve requirement differentials for the various classes of banks, as well as the classes of banks, were carried into the new system.  Recent Congressional legislation, however, ordered the elimination of the classification "central reserve city."  There are now only reserve city banks and country banks.  The reserve requirements and allowable maximum and minimum ratios as of September 1, 1964 are shown in Table 3-3.

---

[3] Net demand deposits means a bank's gross demand deposits, less any demand deposits due from other commercial banks, less cash items in process of collection.

TABLE 3-3  Member Bank Reserve Requirements (per cent of deposits)

| | Net Demand Deposits | (Min–Max) | Time Deposits | (Min–Max) |
|---|---|---|---|---|
| Country banks | 12% | (7–14) | 4% | (3–6) |
| Reserve city banks | 16½% | (10–22) | 4% | (3–6) |

*Source: Federal Reserve Bulletin,* September, 1964.

As shown in Table 3-3 reserve requirements are higher for city banks than for country banks on demand deposits, but are uniform among all banks for time deposits.   Despite recent provisions to count vault cash as legal reserves, the bulk of reserves are held as deposits with the Federal Reserve.   For the four week period ending on June 24, 1964, all member banks had net demand deposits of $109,622 million, time deposits of $98,171 million, and total reserves of $20,431 million of which only $3,168 million was vault cash allowable as reserves.   Since vault cash plays so small a part of the total reserve situation, we shall assume for convenience that all reserves are held in the form of deposits at the Federal Reserve.

These deposits at the Federal Reserve, the commercial banks' reserve balances, can be thought of as analogous to an individual person's demand deposit at a commercial bank.   Indeed, we shall treat the commercial bank's reserve balance at the Federal Reserve as the commercial bank's checking account; and the Federal Reserve becomes, among other things, the banker's bank.   The bank's reserve balance will be increased if the bank deposits coin and currency or checks drawn on other banks.   Similarly, the bank can write checks against this balance or withdraw currency and coin from it.

Originally reserves were required to protect the liquidity of the bank. Now, however, their principal purpose is to provide a means for the monetary authorities to exercise control over the money supply.   The liquidity considerations are safeguarded by the Federal Reserve's ability to furnish additional reserves and currency should this be necessary.   Since the Federal Reserve is the banker's bank, the Federal Reserve can loan to the bank or buy securities from it to increase its reserves or furnish it currency.

### Demand Deposits

Demand deposits are the largest liability item on the balance sheets of the commercial banks.   As we know, these demand deposits constitute the major portion of our money supply.   Since demand deposits are obligations of the bank payable on demand (hence the name, demand deposit), they are obviously liabilities.   But while they are liabilities to the bank they are, at the same time, an asset to the owners of the demand deposit.

Although demand deposits are money, and are the largest single portion of our money supply, this money has no physical existence. As a consequence, some 80 per cent of our money supply has no corporeal existence, unlike the remaining 20 per cent of the money supply which consists of currency and coin.   Demand deposits, that is to say, are nothing more nor less than bookkeeping entries on ledger cards, arrangements of electric impulses on magnetic tapes, etc.   They are only a mass of numbers or some other kind of bookkeeping device.

How do these demand deposits come into being?   To the bank, as we have seen, the demand deposit is a liability, an obligation payable on demand.   For a bank to be willing to incur such an obligation some consideration must be given it in exchange.   This consideration may be the actual depositing with the bank of currency, coins, or checks on other banks.   But these demand deposits may also be created when no "deposit" as such takes place.   What happens is that the bank accepts someone's promise to pay, an IOU, in exchange for a demand deposit. By accepting an IOU in exchange for the demand deposit the bank has created money at the same time, in creating the demand deposit.

The important thing is that the bank must receive some consideration, some kind of asset, in order for it to accept the liability of a demand deposit.   The asset it receives may be currency, coins, checks on other banks, or it may be someone's promise to pay, that is, an IOU. We earlier discussed these IOU's owned by the bank, but at that time we discussed them under the headings of loans and discounts and government securities.   Regardless of the name, they represent someone's debt to the bank, a promise to pay interest and principal to the bank.

The demand-deposit liabilities of the commercial banks are owed principally to the nonbank public (which includes you and me, businesses, and state and local government units) and to the Treasury's Tax and Loan Accounts, into which tax withholdings are deposited until they are needed by the Treasury.

### Time Deposits

Time deposits constitute the second type of deposit liability incurred by a commercial bank.   These time deposits differ from demand deposits in that they are not payable on demand.   The bank may insist on notification of withdrawal prior to the desired withdrawal, though this requirement is seldom invoked.   The technical distinction between demand and time deposits as set forth in the National Bank Act is ". . . demand deposits . . . comprise all deposits payable within thirty days, and time deposits shall comprise all deposits payable after thirty days, all savings accounts . . . which are subject to thirty days notice before payment. . . ."   A further distinction is that banks may pay interest on time deposits but not on demand deposits.   However, the really important point for our analysis is this: demand deposits are money, time deposits are not.   Time deposits are assets to their owners, but they are not directly spendable.[4]

### Summary Balance Sheet: Commercial Banks

The balance sheet for the commercial banks follows.   The items specified constitute only the *principal* asset and liability items of the commercial banks.

Commercial Banks' Balance Sheet, December 20, 1963 (millions of dollars)

| Assets | | | Liabilities | | |
|---|---|---|---|---|---|
| Vault cash | | 4,048 | Demand deposits | | 163,529 |
| Reserve balance at Federal | | | Public | 141,534 | |
| Reserve | | 17,150 | U. S. government | 6,729 | |
| Investments | | 98,155 | Interbank | 15,266 | |
| U. S. government | | | Time deposits | | 111,589 |
| bonds: | 63,196 | | | | |
| Other securities | 34,959 | | Capital account | | 25,677 |
| Loans and discounts | | 159,003 | | | |
| | | | Other liabilities | | 11,978 |
| Other assets | | 34,417 | | | |
| | | 312,773 | | | 312,773 |

*Source: Federal Reserve Bulletin,* August, 1964.

As we shall see shortly, many of these same items will also appear on the balance sheets of the other sectors, the Federal Reserve, the Treasury, and the public.   When they reappear, however, what are

---

[4] Using our definition of money, time deposits are not money.   This definition of money, however, is not accepted by all economists and some interesting empirical studies have been done which include time deposits in the definition of the money supply.   In any event, we must take time deposits and other near moneys into account as important factors influencing how fast and whether or not we spend our money balances.

assets for the commercial banks will be liabilities for someone else, and conversely commercial bank liabilities will be assets for the other sectors.

## THE BALANCE SHEET OF THE FEDERAL RESERVE

As with the commercial bank, we shall pick out only the principal assets and liabilities on the balance sheet of the Federal Reserve Banks. Although there are twelve regional Federal Reserve Banks we shall treat them as one bank.   The presence of twelve banks, instead of one central bank, is a reflection of regional personalities—a distrust of Eastern financial centers.   When the Federal Reserve System was established, twelve district banks were set up so that each could better serve its respective region.   The idea was to have each bank's finger on the pulse of its own district rather than have one "Eastern" bank with a knife at the nation's throat, serving only Eastern financial interests.   Today, however, the policies of the district banks are coordinated, so that little is lost in speaking of the Federal Reserve as one bank, instead of twelve.   We shall adopt the convention of treating the Federal Reserve as a single central bank.

The items that will concern us as the principal assets are gold certificates and United States government securities.   There are other items that appear as assets, but they are on order of 3 per cent of the total, while the assets mentioned constitute 97 per cent of the total.

The principal liability items are Federal Reserve Notes issued, the member banks' reserve deposits, and the Treasury's balance.   These liabilities constitute about 96 per cent of the total Federal Reserve liabilities.   It is apparent that little generality will be lost by concentrating on these principal assets and liabilities.

### Gold Certificates

Gold certificates are not allowed into the hands of the public.   These are noncirculating certificates issued by the Treasury to the Federal Reserve.   Every certificate is backed dollar for dollar by gold.   The certificates are part of the legal reserves backing Federal Reserve note issue and deposit liabilities.   The Federal Reserve is required to hold gold certificates equal to at least 25 per cent of its deposit liabilities and note issue.   The balance of the reserve is composed of United States government securities and eligible commercial paper.   On July 29, 1964 the Federal Reserve Banks owned $15,188 billion of gold certificates.

### United States Securities

These United States securities are obligations of the United States—IOUs of Uncle Sam.   Table 3-4 details recent Federal Reserve holdings of these securities.

TABLE 3-4   Federal Reserve Holdings of United States Government Obligations (millions of dollars)

| Type | Amount |
| --- | --- |
| Treasury bills | 5,137 |
| Certificates of indebtedness | . . . . . . |
| Treasury notes | 24,912 |
| Treasury bonds | 4,711 |
| Total | 34,760 |

*Source: Federal Reserve Bulletin,* August, 1964.   Figures for July 29, 1964.

For the present we shall not distinguish among the various maturities of the government securities held by the Federal Reserve.   It will be convenient simply to call them all "bonds."   Later it will be profitable for us to differentiate among them.

### Federal Reserve Notes

The Federal Reserve notes which have been issued are an obligation of the Federal Reserve to pay on demand.[5]   Because the Federal Reserve has promised to pay they are obviously a liability.   As noted earlier, Federal Reserve notes compose the major part of the currency supply, $32,338 million according to Table 1-1.   These notes range in denomination from $5 and go to the rarely met $10,000 bill.[6]

### Treasury Deposit

The Federal Reserve acts as a bank not only for commercial banks, but for the United States government as well.   Checks written by the

---

[5] They are certainly payable, but only in terms of similar moneys.   They are not redeemable in gold even though backed by at least 25 per cent in gold certificates.

[6] The Treasury issues no currency larger than $10 in denomination.

Federal government are drawn against its deposit balance at the Federal Reserve. This balance, which belongs to the Treasury, constitutes an asset for the Treasury, but since the Federal Reserve must pay checks drawn against this deposit it is a liability item for the Federal Reserve.

While not large in size, the Treasury's working balance at the Federal Reserve is constantly being drawn against and replenished. As we shall presently see, Treasury operations have a significant effect on the monetary system.

### Member Bank Reserve Balances

This is the last item among the principal liabilities of the Federal Reserve. These member bank reserve balances are the legally required reserves backing the deposit liabilities of the commercial banks. At the same time, however, these balances are the commercial bank's checking account. They consequently represent an asset for the commercial banks and a liability for the Federal Reserve since it must stand ready to pay these checks. As of July 29, 1964, member banks had reserve balances of $17,023 million.

### Summary Balance Sheet: Federal Reserve

The balance sheet for the Federal Reserve is displayed below   The items shown are the *principal* assets and liabilities of the Federal Reserve System.

Federal Reserve Balance Sheet, July 29, 1964—(millions of dollars)

| Assets | | Liabilities | |
|---|---|---|---|
| Gold certificates | 15,188 | Federal Reserve notes issued | 32,611 |
| United States government | | Member bank reserve balances | 17,023 |
| bonds | 34,760 | Treasury balance | 674 |
| Other assets | 6,340 | Capital account | 1,633 |
| | | Other liabilities | 4,347 |
| | 56,288 | | 56,288 |

*Source: Federal Reserve Bulletin*, August, 1964.

### THE BALANCE SHEET OF THE TREASURY

The Treasury influences our money supply through its various activities. Accordingly, we shall look at the principal assets and liability items on the Treasury's balance sheet.   First, we shall look at the principal monetary assets and monetary liability items, and then some items that are important for our study, but which "unbalance" the balance sheet.   At this point we shall deal with selected assets and liabilities which are of principal concern to us.

We have already discussed many of the items that will appear on the Treasury's statement.   Among the asset items we find the monetary gold stock and silver coins and bullion, which give us the total monetary metal stock.   These items constitute the Treasury's monetary assets. The monetary liability items of the Treasury are gold certificates issued and outstanding, and its issued coin and currency.   Let us examine these Treasury monetary assets and liabilities in some detail as is done in Table 3-5.

TABLE 3-5   Monetary Assets and Liabilities of the Treasury—June 30, 1964 (millions of dollars)

| Assets | | Liabilities | |
|---|---|---|---|
| Monetary gold stock | 15,461 | Gold certificates | 15,185 |
| Silver coin and bullion | 4,331 | Coins and currency | 5,578 |
| Monetary assets | 19,792 | Monetary liabilities | 20,763 |

Source: Federal Reserve Bulletin, August, 1964.

Table 3-5 shows that the monetary assets and monetary liabilities do not balance.   What has happened?   To begin with, the Treasury has not monetized all of its gold stock.   Some gold remains against which no gold certificates have been issued.   Secondly, the Treasury has made a profit in its silver operations in the past.   It has bought silver at 90.5 cents an ounce, for example, and issued silver certificates to pay for it, whereas for monetary purposes silver is valued at $1.29 an ounce. Thus, against 100 ounces of silver, for which it paid $90.50, the Treasury could issue silver certificates to the amount of $129.

An adjusted balance sheet for the Treasury's monetary assets and monetary liabilities may be obtained in the following manner.   Something is added to both sides of the balance sheet in order to bring about a balance.   When this is done monetary assets equal monetary liabilities.   The two manufactured items are called "Treasury cash," the liability item, and "Treasury currency assets," the asset item.   Treasury cash is roughly the difference between the total monetary gold stock and gold certificates; that is, nonmonetized gold.   The asset item, Treasury currency assets, is formed simply by assuming that the Treasury possesses such assets as silver plus its holdings of other assets exactly equal to its liability for outstanding currency. After these adjustments have been made the Treasury's balance sheet appears as in Table 3-6.

TABLE 3-6   Adjusted Treasury Balance Sheet, June 30, 1964 (millions of dollars)

| Assets | | Liabilities | |
|---|---|---|---|
| Monetary gold stock | 15,461 | Gold certificates | 15,185 |
| Treasury currency assets | 5,578 | Currency and coin issued | 5,578 |
| | | Treasury cash | 276 |
| Total | 21,039 | | 21,039 |

Source: Federal Reserve Bulletin, August, 1964.

Now the balance sheet balances. The only reason for going to this trouble is to have a balanced balance sheet for the Treasury, which may then be merged with the balance sheets of the commercial banks and Federal Reserve to produce a consolidated balance sheet for the monetary system. This we shall not do, however.

It may be noted that the "adjusted" Treasury balance sheet deals with the monetary metal stock only on the asset side. Although the "adjusted" balance sheet is helpful in analyzing the monetary system as a whole, for our purposes the "unbalanced" balance sheet is more useful. Indeed, we shall unbalance it further by the inclusion of a large non-monetary liability, the Federal debt. These government bonds have appeared on other balance sheets so we include them here. Thus, our final Treasury "balance" sheet will list as principal assets the gold and silver metal stock, and the Treasury's deposits at the Federal Reserve and commercial banks. The principal liabilities are gold certificates, Treasury currency and coins issued, and United States government bonds.

## Monetary Gold Stock

The monetary gold stock is the value of the gold owned by the United States Treasury, valued at $35 an ounce. Against this gold, gold certificates are issued. One dollar of gold backs every dollar of gold certificate; in addition, there is a small amount of gold against which no certificates have been issued. Gold certificates can be held legally, as we have said, only by the Federal Reserve.

### Monetary Silver Stock

In addition to gold, the Treasury also owns some monetary reserves in the form of silver. The monetary use of silver is similar to gold in some respects, different in others. The obvious differences are that silver coins and silver certificates, backed by silver, both circulate. Moreover, the Treasury was authorized to buy domestically produced silver at 90.5 cents an ounce, which for many years was generally in excess of the market price. Treasury silver purchases were thus a subsidy to the Western silver interests.

### Deposit at Federal Reserve

The deposit balance of the Treasury at its bank, the Federal Reserve, is an asset to the Treasury, a liability to the Federal Reserve. The Treasury uses this demand deposit in exactly the same way as the public uses its demand deposits at commercial banks. The Treasury makes all its disbursements through checks drawn against its balance at the Federal Reserve. Like the public when its balance gets low, the Treasury has to make additional deposits before more payments can be made. To deposit to this balance the Treasury must collect taxes, issue gold certificates or some type of Treasury currency to the Federal Reserve, or borrow from someone. As we shall see later these different activities have differing effects on the money supply. The Treasury's deposit balance at the Federal Reserve, though kept rather small, is quite active, and the monetary significance of Treasury operations is far out of proportion to the size of this balance.

### Deposit at Commercial Banks

The Treasury also maintains rather substantial balances at commercial banks. But the Treasury does not draw against these balances to make its expenditures. Instead, the Treasury transfers the balances to the Federal Reserve and then makes its disbursements. The deposit balances arise principally through the Treasury designating certain commercial banks as depositories for tax revenues collected through the withholding of income taxes. As these tax deposits build up at the commercial banks the Treasury is meanwhile drawing against its balance at the Federal Reserve. To reestablish its working balance the Treasury simply notifies the commercial banks that on a certain day they will transfer the balance to the Federal Reserve. The operation is very smooth.   Since notification is given the banks prior to the transfer, any necessary reserve adjustments can be made.   In this fashion disturbance to the monetary system is kept to a minimum. Later we shall discuss these Tax and Loan Accounts in greater detail.

### Gold Certificates Issued

The first liability item of the Treasury balance sheet is the Treasury's issuance of gold certificates.   These certificates are issued only to the Federal Reserve.   They are a liability since they are a promise to pay gold if the certificate is presented for redemption.   Because these certificates do not circulate this aspect need not detain us.   Of the very few "old" gold certificates which circulated prior to going off gold in 1933, some $30 million are still outstanding.   These are now redeemable only in other lawful moneys, not in gold.   Since the Treasury cannot spend gold directly, the gold certificates are issued to the Federal Reserve in order to gain a deposit balance against which to write checks.   These same certificates are considered an asset by the Federal Reserve, and also constitute part of the reserve required against the note and deposit liabilities of the Federal Reserve.

### Treasury Currency and Coin Issued

The currency and coin issued by the Treasury are the Treasury's liability.   The currency is a liability because it is a promise to pay, and the coins are liabilities because they are not full-bodied coins, but rather token coins.   The previous statement is not entirely true, since the silver dollar has a dollar's worth of silver in it, at the current market price for silver.   This, however, is a very recent development.   The other coins have a metallic content whose market values are less than their monetary value.   Treasury currency and coin are put into circulation through the Federal Reserve.   The Treasury deposits currency and coin with the Federal Reserve, receiving an equal credit to the Treasury's deposit balance.   Then as the commercial banks request coin and currency the Federal Reserve will pay out the Treasury currency and coin.

### United States Government Obligations

This last Treasury liability is the sum total of Federal debt outstanding.   These United States obligations are issued by the Treasury and consequently are its liability.   As we have already seen, these obligations are issued in various maturities ranging from three months to twenty or thirty years. While these different maturities are technically called Treasury bills, Treasury certificates of indebtedness, Treasury notes, and Treasury bonds, we shall call them all bonds unless we have specific reason to differentiate among them. It should be noted that whereas these bonds are a liability to the Treasury, they are assets to those who own them: the public, the commercial banks, and the Federal Reserve.

## Summary Sheet: Treasury

The Treasury's balance sheet really is not balanced, since we shall include all the principal assets and liabilities and not merely the monetary assets and liabilities. When we do this the summary sheet appears as follows:

Treasury Summary Sheet, June 30, 1964 (millions of dollars)

| Assets | | Liabilities | |
|---|---|---|---|
| Gold stock | 15,461 | Gold certificates | 15,185 |
| Silver stock | 4,331 | Treasury currency | 5,578 |
| Deposit balance at Federal Reserve | 939 | United States government bonds | 312,500 |
| Deposit balance at commercial banks | 9,180 | | |
| Total | 29,911 | | 333,263 |

*Source: Federal Reserve Bulletin, August, 1964.*

The inclusion of the outstanding Federal debt clearly unbalances this "balance" sheet. Nevertheless, because these Treasury obligations play an important role in the working of the monetary system it is useful to include them here.

## THE BALANCE SHEET OF THE PUBLIC

The public's balance sheet obviously includes a tremendous number of asset and liability items. As before, we shall pick out only those particular assets and liabilities of principal significance in analyzing the monetary system. The principal assets of the public are checking accounts at the commercial banks, time deposits at the banks, holdings of currency and coin, and holdings of government bonds. The principal liability item is the debt owed by the public to the banking system.

Since each of these assets and liability items has already been discussed we shall not spend further time discussing them here.   Instead we shall turn to the next section in which the principal items from the four balance sheets are presented in T-account form.

## SUMMARY

The most direct way of summarizing the interrelationships of the asset-liability structure of the monetary system and money using public is to set up the summary statements themselves.   The student should remember, however, that what are presented are the principal assets and liabilities—principal in the sense of their significance to monetary matters.

The T-accounts of the monetary system and of the public are the following:

### Commercial Banks

| Assets | Liabilities |
| --- | --- |
| U. S. government bonds | Demand deposits: |
| Vault cash |   Public's demand deposits |
| Reserve balance at Federal Reserve |   Treasury's demand deposits |
| Loans and discounts | Time deposits |

### Federal Reserve

| Assets | Liabilities |
| --- | --- |
| U. S. government bonds | Reserve balance of commercial banks |
| Gold certificates | Federal Reserve notes issued |
| | Treasury balance |

### Treasury

| Assets | Liabilities |
| --- | --- |
| Gold monetary stock | Gold certificates issued |
| Silver monetary stock | Treasury currency and coin issued |
| Deposit balance at Federal Reserve | U. S. government bonds |
| Deposit balance at commercial banks | |

### Public

| Assets | Liabilities |
| --- | --- |
| Demand deposit at commercial banks | IOU's to commercial banks |
| Currency and coin | |
| Time deposits | |
| U. S. government bonds | |

The student should be quick to see how one sector's liability is another sector's asset. As the volume of these items changes and their ownership shifts monetary consequences are forthcoming. The subject matter for the next chapters is the creation and destruction of these items and how their ownership can be influenced.

## REVIEW QUESTIONS

1. What are gold certificates? What role do they play in our monetary system?
2. Do gold certificates differ significantly from silver certificates in their monetary function?
3. In what sense are gold certificates and commercial bank reserves similar?
4. Draw up the balance sheets for the public, Treasury, Federal Reserve, and commercial banks. Be sure to notice how one sector's liability is another sector's asset.
5. In the current *Federal Reserve Bulletin* look up the composition of commercial bank loans and investments.
6. What are the present commercial bank legal reserve requirements? Consult the current *Federal Reserve Bulletin.*
7. Whose liabilities form the money supply for the public?

PART II

# THE COMMERCIAL BANKING SYSTEM

CHAPTER *4*

# The Commercial Bank System

The class of financial institutions called commercial banks has one important characteristic that distinguishes it from all other kinds of financial institutions. This important distinction is that it alone can hold deposits to be drawn upon by check. As a consequence commercial banks are of considerable importance in understanding the operation of the monetary system, since these demand deposits constitute the major part of our money supply. When we use the term "bank" without qualification, the reference is to commercial banks. The Federal Reserve System, to be called the "Fed" or the central bank, is not to be confused with the commercial banks. The majority of commercial banks, at least from the standpoint of the volume of business they carry on, are members of the Federal Reserve System. We shall discuss commercial banks as if all of them were members of the system.

### The Bank's Balance Sheet

The principal assets and liabilities of the commercial banks are shown in the table on page 62.

Among the principal assets of a bank are its reserves. As we saw in the last chapter, these reserves take the form of deposits at its Federal Reserve Bank.[1] Other principal assets are loans and discounts,

---

[1] As noted earlier, vault cash is also allowable as reserves. The amount of reserves in this form is quite small so we shall ignore this aspect in our analysis.

investments (i.e., government securities), and currency in the vault,
Vault cash is on the order of three per cent of total bank assets.

### Balance Sheet of Commercial Banks

| Assets | Liabilities |
| --- | --- |
| Reserve balance at Federal Reserve | Demand deposits |
| Loans and discounts (IOU's) |    Public's demand deposits |
| U. S. government bonds |    Treasury demand deposits |
| State and local government bonds | Time deposits |
| Vault cash | |

Laws require that a certain percentage of its deposit liabilities—
demand deposits and time deposits—be held in the form of reserves,
that is, as vault cash or deposits at the Federal Reserve. This
percentage, called the legal reserve ratio, is higher for demand deposits
than for time deposits. Thus, against any given volume of deposits
the bank, given the current legal reserve ratios, must maintain minimum reserves. If actual reserves exceed the legal requirements, the
surplus is called excess reserves. If these excess reserves are negative,
required reserves are greater than actual reserves. If the bank should
have a deficit in its reserve position it is expected to make up this
deficiency. Banks are allowed, however, to average their reserve
position over a period of time; reserve city banks average their reserve
requirements over a one-week period, country banks over a two-week
period. Thus, temporary reserve deficiencies are permissible.

### Check Clearing

Since money, as we defined it, is anything spendable and defined in
the unit of account, let us see how demand deposits are spent or transferred to others as a means of payment by their owners. Because
demand deposits are simply batches of numbers in some type of
bookkeeping system, any changes in a deposit account either when
funds are added or checks are drawn, take place by changing the
numbers on the ledgers. The simplest example occurs when the
accounts involved are all in the same bank. In this case an amount is
deducted from one ledger card and added to another. Where several
different banks are involved the process of adding and subtracting
becomes more complicated

Suppose a check payment is made to someone who maintains an

account in a bank other than the one on which the check is drawn. For example, Firm A in San Francisco makes a payment for $500 to Firm B in Chicago. Firm A draws a check on its bank in San Francisco ordering it to make payment to Firm B in Chicago. When it receives the check Firm B will deposit it to its account in a Chicago bank. Once deposited the check becomes the property of the Chicago bank, which has credited Firm B's account, and the Chicago bank must collect from the San Francisco bank on which the check is drawn. This collection is done through the Federal Reserve Banks by means of the clearing process.

The Chicago bank, after crediting Firm B's account, presents the check to the Federal Reserve Bank of Chicago. The Federal Reserve Bank of Chicago credits the Chicago commercial bank's reserve balance and then air mails the check to the Federal Reserve Bank of San Francisco. The Federal Reserve Bank of San Francisco debits the reserve account of the San Francisco commercial bank on which the check is drawn. The check is then forwarded to the commercial bank which finally debits Firm A's account. The settlement between the two Federal Reserve Banks at San Francisco and Chicago is accomplished by wire through the Interdistrict Settlement Fund in Washington, D.C., where all twelve Reserve Banks maintain deposit balances. Thus, the Federal Reserve Bank of San Francisco wires the Settlement Fund to credit the Federal Reserve Bank of Chicago's balance and to debit its (F.R.B. of S.F.) balance. The entire process may be summarized in T-accounts:

San Francisco Commercial Bank

| Assets | Liabilities | |
|---|---|---|
| Reserve balance at FRB of S.F.: −$500 | Demand deposits, Firm A: | −$500 |

Chicago Commercial Bank

| Assets | Liabilities | |
|---|---|---|
| Reserve balance at FRB of Chicago: +$500 | Demand deposits, Firm B: | +$500 |

FRB of San Francisco

| Assets | Liabilities | |
|---|---|---|
| Balance at IDSF: −$500 | Reserve balance of S.F. commercial bank: | −$500 |

### FRB of Chicago

| Assets | | Liabilities | |
| --- | --- | --- | --- |
| Balance at IDSF: | +$500 | Reserve balance of Chicago commercial bank: | +$500 |

### Interdistrict Settlement Fund

| Assets | | Liabilities | |
| --- | --- | --- | --- |
| | | FRB of S.F. balance | −$500 |
| | | FRB of Chicago balance | +$500 |

In the course of an ordinary banking day each bank will have many checks drawn on it and deposited into other banks.  At the same time many checks drawn on other banks will be deposited with it by its own customers.  Most of the claims against the bank will be offset by the claims it has acquired against other banks.  There will typically be a clearing balance each day representing the total change in demand deposits and an equal change in its reserve balance at the Federal Reserve.  If the checks deposited in the bank exceed claims against it the clearing balance is said to be favorable.  On the other hand, if checks presented for payment exceed its claims against other banks the clearing balance is said to be adverse or unfavorable.

The Federal Reserve operates a nation-wide clearing system of amazing efficiency.  Payments between distant cities are made by the adjustment of bookkeeping entries.  Shipments of currency to settle transactions are no longer required.  The number of checks cleared annually run into the billions, and the dollar amounts involved run into the trillions.  The actual operations of the clearing system are, of course, more complex than the foregoing discussion indicates.  Problems arise in the timing of the crediting and debiting of accounts, in accuracy, and so forth.  For example, the Chicago bank may have its reserve balance credited before the San Francisco bank has its reserve balance debited.  But the main outline of the procedure is sufficient for an understanding of the Federal Reserve clearing process.

In addition to the clearing system operated by the Federal Reserve, most cities of any size have a local "clearing house association" which is not directly a part of Federal Reserve System.  Each local bank daily presents to the clearing house the checks it has accumulated against other local banks.  At the same time it is presented with the checks drawn on it which the other local banks have accumulated.  Most of the claims against the bank are offset by the claims it holds against the other banks.  In this process some banks will end the day as net debtors and others as net creditors.  The settlement can be effected by the debtor banks paying the creditor banks by checks drawn against their reserve accounts with the Federal Reserve. The Federal Reserve credits the reserve accounts of the creditor banks and debits the reserve accounts of the debtor banks; thus, the ultimate effect is the same as though the clearing had gone through the Federal Reserve.

## SOME TYPICAL BANK TRANSACTIONS

Now that we have seen what items appear on the bank's balance sheet and have learned how checks get paid, let us look at some transactions in which the bank engages. These transactions will obviously involve the items on the balance sheet. Typical transactions include such things as the deposit of currency and checks by customers of the bank, the purchase and sale of various securities by the bank, and the withdrawal of currency by customers of the bank.

### *The Deposit of Checks and Currency*

Whenever customers of the bank deposit checks and currency, the bank credits the depositors' accounts. Thus, the bank's liabilities increase. However, the inflow of currency increases vault cash, an asset item. The situation with regard to deposited checks presents two possibilities: the checks may be drawn against the bank by others among its customers, or the checks may be drawn on other banks. Should the deposited checks be drawn against itself the bank simply credits the depositer's account and debits the account on which the check is drawn. If, however, the check is on another bank, the bank receiving the check presents it for payment through the clearing process and has its reserve balance at the Federal Reserve increased, while the paying bank has its reserve balance debited.

To show the above latter type of transaction let us trace the changes in the various balance sheets. Let us assume Mr. X deposits to his demand deposit in Bank A currency of $100, a check of $250 written by Mr. Y who is also a customer of Bank A, and a check for $150 written by Mr. Z who is a customer of Bank B.

Bank A

| Assets | | Liabilities | |
|---|---|---|---|
| Currency | +$100 | Demand deposits: Mr. X | +$500 |
| Reserve at FRB | + 150 | Mr. Y | − 250 |
| | +$250 | | +$250 |

### Bank B

| Assets | | Liabilities | |
|---|---|---|---|
| Reserve at FRB | −$150 | Demand deposits: Mr. Z | −$150 |
| | −$150 | | −$150 |

### Federal Reserve Bank

| Assets | | Liabilities | |
|---|---|---|---|
| | | Reserve balance Bank A | +$150 |
| | | Reserve balance Bank B | −$150 |
| | 0 | | 0 |

Should Bank A feel that it now has too much currency on hand it will send the excess currency to the Federal Reserve, thereby increasing its balance by the amount of the currency.   If the currency were Federal Reserve Notes the Federal Reserve would debit the liability item "Federal Reserve Notes issued" and increase the liability item, "reserve balance of Bank A."   Should the currency be Treasury issue, the Federal Reserve would increase its asset item, "Treasury currency."   Were Bank A to deposit the $100 in currency with the Federal Reserve and it comprised $75 in Federal Reserve Notes and $25 of Treasury currency, the balance sheets would look like this:

### Bank A

| Assets | | Liabilities | |
|---|---|---|---|
| Reserve balance at FRB | +$250 | Demand deposits: Mr. X | +$500 |
| | | Mr. Y | − 250 |
| | +$250 | | +$250 |

### Bank B

| Assets | | Liabilities | |
|---|---|---|---|
| Reserve balance at FRB | −$150 | Demand deposits: Mr. Z | −$150 |
| | −$150 | | −$150 |

### Federal Reserve Bank

| Assets | | Liabilities | |
|---|---|---|---|
| Treasury currency | +$ 25 | Reserve balance Bank A | +$250 |
| | | Reserve balance Bank B | − 150 |
| | | Federal Reserve Notes | − 75 |
| | +$ 25 | | +$ 25 |

In this particular series of transactions the banks have not created any money by increasing Mr. X's account; Mr. X's gain has been at the expense of lowering Mr. Y's and Mr. Z's deposit balances and by reducing the amount of currency outside the banks by $100. Thus, no money has been created. Though Mr. X has had an increase in his demand deposit there have been equivalent reductions in other deposit balances and the currency outside the banks.

Let us turn now to a transaction in which the bank *does* create money—that is, a net increase in demand deposits and currency outside banks.

### The Purchase of Loans and Securities by the Bank

Another way that Mr. X can increase his balance at Bank A is to sell the bank a security. This security may be some type of negotiable bond eligible for the bank's portfolio, or it may be Mr. X's own promissory note. In any event, the bank's assets have increased as have its liabilities, the increased demand deposit of Mr. X. That is, the bank pays Mr. X by crediting his account by the amount of the transaction. If we assume Mr. X borrows $1,000—sells his IOU to the bank—the balance sheets show the transaction as:

#### Bank A

| Assets | | Liabilities | |
|---|---|---|---|
| Promissory note: | +$1000 | Demand deposits: Mr. X | +$1000 |
| | +$1000 | | +$1000 |

#### Mr. X

| Assets | | Liabilities | |
|---|---|---|---|
| Demand deposit at Bank A | +$1000 | Note due Bank A | +$1000 |
| | +$1000 | | +$1000 |

If Mr. X had sold a government bond, the only change would be a $1,000 reduction in bonds in his assets, with no increase in his liabilities, thus:

#### Bank A

| Assets | | Liabilities | |
|---|---|---|---|
| Bonds | +$1000 | Demand deposits: Mr. X | +$1000 |
| | +$1000 | | +$1000 |

Mr. X

| Assets | | Liabilities |
|---|---|---|
| Bonds | −$1000 | |
| Demand deposit at Bank A | + 1000 | |
| | 0 | 0 |

Thus, in order for the bank to lend Mr. X $1,000 the bank simply makes a bookkeeping entry in Mr. X's account, crediting him with $1,000. The bank, of course, receives something of value for this, Mr. X's promissory note. But what is important here is that the bank has created money—demand deposits have increased by $1,000.

The contrary situation in which a bank sells a bond out of its own portfolio to a depositor simply reverses the process. The bank's assets decrease as do its liabilities (demand deposits).

If a bank makes a loan to a depositor of a different bank the result is not quite the same. The bank making the loan will lose reserves and increase its loans and investments. But the bank into which loan proceeds are deposited finds both its reserves and its deposit liabilities increased. Hence, even in this situation there is a net increase in the money supply.

### Currency Transactions

We have already indicated how some currency transactions are carried out. When depositors turn in currency to a bank, the bank, in turn, redeposits any excess over its vault cash needs in the Federal Reserve. Thus, we might find the bank crediting the depositors' accounts and having its own reserve account at the Federal Reserve credited by an equivalent amount. Both assets and liabilities of the bank have increased by an equal amount. The Federal Reserve, on the other hand, increases its liability item "commercial bank reserve balances" and reduces its liability item "Federal Reserve Notes issued" if the currency is Federal Reserve Notes, or increases its asset item "Treasury currency" for that part of the currency deposited which is Treasury currency.

Thus, if Mr. X deposits $100 in currency in Bank A comprising $75 in Federal Reserve Notes and $25 in Treasury currency, and if the bank redeposits it with the Federal Reserve, we have the following balance sheet entries:

Bank A

| Assets | | Liabilities | |
|---|---|---|---|
| Reserve at FRB | +$100 | Demand deposits: Mr. X | +$100 |
| | +$100 | | +$100 |

Federal Reserve Bank

| Assets | | Liabilities | |
|---|---|---|---|
| Treasury currency | +$ 25 | Reserve balance of Bank A | +$100 |
| | | Federal Reserve Notes | −  75 |
| | +$ 25 | | +$ 25 |

Conversely, if a depositor withdraws a part of his deposit balance from a bank obtaining currency, the bank has a reduction in its currency assets and also its deposit liabilities.   If the bank needs more currency it will obtain it from the Federal Reserve by writing a check against its reserve account.   The Federal Reserve supplies the currency by reducing its holdings of Treasury currency, increasing its issuance of Federal Reserve Notes, or both.   And at the same time it debits the reserve account of the bank.   This is shown as follows:

Bank A

| Assets | | Liabilities | |
|---|---|---|---|
| Currency | −$100 | Demand deposits | −$100 |
| Restore currency | + 100 | | |
| Reserve balance at FRB | − 100 | | |
| | −$100 | | −$100 |

Federal Reserve Bank

| Assets | | Liabilities | |
|---|---|---|---|
| Treasury currency | −$ 25 | Reserve balance of Bank A | −$100 |
| | | Federal Reserve Notes | + 75 |
| | −$ 25 | | −$ 25 |

## Summary

The above transactions are representative of the business transactions of a commercial bank.   Some of them are essentially of a service nature to its customers: the acceptance of deposits, the provision for withdrawal of currency, etc.   But one type of transaction is of special importance to us, namely the creation of new money by the bank through a stroke of a pen when it buys a customer's promissory note by crediting his demand deposit account. This creation of deposits is quite obviously a simple process for the bank to increase its profits, since the promissory notes earn interest. What, then, is to stop banks from continuously increasing their deposits through lending in order to keep their profits mounting? To this question we now turn.

## THE ROLE OF BANK RESERVES AND CREDIT EXPANSION

The basic factors that limit the extent to which a bank, or the banking system, can expand loans and deposits are the reserve level and the legal reserve ratios. The basic underlying equation is that required reserves must equal the legal reserve ratio multiplied by deposit liabilities. Banks must maintain reserves at least equal to the legally required minimum.

In addition to meeting the legal requirements a bank must, in the interest of bank safety and liquidity, exercise judgment and prudence in its selection of loans. That is, the loans will be limited to those whose default is least likely. Moreover, deposits cannot be increased if the prospect of adverse clearing or currency drains would threaten the liquidity position of the bank.

Originally, the legal reserve requirements were established to protect bank liquidity, to enable banks to pay depositors on demand. Liquidity considerations are now taken care of by the banks' recourse to the Federal Reserve for additional currency and reserves if needed. Thus, the legally required reserve has come to be the central bank authorities' principal means of regulating the money supply.

The reserves in question are the deposits owned by the commercial banks at the Federal Reserve. The banks treat them exactly as an individual treats his deposit at a commercial bank. They deposit to them and withdraw currency and write checks against them. Extending the analogy, the Federal Reserve provides the commercial banks with additional bank services in the form of lending to the banks or buying securities from them. The reserve positions of the banks are simply entries on ledgers, and so may be adjusted by bookkeeping changes.

Having acquired a framework for analyzing credit expansion by the banks, we shall consider two cases: the single bank in the banking system and the banking system as a whole.

### The Single Bank Situation

To begin with, the single bank must weigh the possibility of an adverse clearing drain if it expands its loans and deposits. For example, if a bank purchases securities on the open market it usually finds the seller to be a customer of another bank. This means that the purchasing bank will lose reserves by the amount of the purchase. Even though initiated by the bank itself, this is an unfavorable clearing situation. On the other hand, if the bank lends to one of its own depositors it can expect the borrower to spend the loan among others who are not likely to be its customers. Thus, whether due to its own action or to its depositor's action, the bank making the loan stands to lose reserves through adverse clearing balances. To guard itself against these adverse clearing balances the bank will not lend beyond its excess reserves.

This general rule of thumb, that a single bank lend no more in a day than its excess reserves at the beginning of the day, is reasonably accurate. There are circumstances, however, which may alter it somewhat and allow a bank to lend even more. It is not uncommon that, in granting a loan, the bank may require the customer to maintain some specific minimum balance in his account. Thus, any adverse clearing arising from this loan may be less than the amount of the loan. This is the case if any part of the loan is needed to maintain the minimum balance.

Other circumstances in which banks undertake greater loan expansion than the amount of excess reserves allowed would be when the bank is in a region having a favorable clearing balance, when other banks are expanding their loans rapidly, or when the bank knows the bulk of the amount loaned would be paid to individuals who were its customers. In addition to these factors, currency withdrawals and time deposits further complicate the matter. These considerations will be taken up shortly, but let us first consider an example using the rule of thumb that a single bank may not safely loan more than its excess reserves.

Let us assume that the Z National Bank has the following balance sheet at the beginning of a banking day:

### The Z National Bank

| Assets | | Liabilities | |
|---|---|---|---|
| Reserves at FRB | $10,000 | Demand deposits | $30,000 |
| Loans | 40,000 | Time deposits | 20,000 |
| | $50,000 | | $50,000 |

We assume that legal reserve ratios for this bank are 20 per cent for demand deposits and 5 per cent for time deposits. We shall further assume the bank is interested in maximizing profit, so that when loan opportunities of suitable quality present themselves the bank will, whenever possible, act on them.

We see that the bank has excess reserves:

$$
\begin{aligned}
\$30{,}000 \times 20\% &= \$6{,}000 \text{ required for demand deposits} \\
20{,}000 \times 5\% &= \underline{1{,}000 \text{ required for time deposits}} \\
&= \$7{,}000 \text{ required reserves}
\end{aligned}
$$

Since excess reserves equal actual reserves less required reserves, excess reserves = $10,000 − $7,000 = $3,000. Clearly if the Z National Bank were to make loans or buy securities merely by crediting an account it could purchase securities totaling $15,000, since $3,000 is 20 per cent of $15,000. Assuming that the bank does purchase this amount of promissory notes its balance sheet will now look like this·

### Z National Bank

| Assets | | Liabilities | |
|---|---|---|---|
| Reserves at FRB | $10,000 | Demand deposits | $45,000 |
| Loans | 55,000 | Time deposits | 20,000 |
| | $65,000 | | $65,000 |

The bank is now in equilibrium. It has no excess reserves, and its total reserves are in fact required reserves. But if these newly created deposits are withdrawn by check and deposited into other banks, as is most likely to be the case, what happens?

We know that the banks receiving the checks drawn on Z National Bank will credit their depositors' accounts and then present the checks for payment themselves through the clearing system of the Federal Reserve. When this settlement occurs the Federal Reserve will credit the other banks' reserve accounts $15,000 and debit Z National Bank's reserve $15,000—but Z National Bank has only $10,000 in its reserve balance. It will be forced to liquidate part of its loans or borrow from the Federal Reserve or both in order to obtain an additional $5,000 in reserves just to meet the clearing drain. But this leaves it with $30,000 in demand deposits and $20,000 in time deposits and it requires $7,000 of reserves for these deposit liabilities. Thus, an additional liquidation of assets is in order to bring about a balance. The result of all these manipulations is to end up eventually with deposits totaling $50,000 ($30,000 demand deposits and $20,000 time deposits), required reserves of $7,000, and loans and investments of $43,000. These transactions may be set forth in T-account form as follows.

Z National Bank

| Assets | | | Liabilities | |
|---|---|---|---|---|
| Reserve balance at FRB | | $10,000 | Demand deposits | $30,000 |
| Required: | $7,000 | | Time deposits | 20,000 |
| Excess: | 3,000 | | | |
| Loans | | 40,000 | | |
| | | $50,000 | | $50,000 |

Expanding loans and deposits by the full $15,000 we obtain

| Assets | | | Liabilities | |
|---|---|---|---|---|
| Reserve balance at FRB | | $10,000 | Demand deposits | $45,000 |
| Required: | $10,000 | | Time deposits | 20,000 |
| Excess: | 0 | | | |
| Loans | | 55,000 | | |
| | | $65,000 | | $65.000 |

But when the new deposits are drawn against we find that $5,000 of loans must be liquidated to provide funds to meet the clearing drain.

| Assets | | | Liabilities | |
|---|---|---|---|---|
| Reserve balance at FRB | | $   0 | Demand deposits | $30,000 |
| Required: | $7,000 | | Time deposits | 20,000 |
| Excess: | −7,000 | | | |
| Loans | | 50,000 | | |
| | | $50,000 | | $50,000 |

Since we need required reserves of $7,000, there must be a further liquidation of loans until finally we have

| Assets | | | Liabilities | |
|---|---|---|---|---|
| Reserve balance at FRB | | $ 7,000 | Demand deposits | $30,000 |
| Required: | $7,000 | | Time deposits | 20,000 |
| Excess: | 0 | | | |
| Loans | | 43,000 | | |
| | | $50,000 | | $50,000 |

From this analysis we can see that the final equilibrium consists of the bank having lost reserves equal to $3,000, the original amount of excess reserves, and increased its loans and investments by $3,000. Certainly much less painful would have been a simple increase in loans by the amount of excess reserves, since the clearing drain could then be met by the excess reserves on hand.   Thus, we would have:

### Z National Bank

| Assets | | | Liabilities | |
| --- | --- | --- | --- | --- |
| Reserve balance at FRB | | $10,000 | Demand deposits | $30,000 |
| Required: | $7,000 | | Time deposits | 20,000 |
| Excess: | 3,000 | | | |
| Loans | | 40,000 | | |
| | | $50,000 | | $50,000 |

Increasing loans and deposits by $3,000, the amount of the excess reserves, we have:

| Assets | | | Liabilities | |
| --- | --- | --- | --- | --- |
| Reserve balance at FRB | | $10,000 | Demand deposits | $33,000 |
| Required: | $7,600 | | Time deposits | 20,000 |
| Excess | 2,400 | | | |
| Loans | | 43,000 | | |
| | | $53,000 | | $53,000 |

When the new demand deposits of $3,000 are now drawn against reserves are sufficient to meet the clearing drain and still leave the required reserve amount:

| Assets | | | Liabilities | |
| --- | --- | --- | --- | --- |
| Reserve balance at FRB | | $ 7,000 | Demand deposits | $30,000 |
| Required: | $7,000 | | Time deposits | 20,000 |
| Excess: | 0 | | | |
| Loans | | 43,000 | | |
| | | $50,000 | | $50,000 |

All reserves are now committed, and earning assets have been increased by $3,000, the increase in the bank's loan portfolio.

The reasonableness of this rule of thumb for the single bank should now be evident.   It is only when all the checks are redeposited into Z National Bank that it does not have to face a clearing drain.   If the borrower should want currency the effects are the same as the clearing drain, since to obtain currency the bank must withdraw from its reserve balance.

In any particular situation the rule that an individual bank may expand its loans and deposits by an amount equal to its excess reserves may need some modification, but it certainly provides a useful first approximation of the lending potential of the single bank.

Let us move on to the system of banks.   What is the situation here?

## Expansion for the Banking System

As we have seen, the individual bank is limited in its ability to expand because of adverse clearing balances.   Thus, the individual bank can safely lend only about the amount of its excess reserves.   But the banking system as a whole can lend more than this.   Since the clearing drain simply transfers reserves from one bank to another without destroying the reserves, the clearing drain does not exist for the system as a whole.   What one bank loses through an adverse clearing balance is another bank's gain, a favorable clearing balance for the recipient. As a result, the excess reserves do not disappear until deposits for the banking system as a whole have increased several times the amount of the excess reserves; that is, until the excess reserves have become required reserves through an increase in deposits.

Ignoring for the time being the complications of currency and time deposits, the basic relationship is that loans and deposits, $D$, may be expanded by an amount expressed by the reciprocal of the legal reserve ratio requirement on demand deposits, $R$, times the amount of excess reserves, $X$.   That is, $D = X\left(\dfrac{1}{R}\right)$.   For example, if the legal reserve ratio is 20 per cent and if excess reserves are $1,000, then loans and deposits may be expanded by $D = \$1,000 \times 5 = \$5,000$.

Generally it is better to figure the expansion potential on the basis of excess reserves, rather than trying to use total reserves.   For example, if we were to ask what expansion would be possible from new reserves coming into being on the basis of a currency deposit of $1,000 we would need to be careful.   The depositor has exchanged $1,000 currency for a $1,000 increase in his demand deposit.   And the bank, on depositing the currency at the Federal Reserve, has its reserve balance credited by $1,000.   But excess reserves are only $800, since with increased deposit liabilities of $1,000 the bank must increase its required reserve by $200.   Thus, the potential increase in loans and deposits is $D = \$800 \times 5 = \$4,000$.

Since the commercial bank system is composed of well over 13,000 individual banks, any expansion in deposits for the system must be accomplished through the actions of the individual banks. But if each individual bank can expand its loans and deposits only by the approximate amount of its excess reserves, how can the system effect a multiple expansion of loans and deposits?

As noted earlier, a bank's loss of reserves through the clearing process does not destroy the reserves, but simply transfers them to another bank. Let us continue for the moment to ignore currency drains and time deposits, and trace the process whereby the system of banks can achieve a multiple expansion of loans and deposits.

We shall assume a 20 per cent legal reserve ratio for demand deposits and further assume a deposit of $1,000 in currency into Bank A. This results in an increase in deposit liabilities for Bank A of $1,000 against which it must maintain legally required reserves of $200. But Bank A deposits the currency with its Federal Reserve Bank so it has increased reserves by $1,000, leaving it with $800 excess reserves. Its balance sheet appears as follows:

Bank A

| Assets | | Liabilities | |
|---|---|---|---|
| Reserves | $1,000 | Demand deposits | $1,000 |
| Required res. = | $200 | | • |
| Excess res. = | $800 | | |

This presence of excess reserves gives Bank A the basis for an expansion of its loans and deposits. If Bank A expanded its loans and deposits by the amount of its excess reserves its balance sheet would then change to:

Bank A

| Assets | | Liabilities | |
|---|---|---|---|
| Reserves | $1,000 | Demand deposits | $1,000 (original) |
| Loans | $ 800 | | $ 800 (new) |

But presumably the borrower borrowed in order to spend. Consequently, when the borrower writes checks against his newly created deposit the checks are likely to be deposited into another bank or banks. Let us designate as Bank B the banks receiving these checks drawn on Bank A. Thus, Bank B increases its deposit liabilities by $800 when the checks drawn on Bank A are deposited with it. Bank B sends the checks to the Federal Reserve in order to collect on them. The Federal Reserve credits Bank B's reserve balance by $800 and debits Bank

A's reserve balance by $800. The checks are then returned to Bank A which debits the borrower's account by $800 and returns the cancelled checks to him. The result of this clearing process shows on the balance sheet as:

Bank A

| Assets | | Liabilities | |
|---|---|---|---|
| Reserves ($1000–$800) | $200 | Demand deposits | $1000 (original) |
| Loans | $800 | | |

and for B as:

Bank B

| Assets | | Liabilities | |
|---|---|---|---|
| Reserves | $800 | Demand deposits | $800 |
| Required res. = | $160 | | |
| Excess res. = | $640 | | |

As noted on the balance sheet of Bank B, the increased deposit liabilities of $800 accompanied by an equivalent increase in reserves of $800 has resulted in excess reserves of $640. Thus, Bank B is now in a position to expand its loans and deposits by the amount of its excess reserves. When it does this the balance sheet becomes:

Bank B

| Assets | | Liabilities | |
|---|---|---|---|
| Reserves | $800 | Demand deposits | $800 |
| Loans | $640 | | $640 new |

But here, too, the loan is negotiated in order to make expenditures. Thus, when checks are drawn against the newly created demand deposit and deposited into other banks, Bank B incurs an adverse clearing balance. The receiving banks, call them Bank C, increase their depositors' accounts by $640 and send the checks to the Federal Reserve for collection. The Federal Reserve credits Bank C's reserve balance by $640 and debits Bank B's reserve balance by the same amount. The checks are then sent to Bank B which debits the customer's account and returns the cancelled checks. The result of this on the balance sheet is:

Bank B

| Assets | | Liabilities | |
|---|---|---|---|
| Reserves ($800–$640) | $160 | Demand deposits | $800 |
| Loans | $640 | | |

and for Bank C is:

Bank C

| Assets | | | Liabilities | |
|---|---|---|---|---|
| Reserves | | $640 | Demand deposits | $640 |
| Required res. = | $128 | | | |
| Excess res. = | $512 | | | |

Again we see that excess reserves appear, this time in the amount of $512. In the manner described, Bank C could expand its loans and deposits by $512, incur an adverse clearing balance, and lose $512 of reserves to Bank D, which receives the $512 of checks drawn on Bank C. Bank D would now have the excess reserves of about $410 and the process would continue.

How long will this expansion continue? It will continue to operate until all the original $800 excess reserves have been parcelled out among the various banks and have become required reserves. When all excess reserves have become required reserves the expansion process stops. The sequence of deposit expansion and the reserve position of the single banks and the system may be summarized as follows:

| | Increase in Deposits | | Increase in Reserves |
|---|---|---|---|
| Bank | Each Single Bank | Cumulative Increase for System | Each Single Bank |
| A | $1,000 | $1,000 | $200 |
| B | 800 | 1,800 | 160 |
| C | 640 | 2,440 | 128 |
| D | 512 | 2,952 | 102 |
| E | 410 | 3,362 | 82 |
| — | — | — | — |
| Totals: | $5,000 | | $1,000 = increase in reserves for system |

The ultimate increase of deposits is $5,000, which comprises the initial deposit of $1,000 in currency and a subsequent expansion of $4,000 in deposits on the basis of the $800 excess reserves created by the initial deposit.

Just how fast the expansion process operates is hard to say. Figures on reserve positions seem to indicate, however, that when the banking system obtains new reserves, little time lag in deposit expansion exists though the expansion is faster when city banks get the reserves.

## Currency and Time Deposit Complications

We are now ready to drop the fiction that the public does not hold currency or time deposits.   The public does own time deposits and currency, as well as demand deposits.   Let us assume that the disposition of the public is to hold roughly 50 cents in time deposits and 25 cents in currency for each one dollar of demand deposits.   The presence of these time deposits and currency holdings reduces the expansion potential of any given volume of excess reserves.

Heretofore, we assumed no currency or time deposit complications. Accordingly, we argued that deposit liabilities (demand deposits) could expand in an amount determined by $D = X/R$, where $D$ is deposit expansion, $X$ is excess reserves, and $R$ is the legal reserve ratio against demand deposits.   In our example where $X = \$1,000$ and $R = 20$ per cent we saw deposits increase to $D = \$5,000$.   If loan expansions are accompanied by currency withdrawals we must modify the expansion equation.

Currency withdrawals from banks mean that deposits and reserves decrease by the amount withdrawn.   If the public wishes currency the banks provide it, but the currency is made available at the expense of the reserves.   When a bank requests currency from the Federal Reserve the Federal Reserve simply debits the bank's reserve account and increases its own liability item, Federal Reserve Notes issued.   On the balance sheets these changes appear as follows:

| Bank A | | |
|---|---|---|
| Assets | | Liabilities |
| Reserve balance at FRB | — | |
| Currency (vault cash) | + | |

| Federal Reserve Bank | | |
|---|---|---|
| Assets | | Liabilities |
| | | Reserve balance Bank A   — |
| | | Federal Reserve Notes   + |

It is clear that every dollar of currency drained in this fashion removes a dollar of reserves capable of backing several dollars of deposits.   The effect of this currency withdrawal is effectively to raise the reserve requirements of the bank, since reserves are needed not only to meet the legal requirements on deposits but to meet currency withdrawals as well.

Let us assume that the public chooses to hold $C$ dollars of currency for every dollar of demand deposits. The currency-deposit ratio is therefore $C$ per cent. Consequently, an expansion of demand deposits induces an increase in currency by an amount equal to $D \times C$. The expansion in deposits will cease when the excess reserves have become required reserves. But the introduction of the currency drain means that the excess reserves $X$ are being used to meet the currency drain in the amount $D \times C$ and as legally required reserves of $D \times R$. The transformation of the excess reserves into required reserves may be written as

$$X = D \times R + D \times C$$
$$= D(R + C)$$

From this it immediately follows that new deposit expansion potential is expressed as $D = X/(R + C)$.

The loan expansion is greater than the deposit expansion, however, by an amount equal to the currency withdrawal, $D \times C$. Since currency is money, money expansion is equal to the larger total of currency withdrawn plus the deposit expansion. The currency withdrawal is $D \times C$, so loan expansion $L$ or money expansion $M$ is written as

$$L = M = D + D \times C$$
$$= D(1 + C)$$

In terms of the earlier example, if $C = 25$ per cent and $R$ and $X$ remain as before, the amount of demand deposit expansion now possible becomes \$2,222 ($D = X/(R + C)$) instead of the previous \$5,000. Total money and loan expansion is \$2,778—that is, $L = M = D(1 + C)$. It is quite apparent from this example that the presence of a currency drain amounts to an increase in the reserve requirement, and thus reduces the expansion potential of any given volume of excess reserves.

The currency-deposit ratio is not a particularly stable relationship. The demand for currency fluctuates from year to year and season to season. Although the two tend to move together, there are strong independent factors influencing them. Since they do not always move together, this may raise policy complications. For example, if the Federal Reserve has decided upon a course of restricting monetary expansion and has raised reserve requirements, a fall in the currency-deposit ratio may negate the reserve requirement increase. Thus, if the currency-deposit ratio should jump capriciously it makes the Federal Reserve's task of regulating the money supply that much more difficult. Seasonal movements in the ratio are well enough known to be taken into account, however, and banking panics are much less

likely now than in the past.   When conducting their policy delibera-
tions the monetary authorities can and do make allowance for seasonal
movements in the ratio.

The introduction of time deposits into the analysis further reduces
the demand deposit expansion potential of any given volume of excess
reserves.   Before considering time deposits and currency in conjunction with demand deposits, let us consider time deposits alone.   The
legal reserve ratio for time deposits is lower than for demand deposits.
Let us assume it to be 5 per cent.   Now if an individual owning a
demand deposit of $1,000 were to switch this deposit into a time deposit
of an equivalent amount, what would happen?   First of all, legally
required reserves have fallen from $200 (20% of $1,000) to $50 (5% of
$1,000), thus freeing $150 of reserves.   The potential demand deposit of expansion based on this freeing of required reserves is $750
$\left( D = \dfrac{\$150}{.20} \right)$. The result of the transfer of deposits is to reduce the
money supply by $250, since time deposits are not money.   If the public
wishes to hold time deposits in some proportion to demand deposits,
then as excess reserves permit expansion of demand deposits they will
be accompanied by an increase in time deposits.   The excess reserves
will be used to back both types of deposits, thus restricting the expansion of the money supply (demand deposits) for any given volume of
excess reserves.

If the public's propensity to hold demand deposits, time deposits,
and currency is reasonably stable we can determine the expansion potential of the system.    Say the public holds demand deposits, time deposits,
and currency in the ratio of $4 demand deposits, $2 time deposits, and
$1 currency (the approximate ratio), what may we conclude?   Clearly,
if demand deposits were to increase by $100 this would generate increases
of $50 in time deposits and $25 in currency.   If the legal reserves
against demand and time deposits are 20 per cent and 5 per cent respectively the drain on reserves for these deposits is $22.50.    But the drain
on reserves by currency withdrawals is on a dollar-for-dollar basis.
Hence, reserves are depleted in the amount of $25 by the currency drain.
Expressing these various dollar drains on reserves as percentages of the
demand deposit expansion we have $R + T + C = \$47.50/\$100 = .475$.
Thus, the expansion of demand deposits is expressed as $D = X/(R + T + C)$ where $T$ is the effective reserve ratio on time deposits computed
as the legal reserve ratio on time deposits times the time deposit-
demand deposit ratio, or $.05 \times \frac{2}{4} = .025$.   If $X = \$1,000$, then taking
account of currency and time deposit complications we see that demand
deposits may now be expanded to only $D = \$2,105$, considerably less
than in the original example.

In addition to these limitations on the expansion potential of the bank or the system of banks, we should note one more consideration: that in order to expand deposits, three conditions must be satisfied. These conditions are: (1) the presence of excess reserves; (2) the bank's willingness to make loans; and (3) the willingness of customers to borrow. The lack of any one of these effectively prevents deposit expansion from occurring.

Such situations can exist. Setting aside the question of reserves, let us examine conditions two and three. It is conceivable that general business conditions render banks unwilling to make loans, feeling that those who apply for loans are poor risks. And on the contrary, those whom the bank may consider worthy credit risks may be more interested in getting out of debt than in taking on more debt. During the 1930s both conditions were present; as a result the banking system had substantial excess reserves. Considerations such as these show clearly how monetary policy may fall short of the mark in offsetting slump periods, but be quite effective in offsetting excessive spending in boom times. In other words, in recession periods, though we may provide the banks with excess reserves, we cannot force them to lend or individuals to borrow. But if excessive spending is going on in a boom period, clearly monetary measures, through affecting reserves, may curb expenditures by limiting the available money supply.

### The Contraction of Deposits

So far we have discussed only the expansion of deposits. Deposits can also contract or be destroyed. Essentially, the processes we have explored are reversible. Just as a dollar of excess reserve may result in the creation of several dollars of deposits, the loss of a dollar of reserves *may* result in a severalfold contraction of deposits. If the banks are completely loaned up (total reserves are required reserves), then the loss of a dollar of reserve *must* be accompanied by bank action either to (1) acquire additional reserves, or (2) reduce deposit liabilities.

As we saw earlier, the presence of excess reserves allows the single bank to expand its deposit liabilities by about the amount of its excess reserves and the system to expand by some multiple amount. But what happens when the loan is paid off? If the borrower repays the loan by writing a check against his deposit balance at the bank, the bank has a simultaneous reduction in its assets, the cancelled promissory note, and its liabilities, the demand deposit. Thus, the money supply has been reduced by retirement of debt previously owned by the bank.

Another way in which contraction might occur is through an unex-

pected currency drain.   If a bank is in equilibrium with exactly sufficient reserves, what happens when it is faced by a currency withdrawal?
The situation is presented in T-account form, in the following way:

### Bank A

| Assets | | Liabilities | |
| --- | --- | --- | --- |
| Required reserve | $2000 | Demand deposits | $10,000 |
| Currency | $ 500 | | |
| Loans | $7500 | | |

The legal reserve ratio on demand deposits is 20 per cent.

Clearly, if the currency withdrawal does not exceed $500 the bank
has no problem; it can meet this drain from vault cash.   But what if
the withdrawal exceeds $500?

Let us assume that owners of demand deposits decide to withdraw
$1,000 in currency.   The bank may request an additional $500 in currency from the Federal Reserve, thereby reducing its reserve balance
by that much.   Thus:

### Bank A

| Assets | | Liabilities | |
| --- | --- | --- | --- |
| Reserves | $1500 | Demand deposits | $9,000 |
| (Required res. = $1800) | | | |
| Currency | 0 | | |
| Loans | $7500 | | |

But the bank is now $300 short in required reserves, and it is also out of
vault cash.   This deficiency can be made up in several ways.   The
bank may elect to sell some of its loans to the Federal Reserve, thereby
gaining the necessary required reserves and whatever vault cash it may
desire.   Or, if the bank has loans maturing—and banks usually do by
keeping the maturities of outstanding loans staggered—it can insist on
payment and not relend the moneys received.   If the loans are paid by
drawing checks against deposits of Bank A, it will take $1,500 of deposit
contraction and an equivalent reduction in assets, loans, to reestablish
reserves at the required level.   Thus:

### Bank A

| Assets | | Liabilities | |
| --- | --- | --- | --- |
| Required reserves | $1,500 | Demand deposits | |
| Loans (7,500 − 1,500) | $6,000 | | $7,500 (9,000 − 1,500) |

A multiple contraction in demand deposits has occurred because of a deficit of $300 in reserves.

If, however, repayments of the maturing loans are by currency or checks drawn on other banks then only $300 is needed, since every dollar gained in this fashion is credited to Bank A's reserve balance. Thus, the situation in this event may be shown by offsets in Bank A's asset account:

Bank A

| Assets | | Liabilities | |
|---|---|---|---|
| Reserves (1,500 + 300) | $1,800 | Demand deposits | $9,000 |
| Loans    (7,500 − 300) | $7,200 | | |

This situation, however, means that Bank A's difficulties may well be passed on to other banks in the system, especially if the system as a whole is loaned up and has no excess reserves. In this case, a multiple contraction will occur throughout the system.

This latter possibility, contraction on a massive scale, may cause widespread unemployment and depression. Indeed, among other reasons, it was to avoid just such situations that the Federal Reserve was created. Instead of allowing reserve deficiencies to cause unwarranted contraction the Federal Reserve can provide the banks with additional reserves, if necessary. These reserves may be provided by lending to the commercial banks or buying securities from them, or by adjusting the reserve ratio downward, thereby allowing any dollar in reserve to back a greater volume of deposits. Thus, the Federal Reserve can act to provide the necessary currency and still allow the banks to meet the required reserves.

This is the manner in which our present commercial bank system interacts with the Federal Reserve to provide a flexible money supply and an efficient clearing and payment process.

### REVIEW QUESTIONS

1. "The important fact about the clearing drain is that it does not exist." Assess the validity of this statement.
2. What factors set limits to the commercial banking system's ability to expand loans and deposits?
3. How do banks create money? In order for banks to create money what three conditions must be fulfilled?
4. Why is the individual commercial bank limited in its ability to create deposit liabilities to roughly the amount of its excess reserves?

5. How can the commercial banking system create deposits to some multiple of any newly obtained reserves if each individual bank is limited to expansion equal to its excess reserves?
6. How do time deposits and currency withdrawals affect the expansion potential of any given volume of new reserves?
7. Ignoring time deposit and currency complications and assuming the reserve ratio against demand deposits is 25 per cent, what volume of new deposits can a deposit of $1,000 in currency support?   Trace through the expansion process using T-accounts for at least four banks.
8. Describe the Federal Reserve System check-clearing mechanism.
9. What is the meaning of negative excess reserves?   What sort of adjustment would the bank likely make?

## SUGGESTED REFERENCES

Board of Governors of the Federal Reserve System, *The Federal Reserve System* (Washington: 1961), Chapter II.
Federal Reserve Bank of Chicago, *Modern Money Mechanics* (Chicago: 1961).
Federal Reserve Bank of Philadelphia, Exercises in the *Debits and Credits of Bank Reserves* (Philadelphia: 1955).
Shaw, Edward S., *Money, Income and Monetary Policy* (Homewood: Irwin, 1950). Chapters 6 through 10.

CHAPTER *5*

# *Sources of Commercial Bank Lending Power*

The business of business is to make a profit on the goods or services it sells in the market place. In the banking business, the profit derives largely from the lending of money. So essential is the lending function to the success of commercial banking that the next three chapters are devoted to the subject. The present chapter is concerned with the sources of lending power, the next chapter examines its uses, and the one after that explores the problems faced by banks in the management of their portfolios.

Many of the factors contributing to the lending power of commercial banks and the commercial banking system were introduced during the discussion of the banks' assets and liabilities. Let us now examine the additional roles played by these factors and investigate in particular the nature and characteristics of the principal debt instruments. It should be borne in mind that what might hold for a single commercial bank need not necessarily apply to the commercial banking system as a whole. Because of this prospect, the presentation in this chapter, following a brief digression, first considers the individual commercial bank and then focuses on the entire banking system.

## A DIGRESSION: THE PROBLEM OF BANK CAPITAL

Thus far, in explaining bank assets and liabilities we have ignored the capital account. Now the time has come to pay some attention to this important item. The difference between what banks own (their assets) and what they owe (their liabilities) is their net worth and appears in the capital account.    If the net worth of a bank is less than the par value of its outstanding capital stock, capital is said to be impaired.    The particular supervisory authority that regulates the commercial bank will require the bank to make up the deficiency. Should the value of the bank's assets decline below the amount of its liabilities, the bank would be insolvent and would be closed.

The role played by bank capital is essentially that of a buffer.    It provides a safety fund for creditors to fall back on and averts insolvency for individual banks.    The net worth of a bank is the sum of its capital accounts.    It includes not only the paid-in capital stock previously mentioned, but also surplus, capital reserves, and undivided profits.

Bank stock must have a par value.    Since a newly opened bank almost always operates initially at a loss, bank capital stock is sold at a premium over par value which provides a surplus to prevent the impairment of capital.    After the bank becomes established, this surplus is built up by retained earnings transferred from undivided profits. National banks are required to accumulate net assets until the surplus is at least as large as the par value of outstanding common stock.    Capital reserves represent net assets retained by the bank corporation and withheld from dividends as protection against possible operating losses. They are a share of the difference between assets and liabilities not destined for distribution in dividends to the stockholders.    The undivided profits represent the net assets earned from operations; the bank may distribute these dividends to the stockholders.

From the creditor's—or depositor's—point of view, net worth is the margin of protection for their claims.    That is, if the ratio of capital accounts to total assets is 10 per cent the assets would have to depreciate by 10 per cent before bank liabilities exceeded assets.    Thus, by preventing insolvency, the capital accounts contribute to the maintenance of the "moneyness" of the depositors' claims.    On the other hand, stockholders view net worth as the measure of their interest in the assets of the bank.

In spite of the importance of the capital accounts in maintaining bank solvency and the "moneyness" of bank deposits, government regulations on bank capital requirements are not particularly demanding.    A few states, such as California and Michigan, have more severe capital requirements than those for national banks.    But even Federal requirements on capitalization of national banks are not impressive.    The Federal regulations specify minimum capital requirements depending on the population of the head-office city, and also according to the number of branch offices.

These criteria certainly do not seem to be the most relevant for ward-ing off and preventing bank insolvency. Perhaps capital requirements might better be tied to the total or quality of assets, the total or character of liabilities, the rate of turnover of deposits, or similar aspects which reflect stresses on bank solvency. With the long-run trend of the capital-asset ratio declining, until the ratio in the mid-1950s was about 7 per cent, the margin of net worth has not been overly comforting. Given the public interest in a strong and healthy banking system, it appears that the minimal reform in capital requirements should be to end the competition between Federal and state governments by prescribing uniform capital requirements for all banks.

## SOURCES OF INDIVIDUAL COMMERCIAL BANK LENDING POWER

To return to the main concern of this chapter, the commercial bank has three sources of lending power. The bank acquires funds by which to operate from (1) invested capital, (2) deposits, and (3) bank credit. Let us examine each of these sources of bank funds in turn.

### Capital as a Source of Lending Power

In the process of raising bank capital, the common notion that a bank makes loans by taking money from one person and lending it to another finds some substantiation, but the relationship is not a direct one. If we suppose capital to be raised by selling shares of capital stock, the share purchasers may be assumed to pay for them with a check drawn on a commercial bank. The bank selling the capital stock credits its capital account by the amount of the sale, thus increasing its liabilities. But its assets also increase an equal amount as it deposits the checks received for the sale of stock to its reserve account at the Federal Reserve. At the same time, some bank somewhere else has lower demand deposits and also a reduced reserve balance at the Federal Reserve. These transactions may be recorded in T-account form as follows:

Commercial Bank Selling Stock

| Assets | Liabilities |
| --- | --- |
| Reserve balance at FRB $\quad+$ | Capital account $\quad+$ |

Other Commercial Banks

| Assets | Liabilities |
| --- | --- |
| Reserve balance at FRB $\quad-$ | Demand deposits of public $\quad-$ |

The net effect so far of an individual bank selling shares of capital stock is to lower demand deposits—to extinguish money—and to increase capital liabilities of banks.

If transfers to surplus are considered, the outcome is the same. As the bank accumulates earnings it can transfer some of its assets to the credit of the bank itself, so that a liability item is automatically created. These bank earnings arise from the transfer of money from the public to the bank through interest paid to the bank and from bank service charges. The process of bank earnings is a mechanism which automatically increases capital liabilities and decreases the money supply until such time as the bank may choose to return the earnings back to the public as dividends. If the earnings are retained, clearly the net effect is to decrease the money supply and to increase bank capital.

The idea that banks lend by taking money from one person and lending it to someone else is applicable in the case of bank capital when dealing with an individual bank. The process is not, however, a direct one. As seen above, the increase of bank capital does not simply transfer money from the public to the bank. Rather it destroys money at first. As the T-account shows, the bank increasing its capital has also increased its reserve balance. The bank can thus offset this money destruction by creating money on the basis of the new reserves it has acquired. In effect, this last expansion finances loans with money obtained from stockholders. But it is to be noted that for the banking *system* as a whole there are no more reserves, there has simply been a shifting of existing reserves among individual banks of the system.

### Deposits as a Source of Lending Power

As pointed out earlier, banks accept deposits—that is, increase their liabilities—only in return for some kind of consideration. If the consideration is currency, coin, or checks there is a deposit "created" in the sense of a new entry in the depositor's account, although there has been no net addition to the money supply. But the bank can also create a deposit by the simple expedient of crediting a depositor's account in exchange for a nonmonetary consideration—the depositor's promissory note. In this case the bank has loaned money to the "depositor" by crediting his demand account in exchange for the customer's note. This kind of deposit creation increases the money supply, for new demand deposits have been created.

For the individual bank, reserves are acquired by depositors bringing in currency and coin or checks drawn on other banks. The bank accepts these considerations and increases its deposit liabilities accordingly.  It has, of course, increased its assets an equal amount when it accepts the coin, currency, or checks.  Let us assume the bank in turn forwards these items on to its bank, the district Federal Reserve Bank, for deposit to its reserve account.  In this case the balance sheet of the commercial bank shows the following changes:

Commercial Bank

| Assets | Liabilities |
|---|---|
| Reserve balance at FRB    + | Demand deposit of public    + |

Since banks are required to maintain only fractional reserves, the bank's increased reserve position now includes excess reserves.  This is so because only part of the increased reserve balance is needed to back the increased deposit liabilities.  Thus, by deposits of coin, currency, or checks on other banks, the individual bank gains reserves by which to finance additional loans.

Another source of additional reserves to a bank arises when a customer decides to switch part of his demand deposit into a time deposit.  Since time deposits have a smaller reserve ratio, the switching from demand deposits to time deposits by the bank's customer gives the bank some free reserves.  To illustrate the point, let us assume a 20 per cent reserve ratio for demand deposits and a 5 per cent reserve ratio on time deposits.  Then neglecting other items on the balance sheet we can set up the following T-account:

Commercial Bank

| Assets | | Liabilities | |
|---|---|---|---|
| Required reserve at FRB | $200 | Demand deposits | $1,000 |
| Other assets | 800 | | |
| | $1,000 | | $1,000 |

If the depositors decide to hold, say, half their deposits as time deposits and half a demand deposits required reserves are altered as shown in the table at top of page 91.  By this switch from demand to time deposits the bank has acquired excess reserves with which to back additional loans and deposit expansion.

The individual commercial bank thus has its reserve position enhanced when it has an inflow of coin, currency, or checks drawn on other banks.  Or if depositors elect to hold larger time deposit balances, the bank acquires additional reserves to finance loan operations.  But we must turn presently to the system of commercial banks

Commercial Bank

| Assets | | Liabilities | |
| --- | --- | --- | --- |
| Required reserve at FRB | | Demand deposits | $ 500 |
|   Demand deposits | $ 100 | Time deposits | 500 |
|   Time deposits | 25 | | |
| Excess reserves | 75 | | |
| Other assets | 800 | | |
| | $1,000 | | $1,000 |

as a whole to see if the propositions true for the single bank hold for the banking system.

## Bank Credit as a Source of Lending Power

Member banks are allowed to borrow for short periods of time from the Federal Reserve Banks. This borrowing takes the form of either discounts or advances. A discount (or rediscount) is a loan made to a bank by the Federal Reserve through the purchase of some negotiable instrument that the borrowing bank previously had acquired from one of its customers. The borrowing bank endorses the instrument and sends it to the Federal Reserve Bank. The Reserve Bank discounts it and credits the reserve account of the borrowing bank. Although in effect selling an earning asset to the Reserve Bank, the borrowing bank, by endorsing the paper, incurs a contingent liability with respect to the endorsed paper.

An advance is a direct loan to a member bank by its Reserve Bank. These advances are promissory notes of commercial banks purchased by the Reserve Banks. The notes are secured by collateral acceptable to the lending Reserve Bank, usually Treasury securities.

Discounts and advances differ somewhat in form, but their effect on reserves is the same. The borrowing bank sends the debt instrument in question to the Federal Reserve Bank which then credits the bank's reserve account. The money supply is not immediately affected, but since the borrowing bank's reserve position is changed there can be monetary effects forthcoming. In terms of T-accounts the process assumes the following form:

Commercial Banks

| Assets | | Liabilities | |
| --- | --- | --- | --- |
| Reserve balance at FRB | + | Notes due FRB | + |

Federal Reserve Banks

| Assets | Liabilities |
|---|---|
| Discounts and advances          + | Reserve balance of CB          + |

Another type of member bank borrowing deserves at least brief mention. This is the so-called Federal Funds Market. "Federal Funds" is shorthand for "immediately available Federal Reserve Funds." The Federal Funds Market consists of the buying and selling by banks of reserve balances at Federal Reserve Banks. A bank with excess reserves lends them to another bank which needs additional reserves, transfer being made by telephone. Since reserve balances maintained at the Reserve Banks earn their owners no interest, this Federal Funds Market provides an interest earning outlet for the employment of any temporary surplus reserves. The market is interesting principally because of its sensitivity to credit conditions.

## SOURCES OF LENDING POWER: COMMERCIAL BANK SYSTEM

Sources of lending power for the individual commercial bank, as we have seen, consist of bank capital, deposits, and bank credit. To what extent, if any, do the considerations true of the individual bank carry over to the banking system?

### Capital as a Source of Lending Power

The individual bank situation shows clearly that, whereas a bank can increase its capital liabilities, the corresponding increase in its reserve position occurs at the expense of reserves lost by other banks in the system. The potential expansion in deposit liabilities by the bank acquiring the reserves offsets the money destroyed when the public purchases the shares of capital stock or when earnings are retained. Bank capital is consequently a contractive item and not a source of lending power for the bank system as a whole.

In a later chapter we shall present a monetary equation to show the expansive and contractive items that influence the money supply. At that point we shall again see how the capital accounts of banks act as a contracting element for the bank system as a whole.

### Deposits as a Source of Lending Power

The popular conception of bank lending operations is that banks expand their loans by lending out the funds deposited with them.

This is not the case for the banking system as a whole, except, perhaps, in the case of time deposits.   What may be true for the individual commercial bank is not true for the bank system and vice versa.   Thus, for the banking system loans give rise to the deposits, whereas for the individual bank the contrary is the case.

It should be clear that for the system of banks as a whole, existing demand deposits do not constitute a source of bank lending power. When, for instance, an individual bank receives a check drawn on another bank the recipient emerges with increased reserves.   But these increased reserves are lost by the paying bank on which the check was drawn.   Thus, for the system as a whole there is no increase in reserves, but only a switching or shifting of existing reserves among the banks of the system.

On the other hand, there can be a net inflow of currency to the bank system.   This inflow occurs if the public finds that it is holding too much coin and currency.   In this case the public brings the currency to the banks for deposit, and the banking system acquires additional reserves to finance loan and deposit expansion.   Thus, if the public chooses to hold its money in the form of demand deposits rather than as currency, the banks receive an increase in reserves.   The T-accounts contain these items:

Commercial Banks

| Assets | | Liabilities | |
|---|---|---|---|
| Reserve balance at FRB | + | Demand deposits of public | + |

Public

| Assets | | Liabilities |
|---|---|---|
| Currency holdings | − | |
| Demand deposits at CB | + | |

Similarly, if the public chooses to hold a larger proportion of its assets as time deposits than as demand deposits, the bank system gains excess reserves.   The acquisition of these excess reserves does not arise from any changes in total reserves, but comes about from the considerably lower reserve ratio requirement for time deposits than for demand deposits.   If the banking system is loaned up and has no excess reserves since all reserves are required reserves, any shift by the public of a greater proportion of its deposits into time deposits would give the banks excess reserves.   Other things being equal, then, a source of lending power to the bank system is a greater willingness of the public to hold time deposits.

To summarize the value of deposits as a source of lending power, a net inflow of coin or currency into a bank or the banking system generates additional reserves. Similarly, an increase in public willingness to hold time deposits instead of demand deposits increases excess reserves for both the individual bank and the system. But the deposit of checks drawn on commercial banks affects the individual bank and the system in different ways. For the individual bank, the receiving of a check drawn on another bank produces an increase in reserves. The recipient bank, however, gains reserves at the expense of the paying bank which loses them. For the system of banks as a whole, therefore, demand deposits do not constitute a source of lending power.

### Bank Credit as a Source of Lending Power

We now come to the major source of lending power for the banking system, namely, bank credit. Bank credit is lending that is financed by the creation of demand deposits and Federal Reserve credits. It is money created by the banking system and may be thought of as debt instruments monetized by bank action.

Bank credit can be computed as the total loans and investments of the commercial banks and Federal Reserve Banks less bank capital accounts and time deposits. As we have defined bank credit, it includes the important item of *Federal Reserve credit*. This last item, Federal Reserve credit, is the means through which the Federal Reserve exercises its control over the money supply.

Federal Reserve credit consists principally of the loans and investments of the Federal Reserve Banks. The significance of this lies in the fact that as the Federal Reserve acquires these loans and investments it pays for them by credits on its own books; it monetizes them *and these credits it creates are the reserves of the commercial banking system.* Thus, by increasing its loans and investments (principally Treasury securities) the Federal Reserve can make more reserves available to the commercial banks for the financing of additional loans.

We have seen that for individual commercial banks, lendable funds are derived from bank capital funds, deposits, and by temporary borrowing, either from the Federal Reserve or in the Federal Funds market. Deposits and bank capital, however, are sources of lending power to individual banks only, not to the system of banks as a whole. As a group, the commercial bank system can expand loans and deposits only to the extent that it has or can obtain the reserves needed to support expanded deposits. The availability of bank reserves is largely dependent on Federal Reserve credit.

The reserve balances of commercial banks clearly constitute the source of their lending power, and the reserve requirement ratios set the limits on the extent of lending possible. The Federal Reserve Banks can, however, extend their credit in the form of commercial bank reserve balances or by the issuance of Federal Reserve Notes. This extension of reserve balances is Federal Reserve credit and is accomplished when the Federal Reserve discounts or advances (temporary lending by the Fed) to commercial banks, or when it purchases United States government securities from them.

When the Federal Reserve extends credit by temporary lending (discounts and advances) or permanent credit by purchasing United States government securities, this credit increases commercial bank reserves both individually and as a group. An increase in Federal Reserve Notes, in response to an increase in currency demand which reduces bank reserves, has the effect of cushioning the impact on bank reserves but does not lead to an increase in commercial bank reserves.

The ability of Federal Reserve Banks to extend Federal Reserve credit, either as reserve balances or an increased note issue, is limited by the requirement of a 25 per cent gold certificate reserve against the combined Federal Reserve Note and deposit liabilities. Ultimately, gold and Federal Reserve credit, except as currency circulation may fall, form the principal sources of commercial bank reserves and, hence, the sources of commercial bank lending power. For, as we have seen, the banking system as a whole cannot expand its reserves and its lendable funds unless the Federal Reserve is extending credit, either temporarily by discounts or advances or permanently by the purchase of Treasury securities from the banks or their customers.

Before concluding this section, let us anticipate a result of Chapter 10 where we shall discuss Federal Reserve control over the money supply. The amount of reserves available to the banking system is a basic determinant of the money supply. The determinants of bank reserves are given by a "reserve equation," and a prominent item in this equation will be Federal Reserve credit, which is principally the holdings of discounts and advances and Treasury securities by the Federal Reserve.

If there is any one thing to be stressed here, however, it is precisely that the commercial banking system is heavily dependent on the Federal Reserve for the growth of its aggregate lending power.

## REVIEW QUESTIONS

1. What role is played by bank capital when looked at from the creditor's (the depositor's) viewpoint; from the stockholder's position?
2. Capital is a source of lending power for the individual commercial bank. Comment.
3. For the system of commercial banks, capital is not a source of lending power. Explain why what is true for the individual bank is not true for the system of banks.
4. In what sense are deposits a source of lending power?
5. What is bank credit?
6. In the current *Federal Reserve Bulletin*, look up the volume of Federal Reserve credit. What is the significance of this Federal Reserve credit as a source of member bank lending power?

# CHAPTER *6*

# *Uses of Commercial Banking Lending Power*

Commercial banks use their lending power to acquire earning assets. These particular assets take the form of debt instruments that are composed of loans and investments. They are paid for by the commercial bank's creation of a deposit for the seller of the debt instrument —the borrower. As these deposits are created they, of course, impose new liabilities on the banks.

To facilitate a discussion of debt instruments, we shall divide them into two categories, investments and loans. First, we shall discuss the types of securities which constitute investments for banks. Then we shall take up the topic of loans. In the process, we shall make a general distinction between the two based on the market in which each is handled. Generally, investment securities are purchased in the impersonal open market, whereas loans are acquired in a personal, face-to-face encounter with a borrower.

Commercial banks do not have complete freedom in the purchase of securities. In fact, they are rather circumscribed as to the types and amounts of assets they may acquire. The prohibition on the purchase of corporate stock is almost complete, with only stock in the Federal Reserve Bank, foreign banking corporations, and certain subsidiaries permitted. Similarly, banks are not allowed to acquire real estate other than the banking premises. For member banks of the Federal Reserve System, certain corporate bonds are eligible if they are traded on organized exchanges and are classed as "investment securities" by the Comptroller of the Currency. States also issue "legal lists" which designate the bonds eligible for purchase by the banking institutions under their supervision.

Diversification of bank assets is obtained by limiting the proportion of various forms of assets which may be held.   Further, the amount that may be loaned to any one borrower is commonly limited to no more than 10 per cent of a bank's capital and surplus.   These restrictions apply to all investments except to issues of the United States government, to issues guaranteed by it, or to issues of state and local governments.

There are numerous other restrictions, but without going into them here, it will suffice to indicate that banks are circumscribed in the acquisition of earning assets in order to protect bank solvency.   However, the proscriptions provide only a framework.   Within this framework the individual bank exercises its discretion in the selection of those securities eligible for acquisition.

In this chapter we shall introduce a fundamental problem facing every commercial bank—that is, the managing of the bank's asset portfolio.   Certain general objectives of portfolio management—objectives often somewhat conflicting—will be considered.   A more detailed analysis of these problems will be made in the next chapter.

With this prelude, let us now move on to consideration of the commercial bank's loans and investments.

## INVESTMENT SECURITIES

### Federal Securities

Many issues are sold by the United States government.   Each of these has distinctive features.

Treasury bills are typically 90-day discount obligations, although some of those outstanding have maturities up to one year.   These bills are sold nearly every week in an auction sale conducted by the Treasury.   Interested financial investors inform the Treasury what price they will pay for the securities and what quantity of securities they desire.   The price paid for these securities, which is less than their face value, determines the effective interest rate to be paid on the securities.

Since this market is a competitive one and since it is conducted so frequently in a security so well-known and standardized, the Treasury bill market is a good indicator of credit conditions.   Tight money usually will soon lead to higher bill rates and vice versa.   In the 1930s and the early postwar years, the bill rate went very close to zero, to three-eights of one per cent, as there was an abundance of funds available for such safe and liquid investments.

The next Treasury obligation in terms of maturity are certificates of indebtedness. Certificates of indebtedness usually mature in nine months to a year. They are a favorite investment medium of corporations accumulating funds with which to pay income taxes.

Notes are generally three- to five-year obligations, and for all intents and purposes they are essentially short-term bonds. Bonds are obligations with maturities of five years or longer. Certificates, notes, and bonds are usually sold by the Treasury on such terms as will make them sell at par at the time of issuance; bills, to the contrary, are sold at auction with the Treasury taking the best offers.

Sometimes bonds are issued with a definite maturity date when the principal is to be paid off, but sometimes the Treasury reserves an option to pay off the bonds over a period of years. Such an example occurred in 1953 when an issue of $3\frac{1}{4}$ per cent bonds was sold whose maturity was set at 1978–1983, meaning that the government could pay off the principal at any time after 1978 if it should so desire, provided that it was done before 1983. This procedure is used because the Treasury likes to have some leeway in refunding or paying off maturing obligations in order to be able to take advantage of any changes in credit conditions as the bonds approach maturity. For this purpose it consequently provides itself with a cushion in maturity dates.

Frequently, when an issue is about to mature, the Treasury offers the holders of bonds or notes the right to subscribe to a new issue at prices slightly advantageous to the holder as compared with outstanding issues and as compared to the price available to new purchasers. The old issue is then said to bear "rights," which encourages its holders to purchase the new obligations. The size of Treasury transactions is so large that some kind of mechanism is necessary if credit conditions are not to be upset and Treasury finance to become chaotic.

So far we have dealt only with marketable securities. The general public is probably much more familiar with a nonmarketable security, the savings bond. Savings bonds comprise various types. They all have the common feature of providing stated surrender values, so that the owner can get his principal back at any time, and also earn interest in the interim. The rate of return increases the longer the savings bond is held. These provisions are made in order to appeal to individuals who might otherwise save in other forms where they can get their money back without risk or loss, as in savings deposits. Furthermore, savings bonds are issued in denominations as small as $25 and $50.

This provides the Treasury with access to a pool of savings to which it otherwise would not have access, as the small individual saver is not likely to acquire bonds of $1,000 denomination or larger.

The Treasury also has outstanding certain so-called "special issues." Special issues are mainly those sold to agencies of the government. The Social Security Administration, continually investing funds for old age and retirement benefits, is the most important purchaser of these issues.   The yields on these special issues are set so as to be close to market yields of other government issues.

### State and Local Government Bonds

The number of variations in the types of individual Federal issues is modest when compared to those of state and local authorities.   Thus more than 100,000 public agencies issue securities: states, cities, school districts, sewer districts, counties, toll road authorities, and public housing agencies, to name only a few of them.   Furthermore, each agency may have many issues outstanding.   Some of the local units have good credit ratings, others do not.   Each issue has to be considered separately by the investor.   As a result, the market for state and local obligations is scattered.   Time is usually required before sales can be accomplished advantageously.   For this reason these issues are considered illiquid, and are usually bought with a mind to holding until maturity.   This is especially true of longer-term issues.

General obligation issues are guaranteed by the full credit of the issuing governmental unit.   But governmental units and independent authorities may issue securities not backed by the full faith and credit of the government.   Thus, some obligations may be guaranteed only to the extent of the revenues obtainable by a particular tax or by a particular set of tolls from bridge, road, or other revenue earning property.   These latter bonds are called revenue bonds.   These last are, of course, poorer in credit rating, and in yield give larger returns than general obligation bonds.

In practice many government units sell their issues in serials.   For example, in a given issue it may be provided that 10 per cent matures in two years, 10 per cent in four years, and so on, up to twenty years. This feature provides for the automatic retirement of the issue, and increases the credit rating.   Also various maturities may appeal to particular types of investors; banks, for example, may prefer the short-term issues while pension funds may prefer longer-term ones.

The common feature of state and local bonds is the exemption of interest from Federal income taxes. Thus, an individual or a corporation owning state and local securities receives interest, but all such interest receipts are excluded from taxable income so far as the personal income tax and the corporate income tax are concerned.

### Corporate Bonds

Most corporate bonds are serial issues, but many have various types of sinking fund provisions. A bond may also have a call price which states at what price the management is entitled to pay off the bonds prior to maturity should it so desire. Call prices are a protection against a fall in interest rates to the borrower, and thus are discriminatory to the lender. So-called convertible bonds are convertible into common stock or other securities of the issuing company at the will of the bondholder.

Bonds may be general obligations of a company and, if so, are called debentures, or they may be secured by specific property, stated as collateral. Debentures are of growing importance as compared to secured or mortgage bonds.

Some bond issues are privately placed, which means that the entire issue is sold to one investing institution or to a few such institutions. The terms of the placement of the bonds are negotiated directly between seller and purchaser. Other bonds are publically sold. A group of investors known as underwriters agrees to find a market for the bonds and to guarantee the issuer a certain price. The underwriters then undertake to sell the bonds to any interested person or institution. The issuer does not know in advance who will finally buy the bonds. Publicly issued corporate bonds are sold under much more rigid regulations of the Security Exchange Commission than are privately placed bonds. Among the nonbank financial institutions that accept private placements, the most important are insurance companies, pension funds, and trusts.

### LOAN INSTRUMENTS

Let us now shift our attention to bank loans which include commercial paper, acceptances, call and dealer money, mortgages and consumer credit, and Federal Funds. Mortgages have much of the character of long-term investments such as bonds. A general acquaintance with the general properties of all these types of loans will facilitate the discussion of portfolio management, and also promote keener understanding of the money market.

*Commercial paper* is composed chiefly of the short-term promissory notes of businesses of high credit rating. A considerable share of this paper is sold by sales finance companies, that is, by companies that specialize in the financing of automobiles and other consumer purchases. Such paper is drawn up to be highly negotiable. Since the issuing companies have high credit ratings, and since maturity dates are adapted to the needs of lenders, this paper is highly attractive to lenders and bears a low rate of return. The term "open market paper" is sometimes also used in speaking of commercial paper.

*Acceptances* are usually used in foreign trade. For example, an importer may arrange to pay the exporter with a promissory note. The note is drawn by the exporter and is accepted by the importer for payment in 90 days or some such period; that is, the importer agrees to accept the terms of the promise as stated on the note. The importer as the payer frequently has a credit arrangement whereby a bank also accepts (endorses) the note, thus giving the instrument a high credit rating. The exporter can then obtain his money by selling, that is, discounting, the note to another bank, which holds the note to maturity.

*Dealer money* is usually money lent to firms that make a business of buying and selling United States government securities; these firms realize their profit by charging small fees or "spreads" in the prices and by speculating in price movements of securities. *Call money* is money lent to dealers and brokers in securities, and is so named because it can be called for payment by the bank making the loan. In recent times call money can only be loaned by banks, but inasmuch as dealers and brokers usually have firm understandings with banks about such loans the call provision has little significance. Before 1934, however, call money was dealt in by all types of investors, and the term *call* had real meaning. Both dealer money and call money are secured by securities.

*Mortgages* are loans secured by real estate. *Consumer loans*, on the other hand, are loans to individuals secured by consumer goods or by the general credit of the borrower alone. There is a presumption that mortgage money is used to finance houses or other construction, and that consumer credit is utilized for the purchases of consumer goods, including medical services. In neither case, however, is it possible to determine the ultimate purpose for which a loan is intended. A person or enterprise borrows to be able to spend more than immediate cash resources allow. Any one expenditure may be responsible for the loan, and hence may be said to be the "purpose" of the loan.

Consumer loans occasion higher rates than other loans since they are repaid, as a rule, in monthly installments. Households frequently borrow in this form even when other opportunities are available, perhaps because they like the budgeting which regular repayment entails.

*Federal Funds* are loans among member banks of the Federal Reserve System. Member banks are prohibited from borrowing except from Federal Reserve Banks, but the Federal Funds market is so similar to check-clearing that it is not considered as a prohibited type of borrowing. A member bank having excess reserves lends them, as noted in the last chapter, to another bank with deficient reserves. The borrowing bank obtains the funds immediately by telegraph or telephone transfer, and arranges to repay, usually the next day. Actual documents are only follow-ups. Loans are normally for one day only and bear a low rate of interest, seldom above the discount rate.

### Business Loans

Except for the United States government securities, business loans are the most important part of most commercial banks' business. In 1964 approximately one-fifth of all the assets of commercial banks took this form, and about 40 per cent of assets other than United States government securities were of this form. A typical loan of a commercial bank is to small business. It matures in less than one year and is an unsecured note not readily negotiable. Thus, it is clear that bank loans typically result from the intimate relationship between bank and customer. Most of the information available about the nature of business loans come from the surveys conducted by the Federal Reserve System.

Banks may frequently require a borrower to maintain a certain minimum balance in his account. This is, of course, desirable for the bank from several standpoints. For one thing it makes clearing balances more favorable, or at least less unfavorable. These required balances, called compensating balances, are often 10 to 20 per cent of the amount of the loan. Since interest is charged on the entire loan, this procedure also increases the cost of the loan to the borrower and increases the effective rate of interest to the bank. It may be noted, however, that the likelihood of a borrower's obtaining a loan may well depend upon the balance maintained in his account when he is not borrowing. Hence the question of deposit balance is probably never completely absent from loan negotiations.

The relation of bank and borrower being so personal in many cases, it is clear that loan negotiations are not merely a matter of interest rates. Willingness to lend at time of need, deposit balances, and many other factors enter into the relationships between lender and borrower.

## Mortgages

These loans are usually long-term loans ranging from ten to thirty years in maturity, and are secured by real estate. Approximately one-quarter of all outstanding mortgages are secured by commercial and apartment house properties. The remainder of outstanding mortgages are principally secured by one- to four-family dwellings, although there are some farm mortgages also.

At the present time nearly all mortgages are amortized in monthly payments. At one time, however, it was customary to make single payment loans maturing at a given time, but this practice has disappeared. Prior to 1927, national banks could not make real estate loans of longer than five years maturity.

About 40 per cent of the outstanding mortgages on residential properties are insured or guaranteed by the United States government. The Federal Housing Administration insures approved types of mortgages. The type of construction must be acceptable, and a certain minimum down payment must be made, amounting to 10 per cent or more, generally. If the mortgage is acceptable to the FHA, it insures the holder of the mortgage against loss. This means in event of default the property is transferred to the FHA, and the mortgage is paid in United States government securities. The lender may suffer a loss, but it will be small.

The Veterans Administration operates a little differently. The mortgagee handles the property himself in case of default. Any loss in liquidating the property is paid by the government. The distinction between the insurance program of the FHA and the guarantee program of the VA is not very important, however. The losses to the government under both programs have been inconsequential.

Nonguaranteed mortgage loans are commonly called conventional loans. They tend to carry higher interest rates than guaranteed and insured mortgages.

## Consumer Credit

About three-quarters of consumer credit is installment credit. These loans are paid back in regular amounts, usually monthly. Not only are loans on automobiles, appliances, and home improvements financed this way, but a larger part of personal loans are also installment loans.

Commercial banks did not actively engage in consumer credit until the middle 1930s. There was a long tradition in the banking community against any but the so-called "productive loan," the short-term business loan.   However, the success of specialized nonbank consumer finance institutions led to the entrance of commercial banks into this kind of lending activity.   Today commercial banks engage in all kinds of installment lending, and additionally they are an important source of funds for the lending programs of nonbank financial institutions.

## Money Markets

The term "money" market is not a rigorous one.   It refers in a loose and general way to the trading in short-term obligations, in government bills, acceptances, commercial paper, and dealer money.   The commercial banks, dealers in government securities, corporations, and individuals participate.   There are also a few special dealers in acceptances and commercial paper.   The participants may be either lenders or borrowers.

Longer-term securities, mainly bonds and mortgages, are traded also. This type of trading is usually referred to as the capital market.   The word capital thus implies the commitment of funds for an extended period of time.   Money market transactions are dealings in short-term instruments; capital market transactions involve the trading of long-term debt instruments.

Capital markets are organized about new private placements through insurance companies, pension funds, and the like for bonds, and through the public placement of new securities through underwriters, brokers, and dealers.   Mortgages are placed directly through mortgage companies, mutual savings banks, savings and loan associations, and mortgage companies.   Extensive trading occurs in both bonds and mortgages, through the New York Stock Exchange in the case of bonds, and through a variety of informal market arrangements in other cases. Banks and other mortgage lenders frequently sell their mortgages to insurance companies and other investment institutions.   We shall deal more extensively with these nonbank financial institutions in a later chapter.

## PORTFOLIO PROBLEMS

A detailed discussion of portfolio management will be deferred until the following chapter.   For the present let us be content to note that portfolio management is simply the bank's determination of what constitutes the "best" distribution of assets in its quest for liquidity, solvency, and income—often seemingly conflicting goals.

The asset items appearing on the bank's balance sheet can be divided into three general classes. The classifications are descriptive of the function served by the assets, and one function may blend with another with no clear-cut line of demarcation.

The first functional category is that of cash assets. The bank's holdings of cash assets provide it with immediate liquidity. This liquidity feature is desirable, in fact, necessary. But cash assets earn no income. They consist of vault cash, the reserve balances of the bank at the Federal Reserve, and deposit balances maintained with other banks. From the nature of these assets it is apparent that they are indeed liquid, that they provide the bank with immediate liquidity, for they are immediately available with no risk of loss.

The next class of assets are the so-called "secondary reserves." These reserves are assets which can be converted into cash without delay and with little risk of loss, but which also provide some income in the meantime. For the assets that form the secondary reserve, considerations of yield are subordinated to considerations of liquidity. These secondary reserves consist of high-grade, short-term instruments and are principally short-term Treasury obligations.

The third category of the bank's asset portfolio consists of its loans and investments. This is the portion of the portfolio whose role is principally income generating. That is, these are the assets held first of all for the income they yield. But even here, the bank tends to restrict itself to assets that are generally convertible into cash without either too much loss or too much delay. Thus, the line between the second and third uses of assets is rather indistinct.

Portfolio management boils down to this: the combining of the various assets which may be held in order to achieve the optimum balance to satisfy the needs for liquidity, solvency, and income. Portfolio management is thus a variation on the old economic dictum—"the allocation of scarce means among competing ends." To this problem, we turn in the following chapter.

## REVIEW QUESTIONS

1. Distinguish among the various types of Treasury securities. Using the current *Federal Reserve Bulletin*, determine the holdings of the various kinds of issues by the commercial banking system.
2. Distinguish between mortgage bonds and debentures.
3. What is commercial paper? In what market is it bought and sold?

4. Distinguish between "loans" and "investments" in commercial bank portfolios.
5. Using the current *Federal Reserve Bulletin* determine the composition of commercial bank loans. What are the three principal types of loans?
6. What is consumer credit? What is its purpose and how is it repaid?
7. Is there a difference between the money market and the capital market? Which market is likely to be most competitive?
8. Why would you not expect the rate on Federal Funds to be above the rediscount rate?
9. Generally speaking, banks obtain a higher rate of return on loans than on investments. To what would you attribute this difference?

## SUGGESTED REFERENCES

Beckhart, Benjamin, ed., *Business Loans of American Commercial Banks* (New York: The Ronald Press, 1959).

Federal Reserve Bank of New York, *Money Market Essays*, 1952.

Madden, Carl H., *The Money Side of "The Street"* (Federal Reserve Bank of New York, 1959). Chapters 5 and 6.

CHAPTER 7

# Portfolio Management

The object of portfolio management is to achieve the pattern and distribution of assets necessary to satisfy bank needs for liquidity, solvency, and income. These needs are competitive because the assets that provide maximum liquidity generate little or no income, etc. Consequently, the problem presented to the bank's officers is the familiar one of maximizing well being subject to constraints. The answer, of course, is to equate the marginal return per asset dollar in all directions.

By "equating the marginal return per asset dollar" is meant that a distribution of assets has been achieved so that no further gain can be attained by shifting a dollar from one form of asset into another. That is, the return lost from shifting out of one form is offset by the gain from the acquired asset—no net additional return is possible. When this distribution of assets is achieved, the marginal return per asset dollar is equalized in all uses, and the distribution of assets is optimum.

In order to see how a bank goes about solving this problem of asset distribution we shall look to the ends as well as the means. That is, we shall consider the necessity of providing for liquidity, solvency, and income and then the means whereby these needs are satisfied. We have already discussed the various assets a bank holds; now we are ready to determine why it holds the particular distribution of assets that it does.

In general we can determine four basic uses for bank funds. They are as follows: primary reserves, secondary reserves, customer demands

108

for funds, and open-market purchases of earning assets.[1] Primary reserves consist of the legally required reserves held as deposit balances at the Federal Reserve or as vault cash, plus correspondent bank balances sufficient for assuring efficient operations and service for a bank's customers. These primary reserves constitute the bulk of the bank's cash assets.

Secondary reserves or protective investments perform precisely the role suggested by their name. These are assets that yield some income to the bank, but more importantly, they can be converted from an earning asset into a cash asset with little or no delay or loss of principal. As Professor Robinson puts it, these assets will provide funds, if necessary, "(1) for likely and indeed almost forecastable cash needs, (2) for remote, unlikely, but possible cash needs."[2] These assets serve as a second line of defense in protecting against unforeseen contingencies, above and beyond that provided by the primary reserves or cash assets.

The third priority item is to provide for the bank's customers. The first two priorities serve to insure the bank's ability to continue in business by meeting the claims presented to it for payment. After providing for these the bank now is able to consider its customers' needs for funds. The commercial bank has an important function to fulfill in making funds available to the local community. It is a job for which it should have advantages over competing financial institutions. This simply means that commercial banks will tend to know the local situation thoroughly, extending credit to customers whose operations and needs are intimately known and understood by the banker. But this advantage of banks over other financial institutions does not necessarily carry over into dealings in the open market for investments. In the latter area the insurance companies and trust funds hold sway, with large investment research staffs searching out prime investments.

Thus we arrive at the last use of bank funds, the purchase of investment securities, or earning assets, on the open market. If the first three use-priorities have not exhausted bank lendable funds then, to maximize income, the otherwise idle funds are used in the open market purchase of earning assets. The average commercial bank is too small to maintain a large research staff; for its needs it generally screens the recommendations made by outside rating agencies.

Clearly the asset mix owned by a bank is conditioned by a diversity

---

[1] Roland I. Robinson, *The Management of Bank Funds*, 2nd ed. (New York: McGraw-Hill Company, 1962), pp. 12–18.
[2] *Ibid.*, p. 15.

of factors.   Some assets are held because they are legally required or
because they are necessary for efficient operation.   These are its primary reserves or cash assets.   The rest of the bank's assets comprise
its "loans and investments."   But as we have seen, part of these
investments are held with only secondary consideration given to earnings.   These we termed "secondary reserves," though this term has no
legal significance.   Actually we can classify bank assets in several
ways.   In the previous chapter we considered *classes* of loans and
investments owned by the bank.   Now it is useful to consider the
*function* or role fulfilled by the asset in question.   Thus, from a functional point of view, we divide assets into primary reserves, secondary
reserves, and loans and investments.   But the distinction between the
latter two functions is not hard and fast.   For after all, "secondary
reserves" are loans and investments in the sense of the previous chapter
—that is, classified according to type and not to function.

## THE ENDS OF PORTFOLIO MANAGEMENT

The goals of portfolio management are to provide the bank with
liquidity, solvency, and income.   These particular ends are, of course,
not unique to banking.   Most business activities pursue the same
goals.   But in these latter nonbank business situations, the liquidity
problem may often be subordinated to the other two, especially to
income.   Not so, however, for the commercial bank.

The commercial bank is unique in that almost all of its liabilities
are payable on demand or after rather short notice.   If the bank cannot
meet demands for payment it cannot remain in business.   Hence, the
overriding emphasis on liquidity.

Due to several factors, solvency also presents a problem for the bank.
Insolvency occurs when liabilities exceed the value of assets.   Bank
liabilities are in fixed dollar terms, but asset values are to some extent
subject to variation.   Thus, the market value of securities held by the
bank moves inversely with changes in the market rate of interest.   Or
the value may decline from losses through default or fear of default.

The final goal of commercial bank portfolio management is to
obtain income.   But in the quest for earnings the bank must always
keep in mind the needs for maintaining solvency and liquidity.   There
often appear to be conflicts between the goal of maximizing income
and the other objectives.   For example, in the short run, income
objectives are secondary to liquidity and solvency considerations.
But clearly, to assure long-run earnings the bank must make provision
for these other needs in order to have a continued existence.   Thus,

what may appear inconsistent with respect to short-run profit maximization is perfectly consistent with a long-run view of profit maximizing.

## Liquidity

Commercial banks can appropriately be called dealers in debt. The bulk of commercial banks' assets are the debts or promissory notes of others which have been purchased by creating liabilities or claims against the bank. These liabilities of commercial banks are principally demand deposits and time deposits. The demand deposits are liabilities payable on demand and, although the banks technically can require prior notice for withdrawal of a time deposit, they customarily do not invoke this rule. In any event, what is important here is to understand that the bulk of bank liabilities are contractual obligations to pay fixed dollar amounts on demand or after very short notice.

The ownership of the demand deposits is a factor that a bank considers in determining its policy towards maintaining its liquidity. That is, there are different patterns of deposit and withdrawal between small personal accounts and the accounts of corporate and financial institutions. For example, the small personal accounts are pretty much stable in the aggregate, with deposits and withdrawals tending to offset one another. Furthermore, the fluctuations in totals that do appear are seasonal in nature and may be easily taken into account by the bank. On the other hand, the behavior of commercial accounts is more erratic and subject to wide fluctuations in activity. The accounts of financial institutions especially show great activity and instability. In an effort to provide for liquidity by providing sufficient cash assets and secondary reserves readily convertible into cash, the bank must take into account the ownership of its deposit liabilities, their stability, and the probable behavior of the accounts.

In order that they may more easily calculate their liquidity needs, banks often arrange with large corporate depositors to give them advance knowledge of impending withdrawals. In a similar fashion, the United States Treasury gives advance notice of withdrawals from its Tax and Loan accounts at the commercial banks. By these means banks can arrange to provide for payment when claims are presented to them, without the necessity of undergoing sudden unexpected adjustments in their asset position.

Another common device used by banks to limit the claims presented to them for payment is to require borrowers to maintain "compensating balances." This is the practice of requiring borrowers to maintain certain minimum balances on deposit, instead of allowing them to draw against the entire amount of the loan. Again, this results in the borrower effectively paying a higher rate of interest since he cannot use the entire amount of the loan, but pays interest on the whole amount nevertheless.

To summarize, since the majority of commercial bank liabilities are payable either on demand or after short notice, and since these liabilities are stated in fixed dollar terms, the bank finds it necessary to maintain cash assets in order to meet claims for payment. Since it is most unlikely that all deposit liabilities would be presented simultaneously for payment only a portion of assets must be maintained as cash assets, ready to meet payment demands. The question then becomes, what proportion of assets to hold as cash assets, since such assets earn no income and so are to be economized on. To determine an economical approach to the problem, the bank looks to such factors as the ownership of its deposit liabilities, their stability, seasonal factors, and so forth. But since liquidity needs are not exactly predictable, banks typically provide themselves with secondary reserves. The function of secondary reserves is to provide immediately available cash with little or no loss of principal if liquidation is necessary, and to provide nominal income if they are not needed for liquidity purposes.

## Solvency

As has been repeatedly emphasized, bank liabilities are fixed in dollar terms and, by and large, are payable on demand. Because their liabilities are largely payable on demand, banks must maintain sufficient liquid assets to meet demands for cash as they are made. This is the problem of liquidity; it is essentially the problem of keeping liquid assets equal to liquid liabilities.

But the bank has another problem as well. This is the long-run problem of keeping the realizable value of all assets equal to the value of total liabilities. This is the question of bank solvency. As long as the assets equal liabilities a banking concern is solvent. Should the value of assets decline, but less than the amount of bank capital, then capital is said to be impaired, yet the bank is still solvent. Should the assets decline in value until the margin of bank capital is wiped out, then insolvency exists. Since bank liabilities are in fixed dollars, it follows that the causes of insolvency lie in changes in the value of bank assets. What causes these changes in the value of bank assets?

One source of difficulty is the continual exposure of bank employees and officials to large sums of money. It is by no means unknown that these individuals occasionally bow to temptation and appropriate some of the bank's funds for themselves.   But a much more important source of difficulty are assets that do not turn out as expected when initially acquired.   In an effort to minimize this possibility banks are regulated as to the types of assets they may acquire.

For example, loans to bank officers may not exceed $2,500; mortgage holdings may be restricted to a specified ratio of time deposits or capital; banks typically may not own corporate stock except that acquired as collateral on defaulted loans, and then they are to sell it as soon as reasonably can be done without undue loss; securities issued by any one borrower may be owned in amounts not exceeding 10 per cent of the bank's capital and surplus (government obligations are exempt from this restriction); and so forth.   The purpose of these restrictions is to encourage diversification—to compel it, in fact—and so to reduce the risk of asset depreciation.   The rules also serve to strengthen the bank's independence of any one extremely large borrower, and also to prevent the bank's resources from being used directly to advance its officers' personal fortunes.   But in spite of these safeguards, asset values do deteriorate.

The reasons for declines in the values of assets are many.   For example, loans made now with every expectation of their being sound can turn out poorly because of an unexpected business recession which adversely affects the borrower's ability to discharge the debt.   Even "self-liquidating," short-term commercial loans get into difficulties in such periods, and may necessitate many renewals or extensions before repayment is finally made.   Similarly, long-term commitments which can now be easily handled by the borrower may become impossible due to a future shift of demand away from his product or service.   For these and other reasons reflecting the uncertainty of economic life, default or the fear of possible default may bring about a fall in the market value of assets.

But even if there is absolutely no question at all about the debt being repaid along with the interest paid regularly when due, there can still be changes in the market value of assets held.   Consider, for example, United States Treasury bonds.   Here are obligations certain to be repaid, with the interest paid regularly as due.   How, then, can the value of these bonds change?   The answer is simply by having the *current* market rate of interest change.   Specifically, the market value of securities moves inversely to changes in the current market rate of interest.   Thus, if the going interest rate moves up, the market value of assets owned declines.

To show the inverse relationship between security prices and the interest rate consider the following example.   Assume that one owns a never-maturing bond (a British consol, for instance) which pays $30 annually. What is the value of such an asset? The answer depends on the interest rate. If the current rate of interest is 3 per cent, then the bond is clearly worth $1,000, since 3 per cent of $1,000 is $30. But now note this: if the current market interest rate should rise to 4 per cent the value of the bond falls to $750, for $30 is 4 per cent of $750. That is, with the interest rate at 4 per cent it takes only $750 at this rate to earn $30 per year. Clearly the market value of the bond and the interest rate move in opposite directions.

But the typical loan contract ordinarily specifies a particular number of payments of stated size. In general then, if we are given a stream of future returns and a present value or cost of a loan contract promising to pay such returns, we can compute a rate of interest. Consider, for example, the following. United States Treasury 4s of 1971 were quoted in the June 28, 1963 financial news at about $1,001.20 with an associated yield of 3.95 per cent. This means that for $1,001.20 one could purchase a $1,000 United States Treasury bond with a coupon rate of 4 per cent, yielding annual interest payments of $40. Thus, for $1,001.20 one can purchase $40 a year for eight years until 1971, at which time the principal amount of $1,000 will also be repaid.

A rough method of approximating the effective interest rate is to reduce the return on the $1,001.20 to an annual average. This annual average divided by $1,001.20 will approximate the true effective interest rate. In the course of holding the bond eight years till maturity there is realized a capital loss of $1.20, or about $.15 per year. This means the $40 per year interest payments net only $39.85 per year. This figure of $39.85 divided by $1,001.20 gives 3.98 per cent as the crude approximation to the effective rate, as against the true yield figure quoted of 3.95 per cent.

The point of the exercise is to demonstrate that the purchase of a debt instrument ordinarily involves a stream of future payments, and that given a price this implies an interest rate. Furthermore, as the current market interest rate changes this changes the present value of the stream of future payments; that is, the market price of the security moves inversely to the change in interest rates. Given this relationship between interest rates and security prices, if the interest rate moves up the market value of bank earning assets fall. It is to be noted, however, that the time to maturity also plays a large role. Thus, for any given change in the interest rate, the farther away the maturity date the greater is the change in the market value of the security. As a consequence the bank has additional reasons for holding short-term securities: they are insulated from wide fluctuations in value. This is another aspect of liquidity, then. Even a long-term bond may become part of a bank's secondary reserve as it approaches to, say, within a year of maturity. This means that the realizable price in event of its liquidation is more certain, and differs from its stated redemption value by only a small amount. But, of course, by loading up on short-term securities the bank precludes much chance of capital appreciation should interest rates fall.

The discussion may be summarized by noting the two types of risk to which banks expose themselves by holding debt contracts as the bulk of their assets. The first kind of risk is the *risk of default;* the second risk is the *interest rate risk.* Both risks are due to the uncertainty of future events. The risk of default ranges from practically no risk in instruments such as short-term Treasury obligations or the highest grade of corporate debt, through many shadings or gradations of risk. The problem of judging graduations of risk requires a considerable degree of skill. For what clearly may appear to be currently within a borrowing firm's ability to pay may five years later turn out not to be the case. The firm's prospects may have definitely turned for the worse. Thus, the further into the future the less certain one is about the actual ability of the borrower to carry the debt. Or perhaps additional future debt may be incurred that may cast doubt on the borrower's ability to carry the larger volume of debt. Because of this uncertainty element, the risk of default is present. This risk element must be covered in the price of the security, and banks typically buy debt which has only slight chance of default. Thus, the price differentials among various debt instruments, other factors being equal, presumably reflect the risk of default. This in itself presents the banker with a problem. To maximize profits the banker needs high yields, but these are associated with the riskier opportunities. Thus, skill and judgment are required to evaluate the opportunities open to the bank— for if the loan is defaulted not only does income suffer but solvency is also impaired.

The interest rate risk is inherent in contracts calling for fixed payments over time. As conditions change, the interest rate may rise and so lower the value of the debt instrument. And, if for any reason the contract must be sold, it is the new prevailing conditions that count; thus, a capital loss may be suffered. Hence, bonds that are free of any default risk are still subject to the interest rate risk, for the future level of interest rates is something less than certain.

### Income

In determining the composition of his asset mix the banker must give primary attention to maintaining liquidity and solvency. After satisfying these requirements he is then able to take up the question of providing for bank earnings or profits. Although it may appear that income considerations are being subordinated to liquidity and solvency considerations, in the long run it is clear that the best earnings necessarily entail careful and continual concern for liquidity and solvency. Indeed, these two questions must be satisfactorily answered if the bank is to have any long-run earnings at all. Clearly, if a bank chose only those assets bearing the greatest interest rate it would soon find that as its depositors withdrew their funds it could not make its payments as directed. And a bank which finds itself in this situation will not long survive.

The problem facing the banker is first to satisfy liquidity and solvency needs, and then to worry about maximizing earnings or profits. Assuming that the liquidity and solvency concerns have been satisfied let us turn to the question of earnings. Profits are the difference between income and costs. Since most bank costs, for example, equip ment, vaults, staff, etc. are pretty well fixed in the short run, the maximization of income and minimization of variable costs maximizes profits.

The first thing to consider in evaluating assets for income purposes is to attempt to determine the yields available on the various loan and investment choices open to the bank. In attempting to estimate the yield from some lending opportunity the bank must consider three factors. The first factor to determine is the likeliest value of gross receipts from the asset during the length of its most probable stay in the bank's portfolio. The second factor determining yield is the variable cost involved in ownership of the asset. The third and last determinant of yield is the actual present cost or price of the earning asset. On some of the factors the bank may have considerable information, but only on the last item, the price or cost of the asset, has it an actual datum. The rest are estimates. The yield is thus only an estimated or anticipated yield, and it is the discount rate which makes the known present cost of the asset equal to the expected gross receipts less estimated variable cost associated with ownership of the asset.

The estimation of gross receipts obtainable from some lending opportunity is not without its difficulties. As noted earlier, a loan contract typically specifies a particular number of payments of some stated amount. In some instances repayment is virtually certain, for example, United States Treasury obligations; in other cases, perhaps consumer loans, default is a possibility. There is the risk of default involved here in estimating gross receipts—will the borrower make good his obligations as contracted? But there is also the interest rate risk. A bank may purchase some marketable security expecting to sell it at some future time, but prior to its maturity. Clearly, the market price obtainable in the future is not certain, and the bank will incur a capital loss on resale if interest rates rise during the period the security is in the bank portfolio. Thus, the gross receipts estimate involves both the specified payments being made while the bank owns the asset, and also any capital gain or loss if the security is sold prior to its maturity.

We have called the "investment" portion of a commercial bank's portfolio those financial assets bought and sold in the open market. That is, "investments" are marketable securities. For this type of asset, even for the most gilt-edged security, there always exists the interest rate risk—the possibility of losing money on a later sale of the asset. On the other hand, those assets that constitute "loans" are nonmarketable securities. In buying these nonmarketable securities the bank is not concerned with the interest rate risk, the chance of a capital loss on resale, since it does not plan on disposing of them. But it is concerned with the risk of default that is present here.

From the foregoing discussion it is evident that estimates of gross receipts are subject to wide margins of error. The estimates are not objective fact. They are at best subjective estimates based on as much objective fact as possible.[3]

The second factor that determines yield is the cost of acquiring and holding the asset. Net receipts are the difference between the gross receipts and variable costs associated with holding the asset. It is probably correct to say that it is easier for a bank to forecast the costs associated with the purchase of an earning asset than to estimate the gross receipts. Many banks, especially the larger ones, have rather detailed information on the supplementary costs associated with additions to their holdings of earning assets. These costs constitute the bank's variable costs. Thus, banks generally have a good idea of the costs involved in servicing the various types of loans and investments— for example, the costs associated with handling a purchase of government securities or, perhaps, term loans to businesses. Since for a given class of loan or investment the servicing costs are about the same

---

[3] To illustrate this argument, in 1958 one of the largest West Coast banks, and one of the nation's largest, loaded up on long-term Treasury bonds in the expectation of a light loan demand. Private loan demand turned out to be quite heavy and to meet it required the liquidation of virtually all short-term governments and substantial amounts of the long-terms as well, the latter at a loss. As the annual report wryly put it, "losses were incurred" in the selling of the long-term bonds to obtain necessary reserves to meet the unexpected loan demand.

regardless of the dollar amount of the loan involved, the larger the principal amount the more profitable it is for the bank.  That is, the net receipts are larger since gross receipts are larger on the larger principal amount, but the service costs are the same for any size loan.

The final bit of information needed to determine yield is the price or cost of the earning asset.  This is a concrete, objective datum—the only objective factor of the three, the other two being in some measure subjective estimates.

The estimated yield is the calculated discount rate, which makes the expected gross receipts obtainable from the asset during its stay in the bank's portfolio, less the costs associated with administering the asset, equal to its purchase price.  That is, the yield is the discount rate that serves to equate estimated net receipts to the known asset cost.

Estimation of yield is a crucial matter for banks.  If banks are pessimistic they will refuse to acquire earning assets, holding on to excess reserves.  Then their revenues decline and their fixed costs undermine net worth.  On the other hand, if they are overly optimistic and their estimates turn out badly the result is insolvency.  It seems they are "damned if they do, and damned if they don't."  As we saw earlier, one way to avoid the interest rate risk is to hold only fixed price assets, cash or short-term, gilt-edged securities, but this reduces income.  And to minimize risk or default, diversification is necessary; the bank cannot afford to put all of its loans and investments in one "basket."

One of the interesting aspects of portfolio management is the balancing of short-run profit opportunities against long-run profit maximizing.  What this means is that a bank's loan committee knows that the decision to buy one kind of earning asset likely requires the passing up of an opportunity to buy some other kind of earning asset.  That is, the bank has several different opportunities to lend, but having decided on one it must forego the others.  Thus, if a bank buys a short-term government security instead of lending to a struggling but up-and-coming local firm, the bank will get a definite return with no chance of default and minimum chance of loss if it must liquidate the asset.  But this may also cut down the likelihood of expanding profitable lending activities and of attracting deposits.  For after all, the typical bank is intimately tied to its own particular locale.  Thus, bank loans that favor local businesses and residents may, in the long run, benefit a bank many times over by increasing its earnings over the years.  It follows that a bank may be maximizing profits in the long run by incurring somewhat more risk than short-run profit considerations dictate, by accommodating worthy local customers first, even at the expense, if necessary, of turning down outside borrowers.   For the bulk of the bank's deposits and other income producing activities, such as trust accounts, will be due to its serving local persons and business firms.

## THE MEANS TO THE END OF PORTFOLIO MANAGEMENT

The preceding section was devoted to outlining the needs for maintaining liquidity and solvency while still earning profits.   Now we want to relate these specific ends to the means by which they are attained.

Earlier we saw that four major or basic uses of bank funds can be distinguished.   They are: (1) primary reserves, (2) secondary reserves, (3) customer demands for funds, and (4) open-market purchases of earning assets.   The previous section on "bank income" dealt with customer demands and open-market purchases of earning assets.   Now we must treat uses one and two, primary and secondary reserves.

We are here dealing with bank assets with respect to the *function* or *role* they play in the bank's portfolio.   This is unlike the treatment in the chapter "Uses of Commercial Bank Lending Power" which discussed the various *classes* of loans and investments.   We are now ready to put the pieces together.

### Primary Reserves

Primary reserves, or cash assets, as we now know, consist of the legally required reserves for the bank, held as vault cash or deposit balances at the Federal Reserve, plus correspondent balances with other banks, plus cash items in process of collection.

The legally required reserves were originally thought of as a means of forcing commercial banks to keep prudent standards of liquidity so as to be able to meet withdrawal requests.   Over the years this concept of the role of legal reserves has changed until today it is understood that the legal reserve requirement is one of the principal means of monetary regulation by the Federal Reserve System.   Since we operate on a fractional reserve basis, and the law does not permit extended operation with less than the required reserves, these funds do not provide a major source of liquidity.   That is, assuming a 20 per cent reserve ratio, for every $1.00 withdrawn required reserves fall by twenty cents.   But the remaining eighty cents must be paid out of other assets, principally by drawing on correspondent balances at other banks or by liquidating secondary reserves.

Cash items in process of collection are checks and other matured items which the bank owns for which payment has not yet been received, but which are in the process of being collected on. This item does not actually provide the bank with a source of usable funds, since each bank roughly figures that an equivalent sum of checks is on the way to it for payment.

### Secondary Reserves

Secondary reserves are simply protective investments, assets which can be quickly liquidated into cash with little or no loss of principal. They are typically short-term Treasury obligations, the 90-day Treasury bill for instance. But actually any asset that can be immediately converted to cash can be classed as a part of secondary reserves. Thus, high-grade corporate or Treasury bonds within a year of maturity are quickly marketable at close to their face value. The crucial aspects to which assets held as secondary reserves must conform are: (1) they must be open-market obligations of unimpeachable credit standing; (2) they should be of such short maturity that most of the time they will be held to maturity, but if sold prior to maturity their sale will not produce more than trivial losses.

As the principal purposes for holding secondary reserves is to meet liquidity needs if necessary, yield, if any, is subsidiary. But given the types of securities that fulfill this need they clearly fall into what we earlier called "loans and investments." Recall, however, that by investment is meant simply financial assets that sell on the impersonal open market. Loans, on the other hand, result from the personal dealings of banker *vis à vis* customer. There should be no confusion on this point between the *class* to which an asset is assigned and the *function* it performs.

### Loans and Investments

Loans and investments actually constitute the "(2) secondary reserve, (3) customer demands for funds, and (4) open-market purchases of earning assets" mentioned at the beginning of this section. As noted, the distinguishing characteristic between loans and investments is the personal nature of the former and the impersonal, open-market nature of the latter. These two items constitute the earning assets of the bank, though some investments may also serve as secondary reserves.

The various classes of securities which constitute loans and investments have been discussed earlier and so will not be repeated here. But it is clearly from this "loans and investments" portion of the portfolio that income is derived. Thus, proper portfolio management necessitates a recognition of the various uses to which bank assets may be put, both nonincome as well as income-producing, consistent with the objectives of liquidity, solvency, and income.

## SUMMARY

This chapter has examined the problem of portfolio management. The problem is a common one, namely the maximizing of well-being subject to constraints. What the bank wishes to do is to maximize profit while providing for liquidity and solvency. These ends may well run at cross-purposes, or so it may appear.

The loan opportunities offering the greatest return may well be the riskiest. To loan to a high risk borrower is to increase income if all goes well, but to court insolvency if it does not. Similarly, loans typically offer a greater return than investments, but investments are readily marketable and so serve as protection in case of liquidity needs. In order to protect against risk in an uncertain world, banks will diversify their assets so as to minimize risk and maximize net revenues.

Thus, total assets are allocated between cash assets and earning assets. The cash assets are largely determined by legal and institutional requirements. The earning assets will be divided between gilt-edged, open market investments and loans. The gilt-edged securities will be partly short-term for secondary reserve liquidity purposes and long-term for income purposes. The loans will be similarly divided among classes of borrowers. But presumably the principle for this allocation will be to equalize the marginal rate of return, adjusted for risk factors, on all the various types of assets.

Notice the use of "presumably" in the preceding sentence. Because the real world in which the banker operates is characterized by uncertainty, the marginal rule is probably never fulfilled. The banker operates according to averages and rules of thumb. But, nevertheless, the general considerations raised here are the ones that the banker somehow has to answer.

## REVIEW QUESTIONS

1. What are the goals of commercial bank portfolio management?
2. There are two basic kinds of risk in holding debt securities. What are they?
3. Even if United States Treasury obligations are judged free of risk of default, the interest rate risk still remains. Why is this so?

4. Construct an arithmetic example to show the inverse relationship between security prices and the interest rate.
5. What are primary reserves and what is their function? Are primary reserves legal reserves?
6. What are secondary reserves and what is their function? Are secondary reserves legal reserves?
7. From which side of the balance sheet does the problem of bank solvency originate? Explain.
8. What factors enter into the estimation of the yield to be obtained from an earning asset?
9. Explain the meaning of the marginal principle for determining optimum portfolio asset mix.

## SUGGESTED REFERENCES

Kennedy, Walter, *Bank Management* (Boston: Bankers Publishing Co., 1958).
Lyon, Roger A., *Investment Portfolio Management in the Commercial Bank* (Rutgers University Press, 1960).
Robinson, Roland I., *The Management of Bank Funds*, 2nd ed. (New York: McGraw-Hill Book Co., 1962).

PART **III**

# CENTRAL BANKING AND OTHER MONETARY INSTITUTIONS

# CHAPTER *8*

# *The Federal Reserve System: Structure*

To understand the Federal Reserve System, the central banking organization in American economic life, it is necessary to review briefly the development of the American commercial banking system. This summary will cover the major domestic banking developments which led to the legislation establishing the Federal Reserve System in 1913.

We shall divide our treatment of the Federal Reserve System into three major topical areas. The first of these, the structure of the Federal Reserve System, will be covered in the present chapter. The following chapter will take up the functions of the Federal Reserve System. Finally, the third topic, Federal Reserve controls over the money supply, will be investigated in Chapters 10 and 11.

## MAJOR DEVELOPMENTS IN THE COMMERCIAL BANK SYSTEM

The history and evolution of the American system of commercial banks and their relationship to the central bank is a fascinating topic, worthy of extended treatment in detail. For our purposes, however, certain salient features stand out, and only these aspects of bank history will be examined. The particular features that will help us understand the present sytem are the change in bank liabilities from bank note issue to deposit liabilities, and the change in banking philosophy from the so-called "commercial-loan" theory of banking to the bank's becoming a regular department store for credit.

The first bank in the modern sense of the word in the United States was the Bank of North America, founded in Philadelphia in 1782.

This bank, and others like it that soon followed, was located in a commercial center on the Atlantic seaboard. The loans made by these institutions were short-term loans, secured by goods in the process of exchange and liquidated upon sale of the goods. They were in the strictest sense short-term, self-liquidating loans—and it was this type of loan around which the "commercial-loan" tradition was built. Loans were to be made only for short-term "productive" purposes, and were secured by readily salable goods and inventories. Although this was the accepted banking doctrine for over a hundred years, actual commercial bank practice continually departed from it.

The reason for this departure is easily found. The frontier did not stay near the coastal commercial centers, but moved inland. This movement of the frontier with its attendant agricultural expansion, foundry and mill establishment, etc., absorbed more of the increasing population into these activities than into merchandising. Thus, the interests of the frontier area were more industrial and agricultural in nature than commercial. The accompanying demand for credit for these activities was consequently of a long-term nature, rather than of the short-term, self-liquidating commercial type. This demand for long-term credit made it impossible for most banks to operate in the "commercial-loan" tradition. And today, as we have seen, banks engage in a variety of lending activities, both short-term and long-term.

Although we have discussed the demand on the banks for credit, we have not discussed the form that the extension of bank credit took. In early American banking the extension of credit took the form of an increase in bank note circulation, and not in demand deposits as is now the practice. When loans were made, the borrower received the proceeds of the loan in the form of bank notes issued by the bank. These bank notes circulated from individual to individual and formed the bulk of the money supply.

From 1782 to 1836, the expiration date of the charter of the Second Bank of the United States, there was an increase in state-chartered banks to about 700 in number, with only one federally chartered bank, the Bank of the United States. The note issue of these state-chartered banks over which the Federal government exercised no control formed the bulk of the money supply. In 1838 there occurred a significant change with regard to the establishment of state banks. Until this time it took special legislative action to grant a state bank charter. But in 1838 New York passed the Free Banking Act. This Act provided that anyone could be granted a bank charter without special legislative action by complying with certain general conditions, including the pledging of securities with the state bank supervisory authorities against their circulating notes.    This Free Banking Act resulted from two main considerations: (1) with the rapid growth of the nation, the public was dissatisfied with the limited availability of credit and access to it; (2) at the same time there was mounting public dissatisfaction with the frequent failure of banks to honor their notes, and with the subsequent discounting of the circulating notes.    Thus, the Act attempted to provide a more abundant supply of bank credit, while at the same time provide a better circulating medium.

This "free banking" spread rapidly from New York into other areas. In the remoter frontier regions it frequently degenerated into what was called "wildcat" banking.    Banks were established in regions where, it was claimed, only wildcats lived, and consequently there was little chance that the circulating notes would be presented for redemption.    An additional difficulty was that swindlers often took advantage of frontier ignorance of securities by acquiring bonds of little or no value, pledging them in exchange for their face value in circulating notes, and then vanishing.    The various abuses of free banking—frequent bank failures, failures to redeem notes in specie, limited capital and the evasion of capital requirements, counterfeiting opportunities, etc.,—led to fundamental change in the "freedom" to engage in banking.    Today, instead of having to grant a charter to anyone agreeing to the provisions of the Act, the banking authorities grant charters only when the proposed bank has competent management and reasonable prospects for success.

A major factor contributing to the banking difficulties of the time was the equating of the redemption of bank notes to the securities pledged.    Thus, as long as the bank notes were secured by pledged collateral, the notes were assumed to be safe (retain their face value) even though not redeemable in specie.    Indeed, the New York Free Banking Act which initially required specie reserves of $12\frac{1}{2}$ per cent repealed this provision in 1844.    Specie redemption was generally considered to be a legal technicality, something that the bank promised to do, but which it would make every effort to keep from doing.    But with this type of thinking prevalent, there were numerous bank failures and crises.

However, the importance of adequate bank reserves was brought out in the panic of 1857.    This panic saw the suspension of note redemption by most of the country's commercial banks, the New Orleans banks being the notable exception. Unlike most states, Louisiana imposed substantial reserve requirements on banks under its jurisdiction. The reserve requirements saw each bank maintaining cash assets equal to one-third of its combined note and deposit liabilities, and liquid assets (non-renewable loans maturing within three months) equal to the other two-thirds. The banks might own long-term notes only to the amount of their capital funds. When the Louisiana banks successfully weathered the financial panic without suspending redemption, other banks soon adopted similar reserve requirements against note and deposit liabilities. But only Louisiana and Massachusetts had statutory requirements when the National Bank Act, with such requirements, was adopted in 1863.

At about this time an important shift in the composition of the money supply was occurring. The volume of demand deposits came to exceed the amount of bank notes in circulation. After 1875 bank notes began to decline in volume, their place being taken by other forms of currency and demand deposits. It was not until 1935, however, that private commercial banks finally lost their note issue privilege.

The National Bank Act of 1863 aimed at bringing all banks under Federal authority. Banks chartered under provisions of this National Bank Act were essentially the same as free banks chartered under state laws, except the charters were granted by the Federal government and the collateral securing their notes had to be United States government bonds. The principal features of this Act which concern us are the bank note regulations and the reserve requirements.

Any bank notes issued by national banks were secured by Treasury bonds deposited by the banks with the Comptroller of Currency. Instead of the rush to join the National Banking System, many banks preferred to continue operating under state laws. In an attempt to force these state banks into the system, a 10 per cent annual tax on the notes was passed. The result of this punitive tax was to eliminate state bank notes, but not the state banks. They turned instead to deposit banking in place of bank note issue.

The reserve requirements of the national banks were determined by their location. As we learned earlier, there were three classes of banks: central reserve city banks in New York, Chicago, and St. Louis; reserve city banks in other major financial centers; and so-called country banks. It will be recalled that the reserve requirements were 25 per cent in vault cash against all note and deposit liabilities for the central reserve city banks; 25 per cent for reserve city banks of which half might be held as a deposit with a central reserve city bank; and 15 per cent for country banks, three-fifths of which might be held as deposit balances in reserve or central reserve city banks.

Although the national banks did constitute a considerable advance in banking development, they also brought disadvantages. Their improvements included the establishment of a safe, uniform currency and a reduction in the number of bank failures through strengthening due to more conservative standards of regulation and examination. And finally, there developed a measure of correspondent banking relations through the provision for regarding deposits in reserve and central reserve city banks as reserves. But this last feature also was the system's greatest weakness.

An important feature of the correspondent relationship was the provision that country banks might borrow from their city correspondents should their balances become inadequate, whether because of currency requirements or because of their customers making large payments by check. As long as relatively few country banks wanted to borrow or withdraw funds, the system worked fine. But when all wanted to borrow at the same time trouble resulted. And simultaneous massive demands did occur. For example, every summer and fall banks in agricultural areas had to draw on their reserve balances for funds to finance crops through to harvest. In many cases they had to borrow from the city banks. The currency provided was the city banks' own reserves, and the loss of these cut into their lending ability. They were less able to meet the demands of their country bank correspondents and less able to meet their own customers' demands as well. The big difficulty was the inability of the system to create additional reserves.

Whatever reserves the system as a whole held, that was the limit. The banks had to get along with them whether or not they were adequate. One bank might gain reserves, but at the expense of some other bank's losing reserves. In 1907 the reserves proved to be inadequate. The city banks were suddenly faced by an unusually large demand on their reserves. They were unable to obtain additional reserves so they held on to what reserves they had, obligations to depositors notwithstanding. The system thus provided for the concentration of existing reserves into the city banks, but no provision was made for the creation of new reserves when necessary.

In addition, the amount of currency in circulation bore no necessary relationship to the needs for currency.   The currency supply under the National Bank System was seasonally inelastic and responded not to the needs of trade, but rather to the price of bonds backing the notes. Thus, if the price of the bonds rose, the banks found it profitable to sell them.   This action reduced the amount of circulating currency, whether or not this was desired by the money using public.   Similarly, if the prices on bonds fell, the bank might find it profitable to buy the bonds and issue notes against them, regardless of whether the added currency was necessary.   Treasury finance also complicated the situation.   If the Treasury had a surplus it might retire the bonds, irrespective of whether this action was appropriate for the money supply.   Likewise, a deficit would find the Treasury borrowing, that is, issuing bonds even though the added money supply was not necessary for the public needs.

Difficulties such as these led to the eventual adoption of the Federal Reserve Act in 1913.   This major reform in the banking system culminated years of persistent proposals that a more elastic currency be provided, so that the volume of money in circulation might be responsive to changes in the public's demand for money.   It also provided a central banking mechanism, so that excessive changes in bank credit could be avoided by the creation or destruction of reserves in keeping with the needs of the money using public, and by the ability of the banks to meet those needs.   The next sections will show how the Federal Reserve meets these and other duties assigned to it.

## THE FEDERAL RESERVE SYSTEM: PERSPECTIVE

In 1913 the Federal Reserve Act established the Federal Reserve System.   The legislation embodied many recommendations of a National Monetary Commission appointed by Congress to evaluate the National Banking System following the unusually severe monetary crisis of 1907.

As we have seen, the National Bank System formed what might be called a financial pyramid.   At the top of the pyramid were the national banks located in New York, Chicago, and St. Louis, the central reserve cities.   Banks in these three cities had to maintain all of their required legal reserves as cash in their own vaults.   National Banks in the smaller cities and in rural areas were permitted to keep balances with commercial banks in the larger cities.   These balances were counted as part of the reserves of the smaller banks.   Thus, there resulted a piling up of resources in larger cities and financial centers.   Furthermore, not only did the outlying banks maintain part of their required reserves as correspondent deposit balances with the larger banks, they also maintained these correspondent bank balances over and above the minimum required reserves.[1]

If for any reason banks were pressed for funds by their customers, the demands ultimately converged onto the few commercial banks located in the financial centers.   In ordinary circumstances these large banks could expect demands for funds by outlying banks to be offset by deposits from other out-of-town banks which were building up their balances.    But if there should occur a net demand for the withdrawal of funds by out-of-town banks, the banks in the financial centers might find it difficult to provide the funds requested.

In the National Bank System era, the extension of bank credit took the form of note issue.   Because no facilities were available for providing additional reserves to back additional bank notes, the credit situation could become very tight.   For example, when outlying banks were trying to withdraw funds, the banks in the financial centers would have to sell securities in order to acquire the necessary funds or they would have to call existing loans and refuse to make new loans or to extend old ones.   These actions all tended to lower security prices as loans were liquidated.   Consequently, borrowing from any source became much more difficult, and interest rates tended to increase sharply.   In this situation, with the absence of a central bank to provide additional reserves, the banking system found itself in periodic difficulty.   The system could not generate the necessary reserves to back additional funds which might be needed.

Every few years there occurred large-scale demands on the banks in the financial centers for withdrawal of the funds deposited with them. These withdrawal demands would result in the wholesale liquidation of bank credit, the suspension of payments to depositors by the banks, and general financial chaos.   Such situations occurred in 1873, 1893, and 1907.   As a matter of fact, it was the panic of 1907 that led Congress to establish the Aldrich Commission—the National Monetary Commission—to investigate and recommend legislation to bring monetary order out of monetary chaos.   The commission's work was culminated in the Glass-Owen Bill, better remembered as the Federal Reserve Act.

---

[1] Since they received up to 4 per cent interest on these deposits it was profitable to do so.

The original purposes of the Act as stated in its preamble were to give the nation an elastic currency, responsive to the needs of business and commerce; to provide facilities for the discounting of commercial paper; and to improve the supervision of banking. Although these were the stated purposes of the legislation, there were also the additional implicit objectives of offsetting inflationary or deflationary movements and of providing a monetary climate favorable to sustained growth and employment.

In order to understand the lack of discussion concerning the goals of the System, we need only to review the theory behind the Act. The prevailing theory at the time held that economic instability in the form of periodic panics and depressions was due to imperfections and breakdowns in the money and credit mechanism. Consequently, if the monetary system's mechanical shortcomings could be eliminated the major cause of economic instability would also be removed. This theory of economic instability did seem to coincide with the economic realities of the time. Sometimes the failures of the monetary system took the form of a shortage of currency; other times the monetary system's imperfections took the form of prolonged lags in the collection and payment of checks; and sometimes the breakdowns were the result of sharp regional shifts of currency or deposits which put the financial centers under extreme pressures.

Given the foregoing factors, the objectives put forth in the preamble to the Federal Reserve Act certainly follow. Indeed, Senator Robert Owen, cosponsor of the Act and then Chairman of the Senate Committee on Banking and Currency, stated that the purpose of the Act was ". . . to establish an auxiliary system of banking which will tend to stabilize commerce and finance, to prevent future panics, and place the nation upon an era of enduring prosperity."

Today the original objectives of the Federal Reserve System have been merged into the broader objectives of offsetting inflationary and deflationary movements and maintaining monetary conditions favorable to high levels of employment and stable growth of the economy. To understand the role of the Federal Reserve in achieving these goals it is necessary to consider first the structure and functions of the System before turning to the methods of Federal Reserve control.

## THE STRUCTURE OF THE FEDERAL RESERVE SYSTEM

The Federal Reserve System is a uniquely American institution. It reflects to a considerable degree the debate that preceded its formation as to the extent of centralization or decentralization desirable in a central bank, and also reflects the concern that a single voice or interest should not dictate its policies.

The Federal Reserve System is not one bank, as we have seen, but rather is composed of twelve regional banks. Thus, the United States has not one central bank as most other countries have, but twelve central banks. Although each Federal Reserve Bank is a separate legal entity, the banks nevertheless are welded tightly together and the Federal Reserve System operates as one central bank.

The arguments leading to the regional bank concept were: (1) that the United States encompassed a huge area with diverse characteristics and needs; thus, it was felt that a single central bank could not serve the various conflicting regional interests as well as a system of regional central banks; (2) that a single central bank might succumb to the influence of the Eastern financial centers; and (3) that a single central bank would be dominated by the Federal government.

Although the regional structure of the System remains, it is not amiss to consider the twelve banks composing the Federal Reserve System as a single central bank. With improvements in communications and transportation, the money and credit market has become truly national in scope. The twelve district banks form a coordinated nation-wide unit, while at the same time remaining regional institutions. The organization of the Federal Reserve System consists of the following five segments:

(1) The Board of Governors, (2) The Federal Open Market Committee, (3) The Federal Advisory Council, (4) The Federal Reserve Banks, (5) The Member Banks of the Federal Reserve System.

We shall examine each of these five segments of the Federal Reserve System. In the discussion that follows, it should be kept in mind that only the current institutional structure is of concern to us although occasional reference will be made to the historical development of the System.

### The Board of Governors

The Board of Governors of the Federal Reserve System is located in Washington. The Board consists of seven members appointed by the President of the United States and confirmed by the Senate. The appointments are for a term of fourteen years and a member is not eligible for reappointment after serving a full term. The appointments are staggered so that one member's term expires every two years. No two members of the Board may come from the same Federal Reserve district. Since the Board members are full-time officers of the System, during their term of office they may have no connection with any bank or trust company as employee, director, officer, or stockholder. A member upon serving a full fourteen-year term may, however, become associated with a banking institution at once if he so desires. Any Board member who withdraws from the Board prior to the expiration of his full term must wait at least two years before joining a banking institution. The expenses of the Board of Governors and its staff are paid out of assessments levied upon the twelve Federal Reserve Banks.

The principal duties of the Board of Governors consist of the supervision and regulation of the various Reserve Banks and member banks, and the formulation and execution of general monetary policy. The Board supervises Reserve Bank operations by requiring periodic reports and statements of condition; appoints three of the nine directors, including the chairman and deputy chairman, of each district Federal Reserve Bank; and approves the appointment of the president and first vice-president of each district Reserve Bank. The Board also periodically examines the Reserve Banks and directs Reserve Bank procedures in examining and supervising member bank activities. The Board also decides upon the admission to or expulsion of member banks from the System, makes decisions as to the establishment of branches by state-chartered member banks, and regulates the interest rate paid by member banks on time deposits. The principal monetary powers of the Board are to "review and determine" discount rates set by the Reserve Banks, to determine the character of commercial paper eligible for rediscounting or advances, to control open market operations by constituting a majority representation on the Federal Open Market Committee, to establish reserve requirements, and to regulate margin requirements on stock-market credit.

The Board of Governors also represents the Federal Reserve System in most of its relations with Congressional activities and with various government departments. The Board submits an annual report to Congress and issues its monthly *Federal Reserve Bulletin*. It also publishes a weekly statement of the assets and liabilities of the Federal Reserve Banks.

### The Federal Open Market Committee

As we shall have occasion to see later, the Federal Reserve System's ability to engage in buying and selling operations of government securities constitutes one of its most powerful instruments for regulating the supply, cost, and availability of money.   The decisions about open market policy are made by the Federal Open Market Committee.

During the early years of the System, each individual Reserve Bank used its own discretion in undertaking open market operations.   These uncoordinated activities often ran at cross purposes with the different Reserve Banks pursuing conflicting goals.   Informal attempts to achieve uniformity were made during the 1920s and early 1930s but were only partially successful.   Congress established the Federal Open Market Committee in its present form in 1935.   The purpose of the Federal Open Market Committee is to establish System-wide policy for the purchase and sale of government securities in the open market. The Committee is comprised of the seven members of the Board of Governors and five representatives elected from the Federal Reserve Banks.   The Reserve Bank representatives are either presidents or first vice-presidents of the various banks.[2]   The Committee meets every three weeks to review the national business and credit situation.

Although not all are voting members of the Committee, the presidents of all twelve Reserve Banks also participate in the Committee's discussions.   This means that all decisions about open-market policy and its coordination with other instruments of monetary policy are made in the light of full discussion of both regional and national conditions.   In this way, with this full participation, the Federal Open Market Committee is the principal policy determining group of the System.

The decisions with regard to open-market policy are made by the Committee in Washington, but the actual purchase and sales of securities on the open market are carried out through the Federal Reserve Bank of New York in the name of the System Open Market Account. Each Federal Reserve Bank participates in the Open Market Account in a proportion equal to the ratio of its total assets to the total assets of all Reserve Banks combined.   Thus, all the Banks are represented

---

[2] The President of the Federal Reserve Bank of New York is always a member and is designated as vice chairman of the Committee.   The other four Federal Reserve representatives are selected from the Reserve Banks of Boston, Philadelphia, and Richmond; one from the Reserve Banks of Cleveland and Chicago; one from the Reserve Banks of Atlanta, Dallas, and St. Louis; and one from the Reserve Banks of Kansas City, Philadelphia, and San Francisco.

in the open-market purchases and sales of securities by the Federal Reserve System.

## Federal Advisory Council

The Federal Reserve Act also created the Federal Advisory Council. This Council consists of a representative from each district selected annually by the Board of Directors of each district Reserve Bank. The representatives are usually outstanding local bankers from each district. They meet four times a year in Washington. The Council confers with the Board of Governors on general business conditions and makes recommendations on banking and credit practice and policy, and on general aspects of the System. The role of the Federal Advisory Council is to serve as another link between the Board of Governors and the banking community of each Federal Reserve district.

## Federal Reserve Banks

The presence of twelve regional central banks serves as a reminder of the strong feelings held by many people against the concentration of financial and banking power. Each of the twelve Federal Reserve Banks is a separate corporation chartered by the Federal government. Originally the charters were to run for a period of twenty years, but in 1927 they were made indefinite to continue in force until annulled by Congressional action or for violation of the law. The twelve district Federal Reserve Banks are owned by their stockholders who are the member commercial banks of the Federal Reserve System in the respective district. The capital stock of the district Reserve Banks is subscribed to by the member banks in amounts equal to 6 per cent of their own capital and surplus, and their holdings are adjusted currently in accordance with changes occurring in their own capital and surplus positions. To date, only 3 per cent of each member bank's subscription has actually been paid in, with the remaining 3 per cent subject to call.

Although the Federal Reserve Banks are owned by their stockholders, the member banks of the System, they differ from privately managed commercial banks in that profits for the stockholders are not the goal of their operation. Further, the stockholder member banks do not have the proprietorship rights, powers, and privileges that ordinarily accrue to the stockholders of privately managed corporations.

The member banks receive a fixed statutory dividend (6 per cent) on their shares. Indeed, the "profit" sought by the Federal Reserve Banks is that of providing a smoothly operating, sound money and credit system. Any dollar profits are secondary and incidental to its principal goal.

The Federal Reserve Banks do earn a profit in their operations, however. Out of their earnings they pay the expenses of the Board of Governors, pay the 6 per cent cumulative dividend on their stock, and make any necessary additions to surplus. Since 1959, when the Board of Governors decided that maintenance of each Bank's surplus at a level of twice the paid-in capital was adequate, all earnings above expenses of dividends and required surplus have been paid to the Treasury. The preceding period of 1947–1958 saw 90 per cent of earnings above expenses and dividends paid to the Treasury.

The Boards of Directors of the twelve Reserve Banks further illustrate the Reserve Banks' public nature. The directors of each Federal Reserve Bank are so chosen as to provide the best financial and business leadership and knowledge to the System. The nine directors of each district Reserve Bank are divided into three groups: three Class A directors, three Class B directors, and three Class C directors. The Class A and Class B directors are elected by the district member banks, one director of each class being elected by small banks, one of each class by medium size banks, and one of each class by large banks. The three Class A directors are members of the banking community. The Class B directors must be actively engaged in the district in some commercial, industrial, or agricultural pursuit, and must not be officers, directors, or employees of any banks. The three Class C directors are appointed by the Board of Governors of the Federal Reserve System. They must not be officers, directors, employees, or stockholders of any bank. The Board of Governors designates one of the Class C directors as chairman of the Reserve Bank's Board of Directors and also appoints another as deputy chairman.

There are twelve Federal Reserve Banks serving the twelve Reserve districts. In addition to the main head office Reserve Bank in each district, most of the districts have branch Federal Reserve Banks. The branch Reserve Banks make the System's facilities more readily available in all parts of the country, expedite collections and other services, and perhaps forestall local jealousies against a Federal Reserve city. There are twenty-four branch Reserve Banks so there are thirty-six cities throughout the country with essentially equal central bank facilities. The districts and branches are listed as follows:

| | |
|---|---|
| Federal Reserve Bank of Boston | District Number 1 |
| Federal Reserve Bank of New York | District Number 2 |
|    Branch at Buffalo, New York | |
| Federal Reserve Bank of Philadelphia | District Number 3 |
| Federal Reserve Bank of Cleveland | District Number 4 |
|    Branches: Cincinnati, Ohio | |
|             Pittsburgh, Pennsylvania | |
| Federal Reserve Bank of Richmond | District Number 5 |
|    Branches: Baltimore, Maryland | |
|             Charlotte, North Carolina | |
| Federal Reserve Bank of Atlanta | District Number 6 |
|    Branches: Birmingham, Alabama | |
|             Jacksonville, Florida | |
|             Nashville, Tennessee | |
|             New Orleans, Louisiana | |
| Federal Reserve Bank of Chicago | District Number 7 |
|    Branch at Detroit, Michigan | |
| Federal Reserve Bank of St. Louis | District Number 8 |
|    Branches: Little Rock, Arkansas | |
|             Louisville, Kentucky | |
|             Memphis, Tennessee | |
| Federal Reserve Bank of Minneapolis | District Number 9 |
|    Branch at Helena, Montana | |
| Federal Reserve Bank of Kansas City | District Number 10 |
|    Branches: Denver, Colorado | |
|             Oklahoma City, Oklahoma | |
|             Omaha, Nebraska | |
| Federal Reserve Bank of Dallas | District Number 11 |
|    Branches: El Paso, Texas | |
|             Houston, Texas | |
|             San Antonio, Texas | |
| Federal Reserve Bank of San Francisco | District Number 12 |
|    Branches: Los Angeles, California | |
|             Portland, Oregon | |
|             Salt Lake City, Utah | |
|             Seattle, Washington | |

*Figure 8-1* (*facing page*) The Federal Reserve System. Boundaries of Federal Reserve districts and their branch territories. Source: *Federal Reserve Bulletin.*

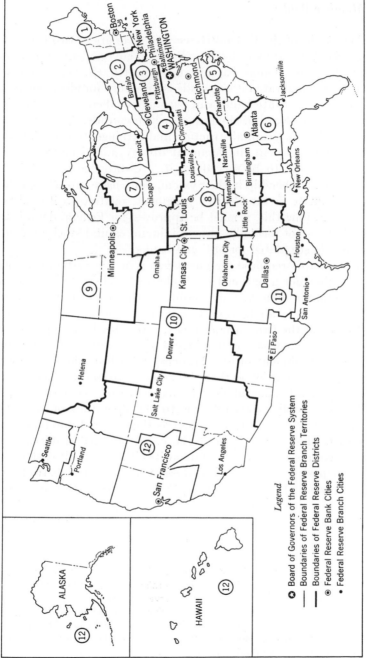

Legend

⊗ Board of Governors of the Federal Reserve System

— Boundaries of Federal Reserve Branch Territories

— Boundaries of Federal Reserve Districts

◉ Federal Reserve Bank Cities

• Federal Reserve Branch Cities

## The Member Banks

Member Banks of the Federal Reserve System are of two types: those having charters granted by the Federal government, the national banks; and those banks having state-granted charters. When the System was inaugurated it was made compulsory for all national banks to be members. State banks can become members if they obtain the approval of the Board of Governors, which considers the adequacy of an applicant bank's capital structure and earnings, the general character of its management, its financial history and condition, and the community needs to be served by it. A state bank, if it is to be admitted to membership in the System, must have capital and surplus that is adequate in the Board's judgment, relative to its assets and deposits. Failing this, it must be approved for Federal deposit insurance if it does not meet the same minimum capital stock and surplus requirements stipulated for national banks.

The standards required for membership in the System are roughly those required for a national bank charter. There are certain minimum capital requirements[3] depending on the size of the city in which the applicant is located. The Board must also be satisfied as to the competency of the bank management. Member banks operate under rules that are somewhat more stringent with regard to lending practices and the establishment of new branches than those imposed by most states. But in addition to the rules and regulations directed primarily toward the maintenance of high standards of banking, there are certain member-bank obligations relating to the operation of the Federal Reserve System itself. One of these is the required purchase of capital stock of the district Reserve Bank. Additional requirements are to hold legal reserves in back of deposits either as vault cash or in the form of deposits[4] at the Federal Reserve Bank of the district, and to remit at par for checks drawn against themselves when presented by a Reserve Bank for payment.

In return for the obligations that they assume, the member banks are entitled to a number of privileges through membership in the

---

[3] The Board of Governors has discretion to modify capital requirements if the specific case under consideration, in the Board's judgment, warrants such action.
[4] Originally only deposits at the district Reserve Bank could count as legal reserves. In 1959 Congress passed legislation authorizing the Board of Governors to permit member banks to count all or part of their currency and coin in meeting reserve requirements. Banks are now permitted to count all their vault cash, along with balances at their Reserve Banks, in meeting their reserve requirements.

Federal Reserve System.   The member banks look upon the Federal Reserve Bank as *their* bank.   That is, the Reserve Bank is a "banker's bank," and the privileges that member banks enjoy correspond to the privileges an individual customer of good standing enjoys at his commercial bank.   The member banks can turn to their district Reserve Bank to obtain needed funds by borrowing or discounting.   They can obtain currency from their Reserve Bank whenever required.   They are further entitled to the use of the services of the System in transferring funds and collecting for checks due them; to obtain information and assistance from experts on various routine and special banking problems; to participate in the election of six of the nine district Bank directors; and to receive the statutory cumulative 6 per cent dividend on their paid-in capital stock of the Federal Reserve Bank.

The member banks of the Federal Reserve System number 6,180 out of a total of 13,669 individual commercial banks.[5]   Somewhat over one-third of the member banks are national banks; the rest are state-chartered institutions.   The member banks, although constituting less than 50 per cent of all commercial banks, represent about 85 per cent of all commercial bank resources.

There are numerous reasons why so many state banks have been reluctant to join the System.   For one thing, restrictions on lending practices of member banks are generally stricter than those imposed by state authorities.   And there are many state banks that cannot join because they cannot meet the capital requirements.   Probably the most onerous requirements of Federal Reserve System membership for many state banks, and thus the reasons for most state banks not belonging to the System, are the reserve requirements and the par clearance provisions.

In many cases a state-chartered, nonmember bank may be subject to a lower reserve requirement, may count both its vault cash and its deposit balances with correspondent banks as reserves, and may also count as part of its reserves certain interest-earning assets, such as state or United States government securities.   By becoming a member bank it would have to sacrifice some of these profit opportunities.

For some nonmember state banks the biggest objection is the par clearance provision.   The par clearance provision prohibits a member bank from levying a charge to cover the cost of providing funds at some out-of-town point to pay for checks drawn against itself and presented to it for payment by another out-of-town bank.   That is, the bank on which the check is drawn may not deduct some charge or fee

---

[5] Figures given as of June 30, 1964, *Federal Reserve Bulletin*, August, 1964.

from the amount it is ordered to pay, meanwhile debiting the depositor's account the full amount. Eight states permit such nonpar payment. Nonpar clearance is a source of nuisance and cost to banks which remit at par, and may lead to inefficient routing of checks in order to avoid nonpar payment. The Federal Reserve System maintains a "par list" consisting of all member banks and those nonmember banks that have agreed to remit at par for checks the Federal Reserve Banks have forwarded to them for payment. Better than 90 per cent of all commercial banks, accounting for about 98 per cent of commercial bank deposits, are on the par list.

A further reason for many state banks not joining the System is that they already are the recipients of most of its benefits. A nonmember bank that maintains a correspondent relationship with a member bank is able to avail itself indirectly of most of the System's facilities. By depositing checks with the correspondent bank it can utilize the System's clearing and collection services, and by discounting paper with the correspondent bank it may make indirect use of the credit facilities of the System. In this fashion, many banks escape the costs and responsibility of membership in the System, but at the same time manage to partake of its advantages.

The less than 100 per cent membership of all commercial banks in the System seems undesirable. The reason, of course, is that commercial banks greatly affect the public interest even though they are themselves private institutions. It is unlikely that the Federal Reserve System can as effectively carry out its purposes if only about one-half of all banks are subject to its controls. The most effective monetary policy is a comprehensive one that covers all banks, not just part of them. Nonmember banks, of course, are not insulated from all Federal Reserve policy, but this policy does not bear directly on them, impinging on them only roundabout.

Since compulsory membership in the System or the confining of bank chartering to the Federal government seems impossible and, at best, an extreme solution to the problem, a possible program for more effective policy control has been proposed. Both a Congressional subcommittee and the Chairman of the Board of Governors have proposed that, first, all commercial banks, or at least all insured commercial banks, with deposits subject to check have the same reserve requirements regardless of membership or not; and second, that all banks be given access to the discount and credit facilities of the Reserve Banks. This would be an important first step to a more effective monetary policy.

## REVIEW QUESTIONS

1. What was the commercial-loan doctrine and why was this banking theory so often not honored in practice in early American banking?
2. Discuss the change over time in the character of bank liabilities. How did the National Bank Act contribute to this change?
3. What is meant by the term "free banking?"
4. Discuss the process whereby bank reserves became concentrated in a few major financial centers under the National Bank System.
5. Discuss the factors which led to the passage of the Federal Reserve Act in 1913.
6. What are the duties and powers of the Board of Governors?
7. Who owns the Federal Reserve Banks? Why are more than 50 per cent of all commercial banks not members of the Federal Reserve System?

## SUGGESTED REFERENCES

Board of Governors, *The Federal Reserve System: Purposes and Functions* (Washington, D.C., 1961).

Hammond, Bray, *Banks and Politics in America from the Revolution to the Civil War* (Princeton University Press, 1957).

Hammond, Bray, "Historical Introduction," in *Banking Studies* (Board of Governors, Washington, D.C., 1941).

Robertson, Ross, *History of the American Economy* (New York: Harcourt, Brace and World, 1955). Chapters 7, 13.

Studenski, Paul and Herman E. Kroos, *Financial History of the United States* (New York: McGraw-Hill Book Company, 1952).

CHAPTER *9*

# *The Federal Reserve System: Functions*

Some of the functions or chores handled by the Federal Reserve System have already been hinted at in preceding chapters. These services are provided to the member banks of the System and to the United States government. The services are supervisory, or they deal with the provision for cash-balance and payment services to member banks, the government, and the public. These payment and cash-balance services are chiefly the following: handling member bank reserve accounts, furnishing currency and making currency shipments, facilitating the clearance and collection of checks, affecting telegraphic transfers of funds, and acting as fiscal agents, custodians, and depositories for the Treasury and other government agencies.

The service functions with which we shall concern ourselves are the supervision of the member banks, the clearing and collection of checks, the issuing of currency, and the acting as fiscal agent for the United States Treasury and other government agencies.

## MEMBER BANK SUPERVISION

An efficient banking system is essential to the smooth functioning of the economy. Because of this fact, the private business of commercial banking is vested with a public interest. As a result of this public interest, banks are subject to governmental supervision and regulation.

The Federal Reserve Act placed upon the Board of Governors and the Federal Reserve Banks the responsibility of supervising the mem-

144

ber banks.   The role of supervision is, however, shared with a number of other government agencies.   At the Federal level, supervision is also exercised by the Comptroller of the Currency and the Federal Deposit Insurance Corporation; state-chartered member banks are subject, in addition, to state supervision.

Bank supervision is directed at safeguarding and serving the community's interests.   The principal objective is to protect the banking structure against any weakness in individual banks and, if possible, to help them to become stronger units.   Thus, the major responsibility of the supervising authorities is to keep informed on the condition, operations, and management of the banks in their jurisdiction, and to prevent and correct unsound situations.

Bank examination is the best known form of supervision.   The purposes of bank examination are: (1) to analyze and appraise assets and liabilities and to determine a bank's solvency; (2) to detect violations of banking laws by the bank and its staff; and (3) to review and appraise the bank management to discover unsound practices or policies.   The bank examiner is a fact-finder.   In the light of the examiner's findings, the supervisory authority formulates the appropriate policy and prescribes any steps which may be necessary to correct any criticized areas of a bank's activities.

Given the complex banking system of this country, there are certain to be some cases of overlapping responsibilities for bank supervision. Since all of the various supervising agencies have similar basic objectives, through cooperation much duplication of effort is avoided.   The Office of the Comptroller of the Currency, a bureau of the Treasury, has the charter and supervisory authority for the national banks.

The Federal Reserve System has supervisory power over all member banks and bank holding companies.   As a matter of practice, however, the System confines its bank examinations to state-chartered member banks and, whenever possible, conducts such examinations jointly with the state supervisory authority.

The Federal Deposit Insurance Corporation has supervisory authority because of its responsibility to insure deposits of member banks and other banks that elect to become members of the Corporation.   The Federal Deposit Insurance Corporation in practice examines only those insured banks that are not subject to examination by another Federal supervisory agency.

The examination of member banks is thus actually carried out by four different authorities, the Comptroller of the Currency, the Federal Reserve Banks, the Federal Deposit Insurance Corporation, and the state banking authorities.   The national banks are subject to examination by the Comptroller of the Currency.   The Comptroller's Chief District Examiners (the Comptroller's office maintains a field staff in each district under the Chief District National Bank Examiner) furnish the Reserve Bank with copies of reports of the examinations of all the national banks in its district.   The Reserve Banks thus do not have to examine the national banks, investigating only special points of weakness or unsound practice uncovered by the national bank examiner's report.   Similarly, since state member banks are subject to examination by the state banking authorities, the Reserve Banks and state supervisory authorities cooperate as much as possible in joint or alternate examinations.   The established policy is, however, for the Reserve Bank to conduct one regular examination of each state member bank each year.

## THE CLEARING AND COLLECTION OF CHECKS

In order to understand and appreciate the clearing and collection of checks through the Federal Reserve System, we must define "clearing" and "collection" and see how these processes operated prior to the System.

As discussed earlier, the principal means of making payment in our economy is by means of checks drawn against demand deposits.   But a check is simply a written order to a bank, signed by a depositor, instructing the bank to pay a certain sum to a designated payee.   If the payee were to come into the bank and present the check for payment, the bank would have to pay the face amount of the check.   Very few checks, however, are collected in this manner.   Collection clearly means the presenting of the items payable to the paying bank, which pays in cash or the equivalent.   Clearance, on the other hand, is the offsetting of mutual claims of one bank against another so that only the net difference need be settled.   The advantages of clearing are that it is more economical and convenient, conserving more time and effort than collection, with a similar conservation of the amount of cash transferred from one bank to another.

Ordinarily the recipient of a check, the payee, deposits the check in his own bank for collection.   The bank increases the depositor's account but generally denies him the right to draw against it until the check has been collected, for initially the bank has received no actual funds but only an item for collection.   Prior to the Federal

Reserve System, if a bank were to mail such checks directly to the bank on which they were drawn the paying bank might refuse to remit at par.   The paying bank might deduct an exchange charge of, say, one tenth of one per cent on the following grounds.

First, since the check was not submitted by the payee but by his bank, the paying banks argued that they were acting as agents of the collecting bank and were therefore entitled to compensation.   The compensation was the remittal of less than the face amount of the check while charging the check writer's account the full face amount.

A second reason for making exchange charges was the claim by the paying bank that the cost of transferring the funds should not fall on it. For after all, the banks argued, it was not their fault if the payee could not come to them for payment.   If the payee wished the paying bank to transfer to him part of the deposit of the one of its customers, the bank had the right to deduct a charge presumably to defray the costs of packaging, shipping, and insuring the currency to be delivered.

In practice, of course, most payments were made by sending the collecting bank a check drawn on some correspondent bank instead of actually shipping currency.   But the maintenance of balances with correspondent banks meant some costs of administration, and so the paying bank would still deduct an exchange charge.   Since the collecting banks did not want to absorb the exchange charges, and since for fear of losing customers they did not want them to absorb the charges, the existence of nonpar banks led to quite complicated and circuitous check routings.   The collecting banks went to considerable effort to collect at par, and this usually required that checks ultimately be forwarded to correspondent banks in the vicinity of the paying banks. Thus, if Bank A received a check drawn on Bank Z which deducted an exchange charge, Bank A would send the check to Bank B which remitted at par, Bank B would send it to Bank C which also remitted at par, and the process would continue until the check finally arrived at some bank to which Bank Z would remit at par.[1]

Since banks could count correspondent bank balances as part of their reserves, as soon as the check had been sent to the correspondent

---

[1] An illustration of the circuitous routing sometimes necessary to collect at par is given in Steiner, Shapiro, and Solomon, *Money and Banking*, 4th ed, (New York: Holt, Rinehart, and Winston, 1958), p. 254.   The illustration involves a check that traveled 1,223 miles and took ten days to pass through ten banks other than the drawee in order to settle a claim involving payer and payee only ninety-three miles apart.

bank the collecting bank would count it as part of its reserves. But since it might be a considerable time before the check was finally collected, a number of banks might simultaneously be counting the amount as part of their reserves. The complicated check routings thus tended to overstate the reserves of the banking system in two ways: the forwarding banks gained reserves before they were actually collected, and the paying bank's reserves were maintained longer than if the check had been directly presented to it for collection. These fictitious reserves were called "float."

The clearing and collection of checks has been greatly expedited by the establishment of the Federal Reserve System. All member banks are required to remit at par, and nonmember banks that agree to remit at par and to maintain a clearing balance at the district Reserve Bank may also use the System's clearing and collection service. In illustrating the clearing and collection process T-accounts are quite useful. Since T-accounts do not show the time dimension the student must keep certain information in mind. A member bank or a nonmember clearing bank get credit for the checks deposited at the Reserve Banks according to a time schedule that roughly reflects the time needed for collection. Each Reserve Bank publishes its availability schedule, which shows when the proceeds of checks deposited with it are available. During this period the funds are neither credited to the depositing banks nor charged against the paying banks. Thus, according to the time necessary for collection, member banks depositing checks receive credit ranging from immediately to two business days. At the end of the period credit is transferred from a deferred account to the member banks' reserve account and is available for use. Checks drawn on the banks in the same city as a Reserve Bank are credited immediately. Checks drawn on more distant banks are credited the next day, and checks on the most distant banks are credited on the second business day.

Since the longest time that credit is deferred is two business days, credit is often granted to a bank before collection is made. Thus, a bank may receive credit before the checks are debited against the accounts of the banks on which they are drawn. As a consequence, the total of "cash items in process of collection"—the checks on the way to the paying banks—tends to exceed "deferred availability cash items"—checks deposited but not yet credited. The difference between cash items in process of collection and deferred availability cash items is "float," which constitutes extra reserves available to the banking system.

Since 1945 the clearing process has been speeded by the use of routing symbols. The routing symbol is a fraction which appears on the check. The numerator consists of two numbers separated by a dash. The first part locates the bank: numbers 1 through 49 are for major cities; 50 through 99 are assigned to states or territories. The second number is the number of the bank assigned by the American Bankers Association. Thus, 98–17 means Washington State (98) and Seattle First National Bank (17). Although this number helps in sorting checks it does not show how the check is to be collected. The denominator of the fraction summarizes the collection routing. Thus, a check drawn on the Walla Walla branch of Seattle First National Bank carries the routing symbol $\dfrac{98-17}{1233}$. The number 1233 means collection should be made through the 12th San Francisco Reserve District (12) and the first 3 shows collection is to be made through the Portland Branch Reserve Bank. The second 3 indicates deferred availability. Whenever the last digit is other than zero it means deferred availability, but does not show how long it is deferred. A denominator of 1210, for instance, indicates the check should be sent to the head office (1) of the 12th District Federal Reserve Bank where credit is immediately available (0).

As a sidelight, checks on the Federal Reserve Banks carry the denominator 000 to indicate that they are immediately payable at any Federal Reserve Bank or branch.

To illustrate the clearing and collection process under the Federal Reserve System let us examine a number of typical situations. First we shall deal with the problem of clearing and collection for member banks within the same city. The second situation will be between two banks in different cities in the same Federal Reserve District. The last situation will concern banks in different Reserve districts.

### Local Clearing and Collection

In our first hypothetical case we assume two local member banks, the First National Bank and the Second National Bank. Let us call the depositors of the First National Bank Mr. A and Mr. B and the depositors of the Second National Bank Mr. Y and Mr. Z.

To illustrate the local collection process assume Mr. A pays $100 by check to Mr. Z. Our T-accounts show Mr. Z depositing A's check in the Second National Bank.

### First National Bank

| Assets | | Liabilities | |
|---|---|---|---|
| Reserve balance at FRB | −$100 | Demand deposit of A | −$100 |

### Second National Bank

| Assets | | Liabilities | |
|---|---|---|---|
| Reserve balance at FRB | +$100 | Demand deposit of Z | +$100 |

### Federal Reserve Bank

| Assets | | Liabilities | |
|---|---|---|---|
| | | Reserve balance of SNB | +$100 |
| | | Reserve balance of FNB | −$100 |

Second National Bank credits Z's account with $100, sends the check to the district Reserve Bank where the Reserve Bank credits Second National's reserve balance $100 and reduces First National's reserve account by $100.   The Reserve Bank then sends the check to First National, notifying it of the changed reserve position and First National now debits A's account by $100.   The T-accounts all balance.   Mr. Z and Second National have both been paid without resort to the cumbersome movement of cash.   Simple bookkeeping entries suffice.

Most major cities operate local clearing houses.   In this case, instead of sending the check to the Reserve Bank, Second National probably wires the Reserve Bank of its claim on First National and the Reserve Bank adjusts its book accordingly.   The end result is the same.

For a better illustration of the offsetting clearing process let us consider checks being exchanged between the banks.   As before let us assume A pays Z $100 by check and in addition that Y pays B $50, also by check.   The T-accounts now show that First National has a net decrease in its liabilities of $50 with a corresponding loss of reserves. Second National has a net increase of $50 in its liabilities and a corresponding increase in its reserves.   The Reserve Bank simply increases the reserve balance of Second National by $50 and decreases the reserve account of First National by the same amount.   The point to be noted is that final payment is made by settling the net amount.   Thus, in practice, each bank in a city at a stated time every day takes to the clearing house all the checks it has accumulated against the other local banks.   The clearing house officials compare the total amounts of checks presented by each bank against the other banks to the total amount of checks brought in by other local banks against it. The net figures so determined are then paid by checks drawn against the reserve balances at the district Reserve Bank, some banks gaining reserves and some banks losing reserves:

First National Bank

| Assets | | Liabilities | |
|---|---|---|---|
| Reserve balance at FRB | −$50 | Demand deposit of A | −$100 |
| | | Demand deposit of B | +$ 50 |
| | −$50 | | −$ 50 |

Second National Bank

| Assets | | Liabilities | |
|---|---|---|---|
| Reserve balance at FRB | +$50 | Demand deposit of Y | −$ 50 |
| | | Demand deposit of Z | +$100 |
| | +$50 | | +$ 50 |

Federal Reserve Bank

| Assets | Liabilities | |
|---|---|---|
| | Reserve balance of FNB | −$50 |
| | Reserve balance of SNB | +$50 |

The individual checks giving rise to the net reserve change may never be sent to the Reserve Bank for clearing at all, but the result is the same whether or not they are.

## Intradistrict Clearing

The procedure is no more complex if the banks are in different cities in the same district. In this case, however, the checks probably pass through the Reserve Bank. Thus, if First National Bank is located in Sacramento, California and Second National Bank is located in Reno, Nevada the clearing process is as follows: If A pays Z by check and Z deposits it in Second National Bank, in order to receive payment Second National forwards it to the Federal Reserve Bank of San Francisco. The Reserve Bank credits Second National's reserve balance according to the availability schedule and debits First National's reserve balance the same amount. The Reserve Bank then forwards the check to First National, notifying it that its reserve balance has been changed. And finally, First National debits A's account. In the T-accounts the items appear as follows:

First National Bank

| Assets | | Liabilities | |
|---|---|---|---|
| Reserve balance at FRB | −$100 | Demand deposit of A | −$100 |

Second National Bank

| Assets | | Liabilities | |
|---|---|---|---|
| Reserve balance at FRB | +$100 | Demand deposit of Z | +$100 |

Federal Reserve Bank

| Assets | Liabilities | |
|---|---|---|
| | Reserve balance of SNB | +$100 |
| | Reserve balance of FNB | −$100 |

This clearing process between cities of the same Reserve district is identical to that of clearing between banks of same city if clearing is through the district Reserve Bank.

### Interdistrict Clearing

Interdistrict clearing is more complicated than intradistrict clearing only because the banks involved do not have their reserve balances in the same Federal Reserve Bank. But since the twelve district Reserve Banks themselves maintain a clearing account in Washington, called the Interdistrict Settlement Fund, the clearing and collection process is expedited. The Reserve Banks have deposited part of their gold certificates in this Interdistrict Settlement Fund acquiring an equivalent credit balance. Thus, the balance sheet of the Settlement Fund looks as follows:

Interdistrict Settlement Fund

| Assets | Liabilities |
|---|---|
| Gold Certificates | District 1 Bank Balance |
| | . . . . . . . . . . . . . . . . . . . . . . |
| | District 12 Bank Balance |

To show interdistrict clearing assume that First National Bank is in Sacramento, California in District Twelve. Assume Second National Bank is in New York City, in District Two. Mr. A pays Mr. Z by check drawn on First National. Mr. Z deposits the check in his bank, Second National. Second National Bank credits Z's account and as it wants payment also, it sends the check to the Federal Reserve Bank of New York. The Federal Reserve Bank of New York will credit

Second National's account, not immediately, but according to the availability schedule. The Federal Reserve Bank of New York airmails the check to the Federal Reserve Bank of San Francisco which debits First National's reserve balance and sends the check on to First National which finally debits A's balance. In the meantime, upon receipt of the check from the Federal Reserve Bank of New York, the Federal Reserve Bank of San Francisco wires the Interdistrict Settlement Fund the amount it has credited to the Federal Reserve Bank of New York. In T-accounts the entries are shown as follows:

First National Bank

| Assets | Liabilities | |
| --- | --- | --- |
| Reserve balance at FRB of SF  −$100 | Demand deposit of A | −$100 |

Second National Bank

| Assets | Liabilities | |
| --- | --- | --- |
| Reserve balance at FRB of NY    +$100 | Demand deposit of Z | +$100 |

Federal Reserve Bank of San Francisco

| Assets | | Liabilities | |
| --- | --- | --- | --- |
| Balance at IDSF | −$100 | Reserve balance of FNB | −$100 |

Federal Reserve Bank of New York

| Assets | | Liabilities | |
| --- | --- | --- | --- |
| Balance at IDSF | +$100 | Reserve balance of SNB | +$100 |

Interdistrict Settlement Fund

| Assets | Liabilities | |
| --- | --- | --- |
| Gold Certificates | Balance of District 2(NY) | +$100 |
| | Balance of District 12(SF) | −$100 |

In actual practice over five billion dollars worth of checks are settled daily through the use of the Settlement Fund. Each Reserve Bank totals the amount it has credited to every other Reserve Bank that day and wires this information to the Settlement Fund. The Fund effects a clearance and wires the final net balances back to the individual Reserve Banks for entry into their books.

In addition to the clearing and collection service just described, the Federal Reserve System also makes available to member banks telegraph facilities for transferring funds to banks in all parts of the country. Within a district the transfer is done by debiting one bank's reserve account and crediting the other bank's account. If the transfer of funds is between member banks in different districts, the reserve account of the bank receiving the funds is credited by its Reserve Bank. Settlement between the two Reserve Banks is made through the Inter-district Settlement Fund. Transfers of funds are provided free of charge for member banks over the System's leased wire network. Transfers of funds for member banks for other accounts are made at cost over commercial wires.

By the Federal Reserve System of clearing, collection, and transfer most of the defects of previous systems have been eliminated. The System permits more direct routing and prompt clearance of checks. Because the cost of clearance and the shipment of currency is absorbed by the Reserve Banks, member banks must remit at par. But, because not all banks are members of the System or are nonmember clearing banks, there are a few nonpar banks. There were 12,020 banks on the par list at the end of June 30, 1964 and 1,567 not on the par list. The nonpar banks are principally rural state-chartered banks in the South and Midwest.

## CURRENCY ISSUE

The amount of currency in circulation depends on the public's demand for it. Under the Federal Reserve System, currency moves into and out of circulation automatically, in response to increases or decreases in public demand.

If the demand for currency increases the commercial banks provide themselves with the amounts and kinds of currency their community wants. This currency is supplied to the banks by the Federal Reserve Banks. If a member bank needs additional currency it orders it from its district Reserve Bank, paying for it by charging its reserve account. A nonmember bank usually gets its necessary currency through correspondent member banks.

All currency is put into circulation through the Federal Reserve Banks. The twelve Reserve Banks keep large inventories of all kinds of currency and coins, issuing it in response to demand. The currency inventory includes not only Federal Reserve Notes, but Treasury currency and coin as well. The Reserve Banks obtain the Treasury currency and coin from the Treasury and pay for it by crediting the Treasury's checking account for the amount of currency and coin obtained.

On the other hand should the public not wish to hold the amount of currency in circulation it will be deposited in commercial banks. The commercial banks may then forward any excess currency over their vault cash needs to their Reserve Bank, receiving a credit to their reserve for the currency deposited.

## FISCAL FUNCTIONS

The Federal Reserve Banks are not only banker's banks, they are also the banks for the United States Treasury and other government agencies. Indeed, the United States government is the Federal Reserve System's biggest customer. The twelve Federal Reserve Banks carry the checking accounts of the Treasury, do much of the work involved in issuing and redeeming government securities, and perform other fiscal duties for the United States government.

The operation of the Treasury involves a tremendous amount of banking business. The Treasury is continuously receiving and disbursing funds all over the country. All of these receipts and disbursements pass through the Federal Reserve System. All Treasury disbursements are made by checks drawn on the Treasury's accounts at the Federal Reserve Banks. But, whereas all Treasury expenditures are through the Federal Reserve Banks, the Federal Reserve Banks are not the sole depositories of Treasury funds.

The Treasury receives its funds from taxes and by selling government securities (borrowing). The funds so received are initially deposited at commercial banks, both member and nonmember, which carry Treasury "Tax and Loan Accounts." These banks are "special depositaries" whose principal special requirement is that with a Federal Reserve Bank they pledge government securities to secure in full the balance in the account. A bank designated as a special depositary credits to the Tax and Loan Account the proceeds of its customers' and its own purchases of government securities. Withheld taxes are also deposited into these Tax and Loan Accounts. But Treasury disbursements are not made from these Treasury accounts in commercial banks. As the Treasury's working balances at the Federal Reserve Banks need replenishing, the Treasury directs the banks having Tax and Loan Accounts to shift the funds to a Federal Reserve Bank.

By carrying the bulk of its deposits in commercial banks, the Treasury minimizes the effect on commercial bank reserves of its fluctuating receipt pattern. To illustrate this point consider the T-account analysis of Treasury receipt of funds from the public in the amount of $100.

## Commercial Bank System

| Assets | | Liabilities | |
|---|---|---|---|
| Reserve balance at FRB | −$100 | Demand deposit of public | −$100 |

## Federal Reserve Banks

| Assets | Liabilities | |
|---|---|---|
| | Reserve balance of CB | −$100 |
| | Treasury balance | +$100 |

## Treasury

| Assets | | Liabilities |
|---|---|---|
| Balance at FRB | +$100 | |

In this illustration the Treasury has deposited the entire proceeds of the borrowing and tax collections to its account at the Federal Reserve. The impact on the reserve position of the commercial banks is apparent. The banks lose reserves to the full amount of the Treasury deposit. On the other hand, if the Treasury maintains these receipts in Tax and Loan Accounts the reserves of commercial banks are maintained. This is illustrated below:

## Commercial Bank System

| Assets | Liabilities | |
|---|---|---|
| Reserve balance at FRB, no change | Demand deposit of public | −$100 |
| | Tax and Loan Account | +$100 |

## Federal Reserve Banks

| Assets | Liabilities |
|---|---|
| | No Change |

## Treasury

| Assets | | Liabilities |
|---|---|---|
| Tax and Loan Account | +$100 | |

The extensive use of Tax and Loan Accounts minimizes the otherwise disturbing impact on bank reserves of the periodic inflow, continuous outgo nature of the Treasury's operation.

The Federal Reserve also serves the Treasury in connection with the public debt. When the Treasury offers a new issue of securities, the Reserve Banks receive the applications from banks, dealers, and others who wish to buy. They make allotments of securities in accordance with Treasury instructions, deliver the securities and receive payment for them, and credit the proceeds to Treasury accounts, principally to Tax and Loan Accounts. The Reserve Banks also redeem government securities as they mature, pay the interest coupons when presented, make exchanges of denominations or kind, and perform other duties necessary in servicing the debt. For example, if an owner of a marketable government security decides to sell it, the Federal Reserve transfers the security in a matter of minutes. If a New York bond dealer buys government bonds from a San Francisco bank, the bank simply takes the bonds to the Federal Reserve Bank of San Francisco which invalidates the bonds and wires the Federal Reserve Bank of New York to issue and deliver new bonds of the same issue and amount.

The Federal Reserve Banks also act as fiscal agents for various United States government agencies and corporations, such as the Reconstruction Finance Corporation and other government lending agencies. Their acting as fiscal agent for the Treasury has twofold benefits. The first is that government funds are safer and fiscal operations carried out far more efficiently than in pre-System days. The second and greater benefit attaches to the coordination now possible of Treasury finance with money market conditions.

## REVIEW QUESTIONS

1. Member bank examination is carried on by a number of different authorities. Discuss how duplication of effort in bank examination is minimized in the examination of member banks.
2. Discuss the difficulties in the clearing and collection of checks caused by the existence of nonpar banks.
3. Trace the steps in the collection of a check drawn on a San Francisco, California bank and deposited in a Cleveland, Ohio bank.
4. What is "float?" In what sense does it represent fictitious reserves for the commercial banking system?
5. How does currency get into circulation? What determines the amount of currency in circulation?
6. What are Tax and Loan Accounts? How does the presence of Treasury Tax and Loan Accounts help to the ease pressure on commercial bank reserves at income tax time?

## SUGGESTED REFERENCES

Board of Governors, *The Federal Reserve System: Purposes and Functions* (Washington, D.C., 1961).

Prochnow, Herbert V., ed, *The Federal Reserve System* (New York: Harper and Brothers, 1960).

CHAPTER *10*

# Bank Reserves, Bank Credit, and the Money Supply

Bank reserves, as we have seen, play a vital and crucial role in the operation of the banking system.   Commercial banks are interested in maximizing profit, just as are other forms of business.   But banks manufacture and sell a rather unusual kind of product—money.   The ability to create money is limited by the establishment of reserve requirements on bank deposits held by the commercial banks.

Today bank reserves serve primarily to limit the creation of demand deposits to pay for the earning assets acquired by the banks in their pursuit of profit.   But this has not always been the case.   Historically, reserve requirements were imposed in order to protect depositors.   Reserves were thought of as providing a liquidity cushion which enabled the bank to meet demands for currency or for paying checks drawn against it.   Although a bank's reserves do provide liquid assets for such purposes, the amount of liquidity so provided is quite small. Banks cannot very well pay out their required reserves to meet payment demands without also depressing their reserves below the required levels.   For instance, if a bank operating under a 20 per cent reserve requirement has no excess reserves—all its reserves are required reserves—a loss of $100 through currency withdrawal or adverse clearing drain pushes it $80 below its required amount.   A $20 drain on reserves it can stand, but it must somehow make up the $80 deficiency. It can sell some assets or else contract its deposits until it has sufficient reserves.

The real liquidity cushion protecting depositors is not required reserves alone but rather excess reserves and "secondary" reserves

158

which can be immediately converted into additional reserves as needed. These secondary reserves, as noted in Chapter 7, are principally short-term government obligations; they can be readily sold without loss or delay whenever the necessity should arise.   The ultimate source of liquidity for the banking system, however, lies in the credit-granting power of the central bank—in the central bank's ability to purchase assets of the commercial bank should the latter need additional reserves.

The factors that influence bank reserves are many and varied. Most of them have already been discussed, but perhaps not in the particular context in which we shall examine them here.   We shall find it convenient to look at the sources of member bank reserves and also at the various competing uses for reserve funds.   These factors may then be conveniently summarized into a reserve equation.   Once we understand the sources of and uses for reserve funds, we can under-take an analysis of the control of bank reserves.

## MEMBER BANK RESERVES

All commercial banks in the United States are required, either by statute or by order of the supervisory authority, to maintain certain prescribed minimum reserves depending on the volume of deposit lia-bilities they owe.   For state-chartered nonmember banks the reserve ratio requirements are set by the state banking authorities.   For all Federal Reserve member banks, whether state or federally chartered, the reserve ratio requirements are specified by the Board of Governors.

The reserve ratios specified by state authorities vary considerably from state to state, and the items that actually constitute the legal reserves also vary.   For example, some states permit vault cash and correspondent balances with other banks to serve as reserves; others allow these items plus government securities.   In order to simplify the discussion we shall continue to make the assumption that all banks are members of the Federal Reserve System.

For member commercial banks, required reserves must be held either as deposits at the district Federal Reserve Bank or as vault cash. Since vault cash is a rather small item, we shall assume that mem-ber bank reserves are maintained as deposit balances at the Federal Reserve Bank of the district.   Reserve requirements have differed as to type of deposit, being higher on demand deposits than on time deposits, and as to class of bank, central reserve city banks, reserve city banks, and country banks.   As discussed earlier this threefold classification of banks was an inheritance from the earlier National

Bank System.   The reserve ratio on time deposits is uniform among the classes of banks, but varies by class for demand deposits.

In Table 10-1 are summarized the reserves required for member banks since the establishment of the Federal Reserve System.   The initial reserve ratios for central reserve city banks, reserve city banks, and country banks were 13 per cent, 10 per cent, and 7 per cent respectively, and 3 per cent for time deposits for all classes.   These requirements remained in effect until 1935.   At that time, the Federal Reserve Act was amended to provide that the Board of Governors might set the actual requirement anywhere between the percentages specified originally in the Federal Reserve Act of 1913 as minimums, to twice these percentages as maximums.[1]   The reason for the passage of this law was that this period was characterized by large amounts of excess reserves and also by a heavy movement of gold into this country. These conditions, as a matter of fact, closely resembled those of the year 1916, which saw for the first time the Federal Reserve Board suggesting that it be given the power to raise reserve requirements for member banks.   It was not until 1933, however, that temporary provision for changing reserve requirements was enacted into law, and the 1935 legislation made this temporary legislation permanent.

In 1959 Congress amended the Federal Reserve Act to eliminate the classification of central reserve city banks.   The 1959 legislation also increased the range of the required reserve ratio from 10–20 per cent to 10-22 per cent for the reserve city banks.   The range for country banks was kept at 7–14 per cent, and the range for time deposits for all member banks was kept at 3–6 per cent.   The legislation terminated the "central reserve city" classification on July 28, 1962.   Thus, the Board of Governors gradually eliminated the reserve ratio differential between central reserve city banks and reserve city banks until in December, 1960, both classes had a requirement of 16½ per cent.   This same 1959 legislation also provided for the counting of vault cash in reserves in order to correct inequities between banks in the same reserve class.   These inequities arise because some banks, as a result of their location or other conditions, need to hold relatively larger amounts of vault cash for operating purposes than other banks.   This, of course, reduces their earning power since vault cash earns no interest.   Thus by counting vault cash as part of reserves this inequity is removed.

---

[1] Congress authorized an increase in the maximums for a brief period in 1948–1949. The authority for the increased maximums lapsed in 1949 and the System did not ask for an extension.

Table 10-1 summarizes the history of legal reserve requirements as a percentage of deposits.

**TABLE 10-1**   Historical Summary of Reserve Requirements as Percentage of Deposits

| | Net Demand Deposits | | | Time Deposits |
| Date | Central Reserve City Banks (%) | Reserve City Banks (%) | Country Banks (%) | All Member Banks (%) |
| --- | --- | --- | --- | --- |
| 1913–1935 | 13 | 10 | 7 | 3 |
| 1935–1959 | 13–26 | 10–20 | 7–14 | 3–6 |
| 1959–1962 | 10–22 | 10–22 | 7–14 | 3–6 |
| Since July 28, 1962 | Classification eliminated | 10–22 | 7–14 | 3–6 |

The reserve ratio requirements for demand deposits apply to *net demand deposits*, that is, gross demand deposits less balances due from other banks (correspondent balances) less cash items in process of collection. Time deposit requirements apply to gross time deposits. The reason for using net demand deposits is to prevent requirements from being duplicated over the entire banking system.

In order to determine reserve requirements, we multiply the required reserve ratio set by the Board of Governors on demand deposits by the volume of net demand deposit liabilities and add the required ratio for time deposits multiplied by the volume of time deposit liabilities. This sum of required reserves on demand deposits and required reserves against time deposits gives total required reserves in dollar amounts.

Actual reserves are the commercial bank's deposits at the Federal Reserve plus its holdings in currency. Excess reserves are simply actual reserves less required reserves. It is possible that excess reserves may be negative, that is, the bank has insufficient reserves. Member banks, however, are not continuously obliged to satisfy reserve requirements. Rather the reserve requirements are averages of daily deposit balances in relation to daily reserves over a period of one week for reserve city banks; country banks' averages extend over half a month. By this process, temporary reserve deficiencies are permitted if they are offset by excess reserves within the period of calculation. If a member bank should fail to meet its required reserve the Federal Reserve Bank imposes a fine of 2 per cent above the rediscount rate based on the average daily deficiencies over the period. Chronic or persistent reserve deficiencies may lead to revocation of membership in the Reserve System for a state-chartered bank, or to the forfeiture of charter for a national bank.

## THE SOURCES OF MEMBER BANK RESERVE FUNDS

In considering sources of bank reserves, the distinction between a single commercial bank and the entire system of commercial banks must be kept in mind. As noted in Chapter 5, a single bank can obtain reserves from other banks, whereas for the system as a whole no additional reserves can be generated except by factors beyond the direct control of the banks. The items that form the reserve base for the commercial banks are Federal Reserve credit, the monetary gold stock, and Treasury currency outstanding.

### *Federal Reserve Credit*

Federal Reserve credit is a principal source of bank reserves. The Federal Reserve provides these reserves simply by creating them when it purchases earning assets. In order to acquire these assets in exchange for creating a liability against itself, the Federal Reserve Banks must themselves fulfill certain reserve requirements. The Federal Reserve Banks must maintain 25 per cent gold certificate reserves against their Federal Reserve note and deposit liabilities. Until the Second World War reserve requirements were higher: 35 per cent on deposit liabilities and 40 per cent on Federal Reserve notes. The remainder of the assets backing these liabilities are United States government securities.

Historically, the gold requirements have approached the legal minimums on only three occasions, in 1920, 1931, and 1945. In the last situation the remedy was found by lowering the required ratio of gold certificates to note and deposit liabilities to 25 per cent. Since about 1957, however, the United States has been experiencing a persistent decline in its monetary gold stock. This situation, coupled with an increase in foreign holdings of dollar balances, is becoming a little uncomfortable. Should foreign-owned dollar obligations be converted into gold at a rapid rate, the situation would become binding, to say the least, since the ratio of gold certificates reserves to Federal Reserve note and deposit liabilities is only about 30 per cent and has been steadily declining. Should the 25 per cent requirement become too restrictive, it would likely be lowered as was done in 1945.

Federal Reserve credit, then, as a source of bank reserves is generated by the Federal Reserve's purchase of earning assets, paying for

these assets by creating deposit liabilities.   Table 10-2 gives Federal
Reserve credit outstanding as of July 31, 1964.

TABLE **10-2**   Federal Reserve Credit Outstanding, July 31, 1964
(millions of dollars)

| | |
|---|---|
| U. S. Government securities held | 35,051 |
| Discounts and advances to member banks | 239 |
| Other discounts, advances, and acceptances | 56 |
| Float | 1,451 |
| Total | 36,797 |

Source: *Federal Reserve Bulletin*, August, 1964.

United States government securities, as the table shows, constitute
by far the biggest part of Federal Reserve credit.   The purchase of
these Treasury obligations are the principal means whereby the Federal
Reserve, of its own initiative, can create Federal Reserve credit.

Discounts and advances to member banks represent loans made to
member banks by the Federal Reserve.   Discounts are the sale by
commercial banks to the Federal Reserve of commercial paper of
acceptable quality.   Advances are the promissory notes of commercial
banks, secured generally by government securities.

Other discounts, advances, and acceptances include holding of
bankers' acceptances or loans made directly to individuals or businesses under Section 13-b of the Reserve Act.

The last item, "float," results from the check clearing and collection
process.   This overstatement of reserves is clearly a form of Federal
Reserve credit, though in this case there has been no purchase of an
earning asset by the Federal Reserve.

## Gold and Treasury Currency

The other sources of bank reserves are Treasury gold and silver transactions.   When the Treasury buys gold it pays for it with a check
written on its account at the Federal Reserve.   The recipient of the
check deposits it to his account at a commercial bank.   When the
check is presented by the commercial bank to the Federal Reserve for
payment, the bank receives this payment through an increase in its
reserve balance at the Federal Reserve.   Total bank reserves have
thus been increased by this gold purchase.   The Treasury, of course,
has a reduced balance at the Federal Reserve and in order to restore
this balance the Treasury issues gold certificates to the Federal Reserve.
The purchase of gold by the Treasury is thus essentially costless to it,

but the Federal Reserve has acquired gold certificates with which to back additional Federal Reserve credit and the commercial banks have gained reserves equal to the amount of the purchases.

Gold sales by the Treasury reverse the process. Just as purchases of gold by the Treasury increase the reserve base, gold sales decrease the reserve base. Consequently a persistent decline in gold holdings will ultimately force a contraction in the reserve base and hence, unless somehow offset, a contraction in the supply of money.

Treasury currency is simply the silver counterpart of gold transactions. Both are taken up more fully in a following chapter.

The sources of member bank reserves as of July 31, 1964 are shown in Table 10-3. The items shown in the table are the sources of member bank reserves, and the predominant role played by Federal Reserve credit is quite evident, providing as it does some 60 per cent of the total sources of member bank reserves.

Our next task is to determine the various uses to which these reserve funds may be put. There are a number of competing uses for these funds besides their use as member bank reserves. If we can determine these competing uses, we shall be able to formulate a "reserve equation" linking the sources and uses of reserve funds in a convenient fashion.

TABLE 10-3   Sources of Member Bank Reserves, July 31, 1964 (millions of dollars)

| | | |
|---|---:|---:|
| 1. Federal Reserve Credit | | 36,797 |
|    a. U. S. Government securities | 35,051 | |
|    b. Discounts and advances to member banks | 239 | |
|    c. Other discounts and advances | 56 | |
|    d. Float | 1,451 | |
| 2. Monetary gold stock | | 15,462 |
| 3. Treasury currency | | 5,571 |
|    Total | | 57,830 |

*Source: Federal Reserve Bulletin, August, 1964.*

## USES OF MEMBER BANK RESERVE FUNDS

As Table 10-3 indicates, the sources of member bank reserves as of July 31, 1964 totaled over $57.8 billion. As we shall see, however, member bank reserves on that date amounted to considerably less than one-half of this total. It follows that a substantial amount of potential member bank reserve funds had been diverted into competing uses.

The principal competing use for reserve funds is currency in circulation.  There are a number of other competing uses for these funds, but they are of a much lesser magnitude than currency in circulation. These other uses are Treasury cash and Treasury deposits at the Federal Reserve, foreign deposits at the Federal Reserve, and other deposits and accounts at the Federal Reserve.

## Currency in Circulation

As discussed earlier, all currency is put into circulation through the Federal Reserve Banks.  Treasury currency is deposited with the Federal Reserve by the Treasury in order to obtain a credit to its account. Then as the public needs it, such currency is provided by the Federal Reserve Banks.  The same is true of Federal Reserve notes, except that the Treasury is not involved.

To recapitulate, commercial banks hold minimum amounts of currency since this earns no income.  Should the money-using public desire more currency, however, the banks provide it.  They order the currency in the desired amount and denominations from their Reserve Bank, paying for it by authorizing the Reserve Bank to charge their reserve accounts.

Conversely, should the public have too much currency, it deposits it with the commercial banks.  If the commercial banks then find themselves with excess currency they ship the surplus to the Reserve Banks, receiving a credit to their reserve accounts.

These operations may be summarized in T-account form.  If the public desires to hold more of its money as currency the result is as follows:

| Public | |
|---|---|
| Assets | Liabilities |
| Demand deposits at commercial bank    — | |
| Currency holdings    + | |

| Commercial Bank | |
|---|---|
| Assets | Liabilities |
| Reserve balance at FRB    — | Demand deposits of public    — |

| Federal Reserve Bank | |
|---|---|
| Assets | Liabilities |
| | Reserve balance of commercial bank    — |
| | Federal Reserve notes outstanding    + |

What is clearly noted is the decline in member bank reserves. Should the public hold too much currency for its needs, the process is reversed: the signs in the T-accounts are changed. That is, a currency inflow yields:

Public

| Assets | | Liabilities |
|---|---|---|
| Demand deposits at commercial bank | + | |
| Currency holdings | − | |

Commercial Bank

| Assets | | Liabilities | |
|---|---|---|---|
| Reserve balance at FRB | + | Demand deposits of public | + |

Federal Reserve Bank

| Assets | Liabilities | |
|---|---|---|
| | Reserve balance of commercial bank | + |
| | Federal Reserve notes outstanding | − |

The significance of the foregoing analysis is this: the amount of currency in circulation at any one time measures the net drain of funds into a competing use, since funds so used might otherwise serve as commercial bank reserves.

### Treasury Cash

The item "Treasury Cash" measures the value of the monetary metal stock that has not been monetized. It is that part of our gold and silver stock against which no gold certificates or silver certificates have been issued. This item is negligible, less than half a billion dollars in total.

### Treasury Deposits at the Federal Reserve

Although this item is rather small, it is, nevertheless, important. The Treasury's deposit is an active one. It is constantly being used and thus needs continual replenishing. Whenever the Treasury switches funds from its Tax and Loan Accounts at member banks to its account at the Federal Reserve, the reserves of member banks fall by this amount. Thus, any time the Treasury's deposit at the Federal Reserve is increasing it constitutes a drain on bank reserve funds.

## Foreign Deposits at the Federal Reserve

These foreign-owned deposits are dollar balances held with the Reserve Banks by foreign governments or central banks. A change in these balances, up or down, represents the net loss or gain of commercial bank reserves.

## Other Deposits and Accounts of the Federal Reserve

This represents a hodge-podge of deposits of government corporations and various international financial institutions. Changes in these balances result in opposite changes in member bank reserves just as with foreign deposits. An increase in these balances constitutes an increase in competing uses for reserve funds. Also included in this item are nonmember bank clearing accounts and the net effect of expenditures by the Reserve System to the public (a source of reserves) and the increase in Federal Reserve Bank capital accounts (a drain of reserve funds).

These various items are presented in Table 10-4 to show the various competing uses for member bank reserve funds as of July 31, 1964.

TABLE 10-4  Competing Uses for Member Bank Reserve Funds, July 31, 1964 (millions of dollars)

| | |
|---|---:|
| Currency in circulation[a] | 34,292 |
| Treasury cash | 438 |
| Treasury deposits at the Federal Reserve | 785 |
| Foreign deposits at the Federal Reserve | 135 |
| Other deposits and accounts at the Federal Reserve | 1,327 |
| Total | 36,977 |

[a] Outside of banks.
Source: Federal Reserve Bulletin, August, 1964.

The task is now virtually complete. We have derived the total for competing uses for member bank reserve funds. The difference between the totals for competing uses and for sources of member bank reserve funds is, in fact, the volume of available member bank reserves. We are now ready to formulate the reserve equation from these totals.

## THE RESERVE EQUATION

The two preceding sections were concerned with the sources of and competing uses for member bank reserve funds. The interplay of these factors determines the volume of member bank reserves at any given time. Consequently, changes in the factors determine the changes in bank reserves over time. In order to understand more easily the problem of control of bank reserves—to be considered in the next chapter—we shall develop the so-called reserve equation, which brings together all the factors influencing member bank reserves.

Let us consolidate into a single statement the several sources and uses of reserve funds, putting sources on the left-hand side and uses on the right-hand side. This is done in Table 10-5.

TABLE 10-5   Member Bank Reserves and Related Items, July 31, 1964 (millions of dollars)

| Federal Reserve Credit | | Currency in circulation[a] | 34,292 |
|---|--:|---|--:|
| U. S. Government securities | 35,051 | | |
| Disc. and Adv. to member | | Treasury Cash | 438 |
| banks | 239 | Treasury deposit at FRB | 785 |
| Other Disc. and Adv. | 56 | Foreign deposits at FRB | 135 |
| Float | 1,451 | | |
| Total Federal Reserve Credit | 36,797 | Other dept. and acct. at FRB | 1,327 |
| Treasury Currency | 3,571 | Total Competing Uses | 36,977 |
| Monetary Gold Stock | 15,462 | Member Bank Reserves | 20,853 |
| Totals | 57,830 | | 57,830 |

[a] Outside of banks.
*Source: Federal Reserve Bulletin,* August, 1964.

Since both columns of the statement are equal, it follows that any one item on the statement may be expressed in terms of the others. The particular item in which we are interested is "member bank reserves." This may be expressed in the following equation: Member bank reserves = sources of member bank reserves − competing uses for member bank reserve funds. Thus, in greater detail:

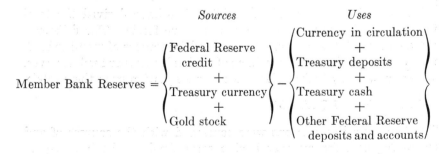

Written in this form, it is clear that member bank reserves vary directly with changes in the "sources" and inversely with changes in the "uses." Thus, in the absence of any offsetting factors, increases in Federal Reserve credit, Treasury currency, and monetary gold stock will operate to increase member bank reserves. On the other hand, increases in currency in circulation, Treasury deposits, etc., will reduce member bank reserves.

To determine the factors giving rise to a change in bank reserves between any two dates, all that is necessary is to write down the reserve equation for the dates in question. To illustrate let us analyze the change in member bank reserves between January 30, 1963 and January 29, 1964. The reserve equation factors are set forth in Table 10-6.

Between January 30, 1963 and the corresponding date one year later Table 10-6 shows that member bank reserves increased in the amount of $589 million. The source factor that increased the greatest was Federal Reserve credit, up some $2,616 million. Discounts and advances and float increased slightly, but offsetting this was a decline of $416 million in the monetary gold stock. Consequently, sources of member bank reserves increased by some $2,488 million. At the same time, "competing use" factors were increasing by $1,870 million, composed principally of an increase in currency in the hands of the public, up $1,953 millions, and a build-up in the Treasury's deposit balance at the Federal Reserve by $32 million, but offset somewhat by falls in Treasury cash, Foreign deposits, and other deposits and accounts at the Federal Reserve.

Over this one year period it is apparent that the principal factors which produced the change in member bank reserves were changes in Federal Reserve credit, Treasury currency, the monetary gold stock, Treasury cash and Treasury deposits at the Federal Reserve, and currency in circulation. The significant fact to be grasped from this is that, of the various factors affecting member bank reserves, only one, Federal Reserve credit, is subject to direct control by the Federal Reserve authorities. The balance of the items lies outside direct control by the Federal Reserve. This notion of dependence and independence of Federal Reserve control will be explored at length in the next chapter. It is sufficient for the moment to note that the only source of member bank reserves directly controllable by the Federal Reserve authorities is Federal Reserve credit. Furthermore, of the various components of Federal Reserve credit only the volume of United States government securities held in the Open Market Account

TABLE 10-6 Analysis of Factors Causing Change in Member Bank Reserves (millions of dollars)

| | January 30, 1963 | January 29, 1964 | Expansive Factors | Contractive Factors |
|---|---|---|---|---|
| Sources: | | | | |
| Federal Reserve Credit | | | | |
| U. S. Govt. Securities | 30,123 | 32,739 | 2,616 | |
| Discounts and Advances | | | | |
| Member Banks | 101 | 209 | 108 | |
| Other Discounts and | | | | |
| Advances | 77 | 68 | | 9 |
| Float | 1,615 | 1,764 | 149 | |
| Total Federal Reserve | | | | |
| Credit | 31,916 | 34,780 | | |
| Treasury Currency | 5,571 | 5,582 | 11 | |
| Gold Stock | 15,928 | 15,512 | | 416 |
| TOTAL SOURCES | 53,415 | 55,874 | | |
| Minus Competing Uses | | | | |
| Currency in Circulation[a] | 31,052 | 33,005 | | 1,953 |
| Treasury Deposit at Federal | | | | |
| Reserve | 837 | 869 | | 32 |
| Treasury Cash | 432 | 410 | 22 | |
| Foreign Deposit at Federal | | | | |
| Reserve | 220 | 141 | 79 | |
| Other Deposits & Accounts | | | | |
| at Federal Reserve | 1,263 | 1,249 | 14 | |
| TOTAL COMPETING | | | | |
| USES | 33,804 | 35,674 | | |
| Member Bank Reserves | 19,611 | 20,200 | | |
| Total Changes Increasing Reserves | | | 2,999 | |
| Total Changes Decreasing Reserves | | | | 2,410 |
| Net Increase: Reserves | | | | 589 |

[a] Currency outside banks.

*Source: Federal Reserve Bulletin,* February, 1964.

is controlled by the bank authorities, the rest being subject only indirectly to control by the Federal Reserve authorities.

## SUMMARY

The purpose of this chapter has been to develop an understanding of the basic interrelationships between bank reserves and the factors that determine their volume. The importance of this becomes clear with the recognition that the bulk of our money supply is demand deposits, whose aggregate volume depends in part on the reserves available to commercial banks. Consequently, an understanding of the determinants of member bank reserves goes a long way towards providing a basis for understanding the means of controlling the money supply.

It is to this problem of monetary control that we shall next turn. But, as we have seen, of the basic determinants of member bank reserves, only one, Federal Reserve credit, is subject to any type of deliberate, conscious control by the monetary authorities. All the other basic factors are not subject to direct control by the Federal Reserve authorities.

The interrelationship between the basic determinants of member bank reserves is summed up in the reserve equation:

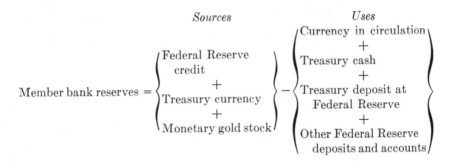

Any increase in the sources of member bank reserve funds, other factors being constant, will increase member bank reserves; any increase in competing uses for reserve funds, other factors remaining constant, will reduce the volume of member bank reserves.

## REVIEW QUESTIONS

1. In the current issue of the *Federal Reserve Bulletin*, look up the present legal reserve ratios on demand and time deposits held by member banks.
2. Define and discuss "float."
3. What are the various items which compose Federal Reserve credit? Discuss each item briefly.
4. What are the sources of member bank reserves?
5. Using the current *Federal Reserve Bulletin*, make up a table showing the present composition of the sources of member bank reserves.
6. List and discuss the various items which make up the competing uses for member bank reserve funds.

7. Again using the current *Federal Reserve Bulletin,* determine the magnitude of competing uses for member bank reserves.
8. What is the "reserve equation?" What is the present magnitude of member bank reserves?
9. Show how member bank reserves vary directly with the sources and inversely with the uses of reserve funds.

## SUGGESTED REFERENCES

Board of Governors, *The Federal Reserve System: Purposes and Functions* (Washington, D.C., 1961).

Federal Reserve Bank of New York, *Bank Reserves, Some Major Factors Affecting Them,* 1951.

Federal Reserve Bank of New York, *Money Market Essays,* 1953.

Madden, Carl H., *The Money Side of "The Street"* (Federal Reserve Bank of New York, 1959).

CHAPTER *11*

# Monetary Powers of the Federal Reserve

The most important aspects of the Federal Reserve System, and the ones with which we are presently concerned, are those that deal with the amount of bank credit and the money supply. The principal powers of the Federal Reserve in this regard are those dealing with open market operations, discounting and member bank borrowing, and reserve requirements. Open market operations are controlled by the Open Market Committee, discount rates are set by the individual Reserve Banks subject to review by the Board of Governors, and reserve requirements are established by the Board of Governors. Clearly the Board of Governors is the chief policy wielding group, as its members form a majority of the Open Market Committee, discount rates are reviewed by the Board, and reserve requirements are the responsibility of the Board alone.

The Federal Reserve exercises its monetary powers through actions directed at the reserve position of member banks. Specifically, the Federal Reserve exercises control over the quantity of bank credit and the money supply by controlling the quantity of Federal Reserve credit. It also controls the multiple expansion potential of member banks by regulating their reserve requirements. Thus, it can both regulate total available reserves and change the level of required reserves. The reserve position of the banking system is the focal point for Federal Reserve control.

The reserve equation derived in the last chapter clearly shows the fashion in which member bank reserves depend on Federal Reserve credit. This reserve equation, as we have seen, shows member bank reserves as the difference between the sources of member bank reserve funds and the competing uses for member bank reserve funds, thus:

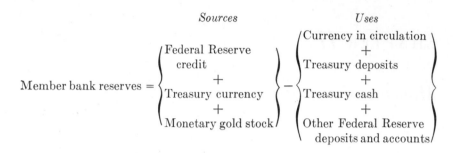

$$
\text{Member bank reserves} = \left\{ \begin{array}{c} \text{Federal Reserve} \\ \text{credit} \\ + \\ \text{Treasury currency} \\ + \\ \text{Monetary gold stock} \end{array} \right\} - \left\{ \begin{array}{c} \text{Currency in circulation} \\ + \\ \text{Treasury deposits} \\ + \\ \text{Treasury cash} \\ + \\ \text{Other Federal Reserve} \\ \text{deposits and accounts} \end{array} \right\}
$$

The only factor in this reserve equation susceptible to any deliberate control is Federal Reserve credit,[1] which it will be recalled, is composed of four elements: United States government bonds held by the Federal Reserve; discounts and advances to member banks; other discounts and advances to nonmember banks (this item is negligible); and float.    Not all of these elements, however, are subject to direct Federal Reserve control.

The volume of float outstanding is a by-product of the check clearing and collection process.    The amount of float outstanding varies both seasonally and cyclically.    But given present arrangements, float is not subject to control.    It could, of course, be eliminated completely by revising the deferred availability schedules used for crediting member bank depositors.    Presumably, the advantages gained from the smooth and rapid transfer of funds offset any disadvantages arising from the lack of control over float.

The volume of discounts and advances held by the Federal Reserve is the other part of Federal Reserve credit not directly controllable. Indirect control, however, is exercised by varying the discount rate and through reserving the right to refuse to lend to the commercial banks.    In discounting the initiative for a loan lies with the borrowing bank; accommodation of the loan request is at the discretion of the Federal Reserve Bank.

The remaining item in Federal Reserve credit, the amount of United

---

[1] As we shall see in the next chapter, this statement must be modified to some degree.    The Treasury does have some monetary power, but by and large it reacts to the initiative of other parties, for example, it stands ready to buy or sell gold at $35 an ounce to qualified persons.    This, of course, has monetary consequences.    The Treasury's ability to engage deliberately in monetary controls is rather limited, however.

States government securities held, is subject to the sole and direct control of the Reserve authorities.   They can vary the holdings of United States government securities on their own initiative by buying and selling in the open market.   As we have seen, this part of Federal Reserve credit provides the bulk of the sources of member bank reserve funds.

Before moving into an examination of the methods of monetary control employed by the Federal Reserve, let us consider possible limits to the control over bank reserves.   In following sections we shall argue that the Federal Reserve can, in fact, exercise almost complete control over bank reserves.   That is, we shall argue that the Reserve authorities can either reinforce, lessen, or neutralize any changes in bank reserves that may arise from changes in the independent factors in the reserve equation.   By operating on those factors over which it does have control, the Federal Reserve can take *dynamic* action to reinforce or *defensive* action to neutralize the effects on reserves expected from changes in the independent factors in order to assure that the net change in the banking system's reserve position will be appropriate for the community's needs for money.   But do the Reserve authorities have this degree of control?

With regard to open market operations in the United States government securities we must look to the sales as well as the purchases of these securities.   With something over $35 billion of government securities in their portfolio, the Reserve authorities are well armed for carrying out open market sales should this be necessary.   But should open market purchases be necessary, then what?   As we know, the Federal Reserve must maintain a 25 per cent gold certificate reserve against its note and deposit liabilities.   When the Federal Reserve purchases securities on the open market its deposit liabilities increase, because the purchases are paid for by credits on its books—its deposit liabilities.   The ratio of gold certificates to note and deposit liabilities as of July 31, 1964 was 29.5 per cent, down from 31.3 per cent a year earlier and from 47.4 in mid-1957.   Thus, while the Reserve authorities have some elbow room, their position is becoming even more binding as the gold drain persists.   If the situation becomes too critical Congress will likely ease the reserve requirement on the Federal Reserve, as it has done twice in the past.

Another limitation to Federal Reserve control over bank reserves can arise if the central bank must maintain or support the government securities market.   For example, during the Second World War and until 1951 the Federal Reserve supported government bond prices.   This meant that the Reserve authorities bought and sold bonds, not to control bank reserves, but to stabilize bond prices.   Control over bank reserves was lost.

In the following sections we shall assume that none of the preceding limitations is present (and currently they are not) and see how the monetary authority exercises its control over bank reserves and the money supply.

## OPEN MARKET OPERATIONS

The instruments of monetary control available to the Reserve authorities range from the flexible and adaptable open market operation to the blunt and inflexible instrument of reserve requirement changes.   In this section we shall examine the open market operation.

The principal tool used for influencing the banks' reserve position is the open market operation.   These operations consist of the purchases and sales by the Federal Reserve of securities in the open market.   The securities traded are primarily United States government obligations, but they sometimes include small amounts of bankers' acceptances.   Since bankers' acceptances constitute a negligible fraction of total transactions we shall assume that the securities traded are United States government obligations.

Dealers who specialize in buying and selling these securities, both for their own accounts and others, maintain an active market in government securities.   Competitive bidding among these dealers determines the terms of trade in any given instance.   The Federal Reserve System conducts open market operations through the open market trading desk in the Federal Reserve Bank of New York, and all purchases and sales are made at this desk.   The total purchases or sales made for the Open Market Account are allocated among the twelve Reserve Banks in proportion to their total assets.   The traders at the trading desk are continually in contact with the credit market and with the reserve position of the banks.   They carry out the policy of the Open Market Committee even though on occasion temporary conditions in the money market may seemingly force them to reverse their field.   For example, currency moves in and out of banks in seasonal, and even weekly, patterns.   The effects of these currency flows on reserves can be offset by open market operations, even though the neutralizing action is apparently contrary to the long-run policy being followed.

Although Federal Reserve open market sales are made outright, open market purchases may be outright or they may be made under a repurchase agreement.   In this latter case, the dealers sell securities to the

Federal Reserve and agree to buy them back within a specified time period of 15 days or less.   The purpose of such arrangements is to provide the Federal Reserve credit on a temporary basis.   But regardless of who sells or who buys the securities from the Federal Reserve, the transactions have a direct impact on the volume of member bank reserves.   The distinguishing feature of open market operations is that they are undertaken solely on the *initiative of the Federal Reserve.*

Open market purchases by the Federal Reserve build up bank reserves and open market sales reduce them.   The most convenient way to analyze the effect of open market operations is through the use of T-accounts.

## Open Market Purchases

When the Federal Reserve goes into the market to purchase securities there is no coercion used to force holders of government securities to sell.   Why, then, do they sell?   The answer is, simply, because it is worthwhile for them to do so.   When the Federal Reserve engages in an open market purchasing operation the prices of the securities are bid up, and the owners of securities can sell their holdings at a profit.

Although the Federal Reserve's open market trading desk deals with only a limited number of security dealers or financial institutions, bondholders generally can trade in these securities through their own banks and security dealers.   Should the Federal Reserve purchase securities from a member bank the transaction is as follows: The bank takes the government securities from its portfolio and exchanges them for an increase in its reserve account at the Federal Reserve.   The commercial bank swaps one kind of asset for another.   The Federal Reserve gains assets, the government securities, paying for them by increasing its deposit liabilities, the member bank reserve balance. In T-accounts this is shown as follows:

Commercial Bank

| Assets | | Liabilities |
|---|---|---|
| Government securities | — | |
| Reserve balance at FRB | + | |

Federal Reserve Bank

| Assets | | Liabilities | |
|---|---|---|---|
| Government securities | + | Reserve balance of commercial bank | + |

What should be clearly understood is that by this open market purchase additional reserves in the amount of the purchase have been channeled into the commercial bank system.

If the seller of the securities is other than a commercial bank the end result is still the same, because all other individuals and institutions maintain their bank accounts with commercial banks. Thus when these individuals and institutions sell securities to the Federal Reserve they take the check received in exchange and deposit it to their account at a commercial bank. When the commercial bank credits its customer's account it sends the check to the Federal Reserve for payment, receiving its payment as a credit to its reserve balance. What has occurred is an exchange of assets by the nonbank public, a trade of securities for a bank deposit. The commercial bank increases both liabilities, the customer's deposit, and assets, its reserve balance; and the Federal Reserve increases both assets, government securities, and liabilities, commercial bank reserve balances. All this is easily summarized in T-accounts:

### Public

| Assets | | Liabilities |
|---|---|---|
| Government securities | — | |
| Demand deposit at commercial bank | + | |

### Commercial Banks

| Assets | | Liabilities | |
|---|---|---|---|
| Reserve balance at FRB | + | Demand deposits of public | + |

### Federal Reserve Bank

| Assets | | Liabilities | |
|---|---|---|---|
| Government securities | + | Reserve balances of commercial banks | + |

Again we see the creation of bank reserves by this open market purchase by the Federal Reserve.

### Open Market Sales

The effect of open market sales by the Federal Reserve is the reverse of that caused by open market purchases. When the Federal Reserve sells securities in the open market it reduces the level of bank reserves. The manner in which buyers are induced to purchase is by an offer of securities at attractive prices; that is, the offering price is lowered with a concurrent increase in the yield.

When commercial banks buy securities from the Federal Reserve they pay for them by having the Reserve Banks charge their reserve balances the amount of the purchase.   The commercial banks exchange assets, part of their reserve balance for government securities.   The Federal Reserve loses an asset, the securities, but reduces its liabilities, member bank reserves.   In T-accounts the open-market sale appears as follows:

### Commercial Banks

| Assets | | Liabilities |
|---|---|---|
| Government securities | + | |
| Reserve balance at FRB | − | |

### Federal Reserve Bank

| Assets | | Liabilities | |
|---|---|---|---|
| Government securities | − | Reserve balance of commercial banks | − |

Note the destruction of bank reserves in the amount of the sale due to this open market sale by the Federal Reserve.

If the purchaser of the securities is the nonbank public, the securities are paid for by checks drawn on commercial banks.   The end result is as before: the public owns government securities instead of bank deposits; the commercial bank reduces its assets, reserve balances, and its liabilities, deposits due the public; and the Federal Reserve reduces its assets, securities, and its liabilities, member bank reserve balances. In T-accounts this shows as follows:

### Public

| Assets | | Liabilities |
|---|---|---|
| Government securities | + | |
| Demand deposits at commercial bank | − | |

### Commercial Banks

| Assets | Liabilities |
|---|---|
| Reserve balance at FRB    —  | Demand deposits of public    — |

### Federal Reserve Bank

| Assets | Liabilities |
|---|---|
| Government securities    —  | Reserve balances of commercial banks    — |

As before, the open market sale has reduced member bank reserves.

### *Indirect Effects of Open Market Operations*

The direct impact of open market operations is clearly on the level of bank reserves.  But there are indirect effects to be accounted for, as well.  In the case of open market purchases, if the member banks are in debt to the Reserve Banks they are likely to use the new reserves to reduce their indebtedness, otherwise they will use them to expand their loans and investments since idle funds earn them no income.  But in order to put these reserves to work, it may be necessary for the banks to lower the interest rate they charge.  On the other hand, open market sales tend to have the reverse effect.  Open market sales deplete member bank reserves, and this may cause the banks to borrow from the Reserve Banks for a temporary meeting of reserve requirements.  Banks, however, either have to obtain additional permanent reserves or run off some of their loans and investments, that is, reduce their deposit liabilities.  And reduced reserves may cause the banks to increase the interest rate on the loans they make during this period.

Another effect of open market operations is the impact on security prices, and hence, on interest rates.  Federal Reserve purchases of securities tend to bid up their prices and lower the effective rate of return; conversely, open market sales lower the securities' prices and increase their yield.  Because government securities are such a large part of the securities market, changes in their effective rate of return tend to spread to the rest of the market causing similar changes in the general pattern of rates on private securities.

Open market operations have not always been an important tool in the Reserve authorities kit for monetary control.  In the early formative years of the Federal Reserve System, the principal instrument of control was thought to be the discount mechanism.  As we shall see, this did not turn out to be the case.  Open market operations were at first used to bolster the earnings of the Reserve Banks.  Through these buying and selling operations Reserve officials became aware of the effects on reserve positions and of their value as a tool for monetary policy.    Starting in 1922 a coordinated approach to open market operations by the various Reserve Banks on a voluntary basis gradually evolved.    Finally, the Banking Act of 1935 set up the twelve-man Federal Open Market Committee.    The decisions of this group are binding and the participation of all district Reserve Banks is compulsory.

## MEMBER BANK BORROWING: DISCOUNTS AND ADVANCES

Member banks may borrow from the Reserve Banks in two ways.    By the first method they rediscount short-term commercial paper or other eligible paper with the Reserve Bank.    Second, they may give their own promissory note secured usually by government securities. Borrowings by the first method are called discounts and by the second method, advances.    Both methods are, however, generally referred to as discounting and the interest rate charged is called the discount rate.

From the point of view of the borrowing member bank, the decision to discount is usually the result of a shortage of required reserves. The bank in this situation can choose to restrict its lending activities, to sell securities in the open market in order to obtain reserves, to borrow reserves from another bank which has excess reserves (Federal Funds), or to borrow from a Reserve Bank.    Since commercial banks attempt to maintain customer good will, recourse is usually had to one of the last three methods—the liquidation of secondary reserves, borrowing in the Federal Funds market, or borrowing from the Reserve Bank.    Which method is used depends on the relative convenience and costs involved.    Discounting is used when it is cheapest or appears most advantageous to the borrowing bank.

The borrowing process is a simple one.    Whether the member banks are discounting some of their customer's notes or borrowing on their own notes, the proceeds are credited to their reserve balances.    The balance sheet of the commercial bank thus has an increase in its notes in the case of an advance and in contingent liabilities in the case of a discount.    Thus, in T-accounts:

Commercial Bank

| Assets | | Liabilities | |
|---|---|---|---|
| Reserve balance at FRB | + | Notes payable (advance) | + |
| | | or | |
| | | Bills payable (discount) | + |

Federal Reserve Bank

| Assets | Liabilities |
|---|---|
| Discounts or advances    + | Reserve balance of<br>commercial bank    + |

By raising or lowering the discount rate, the Reserve Banks can make it costlier or less costly for member banks to obtain additional reserves by borrowing. Such changes in the discount rate affect the general money and credit situation in a number of ways. A direct consequence of changing the discount rate is that it alters the costs of obtaining additional reserves by this method. An indirect effect is the tendency to cause a corresponding change in the interest rates that member banks charge their customers, especially the short-term rate. A further effect of discount rate changes is to indicate to the banking community the thinking of the Federal Reserve authorities as to the current monetary climate. An increase in the rate would indicate concern over credit expansion and would point to a tighter credit policy generally. A reduction in the discount rate would be regarded as pointing toward an easier credit policy.

When the Federal Reserve System was created, it was expected that the discount rate would be the principal tool for making Reserve policy effective. If commercial banks were to obtain additional reserves, they would do so by discounting with the Reserve Banks. They did not. During the 1920s the discount rate frequently could be made effective only by coupling its use with the then emerging open market operation technique. And during the 1930s and 1940s the discount rate became almost ineffective. For how could discount rate changes affect member bank borrowing when member banks had no reason for borrowing? The large gold inflows during the 1930s had built up bank reserves far in excess of required levels, and then also during this period and later during the Second World War there occurred the enormous expansion in government security holdings by the banking system. Thus, reserve positions could be altered by the simple expedient of selling government securities instead of borrowing. Further, the Federal Reserve policy of supporting the government bond market until the Federal Reserve-Treasury "Accord" in March, 1951, meant that whenever commercial banks found it necessary to acquire additional reserves they had a ready market for their government securities and did not have to borrow. They merely sold some of their government securities to the Federal Reserve for additional reserves. Subsequent to the accord, the discount rate has become a more important instrument of monetary policy. But this is a result of the Federal Reserve actively engaging in open market operations to manipulate the reserve position of the banking system, and not to support and stabilize government bond prices.

For discount rate changes to serve effectively as a monetary policy tool, the money and credit situation should be tight. The commercial banks' reserve position must be under pressure with the result that many banks find themselves needing additional reserves and having no cheaper or more advantageous method of obtaining them than by borrowing from the Federal Reserve. Thus, by operating on member bank reserves through open market operations, the more effective become changes in the discount rate. Indeed, the maximum degree of discount rate effectiveness is attained when open market operations force member banks into having to borrow to meet their legal reserve requirements. But this degree of effectiveness is reached as a result of open market policy and not through discount-rate changes alone.

The question may naturally arise that if banks can borrow to obtain additional reserves in order to fulfill their legal reserve requirements, does this not destroy the effectiveness of a policy of credit restraint? The answer to this question is "no." Borrowing fails to nullify restrictive measures because: (1) borrowing is a privilege, not a right, of member banks; and (2) bankers typically are reluctant to borrow. The initiative lies with the member banks. But the Federal Reserve has not encouraged such borrowing, and the tradition has become established that borrowing is a privilege to be used as a temporary source of reserves. Any bank that attempts to keep continuously in debt to its Reserve Bank will have the right to borrow refused. As a result, member banks typically manage their affairs so that they do not need to resort to borrowing except for such contingencies as unforeseen currency withdrawals, unfavorable clearing balances, etc. But, once in debt, it is expected that they repay such debt promptly. Many banks, perhaps as many as one-half of the total number, never borrow, preferring to make necessary adjustments in other ways.

Typically the discount rate is set somewhat above the rate on Treasury bills when the Reserve authorities wish to tighten credit. This discourages borrowing. If the bill rate is 3 per cent and discount rate 3.5 per cent a bank needing additional reserves and owning some Treasury bills will find it cheaper to sell these bills than to borrow. But as these sales are made this forces up the rate of the bills. If the short-term rate rises above the discount rate, banks would have a tendency to start borrowing instead of adjusting through sales of secondary reserves. The Reserve Banks would then likely raise the discount rate in order to keep it serving as a deterrent to credit expansion. Thus, the discount rate usually lags behind changes in the short-term rate.

It appears that discount rate policy when used in conjunction with open market operations provides the monetary authority with another flexible instrument of monetary control. Since member banks are not all alike, the borrowing privilege provides the member bank with a temporary refuge, should it need one, from the undiscriminating impact of restrictive open market operations. Those banks needing time to adjust to the loss of reserves can buy temporary reserves as they adjust permanently to the loss of reserves. And a final significant feature of the member bank borrowing privilege is that should the public desire for cash become very large, the Reserve Banks would loan on almost any type of commercial or business paper presented to them in order to provide the liquidity demanded. Thus, the Reserve Banks would be lenders of last resort in an emergency.

## MEMBER BANK RESERVE REQUIREMENTS

The third principal tool available to the Federal Reserve authorities for influencing the money supply is the authority to change reserve requirements of the member banks. The Board of Governors may set the required reserve ratios for the various member bank classes anywhere within specified limits. For the class "reserve city banks" the limits are 10–22 per cent on demand deposits and 3–6 per cent for time deposits; for "country" banks the limits are 7–14 per cent and 3–6 per cent respectively. Changes in reserve requirements may be applied to one or both classifications at the same time, but they must be kept within the limits set for each class. The Board of Governors has no authority over the reserve requirements of nonmember banks, which total over one-half of all banks but which have only about 15 per cent of total deposits.

In contrast to discounting and open market operations that directly affect the volume of member bank reserves, alterations in the required reserve ratio do not change the level of total reserves. Changes in the reserve ratio change the amount of deposits any given volume of reserves can support. That is, open market operations and member bank borrowing affect the level of available reserves; changes in reserve ratios alter the composition of available reserves as between required reserves and excess reserves.

When the required reserve ratios are changed, two things happen.

First, there is an immediate impact on the secondary reserve position of the member banks.   That is, if the reserve ratio requirements are raised any member banks not having excess reserves will either have to sell some of their secondary reserves, generally their short-term government securities, or else borrow either from banks having excess reserves or borrow from the Reserve Banks.   For the whole system of banks, however, additional reserves can be obtained only if they are provided by Federal Reserve open market operations or by borrowing from the Federal Reserve Banks.

On the other hand, if reserve requirements are reduced the member banks find themselves with excess reserves.   After retiring any indebtedness the banks are likely to increase their holdings of secondary reserves, at least temporarily.

The second major effect of a change in the reserve ratio is the change in the volume of deposits any given amount of reserves can support. Neglecting currency and time deposit complications, if the required reserve ratio is 20 per cent then $1 of reserves can support $5 of deposits.   Increase the required ratio to 25 per cent and this same $1 in reserves can support only $4 in deposits; lower the required reserve ratio to 10 per cent and this same dollar in reserves can support $10 in deposits.

As an instrument of monetary control, changes in required reserve ratios are blunt and inflexible, certainly less flexible than open market operations and discounting.   Indeed, it is not amiss to say that the bluntest and strongest control measure available to the Reserve authorities is the manipulation of reserve ratios.   But this is not a tool to use frequently, however, or to use to produce small changes in the money and credit situation.   For example, member banks for the four weeks ending January 29, 1964 held about $20 billion in reserves. If reserve ratios averaged, say, 20 per cent, the effect of lowering the required reserve ratio 1 per cent from 20 per cent to 19 per cent, neglecting currency and time deposit complications would be to increase the system expansion potential from 5 to about 5.26.   On the reserve base of $20 billions this represents a potential increase in demand deposits of .26 of $20 billion or about $5.2 billions.   This is equivalent to an open market purchase of about $1.04 billion with the reserve ratio held at 20 per cent.   Of course, the lowering of the reserve ratio and thereby making excess reserves available by no means assures an expansion in deposits, but at the very least it provides the potential for deposit expansion.

On the other hand, if the $20 billion in reserves were all required reserves then an increase in the reserve ratio by one per cent from 20 per cent to 21 per cent would force a contraction in deposits unless additional reserves were made available by the Federal Reserve. With an increase in the reserve ratio from 20 per cent to 21 per cent the expansion potential, again neglecting currency and time deposit complications, falls from 5 to about 4.76. This means the $20 billion reserve base can support 0.24 times $20 billion less than before, or about $4.8 billion less in demand deposits. That is, the demand deposits would shrink from $100 to roughly $95 billion if the $20 billion reserves were all required reserves. The increase in reserve ratio of 1 per cent is equivalent to an open market sale of about $1 billion with the reserve ratio left at 20 per cent.

Unless the banks are permitted to obtain additional reserves by borrowing from Reserve Banks or by an open market purchase operation, the increase in reserve requirements will force a contraction in deposits. Thus, the restraining effects of an increase in the reserve ratio are determined in part by the terms on which member banks are permitted to obtain additional reserves from the Federal Reserve. An increase in required reserves will be more effective if accompanied by an increase in the discount rate and a reduction in the Reserve System's buying price for government securities.

Because not all banks are the same in their operating characteristics —their excess reserves, type of business engaged in, etc.—the Reserve authorities are not likely to change the reserve ratio requirement either frequently or by more than 1 per cent or so unless they feel drastic and decisive measures are required. For instance, a bank specializing in loans to businesses and individuals may easily encounter some difficulty in liquidating loans in an amount sufficient to meet increased reserve requirements. Other banks with considerable excess reserves or large holdings of short-term government securities would have less difficulty adapting to increased reserve requirements. And finally, when reserve ratios are changed in one bank classification and not in the other, or changed by different amounts, there exists the embarrassing defense of the burdens assigned to the different bank classes, as well as the different time deposits reserve requirements versus demand deposits reserve requirements.

Thus, the Federal Reserve does not use its power to raise required reserve ratios in such a manner as to force a multiple credit contraction on the economy to a dangerous degree. Rather, the ability to raise reserve requirements allows the Federal Reserve to mop up excess reserves when it is felt that these have become so large and widespread as to threaten inflation from too rapid credit expansion.

## SELECTIVE OR QUALITATIVE CONTROLS

The tools of monetary control discussed above are often referred to as *quantitative* controls. They operate primarily through influencing the cost, volume, and availability of bank reserves. They regulate the supply of credit. They cannot be used effectively to regulate the use of credit in particular areas or sectors of the credit market. In contrast to these "impartial" quantitative controls, the Federal Reserve authorities at various times have had the authority to regulate the terms on which credit is granted in specific sectors. These latter powers are called *qualitative* or *selective* controls. Qualitative controls seek to regulate the *demand* for credit for specific uses by regulating the period of time over which the loan is to be repaid and by setting minimum down payments. Quantitative instruments, on the other hand, seek to influence the *supply* of credit.

The only selective control currently in use is the Federal Reserve's margin requirement that regulates the use of stock-market credit. Margin requirement may be defined as that part of the purchase price of securities listed on national exchanges that may not be borrowed. When the margin requirement is, say, 70 per cent, a buyer of listed stocks with a current market value of $1,000 has to put up at least $700 of his own funds and may borrow no more than $300 using the stock as collateral. Similarly, if the margin were 25 per cent, up to 75 per cent of the transaction might be financed by borrowing. By varying the margin requirement the Board of Governors attempts to influence the amount of credit extended for carrying or purchasing non-exempt securities.

The margin requirement is a product of the stock-market crash of 1929. Prior to the crash, large amounts of borrowed funds were used in stock-market transactions. Since there were no specific means of curbing such use of credit without also curbing other, presumably more legitimate and worthier, users of bank credit, reserve officials hesitated to act to restrict credit. This selective control was granted the Board of Governors in the Securities and Exchange Act of 1934.

Other selective controls have been available in the past. One of these was the regulation of consumer credit during the Second World War and the early postwar years. This regulated the terms on which credit was granted to consumers for the purchase of autos, refrigerators, radios, and other consumer durables. The means of regulation were to impose minimum down payments and maximum payment periods. By increasing the down payment and shortening the payment period many persons who purchase goods by looking only at the size of the monthly payments and the down payment, and not at the total cost, are denied credit, even though the banking system may have ample reserves. For example, an item that costs $2,400 and requires 10 per cent down and allows 24 months to pay means monthly installments of $90. If the down payment becomes 25 per cent and the payment period is shortened to one year, the monthly installments are $150 after a down payment of $600. This could easily discourage a number of would-be buyers.

The other selective control was the regulation of real estate credit. It was similar to consumer credit regulation in specifying loan periods, maximum loan values (minimum down payment), etc. The consumer credit control, regulation W, which expired in 1949, was renewed in 1950. Regulation X, real estate credit, was imposed in 1950. Both regulations expired in 1952.

Thus, the only selective control currently in use is the margin requirement for regulating the flow of credit into the stock market. There is, however, debate among the students of monetary affairs as to the wisdom of this situation. A rather considerable sentiment favors at least standby controls over consumer credit. We shall return to this topic later in our discussion of the objectives and limitations of monetary policy.

## SUMMARY AND EVALUATION

The principal tools of monetary control are open market operations, discounting, and control over reserve requirements. Supplementing these major quantitative instruments is one qualitative or selective control, the stock-market margin requirement. The quantitative controls influence the supply side of the credit market, affecting the volume, cost, and availability of credit. Qualitative controls affect the demand for credit.

When the Federal Reserve authorities determine on the use of one or several of the general quantitative tools, their purpose is to influence, either directly or indirectly, the volume of member bank reserves, in particular the amount of excess reserves available for a further expansion of deposits.

Thus, an important feature of the various instruments is the nature of their direct and indirect effects. Open market operations affect directly both the volume of member bank reserves and deposits, with open market purchases increasing them and sales decreasing them. This direct effect on member bank deposits is unique to this particular instrument.    The amount of excess reserves is modified by changes in the total volume of member bank reserves.    A further consequence of open market purchases and sales is the tendency to raise or depress government security prices.    In contrast, the discount rate does not directly affect either the total amount of reserves or the amount of excess reserves.    Changes in the discount rate merely lower or raise the price of obtaining reserves from Reserve Banks by means of advances or discounts.    Changes in reserve requirements alter the amount of required reserves but do not directly affect the total volume of member bank reserves.    Control over the reserve requirement also affects all member banks of the class to which it is applied.

The indirect effects of the various instruments must also be taken into account in determining the certainty and degree of impact on the member banks.    Open market operations may have rather significant indirect effects.    By affecting the pattern of interest rates open market operations may influence the investment policies of institutions other than commercial banks.    Similarly, changes in the discount rate or reserve requirements can have indirect side effects.    For instance, raising the discount rate may be interpreted as a signal of tighter credit to come, and therefore commercial banks may raise their interest rates and screen loan applications more carefully.    The nature and extent of such side effects depend to a large extent on the general business conditions at the time and to the market psychology then present.    It is impossible to estimate the type of indirect psychological effect the various instruments might have.    Changes in reserve requirements may also indirectly influence interest rates by changing the excess reserve position of member banks.    An increase in reserve requirements, for example, may force some member banks to borrow or to sell securities to obtain reserves to meet the new standards.    Security prices tend to fall and the effective yield rises.

The excess reserve position of the member banks is changed by both open market operations and by changes in reserve requirements.    With either of these tools, the degree of restraint obtained is dependent on how easy or expensive it is to acquire additional reserves.    If the banks can procure fresh reserves at low cost, either by discounting or by selling securities, the restrictive effects of these instruments are seriously reduced.

A second important feature of the various monetary control instruments is the extent to which their impact can be directed into certain channels.    For example, it is next to impossible to say how the effects of open market operations are going to be distributed among the banks. The initial impact is mostly in New York because the open market transactions occur there. Which banks gain or lose reserves is not a decision of the banks themselves, but depends on the extent of the participation of nonbank investors who are buying or selling the securities the Federal Reserve is offering or purchasing. The impact of the open market operation is, therefore, determined by the market forces prevailing. Similarly, the impact of changing the discount rate, by changing the cost of borrowed reserves, affects only those member banks needing additional reserves. Changes in reserve requirements hit all banks in the affected classification; their impact is felt by all the member banks to which the changes apply. But the impact is not, however, necessarily distributed according to the degree of effect needed. Since banks differ, those with excess reserves will not feel the effects of an increase in requirements as much as banks without them.

Flexibility of the various monetary controls is a third important consideration. The point at issue here is whether they can be applied so that the effects will be appropriate, mild or drastic, as the situation requires. On this count open market operations and discount rate changes have the edge over changes in reserve requirements. Open market operations are flexible in that the volume of purchases or sales can be made in any amount according to the needs of a given situation. And even in pursuing some given type of action the instrument is so adaptable that occasional reversals of operation may be taken to offset temporary fluctuations in the factors affecting reserves— to offset, for example, a change in float due to a severe storm disrupting ordinary transportation patterns or unexpected demand for currency by the public, etc. The limitations to the use of this open market instrument lie in the System's holdings of securities that seem more than adequate for any foreseeable selling operation, and on the System's ability to create credit with which to purchase securities. This is limited by the requirement to hold a 25 per cent gold certificate reserve in back of the Federal Reserve's note and deposit liabilities. This may become a more serious problem in the future if the present gold drain continues. The present ratio of about 30 per cent gives the System some elbow room.

Changes in the discount rate are flexible in that they can be small, frequent, and impinge only on those banks needing additional reserves. Changes in reserve requirements are more inflexible. It is an awkward tool to use if changes are made in full percentages, since relatively large amounts of reserve funds are involved. It is less inflexible on this score if changes are made in fractions of 1 per cent, since the impact on reserves can be better gauged to the needs of a particular situation. It is harsh, however, in that any given change affects all banks in the particular class and may cause some banks in the class considerably more adjustment difficulties than others in the same classification. Finally, frequent changes in reserve requirements are ruled out because of the difficulties in adjustment and the need to minimize the obligation to explain the basis for different requirements for different classes of banks and as between time and demand deposits.

Qualitative or selective instruments similarly have both advantages and disadvantages. Qualitative controls influence the demand for credit rather than its supply, and their impact is on a particular segment of the credit market. On the other hand, selective controls are distasteful to many persons because they intrude upon the setting of the terms of a contract between two private parties. They also tend to be discriminatory, since restrictions are placed on some uses of credit and not on other uses. At the present time only one selective control is in use, the regulation of margin requirements in the stock market. Nevertheless, there is some support for control over consumer credit as a supplement to the quantitative instruments presently employed.

## REVIEW QUESTIONS

1. In the reserve equation, what part of Federal Reserve credit is subject to deliberate change at the initiative of the Federal Reserve; what part of Federal Reserve credit can be indirectly influenced by Federal Reserve action?
2. What effects on member bank reserves does a change in legal reserve ratios have? What happens to deposit expansion possibilities?
3. Define open market operations. At whose initiative are they conducted?
4. Trace through the effects on bank reserves of an open-market sale, an open market purchase.
5. What forms may member bank borrowing take?
6. What is the significance of changes in the discount rate?
7. Why is reserve ratio change said to be a blunt instrument of monetary control, while open market operations and discount-rate manipulations are said to be flexible instruments of control?
8. Distinguish between "quantitative" instruments of monetary control and "qualitative" instruments.
9. Look up in the current *Federal Reserve Bulletin* the present margin requirements.

## SUGGESTED REFERENCES

Board of Governors, *The Federal Reserve System: Purposes and Functions* (Washington, D.C., 1961).

Federal Reserve Bank of New York, *Money Market Essays*, 1953.

Federal Reserve Bank of New York, *The Treasury and the Money Market*, 1954.

Federal Reserve Bank of New York, *Open Market Operations*, 1961.

Madden, Carl H., *The Money Side of "The Street"* (New York: Federal Reserve Bank of New York, 1959).

Roosa, Robert V., *Federal Reserve Operations in the Money and Government Securities Market* (New York: Federal Reserve Bank of New York, 1956).

Young, Ralph A., "Tools and Processes of Monetary Policy," in *United States Monetary Policy* (New York: Columbia University, 1958).

CHAPTER *12*

# Monetary Powers of the Treasury

Control of the money supply is not a prerogative vested solely with the Federal Reserve System. Because the Treasury has the authority to buy and sell gold and silver and to mint coins and issue currency, it also possesses substantial monetary powers. But an even more important source of monetary control is the Treasury's discretion with respect to managing its money balances. As the Treasury shifts funds from its Tax and Loan Accounts at the commercial banks to its working balance at the Federal Reserve there is an impact on bank reserves. Thus, the Treasury does have an avenue of control over the money supply.

In addition to these monetary powers the Treasury, unlike the Federal Reserve System, has a number of fiscal powers which are important in determining the level and character of national income and spending. Fiscal powers deal with both government revenues and government expenditures. Later, the role of fiscal policy will be more fully developed. At this point it is sufficient to note that at least one aspect of fiscal operations, namely the acquisition of revenues, clearly has monetary consequences if the revenues are obtained by borrowing. As a matter of fact, in most cases fiscal procedures have monetary consequences. Our task here is to outline the monetary effects of various Treasury operations, assuming, for example, that if the Treasury borrows it proceeds to spend the funds thus acquired. We reserve until later a more extensive treatment of debt management and other fiscal matters.

## GOLD, SILVER, AND THE TREASURY

### Gold Purchases and Sales

Since 1933 the Treasury has bought and sold gold at $35 an ounce. The gold acquired is not coined, however, and it cannot be held by individuals except in jewelry and similar nonmonetary forms.

A typical purchase of gold from a domestic source appears as follows: the Treasury pays for the gold with a check drawn on a Federal Reserve Bank. Thus, the Treasury exchanges one kind of asset for another, namely, the drawing down of its checking account at the Federal Reserve offset by an increase in its monetary gold stock. In the following T-accounts this exchange of assets by the Treasury is numbered "1."

The mining company deposits the Treasury's check in its commercial bank, and the commercial bank forwards the check to its Federal Reserve Bank for credit to its reserve account. These entries are numbered "2" in the T-accounts. The Federal Reserve Bank, upon receipt of the Treasury check from the commercial bank, credits

| Treasury | | | |
|---|---|---|---|
| Assets | | Liabilities | |
| 1. Gold | + | | |
| 1. Deposit balance at FRB | − | | |
| 4. Deposit balance at FRB | + | 4. Gold certificates | + |

| Federal Reserve Bank | | | |
|---|---|---|---|
| Assets | | Liabilities | |
| | | 3. Reserve balance of commercial bank | + |
| | | 3. Treasury deposit balance | − |
| 4. Gold certificates | + | 4. Treasury deposit balance | + |

| Commercial Bank | | | |
|---|---|---|---|
| Assets | | Liabilities | |
| 2. Reserve balance at FRB | + | 2. Demand deposit of public | + |

the commercial bank's reserve account and debits the Treasury deposit balance. These entries are numbered "3." The Treasury may now proceed to restore its working balance at the Federal Reserve by monetizing the gold—that is, by issuing gold certificates against the gold purchased.   The gold certificates are then deposited with the Federal Reserve, which increases its own assets (its holdings of gold certificates) and its liabilities by crediting the Treasury's account for the gold certificates.   These entries are labeled "4."

The final net effects may be summarized as below in the following T-accounts:

Treasury

| Assets | Liabilities |
|---|---|
| Gold                                  + | Gold certificates                          + |

Federal Reserve Bank

| Assets | Liabilities |
|---|---|
| Gold certificates                     + | Reserve balance of commercial bank        + |

Commercial Bank

| Assets | Liabilities |
|---|---|
| Reserve balance at FRB                + | Demand deposit of public                   + |

The consequences of this gold purchase is an increase in money in the hands of the public (the demand deposit of the public) and an increase in the reserves of the commercial banks.   With a fractional reserve requirement excess commercial bank reserves are now available to support a further expansion of bank credit, unless these excess reserves are neutralized by the Federal Reserve through the exercise of open market sales or by raising the reserve ratio requirement.

The Treasury may purchase gold without increasing the money supply or commercial bank reserves by "sterilizing" the gold.   Gold sterilization amounts to not monetizing the gold by not issuing gold certificates against it.   The Treasury pays for the gold by checks drawn against its account with the Federal Reserve, but the Treasury restores its working balance at the Federal Reserve by selling securities to the public or commercial banks.   In effect, the gold is bought with interest-paying securities, and this is nothing more nor less than an open market selling operation conducted by the Treasury.   Thus, if the Treasury sells bonds in the money market and the bonds are purchased by either commercial banks for their own portfolio or by the public, the results are similar.   The process moves through steps 1 to 3 as in the previous example.   But now entries "4" are the issuance of bonds by the Treasury to restore its working balance, the loss of reserves by the commercial banks, and the acquisition of the bonds by the banks or public, as the case may be.  If the bonds are sold to the public, the effects show as:

Treasury

| Assets | Liabilities |
| --- | --- |
| 4. Reserve balance at FRB + | 4. Bonds + |

Federal Reserve Bank

| Assets | Liabilities |
| --- | --- |
|  | 4. Reserve balance of commercial bank — |
|  | 4. Treasury deposit balance + |

Commercial Bank

| Assets | Liabilities |
| --- | --- |
| 4. Reserve balance at FRB — | 4. Demand deposit of public — |

Public

| Assets | Liabilities |
| --- | --- |
| 4. Treasury bonds + | |
| 4. Demand deposit commercial bank — | |

If the bonds are purchased by the commercial banks the results are:

Treasury

| Assets | Liabilities |
| --- | --- |
| 4. Deposit balance at FRB + | 4. Bonds + |

Federal Reserve Bank

| Assets | Liabilities |
| --- | --- |
|  | 4. Reserve balance of commercial bank — |
|  | 4. Treasury deposit balance + |

Commercial Bank

| Assets | Liabilities |
| --- | --- |
| 4. Reserve balance at FRB — | |
| 4. Treasury bonds + | |

Clearly in either case, the sale of bonds to re-establish the Treasury's working balance has resulted in the loss of the reserves acquired by the commercial banks from the Treasury gold purchase.   And by selling to the public there is additionally the destruction of the newly created addition to the public's money supply.   The gold sterilization amounts to an open market selling operation on the part of the Treasury.   Such sterilization operations, however, have been of small importance since 1937 when they were of some importance.

As we can see, the purchase of domestic gold and the issuance of gold certificates (monetization of the gold) result in increases in both commercial bank reserves and in the public's money supply.   Although this transaction represents the essentials of the process, numerous variations occur.   The largest purchases of gold are not from domestic production but rather from foreign central banks.   Whenever such a purchase is made, the immediate effect is to raise the deposits of foreign banks on the books of the Federal Reserve Banks, along with the gold certificates issued against the gold to restore the Treasury's working balance.   Thus, at this stage, bank reserves and deposits in commercial banks are unaffected.   But such sales of gold by foreign banks are usually made to supply the dollar needs for foreign purchase of goods in the United States.   This is to say that when foreign central banks sell gold to the Treasury, money is obtained by exporters.   The dollars so obtained are now spent for American goods, and the dollars end up deposited into domestic commercial banks.   Thus, if gold flows in and goods flow out of the United States, the monetary changes are exactly the same as for a domestic mining company selling its gold production to the Treasury.

Sales of gold by the Treasury have just the opposite effects.   As the gold holdings of the Treasury decline, so also must the gold certificates issued against them be reduced.   Since the Federal Reserve is required to hold gold certificates against its monetary liabilities equal to at least 25 per cent of the liabilities, this explains much of the concern over the present gold outflow sustained by the United States since about 1957. If the gold outflow continues long enough, gold certificates backing Federal Reserve notes and deposits might have to be retired, thus forcing a contraction in Federal Reserve credit.   Because the Federal Reserve holds gold certificates in moderate excess over minimum requirements, this prospect of contraction, even at the height of the outflow, has never been too serious a problem.   A persistent outflow, given the present requirements, could cause difficulties, however.   In this case, since rules seem made to be changed, the gold certificate requirement for the Federal Reserve could be lowered or even abolished.

## Silver Policy

Some things change only gradually, and the price of silver for monetary purposes seems to be one of them. The price of silver for monetary purposes, as we have seen, is $1.29 an ounce, reflecting legislation of 1792 which defined the dollar as 371.25 grains of silver.

The history of silver through the years has been a stormy one, but one thing is clear: the silver bloc in Congress is both vocal and potent. The Silver Purchase Act of 1934 states:

It is hereby declared to be the policy of the United States that the proportion of silver to gold in the monetary stocks of the United States should be increased, with the ultimate objective of having and maintaining, one-fourth of the monetary value of such stock in silver.

To implement this policy the Secretary of Treasury was to purchase silver, both foreign and domestic, so long as the price was less than $1.29 an ounce. The provisions of later legislation in 1939 and 1946 modified the Act. These later acts required the Secretary of Treasury to buy all domestically produced silver at 90.5 cents an ounce or higher. But they also authorized the sale of silver for industrial uses at prices of 90.5 cents an ounce or above. The acts are contradictory. On the one hand, the Secretary was instructed to acquire silver until its value in store was equal to one-third that of gold, but on the other hand he was allowed to sell silver. He certainly could not do both. In a practical sense what this probably says is that the silver interests were satisfied with a price of 90.5 cents an ounce. The world price of silver since the end of the Second World War until 1961 remained around 90 cents an ounce and the Treasury's stock of silver remained fairly stable.

The 1946 legislation authorized the Secretary of Treasury to sell silver to domestic industrial users from its free stocks, that is, the silver not required as currency backing. But until 1959 the world market price of silver was consistently below the Treasury's buying price of 90.5 cents an ounce which constituted a subsidy to domestic producers. Treasury holdings of silver were therefore built up out of domestic production, with industrial users obtaining silver from abroad at cheaper prices. From 1959 to 1961, the world market price rose above 90.5 cents with the result that the Treasury purchased little silver, and industrial users found it cheaper to buy silver from the Treasury.

In 1961 with the stock of free silver running low, President Kennedy directed the Treasury to suspend its silver sales to domestic industrial users. The effect of this suspension was immediate. The market price of silver began to rise and rise rapidly. In June, 1963, the price of silver reached $1.28 per ounce in the New York market.

In June, 1963, the President signed into law new legislation concerning silver. This new legislation repealed the Silver Purchase Acts. The new legislation authorized the Treasury to sell silver freely when its price exceeds its monetary value. This legislation also provided for the gradual retirement of silver certificates from circulation, replacing the familiar "one-dollar bill" by newly authorized one-dollar Federal Reserve notes. When this change-over is completed, the result will be a demonetization of the silver in the United States except for its use in coinage.

The silver released by the gradual retirement of roughly 1.5 billion $1 silver certificates will be used for the minting of needed coins. In this fashion about 1.3 billion ounces of silver valued at $1.29 an ounce will be available for coinage purposes, an estimated twenty-year supply of silver for such purposes. The retirement of the silver certificates and their replacement by the new $1 Federal Reserve notes will proceed gradually because the new Federal Reserve notes require a 25 per cent backing in gold. The gradual introduction of the new Federal Reserve notes, instead of immediately tying up some $400 million in gold as required backing, will allow the earmarking of only about $35 to $40 million of the "free" gold stock a year. In this fashion the gold stock is subjected to less pressure.

The 1963 legislation also repealed the law requiring the Treasury to purchase all newly mined domestic silver presented to it at 90.5 cents an ounce.

The reason for the recent increase in price of silver to the point where it now is at the monetary value of $1.29 an ounce stems principally from the phenomenal growth in its industrial uses. For example, tremendous quantities are used in photography. This use accounts for over 30 per cent of the industrial consumption of silver. Silver is also widely used in the electronics industry. It also has many uses in high-temperature situations because of its high conductivity, resistance to corrosion, and ability to withstand shock and vibration. In addition to these increased industrial uses for silver, larger quantities are also being used for coinage purposes. The increased demand for coinage purposes stems not only from the increased demand for coins for customary purposes, but also because of the development and increasing popularity of coin-operated vending machines.

At the present time the price of silver cannot rise significantly above

$1.29 an ounce so long as silver is available at that price from the Treasury's holdings. At a price slightly above $1.29 an ounce, the silver content of the standard silver dollar would be worth more than its monetary value. At a little over a $1.38 an ounce, the subsidiary coins would become candidates for melting down.[1]

The monetary consequences of silver purchases were similar to those of gold purchases. To illustrate, assume a domestic silver producer sold silver to the Treasury. Using T-accounts the process was as follows: In entries "1" the Treasury accepted the silver and paid for it with a check on the Federal Reserve. The miner then deposited the check at his commercial bank, which credited it to the miner's account and sent it to the Federal Reserve. The Federal Reserve credited the bank's reserve balance and debited the Treasury's balance. These

### Treasury

| Assets | | Liabilities | |
|---|---|---|---|
| 1. Silver | + | | |
| 1. Deposit balance at FRB | — | | |
| 4. Deposit balance at FRB | + | 4. Silver certificates | + |

### Federal Reserve Bank

| Assets | | Liabilities | |
|---|---|---|---|
| | | 3. Treasury deposit balance | — |
| | | 3. Reserve balance of commercial bank | + |
| 4. Silver certificates | + | 4. Treasury deposit balance | + |

### Commercial Bank

| Assets | | Liabilities | |
|---|---|---|---|
| 2. Reserve balance at FRB | + | 2. Demand deposits of public | + |

are entries "2" and "3." In order to restore its working balance, the Treasury issued silver certificates or coin equal to the purchase and deposited it to its account at the Federal Reserve. These are entries "4." The result was that the reserves of the commercial bank system

---

[1] The silver dollar weighs 412.5 grains, and is 90 per cent silver. This is equivalent to 371.25 grains of pure silver. A dollar's worth of subsidiary coins weighs 385.8 grains, containing 90 per cent silver. This is equivalent to roughly 347.22 grains of pure silver. It thus appears that silver has three melting points: 1,762°F, about $1.30 per ounce for standard silver dollars, and about $1.38 per ounce for subsidiary silver coins.

as well as the public's money supply were increased.   Given a fractional reserve requirement, the commercial banks might attempt to expand the money supply still further since they now had excess reserves.

As mentioned, though the Treasury paid 90.5 cents an ounce for silver it could issue currency or coin in amounts equal to $1.29 an ounce, the full monetary value of the silver.   Generally the Treasury issued currency only equal to the cost of the purchase, and thus, in effect, it sterilized part of the silver.   If the Treasury should choose it could desterilize this nonmonetized silver and issue currency and coin, using the proceeds to meet expenses or to retire debt.   The effect of these operations would be to increase bank reserves further if the debt retired were held by the public or the banks.

### Treasury Borrowing and the Money Supply

Whereas Treasury borrowing and expenditures properly constitute a fiscal activity, it will not be amiss to deal with the monetary consequences of these actions at this point.   In a later section we shall deal again with these and other fiscal actions of the Treasury.

We shall assume that when the Treasury undertakes to borrow money it proceeds to spend the funds so acquired.   When the funds are spent, they are spent with the public for all the kinds of goods and services which the government requires.   But although the public is the recipient of the expenditures, there are three sources from which the Treasury may borrow: (1) the public; (2) the commercial bank system; and (3) the Federal Reserve Banks.   Borrowing from these various sources and spending the proceeds have different monetary effects.   Let us see what these effects are.

### Borrowing from the Public

Borrowing is simply the selling of a promissory note by the borrower to the purchaser (lender).   When the Treasury borrows from the public it means that the public buys government bonds.

The effects of Treasury borrowing from the public and spending the proceeds obtained may be conveniently illustrated by the use of T-accounts.   Four sectors are involved: the Treasury, the public, the Federal Reserve Banks, and the commercial banking system.   If the public purchases a newly issued government bond, it simply exchanges one asset for another.   That is, it pays for the bond by drawing against its checking account at the commercial bank.   Thus, as the

Treasury issues the bond to the public the Treasury's liabilities increase and the public gains an asset. This is shown as entries "1." The public gives the Treasury its check on the commercial bank and the Treasury deposits it in its Tax and Loan Account—entries "2." The commercial bank makes the appropriate adjustments on its books crediting the Treasury's Tax and Loan Account and debiting the public's account—entries "3." So far, so good. But we assumed that the Treasury went into debt in order to spend; to do so the Treasury must shift its balance from the commercial bank to the Federal Reserve Bank. The Treasury thus essentially writes a check on the commercial bank and deposits it to its account at the Federal Reserve Bank, which in turn credits the Treasury's account and debits the commercial bank's reserve. These are shown as entries "4," "5," and "6."

Now the Treasury has the proceeds in its working balance at the Federal Reserve, and finally it can spend. And when the Treasury spends, it spends with the public, which, in turn, deposits the Treasury checks drawn on the Federal Reserve in the commercial banks. Thus, the Treasury loses its deposit balance, the public regains its deposit

### Treasury

| Assets | | Liabilities | |
|---|---|---|---|
| | | 1. Bonds | + |
| 2. Deposit balance at commercial bank | + | | |
| 4. Deposit balance at commercial bank | − | | |
| 5. Deposit balance at FRB | + | | |
| 7. Deposit balance at FRB | − | | |

### Public

| Assets | | Liabilities | |
|---|---|---|---|
| 1. Treasury bonds | + | | |
| 2. Demand deposit at commercial bank | − | | |
| 7. Demand deposit at commercial bank | + | | |

### Commercial Bank

| Assets | | Liabilities | |
|---|---|---|---|
| | | 3. Demand deposit of public | − |
| | | 3. Deposit balance of Treasury | + |
| 6. Reserve balance at FRB | − | 4. Deposit balance of Treasury | − |
| 8. Reserve balance at FRB | + | 8. Demand deposit of public | + |

Federal Reserve Bank

| Assets | Liabilities | |
|--------|-------------|---|
| | 5. Treasury deposit balance | + |
| | 6. Reserve balance of commercial bank | − |
| | 9. Treasury deposit balance | − |
| | 9. Reserve balance of commercial bank | + |

balance, and the commercial bank reserve position is restored.    These actions are shown as entries "7" through "9."    The net effect has been to increase the debt of the Treasury, leave the money supply and bank reserves unaffected, and increase the public's asset holdings. Although the money supply is not increased by borrowing from the public, unlike borrowing from the banks or Federal Reserve, there may be changes in spending patterns induced by the increased amounts of liquid assets in the hands of the public.    There could be an increase in the rate of spending, for instance, and this could have effects on prices and income similar to those caused by an increased money supply.    These factors will be discussed later in dealing with monetary theory.

### Borrowing from Commercial Banks

When the Treasury sells bonds to the commercial banks, the immediate effect is to increase the assets and liabilities of both the Treasury and commercial banks.    The Treasury increases its liabilities (bonds) and the commercial banks their assets.    These are entries "1."    The banks pay for the bonds by crediting the Treasury's Tax and Loan Accounts—entries "2."    But to spend the proceeds the Treasury ultimately switches the balance from the commercial banks to the Federal Reserve Banks.    The Federal Reserve credits the Treasury account and debits each commercial bank's reserve account.    These appear as entries "3," "4," and "5."

When the Treasury draws against this balance, the checks it writes are payable to the public.    The public deposits these checks to its accounts at the commercial banks, which then credit the public's account and forward the checks to the Federal Reserve for payment. The Federal Reserve credits the reserve accounts of the commercial banks and debits the balance of the Treasury.    These steps are shown in entries "6," "7," and "8."

## Treasury

| Assets | | Liabilities | |
| --- | --- | --- | --- |
| 2. Deposit balance at commercial bank | + | 1. Bonds | + |
| 3. Deposit balance at commercial bank | − | | |
| 3. Deposit balance at FRB | + | | |
| 6. Deposit balance at FRB | − | | |

## Commercial Bank

| Assets | | Liabilities | |
| --- | --- | --- | --- |
| 1. Treasury bonds | + | 2. Deposit balance of Treasury | + |
| 4. Reserve balance at FRB | − | 4. Deposit balance of Treasury | − |
| 7. Reserve balance at FRB | + | 7. Demand deposit of public | + |

## Public

| Assets | | Liabilities |
| --- | --- | --- |
| 6. Demand deposit at commercial bank | + | |

## Federal Reserve Bank

| Assets | Liabilities | |
| --- | --- | --- |
| | 5. Reserve balance of commercial bank | − |
| | 5. Treasury deposit balance | + |
| | 8. Treasury deposit balance | − |
| | 8. Reserve balance of commercial bank | + |

The net result of this borrowing from the commercial bank system is to increase the indebtedness of the Treasury, to maintain total bank reserves, and to increase the money supply of the public.

### Borrowing from the Federal Reserve System

The Treasury seldom borrows directly from the Federal Reserve, and in fact, the Federal Reserve was for a long time prohibited from purchasing securities directly from the Treasury. During the Second World War, the Federal Reserve System was given authorization to purchase up to five billion dollars of securities directly from the Treasury. In practice, however, most Treasury borrowing is done from the public or commercial banks.    The Federal Reserve provides the banking system with any necessary reserves in order to absorb the security issue.    If the Federal Reserve were to purchase Treasury obligations, the procedure would be as follows.    The Treasury issues bonds to the Federal Reserve, thus increasing the Treasury's liabilities and the Federal Reserve's assets.    This is entry "1."    The Federal Reserve pays for the bonds by crediting the Treasury's balance—entries "2."    When the Treasury draws against its account the checks are received by the public and deposited in the commercial banks.    This is entry "3."  The commercial bank, having credited the public's account, sends the check to the Federal Reserve which credits the bank's reserve account and debits the Treasury's balance—entries "4" and "5."

### Treasury

| Assets | | Liabilities | |
|---|---|---|---|
| 2. Deposit balance at FRB | + | 1. Bonds | + |
| 3. Deposit balance at FRB | − | | |

### Commercial Bank

| Assets | | Liabilities | |
|---|---|---|---|
| 4. Reserve balance at FRB | + | 4. Demand deposit of public | + |

### Public

| Assets | | Liabilities |
|---|---|---|
| 3. Demand deposit at commercial bank | + | |

### Federal Reserve Bank

| Assets | | Liabilities | |
|---|---|---|---|
| 1. Treasury bonds | + | 2. Treasury deposit balance | + |
| | | 5. Treasury deposit balance | − |
| | | 5. Reserve balance of commercial bank | + |

The effects of this Treasury borrowing directly from the central bank are to increase the Treasury's indebtedness and also the money supply and bank reserves by the amount of the borrowing.    Since the public now owns increased demand deposits required reserves are up, but excess reserves are also increased as total bank reserves increase.  Thus, with the excess reserves present, the stage is set for further credit expansion by the commercial banks.    The monetary effects of this type of debt operation are the same as those of a gold purchase.

### Summary of Debt Operations

Let us take a moment to summarize the net monetary consequences of the Treasury borrowing. When the Treasury borrows from the public and then spends the proceeds the net effect is to leave the public's money supply and bank reserves untouched. Thus, the monetary effect is negligible though the public is left in a more liquid position through increased asset holdings.

On the other hand, should the Treasury borrow from the commercial banks the public's money supply is increased, total bank reserves are unchanged, but required reserves are up. Thus, there is a change in the money supply.

It is when the Treasury borrows directly from the Federal Reserve that the monetary effects are most pronounced. In this case both the money supply and bank reserves are increased. And with excess reserves created there exists the potential for still more expansion in the money supply.

### Management of the Working Balance

The management of its deposit balances gives the Treasury a rather powerful instrument of monetary policy. These Treasury balances consist principally of the demand deposits at the Federal Reserve Banks and the Tax and Loan Accounts held at commercial banks.

The way the Treasury chooses to handle these balances gives it a powerful tool for monetary control. As discussed previously, the Treasury maintains a rather small working balance in its account at the Federal Reserve. In contrast to the small working balance, the Tax and Loan Accounts of the Treasury at the commercial banks are much larger.[2] As the flow of cash to the Treasury for tax payments or the receipts of borrowing come in, they are first deposited in the Treasury's Tax and Loan Accounts. Then as the working balance is depleted it is replenished by transferring to it some of the funds deposited in the Tax and Loan Accounts. The importance to monetary control of this switching or transferring of balances is now apparent.

When the Treasury deposits to Tax and Loan Accounts at the com-

---

[2] The balance maintained by the Treasury at Federal Reserve Banks averaged about $826 millions monthly for 1963, whereas the Tax and Loan Accounts were on the order of $5,600 millions. Source: *Federal Reserve Bulletin*, February, 1964.

mercial banks, the latter, as we have seen, simply debit the public's balance and credit the Treasury's balance. The total deposits and reserve position of the commercial banks are unaffected. It is only when the Treasury switches its balance to the Federal Reserve that the commercial banks lose deposits and reserves. Thus, the Treasury has a powerful tool of control over bank reserves at its disposal. The Treasury can decrease commercial bank reserves by increasing its balance at the Federal Reserve through depositing checks on individuals directly to its account at the Federal Reserve or by drawing on its Tax and Loan Accounts at commercial banks, or both. By converse policies reserves can be made more plentiful for the commercial banks.

Occasionally, the Treasury deliberately uses its deposit policy to effect changes in the reserve position of the commercial bank system. But the principal objective of Treasury deposit policy is to minimize the effects of Treasury operations on the banking sytem. Thus, seasonal or other fluctuations in Treasury receipts and disbursement can be insulated away from the operations of the banking system. To achieve this insulation the Treasury: (1) holds the bulk of its balances in Tax and Loan Accounts thereby minimizing the loss of reserves by commercial banks; (2) coordinates the transfer of balances from Tax and Loan Accounts to Treasury working balances with current expenditures so that reserves are quickly restored to the banks; (3) allows its working balance to fall to a minimum just prior to tax collection dates to build up commercial bank reserves so as to provide for the loss of reserves anticipated when the tax collections come due; and (4) sometimes sells tax anticipation notes directly to the Federal Reserve in order to minimize the amount of tax collections withdrawn from its Tax and Loan Accounts.

In summary, the principal objective of the Treasury in its deposit policy is to minimize the effects of its operation on the commercial banks. In this it succeeds quite well. But the ability to build up and shift balances between the commercial banks and the Federal Reserve gives the Treasury a useful and powerful instrument of control over bank reserves.

## REVIEW QUESTIONS

1. What is "sterilized" gold?
2. "When the Treasury purchases gold, the purchase is essentially costless." Explain.
3. Using T-accounts show the effect on commercial bank reserves of a Treasury purchase of domestically produced gold.

4. Why is the persistent gold drain becoming a problem?   What effects does this gold outflow have on Federal Reserve credit?
5. When the Treasury borrows it presumably does so in order to be able to spend.   Using T-accounts, contrast the effects on the money supply and bank reserves of the Treasury borrowing from: (a) the public, (b) the commercial bank system, (c) the Federal Reserve.
6. Show how management of the Treasury's Tax and Loan Accounts influences commercial bank reserves.
7. What is the present status of silver in our monetary system?

## SUGGESTED REFERENCES

Federal Reserve Bank of Chicago, *Modern Money Mechanics.*
Federal Reserve Bank of Philadelphia, *Exercises in the Debits and Credits of Bank Reserves.*

# CHAPTER *13*

# *Nonbank Financial Institutions*

Our primary concern so far has been with the banking system—with the commercial banks and the Federal Reserve. The reason for this preoccupation is that these financial institutions have the ability to create and supply the economic system with money. Now we are ready to consider a new element—the role and significance of nonbank financial institutions.

In contrast to commercial banks, the nonbank financial institutions do not have the ability to create *money*. In a sense, these institutions can create *credit*. They do so by pooling savings, which may also stimulate total saving in the process. These nonbank financial institutions are basically the brokers of funds, rather than the creators of funds. In their role as brokers these institutions fall into two categories: savings intermediaries and borrowing intermediaries. Because they serve as go-betweens for those persons with surplus funds and those needing additional funds, these nonbank financial institutions are often called financial intermediaries.

As we shall learn in the next several chapters, the saving and investment process is a vital one to the growth and stability of the economy. We define saving as not consuming all of one's money income in some accounting period. What is not consumed is, by definition, saved. Investment we define as the accumulation of "productive stuff." But here is the rub. The people who decide to save—who decide to consume less than all their income—are not necessarily the people who decide to invest, to spend for the acquisition of capital goods. Finan-

209

cial intermediaries serve to bridge the gap between savers and investors, between suppliers of funds and users of funds.

There are more than 50,000 companies engaged in financial businesses of one type or another, and of these somewhat fewer than 14,000 are commercial banks. Financial intermediaries outnumber commercial banks by a ratio of nearly 3 to 1. In terms of total assets held, however, commercial banks own approximately one-half of all assets. Nevertheless, financial intermediaries are clearly of considerable importance, in terms of both number and asset holdings.

These financial intermediaries provide a means for facilitating the accumulation of real productive assets by the various economic sectors. They provide the link between financial saving and spending on credit for the accumulation of "productive stuff." A second important function of the financial intermediaries is to make available to the public *financial assets* of various types, such as saving deposits, share accounts, insurance policies, pension rights, etc.[1]

In the present chapter we shall investigate the nature and significance of the financial intermediaries in the saving-investment process. We shall also examine briefly some of the implications of these institutions for monetary policy. Then in the next chapter we shall more closely examine the concept of national income and income accounting, items closely tied to the saving-investment process.

## THE ACCUMULATION OF REAL WEALTH: SAVING AND INVESTMENT

Saving and investment are of paramount importance in economic life. Indeed, economic progress and stability depend on the successful linking of saving to investment in appropriate volume.

Economic progress with its increasing standards of living is dependent on the economy's ability to increase its per capita production of goods and services without equivalent increases in inputs; that is, equivalent increases in man hours and in physical inputs. At any given time there is an existing stock of productive goods. If we assume they are being optimally utilized then little additional output can be obtained. How then does economic progress arise? One basic answer is: provide more or better capital goods per worker. But a second

---

[1] A further aspect is that certain intermediaries may increase the aggregate volume of saving. For example, to the extent that pension plans are compulsory saving may be increased over what it otherwise would be. Similarly, life insurance companies with aggressive sales policies are actually "selling" savings.

question arises: how do we provide these additional capital goods? The answer here is that such capital formation depends on saving.

We have defined saving as the nonconsumption of income. Whatever income is not spent on consumption is, by definition, saved. But because we save does not necessarily mean we wish to accumulate idle cash. Rather than accumulate idle cash most of us buy securities of various types, pay life insurance premiums, acquire savings deposits in commercial banks or savings and loan associations, or repay debts; for example, make payments on mortgages. Some persons, however, acquire capital goods instead of financial assets. Simply because we save we do not necessarily hold more cash. To the extent that capital losses are feared, cash with no rate of return will be held; otherwise the various financial asset choices with positive rates of return will be desired.

A word or two on investment is in order. We have defined investment as the accumulation of "productive stuff." Alternately, investment is the value of *new* real assets produced in a given time period. From these definitions it is clear that investment is not a financial concept. Investment refers to *real goods*, not to stocks, bonds, etc. Unfortunately, in the everyday use of the word, long-term loan instruments such as mortgages and bonds are often called investments— recall the bank portfolio of "investments" which comprises such long-term securities. When we refer to the *investment* of money we shall specify this by using the term *financial investment*, or by adding the word loan. In a similar fashion, we shall use the term *capital goods* to represent the investment items, and to distinguish them from financial capital.

Saving leads to the diversion of part of the current productive capacity away from the production of consumer goods. Investment, in turn, uses these current productive facilities to provide future productive capacity by creating new capital goods.

From the foregoing discussion we can derive the fundamental relationship between saving and investment. Since saving is money income not consumed, it follows that for a given time period saving must equal the net increase in the value of all assets (both real and financial) of all types owned. From this the basic relationship between saving and real investment and financial investment emerges:

Savings = increase in real assets owned
      plus financial accumulation or minus financial disaccumulation.

Financial accumulation for an economic unit is defined as the increased ownership of debt instruments and new equities less any new debt incurred in the time period.

The critical question is to maintain the proper balance between saving and real investment. As we shall see in the next chapter, because of the way in which economists define national income, saving and investment will always be equal in an accounting sense. We may also make use of the savings relation to show the equality of saving and investment for any completed period. That is, we have the following equality:

Saving = increased ownership of real assets plus financial accumulation

or, in other words,

Saving = investment plus financial accumulation.

For the economy as a whole financial accumulation is zero. Any economic unit which has a positive financial accumulation is offset by a negative financial accumulation, or disaccumulation, by some other economic unit. For example, if someone accumulates cash someone else loses cash, or a bank has someone's promissory note offsetting it. Or if some person buys equities someone else sells, or a company has issued new equity stock. In other words, for every lender there must be a borrower. Thus, positive financial accumulation is exactly offset by negative accumulation. Total financial accumulation is zero, and in the aggregate, our basic relationship becomes saving equals investment.

Because different groups of individuals undertake the bulk of saving and investment decisions, the amount of *planned* savings may well differ from what investors *plan* to invest at the beginning of an accounting period. It is the planned (*ex ante*) saving and investment decisions that determine the course of economic progress and stability.

Saving without investment taking place will not add any new productive capacity to an economy. Indeed, as not all goods produced are taken from the market this oversaving generates depression. On the other hand, investment without saving results in inflation. Therefore, if investment is a necessary complement to saving, it is equally necessary that saving must be translated into investment if we are to achieve economic progress. And finally, if this progress is to be reasonably smooth the plans of savers and investors must somehow be coordinated.

It should be clear that what we are discussing here is real saving and real investment. By real saving is meant the release of productive factors from consumption purposes. Similarly, real investment is the utilization of these productive factors to accumulate additional producers goods. The student must acquaint himself with this perhaps unfamiliar usage of the terms saving and investment. As we shall see, in the production of goods and services in a year's time, for example, a money income equal to the value of these goods and services is produced. By not consuming all this money income, saving occurs. This act of saving means current productive capacity is diverted from the production of consumer goods. Investment uses this current capacity to produce capital goods which will increase future productive capacity.

Thus we must never confuse real saving with financial saving, or (real) investment with financial investment. Real saving refers to the release of resources from consumption purposes. Financial saving, however, deals with the use of the money income not consumed for the acquisition of financial assets. Similarly, (real) investment means the actual accumulation of "productive stuff," whereas to most people investment refers to the purchase of stocks, bonds, etc. This latter is not investment to the economist.

We now come to the relationship of this real saving and investment process to the financial system. It is possible, of course, to take money income not consumed, that is, saved, and to use it directly to acquire capital assets, that is, to invest. But this direct channeling of saving to investment is, perhaps, the exceptional case. As we shall see, for the business sector its gross saving from depreciation allowances and retained earnings is probably channeled directly into the accumulation of new capital goods. But for the most part, the financial system enters the scene because most people desire to save by acquiring *financial assets* rather than by acquiring real capital goods. Thus, financial intermediaries exchange desired claims against themselves; that is, they offer such claims as savings deposits, savings and loan association share accounts, life insurance policies with savings features, retirement claims in pension funds, etc., for the savings of those individuals desiring to accumulate these financial assets. These intermediaries then make the funds so acquired (the savings) available to others who wish to spend more than their incomes, usually to purchase capital goods or to finance housing and consumer credit.

Thus, financial intermediaries act as "go-betweens" in the saving-investment mechanism. Basically financial intermediaries obtain funds from savers and supply these funds to business and other borrowers. An important aspect of financial intermediaries is that whereas they acquire the more or less illiquid debts of their borrowing customers, they supply the saver-lenders with claims on themselves which are quite liquid. They thus serve to increase the general liquidity of the economy. The financial intermediaries attract funds by offering interest bearing near liquidity for nonyielding perfect liquidity. The greater the liquidity provided by the institution, the easier it is to attract the funds of the saver. The claims on the financial institutions are considered by the saver-lenders as almost as liquid as the cash given up.

Actually we shall divide financial intermediaries into two specialized categories. Some financial intermediaries specialize in providing outlets for savings, that is, they accumulate savings. These "savings intermediaries" include such institutions as savings and loan associations, savings banks, life insurance companies, investment companies and mutual funds, the savings and trust departments of commercial banks, and the growing number of pension funds. The other class of intermediaries may be termed "borrowing intermediaries." These borrowing intermediaries are specialized financial institutions that assist potential borrowers to tap savings either at their source or at places where savings accumulate. Borrowing intermediaries are institutions such as investment banking houses, mortgage banking houses, and sales finance and personal finance companies which divert funds into consumer credit.

Our next task is to investigate the so-called credit market. It is in this market that lenders and borrowers are brought together, and that savings are provided for investment and other purposes.

## THE MARKET FOR CREDIT

Sometimes the terms *money market* and *capital market* are used for the credit market. Strictly speaking, money market refers to the lending and borrowing of short-term funds involving debt or loan instruments up to one year's maturity. The capital market deals with longer-term funds.

The credit market has no particular meeting place or business address. Participants in the credit market, the lenders and the borrowers, or buyers and sellers of debt instruments, do not gather together in any particular location. Instead, the terms of the transactions are discussed and arranged by telephone, and supporting documents and payments are sent by mail. Despite its decentralization the credit market is highly organized in the sense that there is active competition among lenders and among borrowers, its participants are well informed, and communication is good. Thus, with the exception of a few organized stock exchanges where dealers come together at a specific location, it makes sense to speak of a *credit market* even though it has no specific address.

The aspects of the credit market which are of interest to us are (1) the sources of funds, that is, the sources of savings; (2) the users of the funds, that is, the borrowers; and (3) the financial institutions involved in facilitating the lending-borrowing process.

## The Sources of Funds

The funds traded in the credit market come from four principal supplier groups.   These providers of funds are consumers, nonfinancial businesses, government, and financial institutions themselves.   As we shall see, no one of these groups plays a single role—as lender only. But on balance, some of the groups will be *net lenders* and others *net borrowers*.   That is, savers who make funds available to the market are also often borrowers.   And borrowers become savers as they return funds to the market through debt repayment.   Similarly, financial institutions obtain loanable funds in the credit market by borrowing or by issuing new equity stock, as well as from the flow of savings into savings deposits, savings and loan association shares, life insurance premiums, etc.

CONSUMERS.   The largest source of funds for the credit market is the saving by the household or consumer sector of the economy. Consumers typically save more than any other sector of the economy. The amount of consumer saving and the amount which flows into the credit market is influenced by many factors, including such considerations as incomes, expectations regarding the future, interest rates, etc.

Gross saving of consumers is that part of current income not spent for current consumption purposes.   Part of consumer saving, however, goes directly for purchases of consumer durables—automobiles, appliances, other durable goods, and for homes.   This part of consumer saving is thus utilized for a kind of consumer capital good, for real assets which yield services over an extended lifetime.   Another part of consumer saving is used to acquire financial assets, and often part is used to repay debts contracted earlier.

By purchasing financial assets consumers make funds available to the credit market.   Consumers or savers lend directly when they purchase stocks, bonds, and other loan instruments in the market.   These purchases of financial assets may be from the ultimate borrower who issues a new financial asset in order to finance current expenditure, or the purchase may be from some individual or institution wishing to sell an old (previously issued) financial asset from its portfolio holdings.

When consumers "spend" their savings on savings deposits, savings and loan shares, life insurance premiums, retirement contributions, etc., their saving still enters the credit market through these financial intermediaries. Consumer saving flowing into these institutions reaches the borrowers when the financial intermediaries acquire stocks, bonds, mortgages, and commercial paper.

And finally, of course, the savers may elect to hold their savings by maintaining larger balances in their checking accounts, instead of allocating them to any one of the above uses.

NONFINANCIAL BUSINESS. Another major source of funds for the credit market arises in the nonfinancial business sector. Gross business saving is the amount of funds generated by retained earnings and from depreciation allowances. Most of these gross business savings are used directly to finance the replacement of capital goods or to finance the acquisition of additional capital goods. Some funds from business saving are available to the credit market. On balance, however, the business sector is a net borrower of funds, rather than a lender of funds.

Business saving available to the credit market is usually temporary. That is, an increase in funds supplied by business generally precedes an increase in capital expenditures by business. As expenditures are made, or as liabilities coming due are paid, these funds are withdrawn from the credit market. Because businesses expect to be using their savings in the near future, or want them readily available, these business savings are typically used to purchase highly marketable short-term paper. Should the short-term interest rate be quite low businesses might simply maintain an increased demand deposit balance.

GOVERNMENT. Governmental units both supply funds and use funds in the credit market. Like the business sector, the government sector is usually a net borrower of funds.

Quite clearly governmental units are users (borrowers) of funds when their expenditures exceed their revenues. They, of necessity, must borrow to cover the difference between their receipts and expenditures. On the other hand, governments supply funds to the credit market in several fashions.

First, some of the funds provided the credit market are actually the saving of the consumer, or household, sector. These funds are the retirement contribution by consumers collected by some government agency. The funds so collected are generally used to acquire long-term obligations.

The second way the government sector provides funds to the credit market is by the *net* repayment of debt. This is possible when revenues exceed expenditures. When governments pay off obligations held by financial institutions, funds become available for relending by these institutions. Funds repaid to individuals or businesses may flow into the credit market or they may result in lowered demands on the credit market if used to finance expenditures which otherwise would have been financed by borrowing. However, depending on the source of the surplus revenues and the recipients of the debt repayment, the actual effect on the credit market is difficult to predict.

Another way in which government units influence the credit market is by their involvement in special programs. Although not affecting the total volume of funds in the market, government units may influence the distribution of the funds into particular areas. For example, take the home mortgage programs of the Federal government. The government provides funds directly when a Federal agency purchases mortgages from lenders. These purchases enable the lenders to offer additional mortgage credit. But the principal aspect of government participation in the mortgage market has been the insuring or guaranteeing of home mortgages. These are the FHA and VA home mortgage programs. These programs affect the willingness of private lenders to supply funds for mortgage loans, but rarely do they result in direct government loans.

**FINANCIAL INSTITUTIONS.** The final source of funds for the credit market is financial institutions. The savings intermediaries make funds available by collecting or pooling the savings of others. Thus, the funds that flow initially into savings accounts, pension and retirement funds, life insurance, etc. are channeled through these intermediaries into the credit market. In addition to collecting the current savings of others, funds are also obtained from their own retained earnings, from new stock issues, and finally by borrowing themselves. Of all financial institutions, only the commercial banks have the unique capacity to lend without necessarily having previously acquired the funds being lent. As we know, the amount of lending that commercial banks can do depends upon the availability of reserve funds to them.

## Users of Funds

The same four sectors which supply funds also constitute the users of funds in the credit market. As we have seen, each sector may be both a supplier and a user of funds. Typically, however, certain sectors are net lenders and others net borrowers. Thus consumers, or the household sector, and financial institutions are net lenders; the government sector and the business sector are net borrowers of funds.

CONSUMERS. The household sector uses short-, intermediate-, and long-term credit. The long-term commitments of funds to this consumer sector are principally mortgages for home purchases. The short- and intermediate-term credit is used to finance outlays for such items as automobiles, household appliances, and household repair and improvement. These expenditures constitute a form of investment as they yield services over a considerable period of time. The household sector also makes use of short-term and intermediate-term credit for a variety of other purposes, e.g., education, travel, and various personal emergencies.

### Nonfinancial Business

The nonfinancial business sector is a net borrower or user of funds in the credit market. Businesses raise funds for long-term purposes by issuing bonds, that is, by long-term borrowing; long-term funds are also acquired by issuing new common or preferred stock. Funds needed to finance inventories or for other short-term needs are generally financed by short- or intermediate-term loans from commercial banks or sales finance companies. Often businesses maintain a "line of credit" with banks. This is an arrangement negotiated by a business with a bank which enables it to obtain funds up to a certain amount for a given period of time without additional negotiation.

An increasing number of businesses are raising short-term funds through sales in the open market of their own commercial paper. This is still, however, a rather minor element in the over-all pattern.

### Government

The government sector is also a net borrower of funds. Government units raise funds (borrow) by issuing securities; that is, issuance of promises to repay principal and interest. The Federal government issues marketable debt instruments in varying maturities from three months to thirty years. In addition to its marketable securities, that is, transferable, the Federal government issues nonmarketable securities, principally United States savings bonds sold to the public and also certain special issues held only by government trust funds.

State and local government units borrow mainly by selling long-term bonds. However, some short-term borrowing is done through tax anticipation notes.

FINANCIAL INSTITUTIONS. Although financial institutions on balance are net lenders, there are active users of funds among them. For example, sales finance and personal finance companies are large users of short- and intermediate-term commercial bank credit. So are securities dealers and brokers and mortgage bankers. As will be brought out in the next section, these are the "borrowing" financial intermediaries as contrasted with the "saving" intermediaries, for example, savings and loan associations and life insurance companies. On occasion long-term funds are acquired by financial institutions when additional capital stock is sold.

## PRINCIPAL FINANCIAL INTERMEDIARIES

References have been made to various financial intermediaries. Let us describe briefly the more important of these, and the character of their sources and uses of funds; that is, the kind of liability they issue against themselves, which influences the use to which they put their funds.

We may classify financial intermediaries into two categories: savings intermediaries and borrowing intermediaries. The savings intermediaries are such institutions as savings banks, savings and loan associations, credit unions, life insurance companies, mutual funds, retirement funds, and even commercial banks. They are institutions that collect and pool the funds obtained from many individual savers. The savings intermediaries then channel the funds acquired to various borrowers. In acquiring the funds, the savings institutions issue claims against themselves, and the nature of these liabilities, whether payable on demand or not, influences to a considerable extent the kinds of debt instruments (earning assets) they acquire.

The borrowing intermediaries, on the other hand, are financial institutions which provide services for borrowers by expediting access to the credit market. The borrowing intermediaries borrow against their own credit, and then lend the funds obtained to the ultimate borrower. Examples of such borrowing intermediaries are investment bankers, mortgage banks, and sales finance and personal finance companies.

### Savings Intermediaries

The savings intermediaries which we shall discuss are commercial banks, savings banks, savings and loan associations, the Federal government, and life insurance companies. This list falls short of encompassing all savings intermediaries. Exclusions, for instance, are credit unions, retirement funds, investment companies or mutual funds, retirement and pension funds, trusts, etc. The list, however, is sufficiently inclusive to illustrate the nature and implications of the activities of this class of financial institutions.

COMMERCIAL BANKS. These financial institutions are unique in that their demand deposit liabilities are money. As we have seen, commercial banks can, within limits, create money. Thus, while other lenders are restricted in their lending activities to funds previously acquired, the commercial banks may create the funds that they lend.

Whereas the principal source of commercial banks' loanable funds is their ability to create the funds, it is well to remember that, aside from the major factor of reserve bank credit for the individual commercial bank, the ability to create loanable funds rests on the savings of individuals and businesses. These savings are of diverse form. They may be short term, funds deposited subject to withdrawal on demand, that is, demand deposits; or they may be deposited on a longer term basis, that is, funds deposited in time or savings deposits. Finally, funds are contributed by the owners of the banks in the form of the bank capital funds.

Commercial banks have the shortest-term liabilities of all the various financial institutions. More than 90 per cent of commercial bank liabilities are deposit liabilities, and of these deposit liabilities about three-fifths are demand deposits subject to withdrawal on demand. Since demand deposits show wide seasonal variations and are active accounts, commercial banks must be ready to meet drains on their deposits and reserves.

Due to this preponderance of short-term saving—that is, demand deposits—commercial banks tend to lend on a short- or intermediate-term basis. The two major exceptions to this are installment loans to business, which are often of relatively long maturity, and real estate mortgage loans. In addition to lending on short term, the investment or security portfolio of commercial banks also tends to be composed of short-term instruments, especially United States government issues, which provide considerable liquidity should it be needed.

But we must qualify all this. Bank lending is broader in scope and greater in total amount than that done by any other type of financial institution. In practice, commercial bank lending activities range from one or two day maturities, as in Federal Funds, up to thirty years, as in the case of VA guaranteed mortgage loans and certain long-term bonds. The bank's borrowing customers may be consumers, merchants, farmers, home buyers, business enterprises, and even other financial institutions borrowing in order to be able to provide funds to meet the demands of their own borrowing customers. The wide variety of lending activities engaged in by the commercial bank is shown in Table 13-1. This table gives the distribution of loans in the loan portfolios of commercial banks as of December 20, 1963.

TABLE 13-1 Commercial Bank Loans (millions of dollars, December 20, 1963)

| Type of Loan | Amount |
|---|---|
| Commercial and industrial | 52,947 |
| Agricultural | 7,470 |
| For purchasing or carrying securities | 7,862 |
| To financial institutions | 13,084 |
| To individuals | 34,550 |
| Real estate | 39,056 |
| Other | 4,034 |
| | 159,003 |

Source: Federal Reserve Bulletin, August, 1964.

SAVINGS BANKS. Mutual savings banks are nonprofit organizations. They are owned by and operated for the benefit of their depositors. The majority of these mutual savings banks are found in New England or the Middle Atlantic seaboard states.

The origins of the mutual savings banks go back to the early 1800s. They were organized in order that persons of modest means might constructively and profitably save. By pooling savings the funds could be employed in an economically useful fashion instead of hoarded. The savings of many individuals allowed greater diversification, and hence greater safety, than the individual could obtain by purchasing any of the other financial assets available at that time.

Mutual savings banks provide an outlet for the regular saver of relatively modest income. They afford a convenient place for putting savings where the funds will be safe and readily available if needed. The depositor looks upon these funds as being highly liquid. As a matter of fact, the deposits do not need to be paid on demand. Yet, as a practical consideration, savings banks rarely invoke their legal right of prior notice for withdrawal. Thus, for the individual depositor these deposits are quite liquid. Any concerted wave of withdrawal requests could, however, easily prove troublesome by forcing the liquidation of assets at a loss. To minimize the risk of this the state chartering laws generally place a maximum on any one deposit. Actually the key safeguard is the slow rate of deposit turnover.

As an additional liquidity safeguard, most deposits are insured by the FDIC, though many savings banks do not belong.    In Connecticut and Massachusetts the states operate their own deposit insurance systems.    Altogether, better than 90 per cent of all deposits in mutual savings banks are covered by some type or another of deposit insurance.

The loanable funds of mutual savings banks are obtained from their depositors.    When a savings bank lends, it lends funds previously deposited with it.    Thus, since savings banks cannot create money, when a savings bank lends, its cash withdrawal is equal to the amount of the loan.    This loss of loan funds is also true of commercial bank lending, but commercial banks can expect some amount to be redeposited; this is not the case for the savings banks.    Safety thus becomes of extreme importance in the lending process.    Traditionally the loan policies of savings banks are conservative and in their lending activities every effort is made to minimize the risk element.

Since the deposit liabilities of these savings banks have a low rate of turnover, the assets held by these institutions reflect this factor as well as the desire for safety.    Because of a lower rate of deposit turnover than commercial banks, the mutual savings banks lend long term, principally on mortgage loans.    Other assets held are almost entirely government securities and, perhaps, high-grade utility and industrial bonds.    The distribution of assets for mutual savings banks is shown in Table 13-2.

SAVINGS AND LOAN ASSOCIATIONS.    Another type of mutual association is the savings and loan association.[2]    Individuals who place their savings with these institutions do not actually deposit their funds. Instead they technically purchase "share accounts," and thus become owners of the association.

Should the shareholder (the "depositor") wish to withdraw his funds the association repurchases his shares.    The savings and loan associations are obligated to repurchase the shareholders' shares, but they may invoke a waiting period instead of buying them back immediately.    For many years, however, most savings and loan associations have made the proud boast "every withdrawal request paid on demand" or some similar statement.    The public has consequently come to look upon these "deposits" as being quite liquid.

The public's concern over the liquidity of their accounts with savings and loan associations has been shored up by several factors.    Since

---

[2] Federally chartered savings and loan associations must be mutual associations; state chartered can be either mutual associations or stock companies depending on the laws of the chartering state.

TABLE **13-2**  Mutual Savings Banks, Assets (millions of dollars, May 31, 1963)

| Type of Asset | Amount |
| --- | --- |
| Loans: | |
| Mortgage | 37,601 |
| Other | 714 |
| Securities: | |
| United States Government | 6,052 |
| State and local government | 419 |
| Corporate and other | 5,150 |
| Cash or other assets | 1,674 |
| | 51,610 |

*Source: Federal Reserve Bulletin*, August, 1964.

1932 the Federal Home Loan Bank System has served savings and loan associations in much the same fashion as the Federal Reserve System aids commercial banks.   The FHLBS has eleven regional Federal Home Loan Banks that provide rediscount facilities and lines of credit in the area of urban real estate finance.   These eleven regional home loan banks are owned by member savings and loan associations who subscribe to its capital stock.   In addition, the home loan banks may issue bonds or otherwise borrow funds in order to carry on their operations.

All federally chartered savings and loan associations must be members of the FHLBS and state-chartered institutions may join.   The home loan banks lend to member institutions on both short- and long-term bases.   Long-term advances must be secured by mortgages or government obligations.   Short-term advances may be unsecured. More than 95 per cent of all savings and loan associations are members of the FHLBS.   Member associations must hold at least 6 per cent of their total assets as cash or United States government obligations.

Since 1934 accounts in savings and loan have been insurable by the Federal Savings and Loan Insurance Corporation (FSLIC).   Individual accounts may be insured up to a maximum of $10,000.   Member associations finance the FSLIC by paying an annual premium equal to $1/12$ of 1 per cent of aggregate liabilities.   All associations with a Federal charter must belong to the FSLIC, and state-chartered savings and loan associations may join if they so desire.   Furthermore, some states require state-chartered associations to join both the FHLBS and the FSLIC.

Although the foregoing factors may influence the individual depositor's feeling about the liquidity of his funds entrusted with his savings and loan association, the most important assurance of liquidity is probably the nature of the assets these associations aquire. Savings and loan associations lend almost exclusively to home buyers in their immediate or nearby communities. Because these mortgage loans require repayment in a systematic fashion, the monthly repayment of interest and amortization of principal, there is a steady flow of cash into the associations. Nearly 95 per cent of all savings and loan association earning assets are in the form of these first-mortgage loans. The balance of their earning assets are principally United States government securities.

Due to the low rate of turnover in the share accounts and their essentially time deposit characteristics, the savings and loan associations, like the mutual savings banks, are able to lend on a long-term basis. This contrasts with the commercial banks which, while holding many mortgages, tend to lend at the shorter end of the credit spectrum. The asset structure for savings and loan associations is given in Table 13-3.

TABLE 13-3 Saving and Loan Associations, Assets (millions of dollars, May 31, 1963)

| Type of Asset | Amount |
|---|---|
| Mortgages | 94,971 |
| United States Government securities | 6,712 |
| Cash | 3,504 |
| Other[a] | 6,738 |
| | 111,925 |

Source: Federal Reserve Bulletin, August, 1964.
[a] Includes other loans, stock in Federal Home Loan Bank, other investments, real estate owned and sold on contract, and office buildings and fixtures.

THE FEDERAL GOVERNMENT. At first blush the Federal government may not seem to be a financial intermediary, and a savings intermediary at that! But with over $48 billions of savings bonds outstanding as of February, 1964, the Federal government very clearly offers a financial asset which is quite attractive to a rather large number of savers.

Because of the convenient denominations in which savings bonds are available—as small as $25—they have considerable appeal to the individual saver. The "Series E" savings bond is a redeemable, nonmarketable (nontransferable) bond. These bonds are sold on a discount basis and mature in ten years. Because they are redeemable at any time prior to maturity, though with some sacrifice of interest, the public considers these bonds as highly liquid assets.

The Postal Savings System, the other government savings institution, was established in 1910. The purpose of this system was to make savings facilities available to individuals and communities where other safe savings institutions were not available. Postal savings offered a completely safe place to put funds that were readily available if needed, but that would earn a low rate of interest (2 per cent) in the meantime. Deposits in postal savings grew slowly, reaching their peak of $33 billions in the early 1940s. But with the Treasury pushing Series E savings bonds since 1942 and other financial assets offering a more attractive rate of return, postal savings have steadily declined in importance.

Even though it is not a financial institution in the usual sense, the Treasury by the issuance of savings bonds provides an important outlet for the savings of many individuals. These savings bonds provide a liquid, fixed-value financial asset that is easily understood by the small individual saver.

LIFE INSURANCE COMPANIES. Life insurance companies are savings intermediaries and major lenders in the credit market, second only to the commercial banks. The lending practices of life insurance companies differ from those of commercial banks in that the majority of insurance company earning assets are acquired in the open market, whereas many commercial bank loans are direct customer-bank transactions. The direct placement of security issues with life insurance companies is becoming of increasing importance, however, and even home mortgages are often acquired in direct home buyer-lender transactions. Nevertheless, life insurance company loans to business and industry include large amounts of bonds and stock purchased in the open market, and they even acquire home mortgages in large blocks in the secondary market.

The principal source of funds for life insurance companies is their premium income, on the order of 80 per cent, with investment income making up all but a negligible fraction of the balance. Because all life insurance, except term insurance, has "built-in savings," the standard level premium means that excess payments with regard to mortality expectation are made in early years whereas underpayments are made in later years. Thus enters the savings element. The overpayments in the early years are savings available to the policyholder as "cash-surrender value" should he wish to cancel his policy, or as funds he may borrow should it become necessary.

The premiums that pour into life insurance companies are greater than the funds necessary to pay current operating and contractual expenses—death benefits, etc. These excess funds must be used to acquire earning assets to help pay the underpayments of premiums in the later years of the policies' lives, and to pay the guaranteed rate of interest on the savings or "cash values" of the policies in force.

Because of large sales of savings-type policies, life insurance companies are today an important financial intermediary. As of May, 1964, life insurance companies owned assets valued at over $144 billion. These assets had increased through the 1950s on the average of about $6 billion a year. This is indeed big business. One of the features of this business is its concentration. Although there are more than 1,400 life insurance companies, about three-fifths (60 per cent) of the business was done by the ten largest. At the opposite end of the spectrum, the smallest 80 per cent of the companies did relatively little business— less than 5 per cent of all life insurance sales. The significance of the size problem is that the larger companies receive large amounts of funds which they must use to acquire earning assets. The larger life insurance companies are likely to favor large-sized loans; as a consequence they are becoming more active in the "direct placement" arena by negotiating the purchase of an entire issue of bonds from the borrower.

The composition of life insurance companies' assets as of the end of May, 1964, is shown in Table 13-4.

TABLE   13-4   Life   Insurance   Companies,   Assets (millions of dollars, May 31, 1964)

| Type of Asset | Amount |
|---|---|
| Government securities: | |
| United States Government | 5,731 |
| State and local government | 3,827 |
| Foreign | 2,878 |
| Business securities: | |
| Bonds | 54,674 |
| Stocks | 5,939 |
| Mortgages | 52,117 |
| Real estate | 4,416 |
| Policy loans | 6,909 |
| Other assets | 7,821 |
| | 144,312 |

Source: Federal Reserve Bulletin, August, 1964.

What stands out clearly is that about 90 per cent of life insurance funds are lodged in financial assets of fixed-dollar value.   This in large measure reflects the restrictions imposed by state regulatory laws on the lending activities of life insurance companies.   These state laws establish standards which must be followed by the companies in finding outlets for their accumulated funds.   These standards typically specify fixed-dollar obligations of appropriate quality, and prohibit or regulate the acquisition of common stock.   The emphasis has always been on the safety of principal and stability of income.

Within the limitations set forth by the state regulatory commissions to provide for the safeguarding of policyholders, the aim of the portfolio managers of life insurance companies is that of management generally: to maximize the return on a long-run basis.   Thus, life insurance companies strive, for the most part, to obtain as high a yield rate possible for the types of earning assets they may legally acquire.   Whereas portfolio patterns do not change overnight, shifts of assets are made and new funds are channeled into the most attractive eligible securities. With about $6 billion a year, or $500 million monthly, to lend, life insurance companies are clearly an important financial intermediary.

Because of the contractual nature of life insurance policies and the predictability of benefit payments, the financial assets acquired by life insurance companies are of a long-term nature.   Given the types of financial assets eligible for their portfolios, life insurance companies offer rather diversified credit service.   The bulk of their earning assets, however, are corporate bonds and mortgages.

### Borrowing Intermediaries

The class of financial institutions designated as "borrowing intermediaries" consists of those institutions that assist borrowers to tap savings. Some do this by bringing potential borrowers into contact with lenders; others assist borrowers by using their own credit to borrow funds, and then in turn lend these funds to the ultimate borrower.   The first category of institutions are investment-banking houses, mortgage bankers, and security brokers and dealers.   The second category comprises the sales finance and personal finance companies.

INVESTMENT-BANKING HOUSES.   Investment banking is not banking in the usual sense, and commercial banks are, as a matter of fact, prohibited from engaging in it.   Investment bankers are essentially merchandisers who purchase new issues of securities at wholesale and resell them at retail.

To illustrate the role played by investment-banking houses let us consider the following example.   Corporate businesses obtain funds from the public by selling capital stock or by borrowing, that is, selling bonds. Most corporate securities are sold to the public by the issuing business with the assistance of an investment-banking house. The investment bank, when approached by the company wishing additional funds, advises on the size and terms of the issue, and on whether an issue of common stock, preferred stock, or bonds, or perhaps a combination of these, is likeliest to be sold successfully. In order to determine these factors the investment bank will thoroughly investigate every aspect of the corporation's business—its capitalization, finances, management, etc.

Should the investigation prove satisfactory to both the investment-banking house and the borrowing corporation—that is, the borrower believes the terms are as low as it can get, while the investment banker believes the terms are attractive enough to attract buyers (lenders)—an agreement called an underwriting is drawn. As the term is generally used, underwriting means a firm commitment on the part of the investment bank to purchase outright the entire security issue from the issuing company for resale to the public. The underwriter guarantees the issuer a specific sum of money on a designated date. The underwriter delivers the money upon purchasing the issue, but then it is up to him to dispose of the securities as best he can. If the securities do not sell the loss is borne by the underwriter.

On occasion several investment banks may join in forming a syndicate to arrange and market the issue. This is particularly common when the security issue is a large one.

On acquiring the security issue the underwriter, or underwriting group, attempts to sell the securities to the public. To do this a selling group is generally formed, composed of the underwriters and additional security dealers. Neither the investment banks nor the dealers desire to tie up their financial capital by holding large amounts of the security for more than a brief period. They make their profit from the spread between their purchase price and the price they sell the security for. Securities are their product, and they want to turn over their inventory as rapidly as possible.

At almost every stage of this marketing process bank credit is involved. The underwriting is a promise to pay a specified sum to the security issuer. The underwriter must either have the funds or access to borrowing from commercial banks. And until all the securities are sold to the final purchasers, they are carried in investment-banker and dealer inventories. Finally, it should be noted that the ultimate purchase of the securities may also be partly financed by bank credit.

One aspect of investment banking should be noted at this point. These institutions are quite sensitive to changes in the cost and availability of bank credit because their profit is generated out of large volume with low margins.

MORTGAGE BANKING.  The mortgage banker is the go-between for lenders and borrowers of mortgage loans. Whereas the mortgage banker may lend funds on mortgage loans to builders or persons acquiring real estate, the primary concern is in finding good-quality mortgages which can be sold to life insurance companies, etc. These mortgage banks make the major portion of their income from commissions or loan fees. In many instances they not only place the mortgage loan but also continue to supervise and service the loan by collecting the principal and interest payments for the lender.

SECURITY BROKERS AND DEALERS.  An important source of demand for short-term funds comes from security dealers and brokers. The difference between a dealer and a broker is this: a broker is simply a middleman who brings seller and buyer together and makes his income by charging a commission; a dealer buys and sells on his own account, making his profit from the difference between his buying and selling prices.

So-called "dealer money" consists of short-term bank loans to security dealers to finance inventories of securities.

Stock-brokerage houses are also users of short-term bank credit. These loans are often terminable by either the borrower or the bank without notice and are called *call loans*. These stock-brokerage houses borrow funds in order to lend them to their customers who purchase stock "on margin." Instead of putting up the entire amount of the transaction, the customer need use his own funds for only part of the amount and borrow the rest. As we have seen, if the "margin" is, say, 70 per cent, the customer on $1,000 transaction puts up $700 and borrows $300. Margin requirements, it will be recalled, are regulated by the Board of Governors, and are applicable only to stocks listed on organized stock exchanges.

SALES FINANCE COMPANIES.  The sales finance company is one of several institutions providing consumer credit. Other financial institutions providing consumer credit are, for instance, consumer finance or personal finance companies, commercial banks, and businesses or individuals extending credit in the form of bank credit or charge accounts. We have discussed bank installment loans to consumers. Here we are interested in borrowing intermediaries, among which the principal institutions are sales finance companies and personal (or consumer) finance companies.

Sales finance companies are differentiated from other consumer credit institutions by virtue of their indirect extension of credit. Sales finance companies typically purchase the installment contracts—the notes signed by purchasers of consumer durable goods—from the dealers involved. The other consumer credit sources deal directly with the borrower.

A typical transaction of a sales finance company might go something like this: A dealer in some consumer durable goods (autos, household appliances, etc.) sells some item on the installment plan. The installment contract is then purchased by the sales finance company. The dealer receives his payment from the sales finance company and the installment payments are made directly by the customer to the sales finance company.

The particular details of such transactions may vary widely. But there is always some provision whereby the lender may sell the item should the loan not be repaid. Sometimes a conditional sales contract is used, and often the dealer is relieved from liability for loss. Sometimes a mortgage permitting repossession is used. In any event, the common denominator is the use of the good purchased as collateral for the loan.

Installment finance as an organized industry dates from about 1915. Sales finance companies may be individual proprietorships, partnerships, or of corporate nature, but whatever their form they are frequent visitors to the credit market for funds to relend to their business customers. From 1915 until 1933 sales finance companies purchased almost all the installment contract paper arising from installment sales of consumers durables. While commercial banks were unwilling to finance directly the sale of these goods themselves, they were willing to lend funds to the finance companies using the installment contracts as collateral. Thus, the sales finance companies acted as go-betweens, obtaining credit from commercial banks and channeling it into the purchase of consumption goods.

The sources of funds for sales finance have changed to some degree in recent years. More and more the large sales finance companies—companies like General Motors Acceptance Corporation, C.I.T. Financial Corporation, Commercial Credit Company, etc.—are by-passing the banks and borrowing in the money market on the strength of their own promissory notes. Banks, however, continue to be a principal source of funds for the industry as a whole.

In addition to sales finance companies, since 1933 commercial banks themselves have become active in the consumer installment-credit field. Today many commercial banks purchase installment paper directly from retail dealers or encourage their customers to arrange bank financing for their purchases of autos, appliances, home improvement, etc., through what the Bank of America, for example, calls "Timeplan" credit.

The total of consumer installment credit outstanding as of June 30, 1964 supplied by financial institutions is shown in Table 13-5.   There

TABLE 13-5   Consumer Installment Credit, Financial Institutions (millions of dollars, June 30, 1964)

| | Lending Institution | | |
| Type of Loan | Commercial Banks | Sales Finance Companies | Consumer Finance Companies, Credit Unions, etc. |
| --- | --- | --- | --- |
| Automobile loans | 12,177 | 8,633 | 2,537 |
| Consumer durables | 3,205 | 3,615 | 894 |
| Repair and modernization | 2,355 | 150 | 890 |
| Personal loans | 5,170 | 1,830 | 8,087 |
| | 22,907 | 14,228 | 12,408 |

Source: Federal Reserve Bulletin, August, 1964.

was a total of nearly $49.5 billion of consumer installment credit supplied by financial institutions; the same date there was an additional volume of installment credit in the amount of $6.4 billion supplied by retail outlets such as department stores, furniture and appliance dealers, etc.

PERSONAL FINANCE COMPANIES.   These financial institutions deal directly with the borrowing individual.   As with the sales finance companies, commercial banks are the principal source of their funds for lending.

The typical transaction of personal finance companies involves only a modest sum, since most states limit the amount that may be lent— some states have limits as low as $300 or $600.   The loan is generally unsecured, that is, is a so-called "signature loan."   Sometimes, however, wage assignments are used as security and other times chattel mortgages on household furniture, etc., are used as security for the loan.

CHARGE ACCOUNT CREDIT.   Because it is the most widely used type of consumer credit, charge accounts are deserving of at least brief comment. When an item is purchased and we say "charge it" it means the seller is extending us credit. In order to provide this credit the retailer must have access to funds either by borrowing from banks or else from his working capital funds. Even here, to finance the deferred payments arising from the use of charge accounts there must be funds or access to funds—typically the ability to borrow at commercial banks. In this sense, the retailer acts as a borrowing intermediary by arranging financing with a commercial bank for example, in order to extend to his customer the privilege of using charge-account credit. As of the end of June, 1964, there was outstanding retail charge-account credit amounting to $5.2 billion and service credit of $4.5 billion.

## IMPLICATIONS FOR MONETARY CONTROL

The rapid growth of the nonbank financial intermediaries in recent years has raised some questions with respect to the implementation of monetary policy by the Federal Reserve authorities. These non-bank financial institutions have not only grown in absolute size, but their relative growth has also exceeded that of commercial banks.

This very rapid growth of nonbank financial institutions has raised the question of their significance as a possible offset to monetary policy because of the rapid increase in the public's holding of the liquid assets supplied by them. Since these liquid assets held by the public are "near moneys," changes in their amount may have important effects on the demand for money balances, and thus upon the velocity of circulation. Yet the cyclical and secular factors causing changes in the amount of these liquid assets, and the lending policies of the institutions which create them, lie outside the direct control of the Federal Reserve authorities. Some monetary students argue that this may be a rather serious obstacle between Federal Reserve policy and the goals it is attempting to attain.

In seeking to reach its desired goals the Federal Reserve works to maintain or achieve an appropriate level of expenditures in the economy by fostering a flow of money and credit that will facilitate orderly economic growth. In order to carry on any expenditure act, money is necessary. Money thus performs one of its major functions, it is serving as a means of payment. Now in order to carry on a given level of expenditures, or payments, what are the relevant factors? Let us assume a given price structure. Then if $500 billion of payments are to be made in a year, this could be done by having a money stock of, say, $250 billion which turns over twice in the year or of

$100 billion which turns over five times in the year. This rate of turnover or rate of circulation is termed the *velocity* of the money stock. As we have already seen, the methods of control of the Federal Reserve authorities directly affect the size of the money supply, and indirectly affect its velocity. Thus, a restrictive policy may be offset by an increase in velocity.

It may be argued that the presence of the many "near moneys" available from the widespread growth of nonbank financial institutions affects the level of expenditures by influencing the velocity of money. How does this influence work? Recall that money serves as more than only a means of payment, that it serves also as a store of value. Money is thus an asset that provides its holder with a fixed value and is easily negotiated; that is, it is the most liquid of all assets. Most holders of claims on nonbank financial institutions view these claims as being "money in the bank," as being quite liquid. Thus, when an income recipient has wealth held in a liquid, fixed-value form, his expenditures out of current income may be higher than otherwise.

As one example, assume a restrictive monetary policy. The monetary authorities are attempting to curtail either the level of expenditures or its rate of increase. In so doing, they will be engaged, among other measures, in a policy of open market sales. As these open market sales are made security prices fall and interest rates, or yields, rise. This fall in security prices may make the fixed-value near moneys— savings deposits and savings and loan shares, for instance—more attractive. If holders of *idle* money balances switch to these near moneys, velocity may rise. The money supply has not changed, but borrowers from the financial institutions are *spending* otherwise idle funds; velocity has thus increased.

The Federal Reserve authorities can influence the lending policies of financial intermediaries in at least three ways. First of all, by using open market sales, discount rate increases, etc., they can restrict the ability and willingness of commercial banks to lend to the borrowing intermediaries. Second, their open market sales may directly affect intermediaries if customers withdraw funds to purchase government securities; or loanable funds are reduced if an intermediary itself should purchase government securities. The third avenue of influence is perhaps the most important one. Open market sales are accompanied by a fall in security prices. Financial institutions finance many new loans by selling existing debt instruments in their portfolios. Thus, the capital loss incurred, should existing loan instruments be liquidated, may "lock-in" the intermediaries in their present holdings.

The purpose of this chapter has been to point out how the rapid growth of nonbank financial institutions has certain interesting implications for monetary control. Whether these necessitate extending Federal Reserve control over the intermediaries will be taken up later. For the present it is enough to recognize that these nonbank financial institutions offer the public attractive and diversified outlets for their savings, and that the public looks upon these liquid assets as "money in the bank" and makes plans accordingly.

## SUMMARY

The role of financial intermediaries is to make more efficient the transfer of spending power from those with surplus money income to businesses or individuals wishing to spend in excess of their current income. We have defined saving as the nonconsumption of money income and investment as the accumulation of "productive stuff"—the acquisition of real assets as distinct from financial assets. From these definitions we obtained the basic relationship between saving and investment, or

Saving = increased ownership of real assets plus financial accumulation.

Since for the economy as a whole financial accumulation is zero—one person's accumulation of financial assets is another person's disaccumulation—we obtained the equality of saving and investment. This is always true in an *ex post* or accounting sense. What is of interest is whether or not planned, or *ex ante*, saving equals planned investment. Since savers and investors are generally two distinct groups, the financial intermediaries serve to coordinate their plans.

The financial intermediaries may be placed into two general categories: savings intermediaries and borrowing intermediaries. The first category collects and pools the surplus funds of savers. They do this by offering an attractive and diversified variety of claims against themselves. These claims are such financial assets to their owners as savings deposits, savings and loan association shares, life insurance cash and surrender values, etc. The funds obtained by providing attractive outlets for savings are, in turn, lent by the savings intermediaries to borrowers, usually for real investment purposes. The institutions thus channel funds from savers to investors.

The second class of financial intermediaries, the borrowing intermediaries, operate for the most part in the area of consumer credit. They obtain the funds they lend by borrowing from other financial institutions, chiefly from commercial banks but also by open market sale of their own promises to pay. In this situation also, surplus funds are channeled to those who wish to spend in excess of current income.

The extremely rapid growth of nonbank financial institutions relative to commercial banks in recent years has raised the question of their influence on the effectiveness of Federal Reserve monetary control.   Specifically it is argued that the large and diversified holdings by the public of "near moneys," the claims issued by the various savings intermediaries and regarded as "money in the bank" by the claimholders, serve to increase the income velocity of any given money stock, thus making more difficult the task of regulating the level of expenditures.   That is, the monetary authority may control the level of the money supply but an increased rate of turnover may negate any contraction in the money supply.   We do no more than point out the problem here, reserving for a later chapter its assessment and the possible need for an extension of Federal Reserve control over these nonbank financial institutions.

## REVIEW QUESTIONS

1. Develop the relationship between saving, investment, and financial accumulation.   Why, for the whole economy, does saving equal investment?
2. How do financial intermediaries serve to coordinate the activities of savers and investors?
3. Discuss the sources of and users of funds in the credit market.
4. Discuss the institutions which compose the two general classes of financial intermediaries.
5. The commercial bank plays both a direct and indirect role in consumer credit.   Discuss.
6. What is consumer credit?
7. What is investment banking?
8. Develop the argument that the widespread presence of nonbank financial institutions has led to an increase in the velocity of circulation, and thus has weakened Federal Reserve monetary control.

## SUGGESTED REFERENCES

Federal Reserve Bank of Richmond, "The Money Lenders" in *Readings on Money,* 1957.

Horvitz, Paul M., *Monetary Policy and the Financial System* (Englewood Cliffs: Prentice-Hall, 1963).   Chapters 6–10.

Ludtke, James B., *The American Financial System* (Boston: Allyn and Bacon, 1961).

Robinson, Roland I., ed., *Financial Institutions.* 2nd ed. (Homewood: Richard D. Irwin, 1960).

PART IV

THE THEORY OF AGGREGATE
ECONOMIC ACTIVITY

# CHAPTER *14*

# *The Composition of Income and National Income Accounting*

From description of the American banking and monetary system, we are about to move to the theoretical considerations underlying such factors as the level of income and employment, economic growth and stability. For the next several chapters we shall focus our attention on the forces that determine the total level of economic activity. Yet before we actually move on to this theoretical discussion, it will be useful if we delve into the components of total, or aggregate, income and also gain some understanding of the concepts involved in national income accounting.

To appreciate how aggregate income is determined it is necessary to comprehend the structure of the economic system. This requires a knowledge of the concept of the gross national product which entails an insight into the main aspects of national income. The economic system is composed fundamentally of business units, governmental units, households, and foreign units.[1]

Business units are private organizations engaged in the production of some type of good or service for the purpose of making a profit. These units are corporate, partnership, or individual ownership in form. Although they can be usefully classified into industries, as several government statistical agencies have done, we shall deal with the broad

---

[1] While typical national income accounting procedure includes the foreign sector, we shall deal here with a "closed" economy. That is, for our present purposes little is to be gained by including foreign transactions and so we abstract from them. In a later section we may again take account of this sector.

category of privately owned profit making organizations and call them, for the most part, *firms*.  Strictly speaking, a firm is only a partnership or an individual enterprise, such as a law firm, an engineering firm, an accounting firm, or the like.  A corporate venture is not a firm, but a company or an organization.  Yet for centuries economists have used language loosely, calling both incorporated and unincorporated businesses firms.

Governmental units engage principally in activities that cannot be satisfactorily provided by private firms.  Such things as education, law enforcement, defense, etc., do not manufacture a product which can be readily sold on a profit basis.  Some governmental activities, of course, such as hydroelectric power production and postal service are more nearly of commercial nature.  But, by and large, government activities provide services useful to the community as a whole rather than to the individual.  This puts governments into a considerably different category from business.

The household sector may be considered as the end point of economic activity.  Households enjoy the products and services of business and government.  Since households are the suppliers of labor, one could take the point of view that they use certain raw materials—consumer goods—to raise and train factors of production—children. This, however, is not the customary point of view, and it is more suitable to think of households as the recipients of goods and services that are enjoyed as an end in themselves.  Consumer goods are then an end point, and not another ingredient of production.  This is not to deny that households do not provide labor and capital to business. The household supplies services to business and receives a return, but the two are independent activities, and are not directly integrated activities as is the case for business.

This completes our list of economic sectors: (1) business; (2) government; and (3) households.  What we wish to do now is to derive the concepts of gross national product, national income, etc., and to show the interrelationships among the various sectors.  To do this let us turn to the principal transactions involved.

## SOME IMPORTANT TRANSACTION ACCOUNTS

We shall not attempt to spell out every transaction one might possibly encounter in studying our economy.  What we shall do is to single out those principal transactions, both of market and nonmarket varieties, necessary to develop the concept of gross national product.  The transactions labeled market transactions are principally those engaged in by the business sector; they entail either a receipt or expenditure with some other sector. The nonmarket transactions, on the other hand, generally involve receipt or expenditures between other sectors of the economy and usually do not directly involve the business sector.

## Transactions Involving the Firm

Since the business firm both purchases certain goods and services and sells others, we may list some important types of transactions as follows:

Transactions involving money receipt—or sources of funds

(a) Sales
(b) Interest receipts
(c) Dividend receipts
(d) Rent receipts
(e) Sale of securities (borrowing or equity financing)

Transactions involving money payments—or uses of funds

(f) Materials and services purchases to be used in production (not investment goods)
(g) Investment goods purchases from firms
(h) Labor purchases from households
(i) Interest payments
(j) Rent payments
(k) Dividend payments
(l) Entrepreneurial withdrawals to unincorporated business
(m) Corporate profits tax
(n) Indirect business taxes

All the above transactions are market matters, involving the actual exchange of money. It will be convenient for us to use the letters, $a$ through $n$, to represent the dollar value of these transactions in a given accounting period, usually one year. Similarly we shall use the subscripts 1, 2, or 3 to designate the sector, business, government, or household respectively, with which the transactions are carried on. Thus, for example, we may write:

$$a = a_1 + a_2 + a_3.$$

Here the dollar value of sales of some firm $(a)$ is equal to the dollar value of sales to other firms $(a_1)$ plus the dollar value of sales to government $(a_2)$ plus the dollar value of sales to households $(a_3)$. In a similar fashion dividend payments by the firm to the household is $k_3$. Of the many possible transactions some are of little importance and we may neglect them; an example would be sales of securities to government, $e_2$.

The distinction between purchases of material ($f$) and investment goods ($g$) is important. Investment goods are long lived and may be used repeatedly in production, wearing out only gradually. Materials disappear in the course of production. And of course services, too, such as transportation, may disappear in the process of production.

Three final items concerning the firm must be defined, but these three are not market transactions. These are inventory accumulation, depreciation, and undistributed corporate profits. We shall designate these by the letters $o$, $p$, and $q$ respectively. In a year's time the value of raw materials, goods in process, and finished goods on hand may change. The change may be either positive or negative. If negative, the value of inventories on hand has decreased. This inventory factor we call $o$. The next concept, depreciation, is an estimate of the dollar loss in the value of investment goods on hand. As noted above, most investment goods, such as buildings and machinery, wear out gradually over time and must be maintained or replaced. Depreciation allowances attempt to estimate the dollar amount which should be set aside or spent annually for new investment goods so that the capital goods do not fall behind in quantity. In simplified terms, if depreciation allowances were set aside each year in a lump sum of money, the accumulated sum would be sufficient to replace the investment goods when they wear out. Similarly, if an amount equal to the depreciation is spent each year on new investment goods the capital equipment would be maintained at a uniform quality level. It is to this concept, depreciation, that we give the symbol $p$. The last item, undistributed profits, needs no elaboration, and to it we assign the letter $q$.

### Transactions Not Involving the Business Sector

In addition to the transactions that concern business, there are other transactions that do not involve the sector. Some of these transactions are market transactions, such as the government purchase of labor from the household; others are nonmarket transactions, such as government transfer payments, including interest payments. Since the most important of these transactions involve the government sector, we may set the transactions out as follows:

Transactions involving money receipt by government

($r$) Personal income tax
($s$) Sale of securities to individuals (borrowing)

Transactions involving money payment by government

(*t*) Transfer payments
(*u*) Government wages paid

These last transactions complete our list.   What should be observed
is simply this: these definitions represent types of transactions among
the various economic sectors and consequently show the financial flows
linking all three sectors.   The task is now to put the transactions into
tabular form in order to show more clearly the interdependence of the
sectors to one another.

All of the transactions fall into one of three categories:

1. Factor payments and receipts: that is, returns to the factors of
   production (land, labor, capital)
2. Product payments and receipts: that is, purchases of final
   products
3. Transfer payments and receipts: unilateral cash payments; that
   is, taxes, savings, payments to persons, etc.

We are now ready to set up sectoral transaction accounts.   Let us
denote the total of a particular transaction carried on in a year's time
by a capital letter.   Thus, for example, $A$ denotes all sales by all firms
in a one-year period, including intrasector sales.   Sales excluding sales
between firms, that is, sales by business to other sectors are $A_2 + A_3$.

Our first transactions account is for the business sector.   This is
Table 14-1, which lists in a systematic fashion the sources and uses of
funds by the business sector.

TABLE 14-1   Consolidated Business Income and Product Account

| Uses of Funds | | Sources of Funds | |
|---|---|---|---|
| Compensation of employees | $H$ | Consolidated net sales: | |
| Income of unincorporated enterprise | $L$ | To households | $A_3$ |
| Rental income of persons | $J_3$ | To government | $A_2$ |
| Corporate profits tax | $M$ | To business on capital account | $G$ |
| Corporate dividends paid | $K_3$ | Change in inventories | $O$ |
| Undistributed corporate profit | $Q$ | | |
| Net interest (pd to H.H.) | $B - I$ | | |
| Indirect business taxes | $N$ | | |
| Depreciation | $P$ | | |
| Charges against business gross product | | Business gross product | |

Table 14-1 exhibits in a compact way the sources and uses of funds by the business sector. The various uses to which the funds are put indicate the many payments made to government and households, as well as some business retention of funds. Very clearly the sources of funds to the business sector are principally sales to other sectors. It follows that we should be able to set up similar sources and uses of funds statements for the household sector and for government.

The sources and uses statements for the household sector and government sector are shown in Table 14-2 and Table 14-3 respectively.

**TABLE 14-2**  Personal Income and Expenditure Account

| Uses of Funds | | Sources of Funds | |
|---|---|---|---|
| Net purchases from business | $A_3$ | Wages and salary: | |
| Personal tax | $R$ | From business | $H$ |
| Personal saving | $PS$ | From government | $U$ |
| | | Income of unincorporated enterprise | $L$ |
| | | Rental income of person | $J_3$ |
| | | Dividends received | $K_3$ |
| | | Personal interest income | $I_3 - B_3$ |
| | | Government transfer payments | $T$ |
| Personal outlay and saving | | Personal income | |

**TABLE 14-3**  Consolidated Government Receipts and Expenditure Account

| Uses of Funds | | Sources of Funds | |
|---|---|---|---|
| Compensation of government employees | $U$ | Personal taxes | $R$ |
| Net purchases from business | $A_2$ | Corporate profit taxes | $M$ |
| Transfer payments | $T$ | Indirect business taxes | $N$ |
| | | Deficit $(+)$ or surplus $(-)$ on income and product transactions | |
| Government expenditures | | Government receipts and surplus or deficit | |

By now it should be clear that these financial flows link one sector to another—which is simply to say that one sector's expenditure (use of funds) is some other sector's income (source of funds). It follows that a consolidated statement of receipts and expenditures should be derivable from the foregoing sector accounts. Such is the case, and the consolidated account for the economy as a whole is called the gross national product and income account. If we form this consolidated account we obtain the result shown in Table 14-4.

**TABLE 14-4**  Gross Income and Product Account

| | | | |
|---|---|---|---|
| Compensation of employees: | | Personal consumption | |
| Wages paid by business | $H$ | expenditure | $A_3$ |
| Wages paid by government | $U$ | Gross private domestic | |
| Income of unincorporated | | investment | $G + O$ |
| enterprises | $L$ | Government purchases of | |
| Rental income of persons | $J_3$ | goods and services | $A_2 + U$ |
| Corporate profits tax | $M$ | | |
| Dividends | $K_3$ | | |
| Undistributed corporate profits | $Q$ | | |
| Net interest | $I_3 - B_3$ | | |
| = National income | | | |
| Indirect business taxes | $N$ | | |
| Depreciation allowance | $P$ | | |
| Charges against gross national product (Factor incomes + transfers + taxes) | | Gross national product (Final product sales) | |

Gross national product, or GNP, is the total dollar value of all goods produced (and sold) in the nation in one year, valued at market prices. The goods produced are final products, that is, the consumer goods, investment goods and inventory accumulation, and government services produced. This is another way of saying that the producer's efforts of a year's time must result in some consumer satisfaction, in governmental service, or in provision for future satisfactions and services through investment and inventory accumulation. Thus the uses to which GNP, the market value of final goods produced, may be put are: consumption, investment including inventory accumulation, and government purchases of goods and services.

Government services are valued at cost, as these services inherently have no market value. It is assumed that their value equals their cost. The presumption is that if these services were curtailed an equivalent amount of consumer goods or investment goods could be produced with the resources thus released. For one part of government costs we have a symbol, $A_2$. This is purchases by the government of materials and supplies from business. The other government expense is for labor employed by the government and for the armed forces. For this category the letter $U$ refers to government wages.

## THE MEANING OF NATIONAL INCOME STATISTICS

Gross national product is defined as the total dollar value of all final goods and services produced in a one-year period, valued at market prices. This is the value of all production, before allowance is made for the value of capital goods used up in producing the year's output. Because it does measure total output, it is one of our best indicators of total economic activity. It reflects the level of employment of resources in the production process.

Defined in terms of current market prices, GNP, in order to compare one time period to another, must be adjusted to show changes in real output, not just changes in the prices at which the output is valued. The Department of Commerce publishes figures of GNP in "constant" dollars for the United States. This means that the dollar value of GNP has been deflated by a price index to remove the effects of price changes over time. The resulting series thus purports to show changes from year to year in real output, the goods and services available for use.

Setting aside the index number problem, let us return to the GNP concept. As we have seen, total production is reflected as sales to households, to business for investment, and to government. But a sales transaction has two sides to it. On the one hand, it is a *receipt* of money by the *seller* of the item, and on the other hand, it is an *expenditure* of money by the *purchaser* of the item. Thus we have the obvious, but nevertheless important, equation that sales equal purchases. In terms of national income accounting, this means that the value of production, or GNP, is equal to the expenditures for the goods produced, or GNP.

### GNP and Expenditure

The expenditures on GNP are gross domestic private investment, personal consumption expenditures, and government purchases of goods and services. In a "sources and uses" approach, expenditures assert the "uses" to which the real income and its money income equivalent are put. From this we should be able to show the "sources" of income. This we can do. But before we do so we had best look briefly at the various "uses" of GNP.

GROSS DOMESTIC PRIVATE INVESTMENT. From the definition of investment goods as long-lived goods used in production, as contrasted with the intermediate goods and services used in production, we obtain the expression $G + O$ for gross domestic private investment.

Thus, gross domestic private investment is acquisition of new capital goods, $G$, plus an inventory adjustment, $O$.   Note that net inventory accumulation is investment.   The major categories of gross domestic private investment are: (1) new construction, both residential and business; (2) producers' durable equipment; (3) net changes in business inventory.

Again a word of caution is in order.   The word *investment* is being used in a very specific way, and not in the usual sense of the term. Investment means here the accumulation of "productive stuff."   It does not mean dealing with existing assets, but the purchase of new currently produced capital goods.   This distinction between the every-day sense of investment and the specific sense in which we use it should be noted and understood by the reader.

PERSONAL CONSUMPTION EXPENDITURES.   The category called per-sonal consumption expenditures, or simply consumption, is the pur-chase by the household of newly produced goods and services.   Our symbol for consumption expenditures is $A_3$.   These consumer goods and services are of diverse forms, but the principal categories are: (1) consumer durable goods—for example, major household appliances, such as refrigerators; (2) nondurable goods—for example, food pur-chases; (3) personal services—for example, medical advice or haircuts.

The determinants of consumer expenditures are numerous, but we shall bypass them here.   In a later chapter, we shall discuss the princi-pal determinants of both consumption expenditures and investment expenditure.

GOVERNMENT PURCHASES OF GOODS AND SERVICES.   This category covers all expenditures by government for final products, and pay-ment for the services of those people employed by government.   As mentioned earlier, governmental units often provide services that have no market price—police and fire protection, education, defense, etc. Thus, the services provided by the government are valued in GNP at their cost to the government.   Our symbol for this category is $A_2$ + government wages, or $A_2 + U$.

"Government purchases of goods and services" does not include *all* expenditures by government.   It does not include "transfer" pay-ments.   These are payments, such as pensions and interest on govern-ment debt, for which the government does not receive currently pro-duced goods or services.

Summarizing the preceding items, as was done in Table 14-4, we obtain expenditures for final output—GNP from the expenditure side. These expenditure totals are important for our study.   If, in analyzing them subsequently, we can determine the principal factors that influence the expenditures in the various sectors, we shall be able to assess the performance of the economy.   We shall then be able to prescribe policy to correct or adjust deficiencies or excesses in one or more sectors.

### GNP and Income

The foregoing section concerned GNP as a summary of the various expenditures for final output.   Thus, GNP represents a kind of indication of the level of expenditures in the economy and therefore, of the level of economic activity.   Now let us see how the various sectors in the economy interact to create and change the level of expenditures.

The gross income accruing to the various sectors is the left-hand side of Table 14-4, the Gross Income and Product Account.   If we take now the gross income, which of course equals GNP, we may set forth the sectoral gross income shares.   These gross income shares are illustrated in Table 14-5.

TABLE 14-5   Gross Income Shares

|  | Recipient | | |
| --- | --- | --- | --- |
|  | Household | Business | Government |
| Compensation of employees | $H + U$ | | |
| Interest and rental income of persons | $J_3 + (I_3 - B_3)$ | | |
| Income of unincorporated business | $L$ | | |
| Indirect business taxes | | | $N$ |
| Depreciation allowances | | $P$ | |
| Corporate income tax | | | $M$ |
| Dividends distributed | $K_3$ | | |
| Undistributed corporate profits | | $Q$ | |

As noted from Table 14-5, if we add the total of gross income accruing to households, business, and government we see that they equal the total given for GNP in Table 14-4.   But what we really want is not the gross income of the household, business, or government sectors,[2] but what we may call their *disposable income*.   In other words, since it is out of disposable income that actual expenditures take place, we must determine how much income each sector can spend.

---

[2] Recall our decision to ignore the foreign sector, at least for the present, since it is of relatively negligible importance in terms of total GNP.

**PERSONAL DISPOSABLE INCOME.** This income concept measures the income available to households out of which consumption expenditures are made. Specifically, personal disposable income (PDI) is derived by adding to gross household income any transfer payments received by the household sector, and from this total deducting personal taxes paid. Thus we have:

| | |
|---|---|
| Gross household income | $H + U + L + J_3 + K_3 + I_3 - B_3$ |
| $(+)$ Transfer payments | $T$ |
| $(-)$ Personal taxes | $R$ |
| $(=)$ Personal disposable income | $H + U + L + J_3 + K_3 + I_3 - B_3 + T - R$ |

**BUSINESS DISPOSABLE INCOME.** The business sector's disposable income is the sum of undistributed profits and the depreciation allowance. Hence, the business disposable income (BDI) and gross business income are identical and are given as $(Q + P)$.

**NET GOVERNMENT REVENUE.** (NGR) This income concept is simply the government sector's gross income minus any government transfer payments. Consequently we may write:

| | |
|---|---|
| Business taxes | $M + N$ |
| Personal taxes | $R$ |
| $(-)$ Transfer payments | $T$ |
| $(=)$ Net government revenue | $M + N + R - T$ |

Now clearly if we add these three disposable incomes together (PDI + BDI + NGR) we shall have GNP as shown in Table 14-4. Thus, we have made the full circuit. Starting with expenditures we have traced the circular flow of income back to its origins. We have developed a rather important notion here, namely that expenditures for goods and services—that is, expenditures on GNP—create an equivalent amount of spendable income. But now we come to an important point. The various sectors have some discretion as to whether or not to spend their disposable income. To this important point we must now turn our attention.

## DISCRETIONARY SPENDING BY SECTORS

The disposable income concepts are the sector incomes out of which spending actually takes place. Within limits, the sectors may at their discretion spend amounts that differ from their incomes. That is, a sector may spend beyond its income (borrow or spend accumulated savings), may spend exactly its income, or may save part of its income (not spend all of its income).

Now let us derive an important equation, namely, that saving equals investment. Saving has been defined as disposable income not consumed. Thus, for the household sector it is the difference between personal disposable income and consumption expenditures. Similarly, since business firms do not "consume" as such, all business disposable income goes into business saving. Finally, we may call government saving the difference between net government revenue and government purchases of goods and services. Adding these sectoral savings we find that this exactly equals gross private domestic investment.[3] Since saving by definition is income not spent on consumption, it includes the direct accumulation of "productive stuff" as well as the repayment of debt or the acquisition of financial assets (interest earning assets).

The reasonableness of this result may be seen as follows. Saving can be accomplished by the accumulation of assets. If the assets are old (existing) assets someone has gained them at someone else's expense. There is no net saving. But if a *new* property comes into existence, that is, investment, this property must be owned by someone, and saving has been accomplished. Thus, it is only investment that makes saving possible. There consequently occurs naturally a flow of securities to constitute savings. Households, for example, may acquire securities from government and business firms, leaving the net change in the cash-balance position of all sectors at zero.

Let us now turn to some basic cash-balance relations. Essentially the cash-balance relation is this: cash accumulation = income + borrowing − spending. The spending term may be considered as being composed of two parts, one the expenditure for goods and services and the other the spending on financial assets.

Taking account of the distinction between spending on currently produced goods and services and spending on financial assets, we may reformulate the cash accumulation relationship as:

income − spending on output = cash accumulation
$$+ \text{[spending on financial assets} - \text{borrowing]}.$$

---

[3] These statements may be summarized as: (1) Personal saving $= H + U + L + J_3 + K_3 + I_3 - B_3 + T - R - A_3$; (2) Business saving $= Q + P$; (3) Government saving $= M + N + R - T - A_2 - U$. Adding these to obtain total saving we have (4) Total saving $= H + L + J_3 + K_3 + I_3 - B_3 + M + N + Q + P - A_2 - A_3$. But from Table 14-4 we see that we may write $H + U + L + J_3 + M + K_3 + Q + I_3 - B_3 + N + P = A_3 + G + O + A_2 + U$, so (5) $H + L + J_3 + K_3 + I_3 - B_3 + M + N + Q + P - A_2 - A_3$ (saving) $= G + O$ (investment).

Stated in this fashion it enables us to judge the effect of the actions of any sector on the economic system. The left side of the equation represents the effect of the spending-saving decision. If a sector spends more than its income, or if its expenditures relative to income rise, this is expansionary since incomes of other sectors will rise. But if spending decreases relative to income, this results in a reduced flow of income to other sectors and is basically contractive in nature.

The bracketed expression on the right-hand side of the equation reflects the net amount of funds entering or leaving the sector through financial transactions. It is the difference, in other words, between spending on securities (lending or debt retirement) and selling securities (borrowing). This item might therefore be considered a "money market" effect, whereas the expenditure on output affects what we shall call the "goods" market.

It will be left for subsequent chapters to develop the importance of the concepts introduced in this chapter. We shall attempt to determine the basic factors that influence decisions to consume, save, and invest. Certainly such factors as the level of income will influence spending; and interest rates, and credit conditions generally, will affect desires to lend, borrow, spend, or accumulate cash balances. Similarly, subjective factors such as tastes, expectations, and the like will affect both the goods market and the money market.

Finally, anticipating further discussion, we have seen that saving and investment are always equal over any given accounting period. Although for any accounting period saving *will equal* investment, it is important to note that *planned saving* and *planned investment* may not have been equal. And whenever planned saving and planned investment for a period are not equal, the level of income is going to change. Since the "savers" in the aggregate are not necessarily the "investors" we can see how a divergence between planned investment and planned saving may arise. If households plan to consume more (save less) of their incomes this may be matched through the unplanned reduction in inventories (less investment). Or contrarywise, if the household plans to consume less (save more) of its income, this may be offset by an unplanned increase in inventory stock. In any event, when planned saving and planned investment are not equal, income will change: planned investment greater than planned saving leads to a higher level of income, and planned saving greater than planned investment leads to a decline in income.

The reason for the income change is now clear from our last cash-balance accumulation equation: any change on the left side must be accompanied by an equal change on the right-hand side to maintain the equality. But the left hand side is essentially the spending-saving decision, and we have seen how an increase in spending relative to income leads to an increase in other sectors' incomes. That is, less planned saving, other factors being given, leads to a higher level of income.

These last mentioned concepts will be explored in greater detail in following chapters.

## REVIEW QUESTIONS

1. Discuss the principal market characteristics of the business, government, and household sectors of the economic system.
2. Using data from the current issue of the *Federal Reserve Bulletin* or the *Survey of Current Business*, determine the values of the items entering into the business sector account, the household sector account, and the government sector account.
3. Using the above sources, determine gross national product.
4. Define GNP. Why is it an important indicator of economic activity?
5. Discuss the relationship between GNP and expenditures.
6. Discuss the relationship between GNP and income.
7. Out of what income concept does spending actually take place? Discuss.
8. What is the cash-balance relation? What does it tell us? Discuss.

## SUGGESTED REFERENCES

Most standard principles of economics textbooks contain a section on national income accounting. Especially recommended, however, is:

Hicks, J. R., A. G. Hart, and J. W. Ford, *The Social Framework of the American Economy*, 2nd ed. (New York: Oxford University Press, 1955). Parts IV and V.

Department of Commerce, *National Income*, a supplement to the "Survey of Current Business" (Washington, D.C., 1954). Provides the detailed procedures in developing the various social accounts.

# CHAPTER *15*

# *Introduction to Monetary Theory*

As we turn our attention to economic theory it may be appropriate to introduce the subject with a few remarks that may help to place the role of theory in sharper focus. To do this we shall pose such questions as what is theory, how is a theory developed, and what is the significance of economic theory?

## THE NATURE AND SIGNIFICANCE OF ECONOMIC THEORY

Explanation and prediction are the goals of economic theory. The significance of macroeconomic theory lies in its applicability to solving problems, or at least shedding additional light on problems, concerned with the level of employment, inflation, economic growth, and so forth. What determines the size or level of these variables? Why and how do they change over time? How are they related to one another at any time and over a period of time? These are possible questions; and theory provides the means by which we attempt to answer them.

In place of the word *theory* another term is often encountered. This term is *model*. In a real sense a theory is a model of that part of the real word it purports to describe. To illustrate: astronomers have developed a comprehensive theory of celestial movement, which enables them to predict with great accuracy events such as eclipses and the movement and positions of various elements of the solar system. A model consequently is a device with which we may predict. A theory is a model of some part of the external world which enables us to understand reality better, and to make predictions of what will happen in various circumstances.

A theory of the economic system is, in general, similar to a theory of the solar system. The astronomer's theory explains the interrelations, position, and movement of heavenly bodies. The economist's theory explains the interrelations, magnitude, and change of economic variables. Theories or models are simply compact, systematic statements of the relationships between relevant economic variables.

It is this systemization that a theory provides which makes understanding and prediction possible. How is this systemization achieved? It is attained by a process of abstracting important details and omitting other factors. By this process, however, we are left with incomplete models of reality.[1] Our models are admittedly oversimplified. But what has been omitted is hopefully offset by the increased understanding that the model gives us. This use of ideal abstractions is not unique to the economist. For example, the physicist speaks of frictionless bodies. The economist is not alone, then, in developing a theory on the basis of assumptions that he knows are not universally valid. Why is the economist not more realistic?

First, in some cases we would like to figure out what would happen if the assumptions were true. If the results seem desirable, then it would be a legitimate aim of policy to attempt to bring about the assumed conditions. Second, for working purposes we may make a convenient assumption about some factor whose variation we will not attempt to explain because we consider it outside the scope of our study. That is, we consider the factor as exogenously determined but include it in our model because it may be important in explaining other variables within the model. Third, while explaining one part of the system we may, for purposes of manageability and simplicity, assume other factors to be constant. Fourth, oftener than not, we may believe the assumption to be true, and assuming its universal validity makes the process of theorizing easier. Furthermore, such assumptions may be relaxed as the theory is developed or applied in specific instances. The danger, of course, is that the uninitiated may ignore or be unfamiliar with the more realistic modifications of the theory, and may attempt to apply the original simplified assumptions as if they were universally valid.

After all is said and done, we come to the heart of the matter. These abstractions provide *useful* models, and the important ques-

---

[1] Thus our models are similar to ordinary maps, in that only the most important features are retained.

tion is: Is the error which results from oversimplification significant in any use we make of the theory?

Implicit in the discussion is the use to which the models will be put. We shall single out for examination the various economic variables, their determinants, and the interrelationships among them that are most crucial in the determination of level of income, maintenance of economic stability, etc.   Thus, given some goal, we have a framework in which the variables may be manipulated in order to achieve the objective.   *The purpose of the study of economic theory, then, is to enable an understanding of economic policy.*   For by having a firm grasp of theory, we are in a position to see how best, or in what fashion, some desired goal may be achieved.

The first area of theory to concern us is the area of monetary theory. We shall consider several variants of monetary theory, starting with the so-called "classical" theories and moving to a more recent formulation.   Then in the next chapter we shall take up the theory of income determination.

## CLASSICAL MONETARY THEORIES

The term *classical* is not a very precise one.   We are adopting J. M. Keynes's use of the term to refer to the group of writers represented by such economists as Alfred Marshall, A. C. Pigou, Irving Fisher, D. H. Robertson, and the many others who formulated the trans-actions-velocity and cash-balances approach to money and prices. These writers generally have one feature in common—to them money is principally a means of facilitating exchange.   For them the really fundamental aspects of economic life are the maximizing of individual utility functions or the minimizing of the cost of production, etc.

The classical writers carried out their analysis in "real" terms. Thus, all exchanges are in essence the exchange of one set of goods and services for another set of goods and services.   In this setting money plays no part except to facilitate this exchange—an intermediary for which goods and services are exchanged and which in turn is itself later exchanged for still other goods and services.

In examining the working of the economic system, the classical economist looked beyond the veil of money.   The classical theorist made his abstractions from money and examined economic life as though money did not exist.   This allowed him to concentrate on the fundamental aspects of economic behavior in real terms.   Prices expressed in money terms represent, ideally, the exchange ratios between real goods and services and express these ratios in absolute terms.   As a consequence of this reasoning the role of money in the classical model is to determine the level of absolute prices. Classical monetary theory, then, explains only fluctuations in the general level of absolute prices.

In order to facilitate the discussion of classical monetary theory it will be helpful to set down the two most widely used monetary equations. The first equation is the so-called *Equation of Exchange:* $MV = PT$. In this formulation $M$ stands for the total amount of money in existence; $T$ is the total volume of transactions exchanged for money during the period; and $P$ represents the general price level of the things exchanged. $V$, however, can have either of two different meanings. First, it may be the actual velocity of circulation of the money supply, that is, the average number of times each unit of money turns over or is exchanged during the period. If this definition of $V$ is used then the equation of exchange is a tautology, true by definition. It simply states that sales equal purchases. It may be useful, nevertheless, in showing factors $M$, $V$, and $T$, which are determinants of the general price level, $P$.

Or second, $V$ may be defined as the equilibrium velocity of circulation, that is, that velocity which individual economic units *wish* to continue over time so long as other conditions, $M$ and $T$ in particular, remain constant. If $V$ is defined in this sense, then the equation represents an equilibrium condition.

The second equation is the *Cambridge Equation: $M = kPT$.* In this formulation $M$ is again the total money supply, $T$ the volume of transactions, and $P$ the general price level. In this formulation $k$ is susceptible to two interpretations. The symbol $k$ may represent the actual proportion of the money value of transactions which people hold in the form of money or cash balances. In this event the equation is true by definition. Alternately $k$ may represent the *desired* percentage of the total money value of transactions which people wish to hold, other factors given, in money balances. In this situation the equation is an equilibrium condition.

## THE TRANSACTIONS-VELOCITY MODEL

The transactions-velocity theory of money is a quantity theory of money. That is, the amount of money influences the general level of prices. But the classical version of this theory also recognizes additional factors to money which determine the general price level. These other factors are (1) the velocity of circulation of money, and (2) the volume of the transactions to be carried on. It is necessary to investigate the determinants of each of these factors which interact to determine the general price level.

We have already discussed the determinants of the money supply, $M$. These are all the factors which interact to produce at any given time a determinate quantity of money. These factors are such things as the level of bank reserves, reserve requirements, the public's willingness to borrow and banks' willingness to lend, the public's propensity to hold currency and time deposits as well as demand deposits, and the Federal Reserve's current monetary policy. Thus it is the complex interplay of these factors which determines the amount of money, $M$, in the economic system.

The total volume of transactions, $T$, is affected by such factors as population, natural resources, and the level of technological development. These factors change only slowly over time. The classical economist assumed full employment of resources as the normal situation; thus $T$ may be assumed constant.

This brings us to the analysis of $V$, the velocity of circulation. Basic to the classical scheme is the concept that it is foolish to hold money at all. This seems to imply that velocity should be infinite. Since velocity of circulation is less than infinite, we must discover why. As we determine why velocity is not infinite we are also finding the reasons why most person do, in fact, hold money balances. This will help us to analyze the cash-balance approach to monetary theory, for if a person can obtain interest by lending money, why hold money balances at all?

Money balances can be explained on two general grounds: (1) frictions in the economic process; and (2) uncertainty as to the future. The classical transaction-velocity theory emphasizes frictions.[2]  Generally it is not efficient to make payments as soon as liabilities are incurred. For example, there are costs associated with preparing a payroll, levying taxes, etc. These can be done more efficiently in larger sums than in small. Thus, economies of size make it desirable to aggregate payments into larger quantities before payments are made, or even requested. Similar considerations apply to the financial acts of borrowing and lending. If it cost nothing to lend money or buy securities in terms of transaction charges—service charges, etc.— then it would pay to lend money as soon as received, and to sell securities when money is needed. But it is a fact of economic life that transaction costs do exist. Hence, it does not pay to make very short-term loans because the interest earned does not cover the costs of buying and selling and administering the loans. Consequently it often pays to hold temporary cash balances. These two factors explain the

---

[2] Uncertainty plays a larger role in the cash-balance formulation, and is, indeed, a major contribution of the Keynesian analysis.

existence of cash balances and velocity: (1) discreteness of payments arising from costs of submitting and paying bills, and (2) the discreteness in costs of buying and selling loan instruments.

The frictions resolve themselves into institutionalized patterns and are normally quite stable. For example, Fisher included among the factors which influence velocity the following: individual payment habits; the community's system of payments with respect to such things as the frequency and regularity of receipts and payments; the density of population; and the rapidity of transportation.[3] Since these are institutional factors which change only slowly over time, we may conclude that velocity is stable and constant.

We now can put the foregoing elements together in order to show the causal mechanism by which the general level of prices is determined. First, the supply of money, $M$, is determined by the interplay of factors such as the level of bank reserves, reserve requirements, monetary policy, etc. Second, since transactions, $T$, are technologically determined by the level of employment, and employment is assumed to be at the full-employment level, $T$ is given and constant. Third, whereas the institutional factors that determine velocity, $V$, are slow to change, the velocity term may be regarded as a constant.

From these assumptions, it becomes clear that any fluctuations in the price level, $P$, are due to the fluctuations in $M$, the money supply. This means that: (1) changes in $M$ do not cause opposite changes in $V$; (2) changes in $M$ do not produce similar changes in $T$; (3) nonmonetary factors are not acting to cause changes in $P$ which also cause similar changes in $M$ or $V$, or $MV$ together, or which do not produce an opposite change in $T$. In essence, the three statements assert the independence of $M$, $V$, and $T$. The validity and usefulness of the transactions-velocity model depend on the validity of the assumptions on which it rests.

Even Fisher recognized that in the short run and in "transition" periods one or several of the assumptions might not hold. But he felt that such periods were temporary in nature, and in the long run the more "normal" relationships would be restored.[4] Thus, we are forced to conclude that the transaction-velocity model has usefulness only in the long-run equilibrium situation; but, unfortunately, the long-run is composed of a series of short-run transition periods. In these periods the theory is of limited usefulness, because during them the assumptions of the model are not fulfilled. Instead of the price

---

[3] Irving Fisher, *The Purchasing Power of Money*, rev. ed. (New York: Macmillan Co., 1926), p. 79.

[4] *Ibid.*, p. 169.

level being a passive dependent factor, it is often crucial in determining $T$, the total volume of transactions. Furthermore, the volume of transactions is a function of the business cycle and is not constant. A further complication is that velocity seems to be related to the level of transactions, and transactions are in turn related to prices. The money supply and velocity also may move together, and the upshot of all these interrelations is that the transactions-velocity quantity theory of money is at best an equilibrium theory. It has little usefulness in explaining the short-run transition period.

This is not to deny any usefulness at all to the transactions-velocity model. It serves to point up factors which undoubtedly influence the general level of prices but which do not obey the limitations that the theory sets on them. Actually, the most serious shortcoming of the theory is its mechanistic approach. It tells *how* fast money is spent, but not *why* it is spent as fast as it is. That is, it ignores the motives for spending decisions. But this omission of motivations has been recognized as a weakness which the cash-balances model seeks to remedy. Thus, in the cash-balances approach, emphasis is placed on answering the question of why people hold money balances.

## THE CASH-BALANCES THEORY

The cash-balance model utilizes a rather different approach to the theory of money. The cash-balances model is a *stock* concept, whereas the transactions-velocity model is a *flow* concept. This is to say that the money supply is a given stock at any point in time, whereas the product $PT$, which is the money value of transactions,[5] is a flow concept holding for some period of time, for example, a year. This being the case it is clear that $M$, the money stock, cannot be directly compared with $PT$, the money flow of expenditures over a year's time. Consequently to achieve a comparison of $M$ with $PT$, the stock of money $M$ is multiplied by $V$, a factor whose dimensions are "per year." By this process the dimensions on each side of the equation of exchange can be seen to be comparable:

$$M \times V \text{ or } (\$) \times (1/\text{yr}) = P \times T \text{ or } (\$/\text{unit}) \times (\text{units}/\text{yr})$$
$$\text{or } \$/\text{yr} = \$/\text{yr}.$$

Since our dimensions are dollars per year, we have a flow situation.

---

[5] The term $PT$, the money value of transactions in a year's time, can be considered as being GNP if transactions $T$, are restricted to new final output and services. Thus, we could write $MV = PT = $ GNP with the above restriction to current final output and services.

On the other hand, the cash-balances model is a stock concept. This is clear since the formulation of the cash-balances approach is given as $M = kPT$. The supply of money at any given time is a *fixed stock*. The $k$ is a factor which adjusts the $PT$ term, dollars per year, into only dollars; thus, we can equate dollars to dollars. The factor $k$ tells what proportion of the annual expenditure stream people try to command by the holding of money balances; alternatively $k$ is the length of time a dollar is *held* on the average before being spent.

The perceptive student has probably observed that algebraically $k = 1/V$. Indeed, as has already been pointed out, the two types of equations are simply different aspects of the same phenomena. As one monetary economist has put it, the cash-balances approach may be likened to "money sitting" and the transactions-velocity view to "money on the wing."

Nevertheless, the cash-balance model represents an important advance over the transactions-velocity model. This is because $k$ can be analyzed in terms of what motivates people to hold money balances, as opposed to the mechanistic nature of the velocity approach. As a consequence, in analyzing the determinants of $k$ the theory must widen its scope of inquiry to deal with uncertainty, the interest rate, and other factors left unconsidered in the transactions-velocity approach.

As pointed out earlier, monetary equations with which we are dealing, the transactions-velocity model equation of $MV = PT$ and the Cambridge cash-balance equation of $M = kPT$, can be looked at two ways. First, they may be considered as definitionally true, as long as the dimensions of the variables are properly defined. Second, the two equations may be considered as equilibrium statements. It is in this latter form that they are of interest to us. For if the equations are construed as representing equilibrium conditions, then $V$ tells us how fast people *wish* to spend their money incomes. Similarly, $k$ tells us the proportions of the annual value of expenditures (income) which people *wish* to hold in money balances.

Given this equilibrium connotation, it is evident that $V$ is to be considered a constant value, and not a variable factor. As a matter of fact, Fisher and other writers[6] did devote some time to examining velocity as a variable term. But because of the rather mechanical nature of $V$, it does not lend itself readily to analysis as a variable factor. One might expect the same to be said of $k$—that $k$ is a con-

---

[6] Cf. Fisher, *op. cit.*, and L. V. Chandler, *Introduction to Monetary Theory* (New York: Harper and Brothers, 1940). Chapter III.

stant.   Indeed, since the factors that explain $V$ also determine $k$ we are reinforced in this belief that $k$ is a constant.   But such is not the case.   Because $k$ is determined by people's motives to hold money, it means that $k$ may be treated as a variable.   Hence, the expression $M = kPT$ may be used as a framework for analyzing changes in the price level, $P$, due to changes in $k$, as well as modifications in $P$ due to changes in $M$, the money supply.

The expression $M = kPT$ states that the supply of money, $M$, is equal to the demand for money, $kPT$—an equilibrium situation in the usual sense.   But what happens if the supply of and demand for money to hold are not equal—that is, if we have a disequilibrium situation? The answer is that equilibrium is attained by changing one or several of the variables $M$, $P$, $T$, or $k$.   If, however, we choose to consider $k$ as given by exogenous factors, then the adjustment must be brought about by changing $M$, $P$, or $T$, but not by $k$.   And assuming full employment, if $T$ is technologically determined by employment, then $T$ is also given and constant.   This reduces our equilibrating variables to two, namely, $M$ and $P$.

However, the community taken as a whole cannot change the amount of money, $M$, in the system.   One individual can increase or decrease his own money balances—but only by having some other individual or individuals offset the first person's change.   For example, what one person manages to spend, thus reducing his balances, becomes someone else's receipts, and thus adds to the latter's balances.   If, according to the full-employment assumption, $T$ is constant and $k$ is exogenously determined, then the effect of individuals' increased spending of money balances for goods, services, securities, or any- thing else can have only one outcome—the general price level must increase.   In the contrary case, any general attempt to increase money balances results in decreased expenditures and a consequent decline in the general price level.

Or consider an increase in the money supply.   Assuming that $k$ is fixed, as is $T$, then until and unless the money value of $PT$ changes, this additional money is superfluous.   That is, with the given desire to hold money balances of $k$ per cent of the money value of $PT$, we have more money than we need.   We thus try to exchange the excess money for goods or securities, but the only way we can effect the exchange is to bid up the price level, $P$.   This bidding-up process continues until the price level has risen sufficiently so that with the new value of $PT$, $M$ now is just $k$ per cent of this new value of $PT$.   Equilibrium is thus restored.

Such changes in the price level continue until the supply of money to hold and the demand for money are equalized, that is, until $M = kPT$. But this conclusion is the same as reached by the transactions-velocity model, namely, that given $k$ (that is, $V$) and $T$, changes in $M$, the money supply, produce proportional changes in the same direction in $P$, the general price level.

On the other hand, to illustrate the manner in which $k$ can be considered a variable consider the following example. Let us assume an initial equilibrium between the supply of and demand for money balances for a given value of $k$. Specifically, let us assume that $M$ is \$10 million, $PT$ is \$100 million, and $k$ is $1/10$. Thus with $M = kPT$ we have \$10 million $= 1/10 \times$ \$100 million. By definition this is an equilibrium situation. The annual money value of all transactions is \$100 million and the money supply is \$10 million. Furthermore, since $k$ is $1/10$, the amount of money the economy wants to hold as purchasing power over the annual stream of expenditure on goods and services valued at \$100 million is $1/10$ of \$100 million, or \$10 million— and this is equal to the supply of money.

But if at this juncture, for reasons which we shall investigate shortly, the community's desire to hold a given proportion of $PT$ in the form of money should change, what will result? How may we analyze the effects of a change in $k$? Given the supply of money $M$ and a constant $T$, it is clear that by changing $k$ the community as a whole is attempting either to increase or decrease its holdings of money relative to the money value of the volume of transactions. Since $M$ and $T$ are fixed, the adjusting factor must be the price level. That is, the price level adjusts until the new $k$ is the desired proportion of the money value of transactions. In our example assume that $k$ changes from $k = 1/10$ to $k = 1/5$. In other words, people in the aggregate wish to increase their money balances. Since the money supply available for holding in cash balances is \$10 million, what must occur as people attempt to acquire larger balances is a fall in the level of prices. This price decline continues until the money available to be held is exactly the desired proportion of the money value of the transactions. And since $M$ and $T$ are fixed the price level must fall. In our example if $k$ becomes $1/5$ then the price level $P$ must fall by one-half its original level, so that with the given $T$, the value $PT$ becomes \$50 million. Now we see that $M = kPT$, where $M$ is \$10 million, $k$ is $1/5$, and $PT$ is \$50 million, has the value \$10 million $= 1/5 \times$ \$50 million.

At this point the student may ask, "so what?" It still is not clear how the $k$ factor represents an advance over the velocity concept. Let us recall the reasons we explained for holding cash balances. These were (1) frictions in the economic process with respect to receipts and disbursement in both the commodity market for goods and services and in the money market in buying and selling loan instruments, and (2) the presence of uncertainty.   These considerations explain the existence of cash-balances, and the *motives* for holding cash-balances may then be described under three general headings.   The first of these motives for holding money balances is the transactions motive, the second is the precautionary or contingency motive, and the third motive is the speculative motive.

Even though we may state the general motives for the holding of money balances, it is next to impossible to put the actual money balances of an individual into one-to-one correspondence with these motives.   This is due to the same dollar doing double duty in many instances.   For example, an individual may have so much money on hand that the transactions motive and precautionary motive for holding money balances may merge together.   As a matter of fact, the three motives likely gradually merge into one another and no sharp lines of demarcation separate them.

In summary, the basic difference between the transaction-velocity approach and the cash-balance approach can be put in terms of the functions of money.   As we know, money serves as both a means of exchange and as a store value.   The transaction-velocity model singles out only the medium-of-exchange function.   That is, it is the *spending* that can be done with a given money supply and given velocity which is considered in the transaction-velocity model.

The cash-balance approach, by introducing motives for holding money balances into the picture, extends the analysis.   For not only are money balances held with a view to spending them, money balances are also held because they are a *store of value*.

## THE MOTIVES FOR HOLDING MONEY BALANCES

### The Transactions Motive

The first motive for holding cash-balances is called the *transactions motive*.   It is exactly what is implied by its name—the holding of sufficient money balances to make regular expenditures out of income that is received only periodically.   For example, persons paid every two weeks need smaller balances than individuals paid monthly; extensive use of credit minimizes the need for large balances, etc.   These are factors which Fisher discussed in connection with velocity determinants.   We may say that the size of the transaction balance is determined by frequency and correspondence of receipts and disbursements,

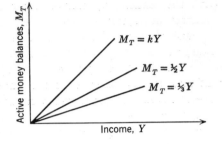

*Figure 15-1* The transaction demand for money balances.

by the use of credit, and similar features of the economic system. But these factors change relatively slowly. Consequently, it seems reasonable to postulate the size of balances held for transactions purposes as essentially a function of or dependent on two variables: (1) the level of transactions to be carried out, that is, the level of income; and (2) the level of prices. Thus, the higher the level of income—the greater the volume of transactions to be carried on—the greater is the need for transaction balances. If employment is high and times are prosperous, larger money balances are needed than if employment and production are low. The second variable says that if the price level is high the transaction need for money is higher than if the price level is low.

It is convenient to show the relationship between the size of transaction balances and the level of income in diagrammatic form. This is done in Figure 15-1. The size of transaction balances lies on the vertical axis, the level of income on the horizontal axis. The diagram shows that larger transaction balances are associated with higher levels of income. In the figure $M_T$ represents the demand function for transaction balances and $Y$ represents income.[7]

In Figure 15-1, the size of the transaction balance is made proportional to the level of income (or money value of transactions) to be carried on; that is, $M_T = kY$. The factor $k$, which gives the slope of the transaction-balance demand curve, is that proportion of income to be held in transaction balances. With $k$ given, higher levels of income require larger transaction balances to be held. If velocity of spending should change, then $k$ would change (since $k = 1/V$) and so the trans-

---

[7] We shall use the symbol $Y$ to represent the money value of *current* production, or GNP. That is, in terms of $PT$, the $T$ is restricted to transactions in currently produced goods and services. Thus $Y = \text{GNP} = PT$, where $T$ is so restricted to currently produced goods and services.

action-balance demand curve would shift. For instance, if $V = 3$ then $k = 1/3$; that is, the slope of the line $kY$ is $1/3$. If velocity falls to, say, 2, then $k = 1/2$; the line $kY$ shifts, becoming steeper, which indicates larger transaction balances held at each income level than with the higher velocity. This means that a given money balance can finance greater total expenditures the faster it turns over, that is, the higher its velocity and so the lower $k$.

## The Precautionary Motive

The second reason for holding money balances is the *precautionary motive*. This motive says that some money may be held to provide for unexpected contingencies—events such as illness, loss of a job, a bargain too good to pass up, or similar situations. It should be noted that these conditions are impossible to predict—the balance is held to provide against unforeseen contingencies. Thus, when uncertainty is present people tend to hold money balances to act as a buffer against unplanned contingencies.

## The Speculative Motive

Like the precautionary motive, the *speculative motive* is hinged upon uncertainty. The speculative demand for money balances is tied to the expected, though by no means certain, changes in the general price level. For example, if prices in general are expected to fall then it is advantageous to individuals to hold large money balances rather than physical assets, whose values are expected to fall in money terms. Conversely, if a price rise is anticipated one decreases money balances and holds goods and securities, whose money values are rising. The choice is one between holding assets with a variety of degrees of liquidity and the holding of money, the asset of "perfect" liquidity—that is, spendability.

Ordinarily we might expect that one would be unwilling to hold cash balances when interest could be earned by lending out the funds. But as an offset to the advantage of interest earning assets there are two disadvantages: (1) Interest earning assets are not as liquid as money. (2) The value of many interest earning assets is not fixed except at the redemption date; thus, if the owner is forced to sell them prior to maturity there exists the possibility of incurring a capital loss. These aspects are related to the rate of interest.

Assume that we buy some type of debt instrument at par; that, for example, we pay $1,000 for a government bond paying 3 per cent

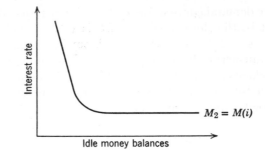

*Figure 15-2* Speculative demand for idle money balances.

annual interest. This means we receive $30 annually in interest payments. Now assume that the going market rate of interest increases to 4 per cent. If, after the rate of interest rises to 4 per cent, we are faced with the necessity of selling our bond no one will pay $1,000 for it. Why should they? Their $1,000 can now purchase an annual interest income of $40. Therefore, in order for us to sell the bond we must offer it at less than $1,000, namely, at a price that would make the annual $30 interest exactly 4 per cent of the purchase price. For a perpetuity bond, the price would become $750 (4 per cent of $750 is $30). Thus, we incur a capital loss. Note that the interest rate and market price move in *opposite* directions.

Now let us consider two extreme situations, one in which the interest rate is quite high and another in which the interest rate is quite low. In the first instance, the most probable change in the rate of interest is downward. In this situation we would keep cash balances at a minimum because (1) we are receiving a high current return, and (2) if the rate of interest does fall we can make a capital gain by selling interest earning assets. But if the interest rate is at a low level, the most probable change in the rate is upward. In this case we would add to our money balances because (1) the low rate of return might not, or only just, cover our transactions charges, and (2) if the interest rate does rise and we are forced to liquidate we could incur capital losses which might easily wipe out the small return received for many previous periods. As a consequence, we may depict the speculative motive as being a function of the rate of interest. With a high interest rate speculative balances are minimal; with a low rate of interest the demand for speculative balances may become insatiable.

The general shape of the speculative demand function for money balances, $M_2$, is depicted in Figure 15-2. The interest rate lies on the vertical axis, the demand curve for speculative balances is represented by $M_2$, and money balances are measured on the horizontal axis.

### The Liquidity Preference Function

The three basic motives for holding money balances, the transactions motive, the precautionary motive, and the speculative motive, can be usefully combined into a single demand function for money balances. This function is called the *liquidity preference* function.

This liquidity preference function can be considered as composed of two basic demands for money balances: a demand for money balances held for known spending requirements is clearly an active demand for money balances. The precautionary demand, on the other hand, is for possible but presently unforeseen expenditures. It is customary to lump the transactions demand for money balances and the precautionary demand for money balances into the so-called *active demand* for money balances. This active demand for money is often denoted by the symbol $M_1$. The demand for active balances can thus be depicted as in Figure 15-3, which is similar to Figure 15-1. Now instead of including only transaction balances as a function of the level of income, both transaction and precautionary balances are included. This is the demand for money balances for expenditures—the demand for money as a medium of exchange.

The demand for idle balances is the speculative demand for money balances. It is a function of the rate of interest. This demand for idle money balances is denoted by $M_2$. This demand for idle money balances is the demand for money as a store of value.

The liquidity preference function may now be derived by adding the active demand to the idle demand for money balances. Since $M_1$, the active demand for money balances is assumed to depend on $k$ and the

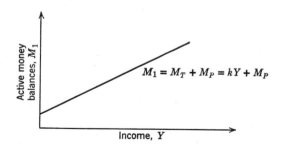

**Figure 15-3** The demand for active money balances.

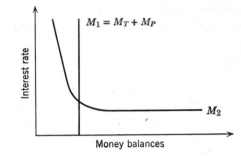

*Figure 15-4*  The demands for money balances for given income level.

level of income, and not on the rate of interest, it can be drawn as in
Figure 15-4.  That is, for some given level of income, $M_1$, the sum of
transaction balances demanded at that level of income plus the precautionary balances demanded, is independent of the interest rate.
This is shown by drawing $M_1$ as a vertical line at the appropriately
sized money balance.

The demand for idle balances, a function of the rate of interest,
can now be added to $M_1$.  The result of adding $M_1$ plus $M_2$ is the
liquidity preference function, which is simply the demand schedule for
money balances.  It shows the money balances demanded at various
rates of interest.  This liquidity preference function is shown in Figure
15-5 as $M_D$.

### The Price of Liquidity

Having determined the demand for money balances, the liquidity
preference function, we can find the "price" of money, namely, the

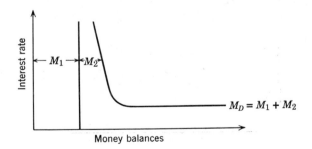

*Figure 15-5*  The liquidity preference function, or demand for money balances.

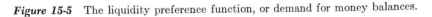

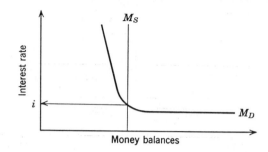

**Figure 15-6**  Determination of the "price" of liquidity.

market rate of interest, if we now introduce the supply of money into the analysis.  Thus, in Figure 15-6, we introduce the existing supply of money available to be held.  This money supply is denoted by $M_S$. The *price of liquidity*, the interest rate paid for giving up liquidity, is determined by the intersection of $M_D$, the demand schedule for money balances, and the supply of money, $M_S$.  The interest rate thus obtained is the rate that equates money balances demanded to the available money supply.

Anticipating results to come later, it is evident that of all the factors involved in the supply of and demand for money balances, only the money supply is subject to manipulation by the monetary authorities. Thus, for example, if the Federal Reserve is engaged in a policy of monetary ease the interest rate falls, since the actions of the Federal Reserve will increase the money supply.  It will be recalled that to bring about a climate of easy money, the Federal Reserve will engage in open-market purchasing operations, reduce the discount rate, and perhaps lower reserve ratio requirements.

## MONEY-MARKET EQUILIBRIUM

At this juncture it is desirable to connect the level of income and the rate of interest.  It will be recalled that the demand for active balances—that is, the demand for transaction and precautionary balances—or *for money as a means of exchange*, was assumed to be independent of the rate of interest and to depend, rather, on the level of income.  On the other hand, the demand for idle balances, the speculative motive—or *for money as a store of value*, was assumed to depend on the rate of interest.  At high interest rates minimal idle balances are demanded.  As the interest falls, larger idle balances may be held.

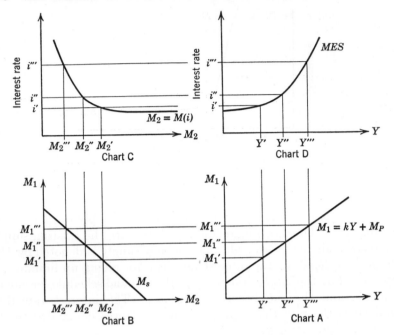

*Figure 15-7*   The determination of the money equilibrium schedule.

At quite low rates of interest the balances demanded for idle purposes may become infinitely large.

The demand for money balances thus depends on both the level of income and the rate of interest. What we wish to do is to determine the relationship between these two variables when there exists an equilibrium in the money market—that is, when the money supply is equal to the demand for money balances. In order to determine the relationship between the level of income and the rate of interest, consider the following set of charts, Figure 15-7.

Chart A depicts the familiar demand for *active* balances, which, according to our assumptions, depends on the level of income, given the value of $k$.

The available money supply is shown in Chart B. This money stock $M_S$ may be held entirely in active balances, entirely in idle balances, or be split between the two. The vertical axis measures the amount of money held in active balances. If the entire money supply were held in active balances this would be at $M_1 = M_S$. Similarly, if the entire money stock were held idle this would be at $M_2 = M_S$.

The line joining the two extreme situations shows how the money supply can be divided between the two competing demands.

Chart C is the demand curve for *idle* funds.  According to our assumptions, this speculative demand for money balances is a function of the interest rate.  At high rates of interest idle balances demanded are negligible, with increasingly larger idle balances demanded as the interest rate becomes progressively lower until, at some minimum interest rate, the demand for idle balances may become perfectly elastic.

Chart D summarizes the results of the Charts A, B, and C.  That is, the schedule labeled MES in Chart D is the *money equilibrium schedule* which relates levels of income and rates of interest when the money market is in equilibrium.

To derive the money equilibrium schedule we proceed as follows. We take as given the two demand schedules for money balances; that is, $M_1 = kY$ and $M_2 = M(i)$.  Also given is the supply of money, $M_S$. Now in Chart A pick some level of income, say, income $Y'$.  This level of income requires, according to the transactions demand schedule, active money balances in the amount $M_1'$.

If we transfer the required active money balance just determined to Chart B, we see that after deducting $M_1'$ from the money supply $M_S$ there is left the amount $M_2'$ for holding in idle balances.  Feeding this amount of funds available to be held idle into Chart C, we find that given the demand schedule for idle balances the interest rate equating the amount of idle balances to the demand for them is rate $i'$.  Thus, we started with an income level $Y'$ and now have interest rate $i'$ associated with it when the supply and demand for money balance are equated.  Chart D contains a plot of the initial income level $Y'$ and the rate of interest associated with it, $i'$.

Repeating the process for income levels $Y''$, $Y'''$, etc., and finding the associated rates of interest enables us to plot additional points of the money equilibrium schedule.  The MES so derived holds only for the *given* supply of money and demands for money balances: let any of these change and the MES shifts.

This raises the interesting question of which, if any, of the determinants of the MES are subject to manipulation by the monetary authority.  That is, to what extent can the monetary authority shift the position of the MES?  If we assume the demands for money balances are given, then only the money supply is left as a policy variable. This money supply is subject to a substantial degree of control by the monetary authorities.  By manipulating bank reserve positions through open market operations, discount rate changes, or reserve ratio changes, the central bank can increase or decrease the money supply, $M_S$. The student should work through the effects of increases and decreases in $M_S$, showing that the MES shifts to the right (increases) in the case of an increase in the money supply, and falls in the case of a contraction in the money supply.

On the other hand, a tight money policy may force individuals to economize on their money balances, which is to say that velocity is likely to rise in a period of tight credit conditions. That is, active balances are turned over faster, which is reflected by a fall in $k$; if $V$ rises from 2 to 3, then $k$ falls from 1/2 to 1/3. The demand schedule for transaction balances, for active balances, shifts to the right. Increases in velocity thus give rise to a shift to the right (an increase) in the MES. This means that even with a constant money supply, the *effective* money supply increases if the rate of spending increases. Thus, if the central bank is trying to hold constant or contract the money supply, a rise in velocity can possibly negate, or nullify to a large extent, the efforts of the monetary authority. We shall return to this consideration in our discussion of monetary policy.

## REVIEW QUESTIONS

1. In what sense are theories like road maps; why is this necessary?
2. Discuss the reasons why a firm grasp of economic theory is desirable.
3. How did the classical monetary theorists look at money?
4. Write an essay on the determinants of $M$, $V$, $P$, and $T$.
5. Write an essay on the factor $k$ in the cash-balance equation. What is its relation to $V$?
6. Discuss the motives for acquiring money balances.
7. What is the liquidity preference function?
8. Trace out the effects on the money equilibrium schedule of: (a) an increase in the money supply; (b) an increase in the demand for idle balances; (c) a fall in velocity (i.e., a rise in $k$).

## SUGGESTED REFERENCES

Dernburg, Thomas F. and D. M. McDougall, *Macro-economics*, 2nd ed. (New York: McGraw-Hill Book Company, 1963).

Fisher, Irving, *The Purchasing Power of Money*, rev. ed. (New York: Macmillan Co., 1926).

Robertson, Dennis H., *Money* (New York: Harcourt Brace, 1929).

CHAPTER *16*

# *The Income-Expenditure Theory*

Money balances are demanded, as we have learned, because of money's importance as both a medium of exchange and as a store of value. When money is a means of exchange, the money balances are needed in order to be spent. Thus, transaction balances, the *active* money balances, are expended on the nation's output of goods and services. These expenditures on final output equal gross national product. Further, they can be broken into the major categories of consumer spending, investment spending (including inventories), and government spending on goods and services.

The present chapter examines the determinants of consumption spending and investment spending. Government expenditures will be taken as given, and no attempt will be made here to explain them. The chapter, then, is a logical extension of the preceding material. We are now seeking to pinpoint the factors upon which decisions to spend for consumption and investment purposes are based. That is, we propose to analyze the factors that largely determine the level and composition of GNP.

The income-expenditure model may also be expressed in the form of equations. The equations basic to this formulation are $Y = C + I + G$ and $Y = C + S + T$. In these equations $Y$ represents income (output), $C$ is consumption, $I$ is investment, $G$ is expenditures by government, $T$ is taxes, and $S$ stands for saving. More precisely $Y$, $C$, $I$, and $G$ are expenditure streams. Income is the sum of expenditures on output, which is composed of consumer goods, investment goods, and the goods and services purchased by government. Hence, the equation $Y = C + I + G$ states the *sources* of income from consumption expenditures plus investment expenditures plus government expenditures. The equation $Y = C + S + T$ gives the *uses* of income: one may spend income for consumption purposes, save it, and pay taxes with it. It follows that in any given period $S + T = I + G$.

These equations $Y = C + I + G$, $Y = C + S + T$, and $S + T = I + G$ are subject to two interpretations. They may be considered as accounting identities, true by definition, or they may be considered as equilibrium formulations. In the first case $C$ and $S$ may be defined as actual consumption and saving. In the second case, the equilibrium situation, they represent the amounts the community would, in equilibrium, consume and save.

We shall now turn to the various components of the income-expenditure model and their determination.

## CONSUMPTION AND SAVING

The first task is to analyze the factors underlying expenditures on consumption. To help start the analysis let us formulate the propensity to consume, or the *consumption function*. This is a schedule relationship which relates levels of consumption to levels of income; specifically, $C$ is the consumption out of a given income $Y$, hence $C = f(Y)$ which may be read as "consumption depends on income."

In formulating the consumption function we shall assume that the principal determinant of consumption is income. But though income is considered as the most important single factor determining the level of consumption expenditures there are recognized, nevertheless, a number of other factors which influence it. These other factors may be divided into two categories, (1) objective factors, and (2) subjective factors. It is these factors, in addition to income, which determine the shape and position of the consumption function. That is, these factors determine how high the consumption function lies and how steeply it rises. A typical consumption function is shown in Figure 16-1. The vertical axis measures consumption, and the horizontal axis the level of income. The consumption function discloses that at a level of income $Y_1$ the amount $C_1$ is consumed, at a level of income $Y_2$ the amount $C_2$ is consumed, and so forth.

It may be argued that the consumption function is relatively stable, and that this stability is due to subjective factors. Among these subjective factors are the community attitudes toward spending or saving, institutional aspects such as corporate views on dividend distribution, etc., and social institutions such as the distribution of income. These

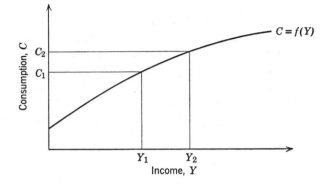

**Figure 16-1** The consumption function.

are factors which change, but change rather slowly.   Hence, the conclusion that short-run changes in consumption are due to changes in
income and not to shifts in the consumption function itself.   Any shifts
in the consumption function are the result of changes in the objective
factors.   Among the objective factors we may mention the following:
(1) windfall gains or losses; (2) changes in government fiscal policy;
(3) changes in expectations; and (4) changes in the rate of interest.

It is the subjective factors, those slow to change, which determine
the basic shape and position of the consumption function.   They are
the factors whose interaction determines the amount of consumption
out of any given income.   This determines how high the function lies.
These same subjective factors also tell us how the amount of consumption spending changes as income changes.   This change in consumption spending with respect to changes in income determines the
slope of the consumption function.

Changes in the objective factors may cause a shift in the position
of the consumption.   This means at each level of income a different
amount of consumption spending is generated.   Hence, the shape and
position of the consumption function is altered due to changes in the
objective factors.

Before further study of the shape and position of the propensity to
consume, let us consider some of the factors which, in addition to
income, influence consumption spending.

## Stocks of Goods

It seems reasonable that the larger the stock of consumer durables,
the lower is the consumer function.   At the close of the Second World

War the nation had virtually depleted its stock of consumer durables. As a consequence of this, the great demand for consumer durables certainly pushed up the consumption function. One simple way of handling this notion is to assume that the level of purchases of these items is dependent on the stock of consumer durables, but that the rate of purchases is determined by income. Thus, a depleted stock of consumer durables would tend to make spending on these items larger than it would otherwise be, and thus the consumption function rises.

### Monetary Assets

By the term *monetary asset* we mean stocks of money, of course, but also *near moneys* such as time deposits, savings accounts, bonds, mortgages, etc., of varying degrees of liquidity. The possession of such fixed value monetary assets increases one's willingness to spend current income. This raises the consumption function higher than it would be in the absence of these assets. One consequence of having a stock of monetary assets is that their purchasing power changes when the price level changes. The consumer must constantly evaluate his asset holdings in terms of the price level, that is, in terms of their purchasing power. Generally, then, we would expect a fall in the price level to result in a higher level of consumption given the income level, since the monetary assets have increased in value (purchasing power).

### Distribution of Income

One does not have to be a student of economics to know that the distribution of income is far from equal. But of what significance is this to our study? Simply this: if income were more evenly distributed the consumption function would likely be higher. It would also probably be somewhat steeper, but probably not significantly so. Thus, if income were more evenly distributed, the level of consumption would probably be higher at each level of income. The distribution of income changes only slowly, so this factor contributes to the stability, as well as the shape and position, of the consumption function.

### Tastes and Habits

Although tastes and habits undoubtedly influence consumption, their incorporation into the consumption function is difficult. Several interesting attempts at this have been made, however, in the derivation of statistical consumption functions. One way has been to use an average of the last several preceding years' income as well as current income. Another method suggests using the highest income previously attained. If either of these formulations is used, consumption is made a function of income in an earlier period as well as a function of current income. The assumption is that people adjust to a standard of living and will resist forces that would tend to lower their consumption standards.

These considerations are factors that determine the shape and position of the consumption function. There are two special terms used to describe the shape and position of the propensity to consume, or the consumption function. These terms are marginal propensity to consume and average propensity to consume.

### The Consumption Function

The *marginal propensity to consume* is the ratio between changes in consumption and changes in income, and expresses the percentage change in income that would be spent on consumption. The value of the marginal propensity to consume is a fraction between zero and one, for at the extremes one may spend none of the change in income for consumption purposes up to a maximum of spending all the change in income on consumption. Hence $0 < (\Delta C / \Delta Y) < 1$, where $\Delta C$ stands for the change in consumption and $\Delta Y$ represents the change in income. The changes in consumption and changes in income move together in the same direction. If income increases consumption increases also, but by not as much; and if income declines so does consumption, but by a lesser amount. Thus the ratio $\Delta C / \Delta Y$, the marginal propensity to consume, is a positive number between zero and one. The marginal propensity to consume, by telling how consumption changes as income changes, yields information about the shape of the consumption function. It seems reasonable to assume that as income reaches higher levels, the consumption function tends to flatten out, that is, the marginal propensity to consume becomes smaller.

The second term, the *average propensity to consume*, is the ratio between consumption spending and income at any given level of income. Thus, the average propensity to consume is given as $C/Y$. This concept obviously tells how high the consumption function is.

These two concepts are illustrated in Figure 16-2, where a typical consumption function is depicted. The marginal propensity to consume is $(\Delta C / \Delta Y) = (C_2 - C_1)/(Y_2 - Y_1)$, that is, the percentage of the increase of income spent on consumption as income increases from $Y_1$ to $Y_2$. The average propensity to consume is at income level $Y_1$ given as $C_1/Y_1$; at income level $Y_2$ it is $C_2/Y_2$.

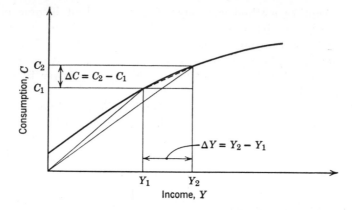

***Figure 16-2***   The marginal and average propensities to consume.

Though the consumption function as shown in Figure 16-2 probably gives a more realistic picture, we shall draw our consumption functions as though they were linear. That is, we shall draw them as straight lines, as in Figure 16-3. This means that the marginal propensity to consume will be constant, but we shall have a declining value for the average propensity to consume. This is illustrated in Figure 16-3 where the consumption function has the form $C = a + bY$. That is, $a$ is the basic level of consumption even when income is zero. The term $b$ is the marginal propensity to consume, and indicates how consumption changes as income changes. As a case in point, assume the following values for $a$ and $b$: $a = 50$ and $b = 2/3$. Thus: $C = a + bY = 50 + 2/3Y$.

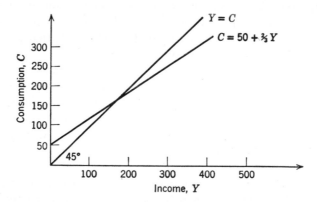

***Figure 16-3***   The consumption function, $C = 50 + 2/3Y$.

For the following values of $Y$ the corresponding values of $C$, $\Delta C / \Delta Y$, and $C/Y$ are:

**TABLE 16-1**

| Income: $Y$ | Consumption: $C$ | Average Propensity to Consume: $C/Y$ | Marginal Propensity to Consume: $\Delta C / \Delta Y$ |
|---|---|---|---|
| 0 | 50 | | |
| 60 | 90 | $90/60 = 1.50$ | $40/60 = 2/3$ |
| 120 | 130 | $130/120 = 1.08$ | $40/60 = 2/3$ |
| 180 | 170 | $170/180 = .94$ | $40/60 = 2/3$ |
| 240 | 210 | $210/240 = .88$ | $40/60 = 2/3$ |
| 300 | 250 | $250/300 = .83$ | $40/60 = 2/3$ |
| 360 | 290 | $290/360 = .81$ | $40/60 = 2/3$ |

This illustrates the proposition that although the marginal propensity to consume is constant, $\Delta C / \Delta Y = 2/3$, the average propensity to consume $C/Y$ steadily declines in value as the income level increases.

The 45° line $Y = C$ in Figure 16-3 is drawn for references purposes only. Since we measure both income and consumption in dollar terms, this line represents equal values of consumption and income. That is, all income is devoted to consumption purposes. The vertical distance between the consumption function and the reference line gives the amounts that people wish to save at various levels of income, since saving is defined as not consuming income. At low levels of income savings may be negative, that is, the consumption function may lie above the reference line.

It follows from the discussion of the consumption function that we could formulate a similar concept, *the savings function*. Indeed, since the consumption function deals with the spending of income for consumption purposes it simultaneously deals with not spending for consumption purposes, which by definition is saving. Thus, the same factors that influence consumption also determine saving, and everything said about the consumption function essentially carries over to the saving function. Therefore, we may define the marginal propensity to save and the average propensity to save. The marginal propensity to save is the ratio of the change in saving to the change in income. The marginal propensity to save, $\Delta S / \Delta Y$, has a value between zero and one. The average propensity to save is defined as the ratio of saving to income. If the marginal and average propensities to consume decline as higher levels of income are reached, the marginal and average propensities to save increase. If the marginal

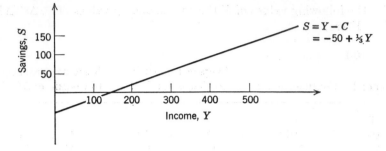

*Figure 16-4*   The savings function, $S = -50 + \frac{1}{3}Y$.

propensity to consume is a constant value so is the marginal propensity to save.   The propositions are illustrated in Figure 16-4.

The amounts that people wish to consume or save may be regarded as basically determined by the level of income.   Further, these relationships may be considered as stable and not subject to violent fluctuation.   We have seen, however, that changes in the objective factors may give rise to shifts in the consumption and savings functions.   A basic assumption is that both the marginal propensity to consume and the marginal propensity to save have a value between zero and unity.   That is, as income changes both consumption and saving change in the same direction, but neither alone by the full amount of the change in income.   The change in income is distributed between a change in consumption and a change in saving.

## THE DETERMINATION OF THE LEVEL OF INCOME

In order to illustrate the process of income determination we shall consider two basic models.   The first will ignore the government sector, but the second will include it.

We defined income in a "sources of income" sense as the sum of expenditures for consumer goods, investment goods, and government expenditures on goods and services; that is, $Y = C + I + G$.   For convenience let us consider $G$, government expenditures, as *public* investment, and lump together private and public investment expenditures, calling them $I$.   Thus, the expenditure definition of income becomes $Y = C + I$.   Correspondingly, in the "uses of income" definition of income as $Y = C + S + T$, let us lump voluntary saving (nonconsumption of income) $S$ with taxes $T$, a form of "forced" saving, calling these consolidated withdrawals from the income stream $S$.   Now the uses definition of income becomes $Y = C + S$.

Thus, we have defined income as the sum of expenditures for consumption and investment purposes. And output—real income—is composed of consumer and investment goods. Assuming for the present that the level of investment expenditures is given, the levels of income and consumption are established by the interaction of investment with the consumption function. This is not merely a matter of adding investment expenditures and consumption spending together, since we do not know the level of consumption spending—because we don't know the level of income. But with a known level of investment expenditures and a given consumption function, we can simultaneously determine the levels of income and consumption.

The actual rates of saving and investment must be equal in an accounting sense, since $Y = C + I$ and $Y = C + S$; that is, $S = I$. But for equilibrium the level of income must be such that people *wish to save* as much as people *wish to invest*—that is, planned saving equals planned investment. If we take as our consumption function the expression $C = 50 + 2/3Y$ and assume investment as $I = 50$, what is the equilibrium level of income?

Plotting the consumption function and the investment schedule in Figure 16-5 and then adding the investment schedule and consumption function to obtain $C + I$, we see that the schedule $C + I$ and $Y = Y$ intersect. What does this mean?

We may call $C + I$ the *aggregate demand* function, since it shows

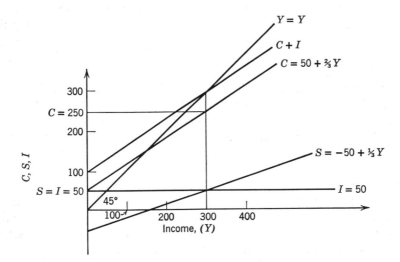

**Figure 16-5**  The determination of the level of income.

how much is spent for consumers goods and investment goods at each income level. And the line $Y = Y$ may be interpreted as *aggregate supply*, in the sense that it shows total output available. The intersection of the supply and demand relations establishes the equilibrium level of income—the income level at which the output supplied equals the output demanded—and an income level at which the amount people wish to save is exactly equal to the amount they wish to invest.

From the consumption data of Table 16-1 together with the assumed investment spending of 50 units we see from Table 16-2 that planned or desired saving equals planned investment at the equilibrium income of 300.

**TABLE 16-2**

| Income (Y) | Consumption (C = 50 + 2/3Y) | Savings (S = Y − C = −50 + 1/3Y) | | Investment (I) |
|---|---|---|---|---|
| 0 | 50 | −50 | | 50 |
| 60 | 90 | −30 | | 50 |
| 120 | 130 | −10 | | 50 |
| 180 | 170 | 10 | | 50 |
| 240 | 210 | 30 | | 50 |
| 300 | 250 | 50 | ← S = I → | 50 |
| 360 | 290 | 70 | | 50 |

Only at income level $Y = 300$ do the consumption expenditures, as determined by the consumption function, plus investment expenditures total 300. Alternately, only at income $Y = 300$ does the amount being saved, as determined by the saving function, equal the amount being invested.

The graphic solution of the above arithmetic example is shown in Figure 16-5. We see that $Y = C + I$ at $Y = 300$ with $C$ of 250 and $I$ of 50; we also see that $S = I = 50$ at income $Y = 300$.

It is important to understand that the level of income generated is not necessarily a full-employment level of income. Indeed, unless the amount of investment is exactly equal to what people wish to save out of the full-employment level of income, the level of income will be something other than the full-employment level. Keynes, of course, argued that a level of income at less than full employment was the rule rather than the exception, and this is a reversal of the classical thinking.

We are now in a position to answer the question of what would happen if the level of investment expenditures were suddenly to change—say, for example, to increase. Graphically this is easily por-

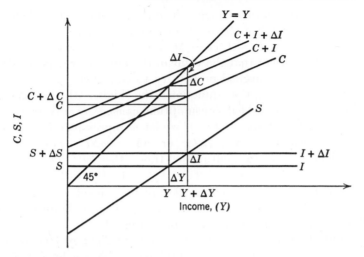

*Figure 16-6*   The change in income due to change in investment.

trayed.   Given the consumption function it simply means an increase
in the investment schedule from $I$ to $I + \Delta I$.   The vertical distance
between $C$ and $C + I$ increases to $I + \Delta I$.   This produces higher
levels of income, consumption, investment, and saving, with the latter
two being necessarily equal.   This process is shown in Figure 16-6.

As a minimum, we know that the increase in investment must
increase income by at least as much, for the increased investment
expenditures immediately generate an equal amount of income.   But
unless all of this additional income is saved—unless the marginal propensity to save equals one—some of this additional investment will
draw forth some additional consumption spending.   The amount of
this additional consumption is determined by the marginal propensity
to consume.   Thus, income will increase by more than just the amount
of the additional investment; how much more depends on the magni-
tudes of $(\Delta C)/(\Delta Y)$ and $(\Delta S)/(\Delta Y)$, the marginal propensities to consume and to save.   Income will rise until people are saving out of the
added income an amount equal to the additional investment.   Thus,
in Figure 16-6 we start from an equilibrium income $Y$ at which $S = I$.
We then increase investment expenditures to a higher level of $I + \Delta I$.
The new equilibrium income is $Y + \Delta Y$.   It is clear from the graph
the change in income $\Delta Y$ is equal to the sum of the increased investment expenditures, $\Delta I$, plus increased consumption expenditures, $\Delta C$.
That is, $\Delta Y = \Delta C + \Delta I$.

The ratio between the change in income $\Delta Y$ and the initial change in investment $\Delta I$ is called the multiplier and is given as $\Delta Y/\Delta I$. This expression $(\Delta Y)/(\Delta I) = 1/(1 - \Delta C/\Delta Y) = 1/(\Delta S/\Delta Y)$. From this formulation it is clear that the value of the multiplier depends directly on the size of the marginal propensity to consume. This means the steeper the consumption function (the higher the $\Delta C/\Delta Y$), the greater will be the added consumption caused by any given increment to investment spending. If we let $m$ represent the value of the multiplier then $m = (\Delta Y)/(\Delta I)$, or $\Delta Y = m\Delta I$. This says that income increases by a multiple $m$ times the $\Delta I$. For example if $(\Delta C)/(\Delta Y) = \frac{1}{2}$ then $m = 1/(1 - \frac{1}{2}) = 1/(\frac{1}{2}) = 2$: for every \$1 of added investment spending the income level changes \$2. If $(\Delta C)/(\Delta Y) = \frac{3}{4}$ then $m = 1/(1 - \frac{3}{4}) = 1/(\frac{1}{4}) = 4$: for every \$1 of additional investment spending income rises \$4.

It should be noted that if we are to stay at the new level of income $Y + \Delta Y$, investment must be maintained at the new level of $I + \Delta I$. If investment expenditures fall back to the original level of $I$ then, with the given consumption function, the income level will fall back to $Y$. The difference between a single shot of additional investment and sustained investment may be easily shown, as in Figure 16-7. Assume $\Delta C/\Delta Y = \frac{1}{2}$ and added investment $\Delta I$. Income is on the vertical axis, time on the horizontal axis. The initial income $Y_0$ is the sum of the initial levels of consumption and investment expenditures, $C_0$ and $I_0$.

Figure 16-7A shows that the total cumulative change is $\Delta Y = \Delta I + \Delta C_1 + \Delta C_2 + \Delta C_3 + \cdots$. The income level initially rises to $Y_0 + \Delta I$, but then with diminishing consumption expenditures over time, drifts back down to the original level $Y_0$. In Figure 16-7B, however, in each time period the investment increment is repeated and the level of income climbs to, and stays at, income level $Y_0 + \Delta Y$. The $\Delta Y$ is shown as the vertical sum of all previous spending effects. If $\Delta C/\Delta Y$ were larger, say $\frac{3}{4}$, then each consumption expenditure would be $\frac{3}{4}$ of the preceding $\Delta I$ or $\Delta C$ and thus the total of $\Delta I + \Delta C$ would be larger; hence, $\Delta Y$ would be larger.

With the initial spending of $\Delta I$, income increases to $Y_0 + \Delta I$ and at this new level of income consumption is $C_0 + \Delta C_1$; but this additional consumption spending $\Delta C_1$ is someone's income and thus income rises to $Y_0 + \Delta I + \Delta C_1 + \Delta C_2$. At this higher income level still more consumption spending is forthcoming, and so the analysis goes on. Since part of each additional round of spending is saved, the process of income expansion stops when the amount of savings generated out of the additional income is exactly equal to the additional investment.

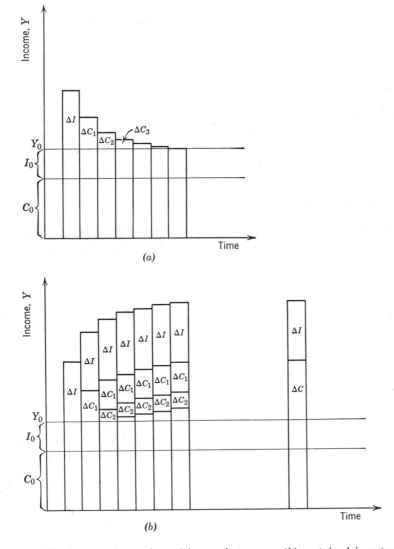

*Figure 16-7*   Income change from (a) one-shot versus (b) sustained investment spending.

Hence, if initially $S_0 = I_0$ then at $Y_0 + \Delta Y$ we have $S_0 + \Delta S = I_0 + \Delta I$, indicating an equilibrium income.

So much for the determination of the level of income, and the process of income change.   We now turn to the determination of investment spending, which until now has been assumed as given.

## THE DETERMINATION OF INVESTMENT EXPENDITURES

The determination of investment expenditures is based on the interplay of two factors. These factors are (1) the so-called marginal efficiency of capital, and (2) the rate of interest. It will be instructive to investigate the nature of each of these factors before attempting to observe how their interaction determines the volume of investment expenditures. In the preceding section we assumed investment expenditures as given. Now we shall see how investment expenditures are determined as well as the sources of changes in these expenditures.

### *The Marginal Efficiency of Capital*

The *marginal efficiency of capital* is the Keynesian counterpart of the classicists' marginal productivity of capital. The two concepts are distinct, even though they are both investment demand schedules. The important aspect of the marginal efficiency of capital (MEC) is the emphasis placed on expectations—expectations about the uncertain future. The simplest explanation of investment is profits. But these profits are not certain—they are *expected* profits.

The MEC is that rate of discount which equates *expected* net revenues of the future back to today's known costs. The net revenues $R_i$ are expected gross receipts for each of the $i$ accounting periods, less the expected variable costs (but not depreciation) for the periods involved. For example, assume a machine costing \$200 today is expected to last for two years and to yield net revenues of \$110 in the first year and of \$121 in the second year, and will be worn out and have no scrap value at the end of the two-year period. What is the MEC of this investment?

Using the familiar discounting formula we have Cost = $R_1/(1 + r) + R_2/(1 + r)^2 + \cdot \cdot \cdot + R_n/(1 + r)^n$ where $r$ is the rate of discount—the marginal efficiency of capital—which balances the two sides of the equation. In this formula given the cost and $R_1$, $R_2$, the expected net revenues, then $r$ is the MEC, the *discount rate* which equates expected revenues to known costs. Thus, in our example where Cost = \$200, $R_1$ = \$110, and $R_2$ = \$121, our problem is to find $r$, the MEC. Simple algebraic manipulation yields the answer that $r$, the MEC, is 10%. Checking this result we see that it is correct since \$200 = \$110/1.10 + \$121/1.21. In more complicated problems $r$ may have to be found by a series of approximations, but in any event it is clear that there is only one value of $r$—the MEC—which will equate \$200 now to \$110 one-year off plus \$121 two years' distant, and it is obvious $110 and $121 must be discounted since $110 plus $121 do not equal $200.

Since the MEC is a *rate* we may compare it to the interest rate. The MEC gives an expected rate of return, and the interest rate is a cost. If the MEC is greater than the rate of interest, it will pay to undertake the investment. Since there are many different investment opportunities available, the MEC for each of them may be calculated. The various individual MEC's and their associated volumes of investment opportunities may then be aggregated into the marginal efficiency of capital schedule. There are a few investment opportunities with a high rate of discount, and relatively more at successively lower rates. Graphically, if we put the rate of discount on the vertical axis and the volume of investment opportunities in the horizontal axis, the MEC schedule slopes down to the right. (There exist probably limitless opportunities where the MEC is negative, but we shall not consider these.) The MEC schedule is shown in Figure 16-8.

On this same diagram we can also add the current rate of interest, $i$. Since it is a rate, the rate of interest is also measured on the vertical axis. The intersection of the MEC schedule and the $i$ schedule determine the volume of investment to be undertaken. Investment will proceed up to the point where the MEC of the last project undertaken is just equal to the interest rate. In Figure 16-8 investment of $I^*$ will be undertaken.

This means that in the desire for profit maximization it pays to carry investment up to this point. Consider the two following cases: (1) investing with borrowed funds, and (2) investing with one's own funds. Clearly in Case 1 it pays to invest with borrowed funds if the

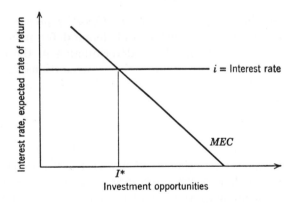

*Figure 16-8* The marginal efficiency of capital schedule.

expected rate of discount exceeds the interest rate—that is, if the MEC is greater than $i$. It will pay to borrow in order to invest until the MEC is equal to the interest rate. In Case 2, when working with one's own funds, two choices are open. One may lend out the funds or may use them oneself. So long as the MEC exceeds the interest rate, it pays to use the funds oneself. But if the rate of interest exceeds the MEC of the contemplated investment, then one is ahead by lending the funds at the going rate of interest. This means that interest is to be considered as a *cost*.

Note the emphasis placed on expectations. It is *expected* revenues which are discounted back to known costs. If for any reason whatsoever expectations change—whether due to real or imagined circumstances—the marginal efficiency of capital also changes. As a consequence, even if nothing has occurred which would alter the future revenues, but one thinks they are changed, then the MEC changes. Thus, even though there is always the use of as much objective information as possible, subjective factors may do much to alter expectations, because the future is uncertain. What seemed profitable yesterday may not seem so today even though no real factor has changed. In contrast to the stability of the consumption function, investment demand may be a rather unstable element, subject as it is to changes in expectations.

But the MEC is only one aspect in the determination of the level of investment expenditures. As we have noted, it takes both the MEC and the interest rate to determine investment spending. How is the rate of interest established?

### The Liquidity Preference Theory of Interest

The Keynesian interest-rate theory, *the liquidity preference theory of interest*, is based on the supply of and demand for money. In the preceding chapter we discussed the determinants of the demand for money balances, that is, the transactions, precautionary, and speculative motives. These we formulated into a liquidity preference function, a schedule showing the amounts of money people wish to hold at different rates of interest. It thus is a demand curve for money to hold.

In Figure 16-9 we assume that given some level of income, people wish to hold transaction balances of $M_T$ and precautionary balances of $M_P$. These balances are interest inelastic—that is, the rate of interest does not influence the size of the balances held for these purposes. The size of the speculative balances is, however, influenced

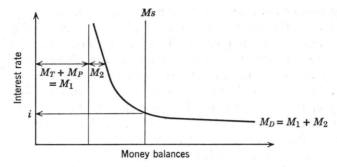

*Figure 16-9*  Liquidity preference determination of the rate of interest.

by the interest rate.  At high rates of interest these speculative balances are minimal, at lower rates they increase in size, and at extremely
low rates of interest the demand for speculative balances may be insatiable.  If we add these three demands for money to hold we get the
liquidity preference function depicted in Figure 16-9.  The supply of
money is taken as given, at any time, by the monetary authority.  In
the diagram the money supply is denoted by $M_S$; we assume the money
supply is interest inelastic.

The interaction of the money supply and the liquidity preference
schedule determines the interest rate, $i$.  Interest in this theory
becomes the price paid to forego liquidity—it is the price necessary
to induce individuals to give up a noninterest earning asset, money,
for assets which pay interest, securities of various types, but which
are not money and hence have varying degrees of liquidity.  This
determination of the interest rate is quite simple.  At any given time
there is only so much money in the system and it must be held by the
community.  Similarly at any given time there are only so many
interest earning securities in the system and they must be owned.
In equilibrium those individuals who want to hold money and those
who want to hold securities must be satisfied.  A process of swapping
one type of asset for another—money for securities and vice versa—
occurs until everyone is satisfied.  But the way the swaps take place
is for the price of the securities to change.  If a person wants to hold
money, a high rate of interest—a bargain basement price on the
security—is necessary to coax him to part with money.  Or if a
person wants to hold securities he must bid up the price on them,
thus lowering the interest rate.  The equilibrium rate of interest is
the rate that leaves everyone satisfied—those who wish to hold money

or securities, or both, are satisfied in their desires.   If anyone is not satisfied then the interest rate must adjust—the price of securities change—until, with the given stocks of money and securities, all the money is held by those who want to hold it, and all the securities are owned by those who want to own securities.

Instead of just one liquidity preference function, there is probably a family of them.   As we noted earlier, the principal determinant of the transaction balance is level of income.   A higher level of income necessitates larger balances for transaction purposes.   For every level of income we have a liquidity preference curve, which is shown in Figure 16-10.   The shift to the right of the liquidity preference functions is due to the increase in $M_1$—the transaction demand for money— as income increases from $Y_1$ to $Y_2$ to $Y_3$, etc.   Thus, any given money supply can give several rates of interest, corresponding to different levels of income.   But for any given level of income, there is only one interest rate which satisfies all individuals' liquidity preferences.   If the money supply is $M_S$, as in Figure 16-10, and the income level is $Y_2$, then the interaction of $M_{D2}$ and $M_S$ yields an interest rate of $i_2$.   But the same money supply, if income is higher at $Y_3$, produces a higher rate of interest, $i_3$, because the increase in the transaction balance demand at the higher income $Y_3$ leaves less of the money supply $M_S$ to satisfy the speculative or hoarding motive.   Thus, in order to obtain money the interest rate, the price paid for money, of necessity must rise.

This concludes our preliminary discussion of the liquidity preference theory of interest.   We shall return to it later.   For now note that it appears to be a purely monetary theory based solely on the supply and demand for money balances.

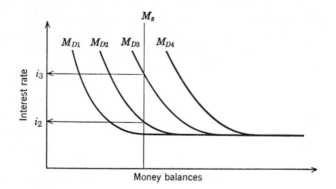

*Figure 16-10*   A family of liquidity preference functions.

## Some Additional Complications

Having defined the notions of the marginal efficiency of capital and the liquidity preference theory of interest, we now return to determination of the volume of investment. As we have seen, the level of income is determined by consumption expenditures, which are themselves dependent on income, and by investment expenditures. Further, we have seen that the equilibrium level of income is not necessarily at full-employment income.

If we assume our situation is a less than full-employment income, what can be done to remedy the situation—to achieve a full-employment level of income, or one at least closer to it? The obvious answer is to increase expenditures both for consumption and investment. Since the consumption function is a relatively stable relationship, it seems unlikely that an upward shift in it will occur.[1] The burden for attaining a higher income level consequently falls on investment.

What will lead to an increase in investment spending? First, with a given MEC schedule, a decline in the interest rate should increase investment spending and, hence, the level of income. But will a decrease in the interest rate accomplish this result? Assume the interest rate is $i_1$ and the volume of investment is $I_1$, as in Figure 16-11. This, we are assuming, generates a level of income short of full employment. If we achieve a fall in the interest rate to $i_2$ investment expenditures increase to $I_2$, which may or may not be enough to achieve full employment, but we at least get a higher income level. This result, however, depends on the MEC schedule being interest elastic.

If the MEC schedule were interest inelastic, then the fall in the interest rate at best would increase investment only slightly, or not at all. This is depicted in Figure 16-12.

But this is not all the difficulty. We assumed a fall in the rate of interest, but how was it accomplished? To show this, we postulate the liquidity preference function and money supply shown in Figure 16-13. The given money supply $M_S$ and the liquidity preference function determine the interest rate $i_1$. To lower the interest rate the monetary authority increases the money supply to $M_{S2}$, thus dropping the interest rate to $i_2$.

This is fine. The interest rate falls, and if the MEC is elastic invest-

---

[1] As incomes increase, consumption spending will increase also, but this is a movement *along*—not a shift of—the consumption function.

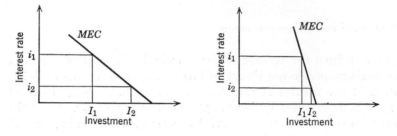

**Figure 16-11** Elastic MEC schedule. **Figure 16-12** Inelastic MEC schedule.

ment spending increases. But if the MEC schedule is inelastic, even though the monetary measures succeed in lowering the interest rate, investment fails to increase. Moreover, even if the MEC schedule is elastic and investment does increase with a drop in the interest rate, there is a lower limit to how far the interest rate can fall. The monetary authority by increasing the money supply to $M_{S3}$ can lower the interest to $i_3$, but no lower. This is the *liquidity trap* zone. The interest rate is now so low that most people prefer to absorb unlimited amounts of idle money balances in preference to risking a capital loss by buying securities. This, then, poses a further difficulty. If the interest $i_3$ is not low enough to induce sufficient investment spending to bring about full employment, then further monetary measures fail, because we cannot force the interest rate any lower.

These two difficulties, the possibilities of an inelastic MEC schedule and of a perfectly elastic liquidity preference function, either singly or together, led Keynes to advocate certain fiscal measures which pro-

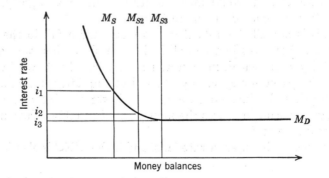

**Figure 16-13** The "liquidity trap."

voked a stir of controversy; namely, the advocacy of public expenditures if private expenditures on consumption and investment were insufficient to generate a full-employment level of income.

## THE INCOME MODEL INCLUDING GOVERNMENT

Beginning in the 1940s, the world began to take for granted the notion that one of government's key functions is to promote high levels of employment and income. In the United States, for example, this was defined as national policy in the so-called Employment Act of 1946.

The introduction of the public, or government, sector into the income model adds a term to both the source and use definitions of income. To the sources of income definition we now include as expenditures on consumption goods and investment goods, expenditures by the government sector; thus, income may be defined as the sum of expenditures on final output and services, and is given as $Y = C + I + G$.

By the same token, the inclusion of the government sector adds a new use for income, that of using income to pay taxes. The use definition of income becomes $Y = C + S + T$. In this formulation with the government sector included, the equilibrium condition now becomes $S + T = I + G$. That is, withdrawals or leakages from the income stream in the form of saving and taxes must be offset by additions to the income stream as investment expenditures and government expenditures. The equilibrium relation that $S + T = I + G$ can be reformulated as $S = I + (G - T)$, where the term $(G - T)$ is the government surplus or deficit. If government expenditures exceed government tax receipts, then $(G - T)$ is positive and a government deficit is an expansive factor in income determination, since it is a net addition to the income stream. On the other hand, if taxes exceed government expenditures, then $(G - T)$ is negative and a government surplus is a contractive factor, since it constitutes a net withdrawal of funds from the income circuit.

### The Effect of Taxes

Once taxes are introduced into the model so is the concept of disposable income. Disposable income is income after taxes, the income out of which consumption and saving take place.

The original formulation of the consumption function had consumption depending on income. The effect of introducing taxes is to shift the original consumption function downward. Thus, at each income level, with taxes present, there is less consumption than otherwise.

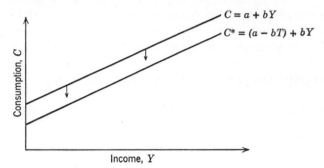

**Figure 16-14**   Tax induced shift in consumption function.

This downward shift of the consumption function is shown in Figure 16-14. If the original consumption function is expressed by $C = a + bY$, then if consumption takes place out of disposable income the new consumption function becomes $C^* = a + b(Y - T) = (a - bT) + bY$. The function shifts down but not by the entire amount of the tax, but only by a fraction of the tax, namely $bT$. At each income level consumption declines in an amount given by the marginal propensity to consume (that is, $b$) times the tax.

If the introduction of taxes causes the consumption function to shift, then by the same token the propensity to save or saving function must also shift.   The saving function prior to taxes is $S = a + (1 - b)Y$, but after taxes are introduced and saving becomes a function of disposable income the new propensity to save function becomes $S^* = a + (1 - b)(Y - T) = a - (1 - b)T + (1 - b)Y$.   That is to say, the saving schedule has shifted downward by $(1 - b)T$, or an amount equal to the marginal propensity to save (that is, $1 - b$) times taxes.   The shift downward in the saving function with the introduction of taxes is shown in Figure 16-15.

It will be recalled that in the simple model of income determination, equilibrium income was attained when the level of income reached the point at which saving equalled investment.   This was shown in Figure 16-5 as occurring at the income level where the saving schedule intersected the investment schedule that is, where $S = I$.   In this new formulation, including government expenditures and tax withdrawals, the equilibrium condition becomes $S + T = I + G$.

The new equilibrium conditions can be presented graphically in a manner similar to Figure 16-5.   Let us redraw the original saving schedule $S$ and the new after-tax saving schedule $S^*$.   The schedule

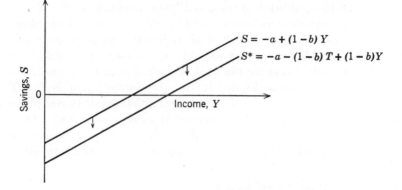

**Figure 16-15** Tax induced shift in savings function.

showing *total withdrawals* from the income circuit is now $S^* + T$; that is, the new shifted saving schedule *plus* taxes. The withdrawal schedule $S^* + T$ lies above the original propensity to save function. The introduction of taxes shifted the saving function down by $(1 - b)T$; that is, at each income level we save less than previously in an amount equal to the marginal propensity to save times the tax. Since the marginal propensity to save is less than one, saving at each income level falls by less than the tax. But then the *full* amount of the tax is added to the new saving schedule $S^*$, so the aggregate withdrawal schedule $S^* + T$ *lies above* the original propensity to save function. The schedule showing additions to the income stream is $I + G$. Thus,

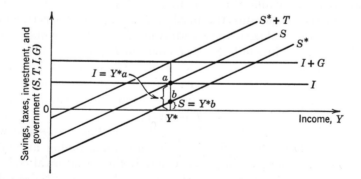

**Figure 16-16** Determination of income level with government and taxes.

in Figure 16-16 equilibrium income is $Y^*$, the income level at which saving plus taxes equals investment spending plus government spending.

It is of interest to note that desired investment plus government spending equals desired saving plus taxes, but no longer does planned or desired investment equal planned or desired saving for equilibrium. This is clearly shown in Figure 16-16, where investment is $I = Y^*a$ greater than desired saving of $Y^*b$. The difference between planned saving and investment is the government surplus or deficit. Only if the government has a balanced budget (that is, $G = T$) will desired saving necessarily equal planned investment for an equilibrium income.

### The Product-Market Equilibrium

In the previous chapter we derived the money equilibrium schedule, or MES. This MES is a schedule relating the rate of interest to levels of income when the supply of and the demand for money balances are in equilibrium. In similar fashion we shall now derive the *goods equilibrium schedule*, or GES. The GES relates the rate of interest to levels of income when the product market is in equilibrium; that is, when $S^* + T = I + G$.

The procedure for deriving the GES is simple and proceeds as follows. Given the marginal efficiency of capital schedule or MEC, assume some interest rate $i_1$. The interaction of this interest rate with the MEC schedule determines investment expenditures of $I_1$. If we assume the level of government expenditures $G$ as given, then we may add $G$ to the MEC schedule to get MEC $+ G$ which tells us total *investment* spending, private plus public, forthcoming at various rates of interest. Thus in Chart A of Figure 16-17, we see that, for interest rate $i_1$, investment and government expenditures total $I_1 + G$.

Chart B is the equilibrium condition: $S^* + T = I + G$. On the horizontal axis we measure the total of $I + G$. On the vertical axis we measure the leakages or withdrawals from the income circuit, $S^* + T$. The 45° line puts $S^* + T$ equal to $I + G$.

Having chosen interest rate $i_1$, we find in Chart A that investment plus government spending is $I_1 + G$. We now put $I_1 + G$ into Chart B to determine the amount of leakage from the income stream. Thus we find $I_1 + G = S_1^* + T$, where $T$ is given.

Chart C is the $S^* + T$ function. This schedule shows the withdrawals from the income circuit which are forthcoming at various income levels. Thus, taking from Chart B the withdrawal $S_1^* + T$ (which equals $I_1 + G$), we find that this volume of withdrawals is generated at income level $Y_1$.

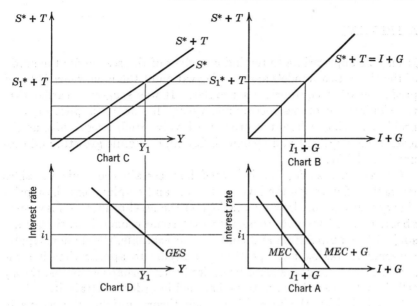

*Figure 16-17*  The determination of the goods equilibrium schedule (GES).

In Chart D these steps are summarized.   The initial interest rate $i_1$ is plotted together with its associated equilibrium income, $Y_1$. Repeating the process for various interest rates, we obtain the associated equilibrium income levels.   The locus of these points traces out the GES.   Thus, given the marginal efficiency of capital schedule, the propensity to save, the level of government expenditures, and taxes, we have found the equilibrium level of income associated with any rate of interest.

If any of the given factors change, then a new GES is produced. For example, if the MEC schedule shifts to the right, or if government expenditures increase, or both, the GES shifts to the right, also. That is, at each interest rate the associated income level is higher. Similarly if taxes are lowered, $S^* + T$ falls and the GES increases.   On the other hand, declines in investment and government spending or increased taxes lead to a fall, a shift to the left, in the GES.   The student should work these changes through for himself.

One further observation may be in order.   Nothing has been said about balancing government expenditures against taxes.   Government expenditures may equal, exceed, or fall short of tax revenues. Clearly alterations in these magnitudes provide a means for implementing economic policy.

## A PREVIEW

It may be appropriate to remind ourselves of the reason for the study of the theoretical models and the derivation of the money-market and product-market equilibrium schedules. It was suggested earlier that the significance of macroeconomic theory lies in its applicability to problem solving, where the problems involve such magnitudes as the level of employment and income, inflation, economic growth, and economic stability.

Our analysis so far has indicated how certain economic variables interact to determine the level of income and employment, how price changes may occur, how fluctuations in the level of income may come about, etc. If we now remember that some economic variables are subject to manipulation and control—for example, the money supply, government taxing and spending—it begins to appear that if some specific economic goal should be desired then perhaps economic theory tells how the variables are to be handled in order to attain it.

This is indeed the case. Economic theory unfolds the *means* to employ to attain the desired *end*. Economic policy must rest upon a firm theoretical foundation. Policy sets forth the desired goals; theory indicates which variables and what kind of action will yield it.

In a later chapter we shall consider the topic of economic policy. At that time we shall review the basic considerations of the macroeconomic theory just developed. But the *use* to which we shall put theory is the prime concern: theory is a tool to be used in the attempt to achieve and maintain the desired economic goal. It suggests the means to gain the end.

## REVIEW QUESTIONS

1. Write an essay on the factors that determine the shape, position, and stability of the consumption function.
2. What is the marginal efficiency of capital? Upon what factors is it based?
3. If a capital asset costs $3,000, is expected to last three years, has no scrap value, and is expected to yield net revenues of $1,100, $1,210, and $1,331 for the first, second, and third years respectively, what is the marginal efficiency of capital for this particular capital asset.
4. What is the multiplier? Why does the multiplier stop multiplying, that is, why is the multiplier of finite value?
5. Trace through the process of income determination in the simple expenditure model. What is the equilibrium condition?

6. Now include government in the model and trace the process of income determination. When is an equilibrium income level achieved?
7. Derive the goods equilibrium schedule. Show the effects on the GES of: increasing $G$ holding other variables as given; increasing $G$ while simultaneously lowering taxes; increasing taxes holding other variables as given.

## SUGGESTED REFERENCES

Dernburg, Thomas F. and D. M. McDougall, *Macro-Economics*, 2nd ed. (New York: McGraw-Hill Book Co., 1963).

Keynes, John Maynard, *The General Theory of Employment, Interest, and Money* (New York: Harcourt, Brace and World, 1936).

McKenna, Joseph, *Aggregate Economic Analysis* (New York: Dryden Press, 1955).

# CHAPTER *17*

# *The Theory of the Rate of Interest*

*The theory of the rate of interest* has had a rather stormy history. Economists have engaged in many disputes with respect to (1) the determinants of the rate of interest, (2) the significance of the interest rate, and (3) the best interest rate policy.[1]  Of these areas of controversy, the one of concern in this chapter is the first—the determinants of the interest rate.  We wish to determine whether, or to what degree, the interest rate depends on the *real* factors of productivity and thrift, as compared with *monetary* factors, in particular, the supply of and demand for money.

We shall deal with three basic theoretical models: (1) the savings-investment theory; (2) the loanable funds theory; and (3) the liquidity preference theory.  The savings-investment theory is generally associated with classical theory, whereas the loanable funds theory is a more modern and refined modification of the savings-investment theory. The liquidity preference theory is the Keynesian interest rate theory.

---

[1] Most discussions are carried on in terms of *the* rate of interest.  But this is an over-simplication, since there is not one interest rate but a whole pattern of interest rates depending on factors such as risk, maturity, and a host of other considerations.  For an excellent discussion of the interest rate pattern and its determinants see E. S. Shaw, *Money, Income and Monetary Policy*, (Homewood: Richard D. Irwin, 1950).  Nevertheless, we shall adopt the usual simplification and speak of *the* rate of interest.

## THE SAVINGS-INVESTMENT THEORY OF INTEREST

We shall start the discussion of interest rate theories with the classical savings-investment theory. Then, after developing the savings-investment theory, it is easy to modify it to take account of more recent developments in order to derive the loanable funds model.

Briefly, in the savings-investment theory the interest rate is determined by the interaction of a demand function and a supply function for capital. Specifically, the interest rate is determined by (1) the demand for funds to finance investment, which varies inversely with the rate of interest, and (2) the supply of savings that people are willing to withhold from their incomes and lend, which is assumed to vary directly with the interest rate. The intersection of these two schedules determines the rate of interest, and only at this interest rate does the amount of saving equal the amount of investment.

### The Savings Schedule

The supply schedule of savings is assumed to be an increasing function relative to the interest rate. That is, people save more at higher interest rates than at low interest rates: savings vary *directly* with the interest rate. This belief is based squarely on an assumption of utility maximization. An individual is assumed to have some preference function which relates the satisfaction he will get from using his income for current consumption to the satisfaction he will receive by deferring his consumption to some future period. To maximize his *total* satisfaction over time, the individual will allocate his income to the time periods in which it yields the greatest over-all satisfaction. But in this income allocation process, the individual must take into account the interest rate. For by foregoing current consumption and lending part of one's income, in the future satisfaction is derived not only from the consumption of the principal amount, but from interest earnings as well.

Other things being equal, it is assumed that a person would prefer current to future consumption. If this is the case an individual would save—forego current consumption—only to the extent that his preference for current consumption would be offset by the interest paid for deferment of consumption.

Several attacks have been made on the assumption that savings vary directly with the interest rate. For example, if a person is saving to obtain a specific sum, the higher the rate of interest the less that has to be saved due to the increase in interest earnings which contribute to the growth of the fund. In this case the saving schedule would slope downward—that is, be inversely related to the interest rate.

A more fundamental objection to the classical savings-investment model is the Keynesian argument: that there is really no significant connection between saving and the interest rate. This view maintains that savings are primarily influenced by the level of income, not by the rate of interest. How would the classical school answer this objection? First, the classical economist would probably agree that saving will vary with the level of income. But then he would argue that the level of real income is not determined in the savings-investment arena, but in the labor market and by the production function which relates total employment to total output. The role of the savings-investment market, contends the classicist, is simply to divide income between consumption and saving.

We clearly have not assessed the importance of the attack on the classical savings function, and, in fact, have only restated the classical position of the role of the interest rate. The answer as to the importance of the interest rate or income level as determinants of saving really depends on the period of time under consideration. In the short run, it seems less probable that the interest rate will be a significant factor. In the long run, the interest rate probably becomes more important.

### The Investment Demand Schedule

The derivation of the investment demand schedule, the second of the basic determinants of the interest rate in the savings-investment theory, proceeds in a straightforward manner. The classical model operated on the assumption of a constant—that is, full employment—level of real income (output). Given the assumption of constant real income, a downward sloping investment demand schedule is easily obtained from the law of diminishing returns. For both the classical marginal productivity of capital or the Keynesian marginal efficiency of capital counterpart, the schedule relating investment demand to the interest rate slopes downward. The lower the price, the interest rate, the more "productive stuff," capital, that will be demanded.

In the classical model the investment demand curve is downward sloping—more investment at lower interest rates—only to substitute relatively cheaper capital for the now relatively more expensive other factors. What is involved here is not the production of additional output, but rather the production of a given output mix in a more

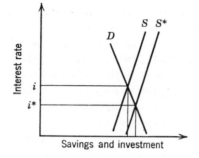

*Figure 17-1*  The saving-investment theory of the rate of interest.

capital intense fashion.    It seems unlikely that the elasticity of this investment demand schedule can be very large.

It is also rather unlikely that the savings function is very interest elastic, at least for the short run.    This means that we have a situation in which the supply of savings function and the investment demand function are both interest inelastic.    In this type of situation any changes in the functions—in the desire to save or desire to invest—necessitate a rather large change in the interest rate in order to equate savings and investment.    Thus, the maintenance of a constant level of real income requires a very flexible interest rate.    That is, stability of income requires perhaps rather extreme instability in the interest rate.

Figure 17-1 shows the interaction of the supply of and demand for capital in the determination of the interest rate.    In this savings-investment theory, the interest rate is the price paid for capital.    The intersection of the supply schedule of capital (the saving function) and the demand schedule for capital (the investment function) yields interest rate $i$.    This is the equilibrium rate of interest, which equates desired saving to desired investment.

To demonstrate the instability of the interest rate, an increase in thriftiness, that is, an increase in the willingness to save at every interest rate, shifts the $S$ function to the right to $S^*$.    The interest rate falls from $i$ to $i^*$, a rather substantial fall, even though saving and investment have increased only slightly.    Although saving and investment have increased, the level of real income is unchanged because of the assumption of full employment of resources.    Thus, the level of income is unchanged, but the composition of income has changed to *less* output of consumption goods—this corresponds to increased saving—and *more* investment good production.

This possibility of a widely fluctuating rate of interest is significant.

Whenever a price fluctuates, opportunities exist for speculators to enter the market.  By the proper timing of their buying and selling (here, lending and borrowing) the speculators profit from these price variations.  It is quite possible that speculative activity of this sort in the money market may interfere with normal market equilibrating forces. At best, the adjustment process may be somewhat delayed.  At worst, the interference of speculative activities may result in a fall in the level of income.  This fall in income may arise if, in the money market, speculators prevent the interest rate from dropping to a low enough level to equate saving to investment.  This means there is an excess of saving over investment.  These excess savings must find some outlet other than investment.  If they are diverted back to consumption spending the result is an unchanged level of income, but a shift in the composition of the income.  But if these funds do not find an outlet, if they are diverted into idle hoards, then the result is a drop in aggregate demand, with a resulting decline in the price level, real income, or likelier both.

### The Pigou Effect

The reason for mentioning the interest inelasticities of the saving function and investment demand schedule, and the resultant need for interest rate flexibility, is to point up the demand for money in the savings-investment theory.  The savings-investment theory apparently implies that there exist two alternatives for the use of income: (1) it may be spent for consumption purposes, or (2) it may be "spent" by lending it in the investment market.  As we have seen, the classical economist could see very little sense in using income simply to accumulate idle hoards—especially when it could be loaned out at interest. But there is also the alternative, and it must be considered, that people *do* wish to add to their money balance and that there does exist a propensity to hoard.  Given this third course, what would happen if an increase in the desire to save were met with an inflexible rate of interest, one which did not fall?  In this case, if people still insisted on saving regardless of whether they found borrowers for these savings, there would occur a gap in the income circuit, the gap being equal to the excess of savings over investment.

The answer to this difficulty is implicit in classical theory, but the Keynesian attack brought forth a restatement and examination of the classical position.  The outstanding spokesman for the classical theory was Professor A. C. Pigou.  The answer to the situation posed is that the fall in aggregate demand—that is, the decline in consumption plus

investment demand—would, if prices were flexible, result in a fall in
the general price level.  This fall in the general price level raises the
real value of existing money stocks; that is, the given money stocks,
with the lower price level, represent increased purchasing power over
goods and services.  As the value of money stocks rises, the desire to
save declines.  This is a shift to the left in the saving schedule until
the saving schedule intersects the investment demand schedule at the
existing inflexible interest rate.  Similarly, a market rate of interest
below the equilibrium rate results in a rise in the general price level,
a fall in the real value of money stocks, and an increase in the desire
to save.  This is the so-called *Pigou Effect*.  The important question
is, of course, whether this process can operate rapidly enough to prevent fluctuations in money income.  The effectiveness of the Pigou
effect is undoubtedly a function of the time period involved, being
more valid in the long-run classical model than in the short-run
Keynesian model.

## THE LOANABLE FUNDS THEORY OF INTEREST

One of the conspicuous features of the savings-investment theory of
interest is the absence of money.  The reasoning behind this omission
is that any influence money might have would be in dynamic, changing
situations, and not in the long-run equilibrium situation; thus, money
would have no lasting effect on the interest rate in the long-run situation.  In other words, money is a medium of exchange and has no
effects on the real economic variables.  But this classical version of
interest-rate theory has to be modified to take into account practical
considerations along several lines.

Since interest is, after all, the price paid for the use of money, and
because there are sources of money other than voluntary saving out of
income, because there do exist demands for money besides the investment demand, and because changes in the money supply do seem to
have effects on the interest rate, even if only in the short run, many
economists regretted the leaving out of factors that in actual practice
seem important in determining the interest rate.  As a result of this
dissatisfaction with the classical savings-investment theory, an alternative theory of the rate of interest was developed.  This theory that
grew out of the classical version is an elaboration of the savings-investment theory and incorporates some additional factors.  This version
of interest rate theory is known as the loanable funds theory.  In this
loanable funds theory the interest rate is determined by the total
demand for and supply of loanable funds.

### The Demand for Loanable Funds

We have said that the loanable funds theory is an extension and elaboration of the savings-investment theory. This is true of both the supply and demand sides of the analysis. Let us see what the loanable funds theorists have added to the savings-investment analysis.

Loanable funds may be demanded for the following purposes:

$D_1$. Financing additional net investment.

$D_2$. Financing the replacement or maintenance of existing capital.

$D_3$. Financing consumption expenditures in excess of one's current income.

$D_4$. Adding to cash balances.

Certainly $D_1$ is included in the demand function of the savings-investment theory. And if we interpret investment in a gross sense $D_2$, replacement demand, is also included in the savings-investment analysis. Similarly, we can handle $D_3$ in the savings-investment theory without altering the real significance of that analysis. Thus, we come to item $D_4$, the demand for money to add to cash balances. This last factor, $D_4$, is a monetary factor whereas the others are of a *real* nature. It is the important addition on the demand side. And on the supply side a similar situation is encountered.

### The Supply of Loanable Funds

The loanable funds theory includes in the supply side the following sources of loanable funds:

$S_1$. Current savings.

$S_2$. The liquidation of previous savings from fixed capital.

$S_3$. Dishoarding of previously accumulated cash balances.

$S_4$. Net addition to the amount of bank credit.

As with the demand side of the theory, which of these sources of loanable funds constitute real changes from the savings-investment theory? If we interpret the savings-investment theory in a gross sense then certainly $S_1$ and $S_2$ are included in it. Thus, the additions to the savings-investment theory incorporated in the loanable funds analysis are items $S_3$, dishoarding, and $S_4$, bank credit. Both $S_3$ and $S_4$ are monetary factors.

We see now that some elements of the loanable funds theory are elements of the savings-investment theory: Thus $D_1$, $D_2$, and $D_3$ and $S_1$ plus $S_2$ are the demand and supply functions respectively of the savings-investment analysis and are real factors. The additional factors of the loanable funds model (that is, $D_4$ and $S_3$ and $S_4$) are the introduction of monetary factors into the analysis. Thus, the loanable funds theory presumably takes into account both real factors as well as monetary factors.

### The Rate of Interest

Perhaps the principal weakness of the loanable funds theory is that it obscures certain relationships between the supply of and demand for money and between saving and investment, by combining both the markets—the money market and the goods market—into one. In order to point up this difficulty let us consider Figure 17-2. The various schedules shown in Figure 17-2 are defined as follows: $S = S_1 + S_2$, $M_S = S_3 + S_4$, where $S$ is savings schedule and $M_S$ is money supplied. The total loanable funds supply schedule is $LF_S = S + M_S = S_1 + S_2 + S_3 + S_4$. The demand function for loanable funds is $LF_D$ which is the sum of investment demand schedule, $I = D_1 + D_2 + D_3$, and the money demand schedule, $M_D = D_4$.

The situation depicted in Figure 17-2 seems to say an equilibrium is possible where $S + M_S = I + M_D$, where $LF_S = LF_D$, but such an equilibrium will be quite unstable unless we have also satisfied the equalities $S = I$ and $M_S = M_D$. Thus in Figure 17-2, at the "equilibrium" rate of interest $i$, we have the supply of loanable funds equal to the demand for loanable funds ($LF_S = LF_D$), but saving at this rate of interest is clearly in excess of investment ($S > I$), and also at this rate of interest money demanded is greater than money supplied ($M_D > M_S$). The situation as depicted is clearly deflationary, which will lead to a lower level of money income, and which, finally, will

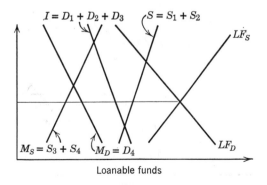

*Figure 17-2* The loanable funds theory of the rate of interest.

cause shifts in the various functions until a true equilibrium is reached. Then all three equalities, $LF_S = LF_D$, $S = I$, and $M_S = M_D$, are fulfilled.

### The Pigou Effect Again

If we can have no real equilibrium rate of interest unless we achieve an equality of savings and investment, does this mean that, fundamentally, the loanable funds advocates believe the interest rate is determined exclusively by the real factors of productivity and thrift? To answer this question let us consider the following example.

Let us start our analysis from an equilibrium situation in which all three equations $S = I$, $M_S = M_D$, and $LF_S = LF_D$ are satisfied. This is shown in Figure 17-3.

Let us now assume that there occurs an increase in the money supply—that $M_S$ shifts to the right which also causes $LF_S$ to shift to the right. These shifts are shown by the starred schedules $M_S^*$ and $LF_S^*$. What will be the results of this increase in the money supply?

First, it is clear that at the equilibrium interest rate $i$ the supply of money exceeds the demand for money. If the reaction to this is a fall in the interest rate to $i^*$ so that the supply and demand for loanable funds are equated we have an equilibrium rate of interest of sorts. But at this interest rate $i^*$ the desire to invest exceeds the desire to save, and an income expansion follows.

This income expansion process will continue until the functions shift so as to achieve the equality in all three equations: that is, the functions shift until $S = I$, $M_S = M_D$, and $LF_S = LF_D$. To answer the question posed earlier, whether monetary factors have any permanent effect on the interest rate or whether the latter in equilibrium is determined by only the real factors of saving and investment, we must

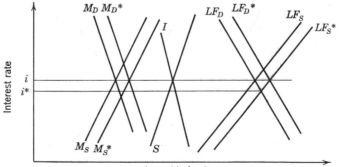

*Figure 17-3*

specify this process of change. That is, we must specify the functions to be shifted and how the final equilibrium is obtained.

If the expansion is simply one of increased prices, and the only functions to shift as money income rises, while real income remains constant, are the supply and demand schedules for money, then the final equilibrium interest rate will be that rate at which saving and investment would have been equated all along. That is, the increase in the money supply has increased the demand for money balances, shifting the $M_D$ schedule to the right to $M_D{}^*$, thus raising the interest rate which equates the supply of and demand for money balances from $i^*$ back to the level which equates saving and investment, $i$. In this case the monetary factors have no effect on the interest rate except during the transition period. We can, therefore, say that the rate of interest is determined by the saving and investment functions. The price level and the supply and demand for money simply adjust to the interest rate basically determined by the saving and investment relations. Thus, the loanable funds theory yields the same answer as reached by the classical savings-investment theory.

On the other hand, if the increase in the money supply had some effect on the saving and investment schedules, we could say that monetary factors may have an effect on the interest rate even in equilibrium conditions. For example, if at the higher level of money income individuals wanted to save more than at the lower level, due perhaps to the fact that the real value of their cash balances was diminished by the price rise, then the new final equilibrium interest rate would be lower than the old equilibrium rate of interest. In other words, the question is whether the saving and investment schedules are solely functions of the interest rate and real income, in which case the classical conclusion holds, or whether these schedules are affected by the price level as well. If the latter is the case—that the schedules are a function of the price level as well as real income—the rate of interest is at least partially a monetary phenomenon.

Earlier we put forth the possibility that an excess of saving over investment would cause a downward movement in the price level until the saving function shifted to the left, raising the interest rate, which equates saving and investment, to the level of the inflexible market rate of interest. This we called the *Pigou effect*. This possibility is significant for it means that Pigou, by making saving a function of the price level as well as of the level of real income and the interest rate, has introduced a monetary factor into his interest rate theory. Thus, classical and neoclassical theory, when it incorporates the Pigou effect, holds that the rate of interest is partially determined by monetary factors as well as the real factors of productivity and thrift. In other words, monetary factors have entered even classical interest rate theories.

## THE LIQUIDITY PREFERENCE THEORY OF INTEREST

We have already seen that the liquidity preference theory of the interest rate appears to be based solely on monetary factors. In this theory the interest rate is given by the money supply—assumed as fixed at any time—and the demand for money, called liquidity preference. This liquidity preference comprises two elements, the transactions and precautionary motives, which relate the demand for money balances to the level of money income, and a third, the speculative motive, which relates the demand for money to present and expected future interest rates.

The possibility of a *liquidity trap* has been mentioned. This is a rate of interest so low that, anticipating future increases in the rate, individuals would rather hold any quantities of money that may be added to the money supply than lend the money at the low interest rate and run the risk of incurring a capital loss if and when the rate rises. In other words, the liquidity trap is a perfectly elastic demand for money balances at a low interest rate.

The liquidity preference theory of interest has been vigorously attacked on several points, counting among them the charges that the real factors of productivity and thrift have been ignored and that the theory is based solely on expectations, which are based on other expectations.[2] It is undoubtedly true that the emphasis by Keynes and his followers on the purely monetary aspects of the theory left them open to such criticisms. Examination of the Keynesian model, however, shows that the real factors are not missing, but only hidden. Furthermore, the expectation as to the future course of the interest is related to real forces, though perhaps only indirectly. After all, expectations are influenced by past circumstances, and if real forces have played a part in shaping them those circumstances have some influence[3] on the interest rate or how it may be expected to change.

Suppose we attempt to answer the charges leveled at the liquidity preference theory. Let us illustrate the relationship between investment productivity and the interest rate through an example. Starting from an equilibrium situation, in which the interest rate equals the

[2] See D. H. Robertson "Mr. Keynes and the Rate of Interest," in *Essays in Monetary Theory*, (London: Staples Press, 1940), p. 25.
[3] See Joan Robinson, "The Rate of Interest," in *The Rate of Interest and Other Essays*, (London: Macmillan, 1952), p. 4–5.

expected productivity of the last unit of investment, we note the effects of an increase in the marginal efficiency of capital schedule, both in the classical and in the Keynesian models.   In the classical system it will cause an increase in the interest rate because the investment demand schedule has shifted to the right.   The higher interest rate will call forth additional savings to match the increased investment.   In the Keynesian model, the increase in the marginal efficiency of capital *might* be accompanied by an increased demand for money which would cause an immediate rise in the interest rate as funds are demanded to finance investment.   Regardless of this possibility, as the level of investment rises due to the shift to the right of the marginal efficiency of capital, income rises by a multiple of the investment increase and prices may rise.   Either eventuality will bring about an increased money demand for transactions purposes, which will cause the interest rate to rise.

Both classical and Keynesian theories agree that in equilibrium the rate of interest must be equal to the marginal productivity of capital or, in Keynesian terms, to the marginal efficiency of capital.   The classical model says any gap between the interest rate and the marginal productivity of capital is closed by two simultaneous movements: (1) the rise in the interest rate; and (2) a fall in the marginal product of capital as investment increases.   The Keynesian model suggests that if a gap exists between the interest rate and the marginal product of capital, the entire adjustment is made by a change in investment, since there is no *obvious* way for a change in the desire to invest to cause a change in the interest rate.   This corresponds to (2) in the classical explanation.   But if we take into account the indirect effects described in the preceding paragraph we see that (1) of the classical view is also included, though in a roundabout fashion.   That is, even in the Keynesian model the rate of interest rises as investment increases.

But what of the criticism that the interest rate is what it is because it is expected to be other than what it is—that is, what of the liquidity trap in the liquidity preference theory?   First, the notion of a very elastic, but not *perfectly* elastic, demand for money could easily be incorporated into the classical model.   Second, the liquidity preference function cannot be perfectly elastic in the long run.   This is so because it depends on expectations as to the future course of the interest rate—in this case, the rate is low and so the expected change is upward—which, as time passes, are shown to be erroneous.

Thus we may conclude that the liquidity trap is essentially a short-run, dynamic, theoretical consideration which is (1) inconsistent with a long-run static model, but (2) can perform an important role in short-run situations.

## SUMMARY

As we remarked at the beginning of this chapter, the theory of the rate of interest has often been steeped in controversy. This controversy is not something of the past; the debate still continues today. To facilitate the comparison of these interest-rate theories, let us compare the factors which enter into each analysis.

Let us take up the investment function first. It is included *explicitly* in the loanable funds schedule of the demand for loanable funds. It is not included explicitly in the liquidity preference model. But it is present in the liquidity preference theory, even if only *implicitly*, as it works behind the scenes, as we have seen. Thus, due to the change in income brought about by a change in investment, investment demand can, in the liquidity preference model, affect the interest rate through changing the demand for cash balances.

So much for the investment component of the two interest rate theories. A more fundamental difference lies in their treatment of saving. The loanable funds theory treats saving as a function of the interest rate; the liquidity preference theory does not. This seems to be a vital distinction, for if either theory would adopt the other's assumption as to the interest rate and saving, the two theories would easily resolve into one.

Leaving in the assumption that saving is a function of the interest rate makes a separate theory of the loanable funds approach. Let us assume that saving *is not* a function of the interest rate: the consequence of this assumption is that the interest rate determines only how much of some fixed or given amount of saving is to be devoted to securities and how much to money. But the loanable funds approach assumes that the interest rate establishes the division of income between consumption and saving. Thus, there is no given amount of saving to be divided between money and securities, but rather an amount of saving varying with the interest rate.

Now what have we said? We have said that one rate of interest is not sufficient to determine *two* allocations: between consumption and saving, and between securities and money. As we have seen in Figure 17-2, there is no reason to assume that the interest rate which equates the supply of and demand for money will also be the rate which equates saving and investment. In order to remedy this problem, the loanable funds theory has to seek help from another source, the level of money income—that is, the price level. In a rather mixed-up way, it takes the rate of interest *and* the price level to determine the allocation of income among the three uses. Neither "price" alone is sufficient to determine any one part of the division of income.

Certainly nothing said here will foreclose debate between the two theories, but perhaps we are now better able to make an evaluation of the relative merits of the theories. We have seen that the differences between the two principal theories examined are not so great as superficial examination indicated. The classical theory is not always a real theory. First, in transition periods, or where inflexibilities are present, monetary factors enter. Second, with the Pigou effect money may have a permanent bearing on the interest rate. Nor is the liquidity preference model strictly a monetary theory, for real factors enter the analysis indirectly through the influence of investment on the level of income and thus, on the demand for money balances.

The net effect seems to be this: in the long-run the real factors of the classical model are the relevant variables; the monetary factors have more influence in the short-run. Interest rate determination turns out to be really a matter of general equilibrium, and cannot be adequately treated in any one particular market. Thus we shall present a simple two-sector general equilibrium model in the next chapter.

## REVIEW QUESTIONS

1. Develop the classical savings-investment interest rate theory. What factors determine the supply of and demand for capital schedules?
2. In the savings-investment theory, the rate of interest allocates income into consumption goods and investment goods production but does not influence the level of income. Why not? Discuss.
3. What are the significant additions of the loanable funds theory to the savings-investment theory?
4. What is the *Pigou effect?*
5. Develop the place of investment demand in the liquidity preference theory of interest rate determination.
6. Compare and contrast the loanable funds theory with the liquidity preference theory and evaluate the contribution of each.

## SUGGESTED REFERENCES

Conard, Joseph W., *An Introduction to the Theory of Interest* (Berkeley: University of California Press, 1959).

Robertson, Dennis H., "Mr. Keynes and the Rate of Interest," in *Essays in Monetary Theory* (London: Staples Press, 1940).

Robinson, Joan, "The Rate of Interest," in *The Rate of Interest and Other Essays* (London: Macmillan Co., 1952).

Shaw, Edward S., *Money, Income, and Monetary Policy* (Homewood: Richard D. Irwin, 1950).

# CHAPTER *18*

# *A General Equilibrium Model of Income Determination*

In Chapter 15 we discussed the money market and in Chapter 16 the market for goods and services. In each case we developed the conditions for equilibrium in the particular market. Now it is time to relate the separate threads of analysis into a more general pattern.

In the analysis of the money market we developed the money equilibrium schedule, or MES. This MES, it will be recalled, relates levels of income and associated rates of interest when the money market is in equilibrium, that is, when the supply of money is equal to the demand for money balances. The relationships involved in the determination of the MES are the supply of money, the transactions demand or active demand for money balances, and the demand for idle balances or speculative demand for money balances.

The goods equilibrium schedule, or GES, relates levels of income and the associated rates of interest when the goods market is in equilibrium. The equilibrium condition for the goods market is that withdrawals or leakages from the income stream (savings plus taxes) are equal to injections to the income stream (investment expenditures plus government expenditures). The relations involved in determining the GES are the marginal efficiency of capital schedule, the level of government expenditures on the one hand and tax collections on the other, and the economy's propensity to save function—or its complement, the consumption schedule.

In the following sections we shall review the determination of the two equilibrium schedules. However, we shall not stop with this review of the separate markets, but shall bring the two markets into a

314

single structure, and then simultaneously achieve equilibrium in both—and hence, in the entire economy. That is, equilibrium will be said to exist for the entire economy when both the money market and goods market are simultaneously in equilibrium.

## THE MONEY MARKET EQUILIBRIUM

We have discussed the demand for money in two senses: (1) the transactions and precautionary demands for money, or active demand for money balances; and (2) the demand for idle money balances. These two demands for money reflect respectively the demand for money as a medium of exchange and the demand for money as a store of value.

As a medium of exchange money is necessary to finance both known as well as possible transactions. The question then arises how much money is needed to finance these transactions. Although no precise answer to this question can be given, it is possible to suggest certain considerations. Given the state of advancement, integration, etc., of the economic system, the higher the level of income the larger become the necessary money balances to finance it. Also the higher the price level the greater will be the necessary active money balances. If we single out the income level as the principal factor determining the size of the transaction balances, that is, assume prices relatively constant, then we can write the transactions demand for money balances as a function of income. Representing the transactions demand for money as $M_1$, we write this demand as $M_1 = kY$. Let us represent this graphically as shown in Figure 18-1. At higher income levels larger money balances are needed; at lower income levels smaller money balances suffice.

The second demand for money as a store of value is a demand for

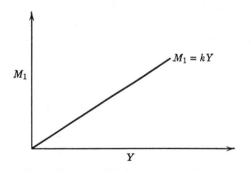

*Figure 18-1* The demand for active money balances.

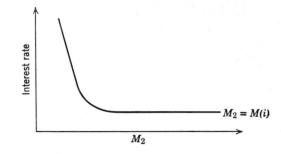

*Figure 18-2* The demand for idle money balances.

idle money balances. We have already studied this demand for idle money balances and have found it to be a function of the interest rate. This functional relationship between demand for idle money balances and the rate of interest we called $M_2$. This demand for idle money balances may be written $M_2 = M(i)$. This is depicted in Figure 18-2. Given the two demands for money balances, equilibrium in the money market occurs when the money supply equals the money demand; that is, when $M_S = M_1 + M_2$. Given this equilibrium condition, let us now derive levels of income and rates of interest consistent with equilibrium in the money market.

The diagram in Figure 18-3 labeled "Chart A" is the function $M_1 = kY$; it relates the demand for money balances for transactions purposes to the various levels of income. The second diagram, Chart B, is the supply of money available to be held.

The line $M_1 + M_2$ (the sum of $M_1 + M_2$ equals $M_S$) intersects the horizontal axis indicating the entire money supply is demanded for idle balances; it intersects the vertical axis showing the entire money supply is demanded for active transactions purposes; and any other point on the line shows the disposition of the money supply between the two demands, active and idle. The third diagram, Chart C, is the familiar demand for idle money balances—that is, $M_2 = M(i)$ or the demand for money as a store of value. The last diagram, Chart D, is the money equilibrium schedule, or MES. This money equilibrium schedule relates equilibrium rates of interest and associated levels of income. Let us see how it is derived.

Starting with Chart A choose a level of income, say $Y'$. At this income $Y'$ the transactions demand for money is $M_1'$. Taking this transactions demand $M_1'$ we introduce it into Chart B. Since the money supply is $M_S$ in order to have equilibrium $M_2$ must equal

$M_S - M_1'$.   Specifically, we find that the demand for idle balances is $M_2' = M_S - M_1'$.   Having now obtained the amount of money available for hoarding purposes we can feed this information into the demand for idle money balances in Chart C in order to find the associated rate of interest, $i'$.   The last step is to plot the rate of interest $i'$ just determined with the original income level $Y'$ from which we started.   The completed process gives one point of the money equilibrium schedule.   By repeating it starting with different levels of income we obtain other points on the schedule.   In fact, this traces out the money equilibrium schedule.   This process is depicted in Figure 18-3.

What is this money equilibrium schedule?   It is a schedule that tells the relationship between the rate of interest and the level of income which will provide equilibrium in the money market.   On what factors does this depend?   The money equilibrium schedule is obviously a function of the transactions or active demand for money balances, the demand for idle money balances, and the money supply.   We have already discussed the determinants of these factors.   If any of the basic determinants of these relations alter, if, for instance, the demands

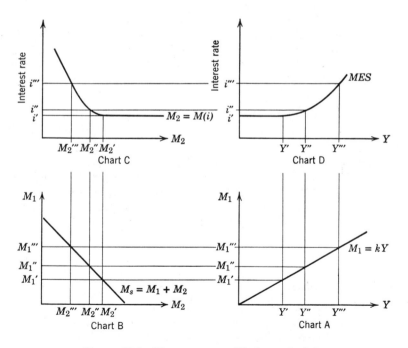

*Figure 18-3*   The money equilibrium schedule.

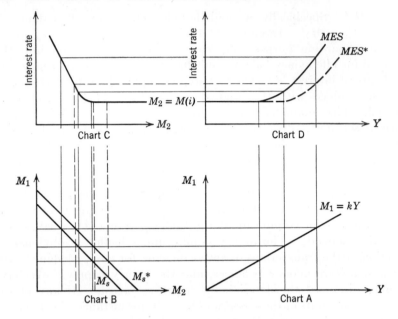

***Figure 18-4***   An increase in the MES.

for money balances shift, or if the money authority changes the amount of money in the system, or perhaps both supply and demand elements have changed; in any of these situations the money equilibrium schedule will shift.   Let us illustrate this process in Figure 18-4.

For example, assume that the functions defining the MES are $M_1 = kY$, $M_S = M_1 + M_2$, $M_2 = M(i)$; now increase the money supply from $M_S$ to $M_S^*$.   We see that the increase in the money supply shifts the MES to MES*, so that a lower interest rate is associated with each income level except at the liquidity trap rate of interest. In a similar fashion if $M_1 = kY$ shifts to the right, that is, if smaller active money balances are held at each income level due to a rise in velocity, then the MES shifts to the right.   Or if the demand function for idle money balances shifts to the left, this results in a shift to the right of the MES.   The student will be well advised to work through these cases, the contrary cases, and possibly some combination of shifts of the original functions.

These relations put together to form the MES are monetary factors. But the money market is only one market.   We must also consider the market for real goods and services, the goods market.   As a matter of fact, our analysis is scarcely complete until we do so.   For as the MES relates the interest rate and income levels, given equilibrium in the money market, so does the GES (goods equilibrium schedule) relate the interest rate and income levels when the goods and services market is in equilibrium.   In order to have a true equilibrium we must have equilibrium in both markets, and this equilibrium must then yield a unique rate of interest and level of income.

## THE GOODS-MARKET EQUILIBRIUM

The derivation of the goods equilibrium schedule proceeds in a manner quite similar to the derivation of the MES.   We deal with the market for goods and services instead of the money market.   And the condition for the goods market to be in equilibrium is that saving plus taxes equal investment expenditures plus government expenditures; that is, $S^* + T = I + G$.

The set of basic relationships with which we work are the following: the marginal efficiency of capital schedule; the equilibrium condition $S^* + T = I + G$; and the saving plus taxes, or $S^* + T$, function. The process of relating the rate of interest to income levels, given equilibrium in the goods market, is as follows.   First, given the MEC schedule assume an interest rate.   This interest rate and the MEC schedule generate the volume of private investment expenditures.   To this volume of private investment expenditures we add the level of government expenditures.[1]   The sum of these two expenditure streams, $I + G$, in equilibrium, is equal to the sum of withdrawals through saving plus taxes, $S^* + T$.   Consequently by going to the $S^* + T$ function, knowing $S^* + T = I + G$, we may determine the income level which is required to generate $S^* + T$ equal to $I + G$.   Thus, we have completed our task; we have related an equilibrium level of income to a rate of interest.   By repeating the process with different rates of interest we determine other levels of income, and the locus of these points is the goods equilibrium schedule, the GES.

We may graphically depict the above described process through the four charts E through H in Figure 18-5.   Thus Chart E contains the MEC schedule and the given interest rate, $i$.   Together the MEC schedule and the interest rate $i$ determine investment expenditures of $I$. The amount of governmental expenditures are given as the difference

---

[1] Government expenditures are assumed to be independent of the level of income. Although this assumption is unrealistic, any other functional relationship would appear to be even less satisfactory.   Thus, it seems best to treat it as an independent factor.

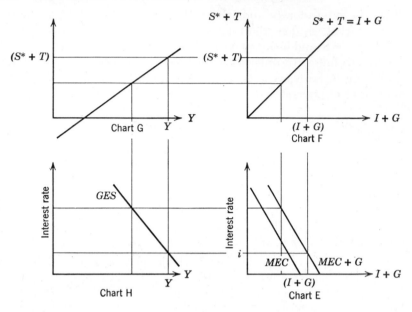

**Figure 18-5**   The goods equilibrium schedule (GES).

between the MEC schedule and the (MEC + $G$) schedule.   In effect, (MEC + $G$) represents an aggregate investment demand function (private plus public investment) with the government expenditures assumed as given and interest inelastic.   Thus the interest rate $i$ and the (MEC + $G$) schedule generate the level of investment expenditures and government expenditures, $I + G$.

Chart F is the equilibrium relation that $S^* + T = I + G$.   Since these terms are all measured in the same units, dollars, the 45° line from the origin represents all points at which $I + G$ on the horizontal axis equals $S^* + T$ on the vertical axis.   Consequently, having found $I + G$ in "E," we find by bringing it into Chart F the equivalent volume of withdrawals from the income stream, saving plus taxes, or $S^* + T$.

Having determined $S^* + T$ we need to know the income level which generates this amount of saving plus taxes.   This is readily obtained by moving to Chart G, which is the "saving plus taxes" function.   By knowing the level of $S^* + T$ we can, from the saving plus taxes function, find the associated level of income, $Y$.   We have now come full circle: we have an equilibrium level of income, $Y$, to pair off with the original rate of interest, $i$, with which we started. By repeating the process we may obtain other such points and trace out the GES.

The GES is valid only as long as the given functions persist; that is, it holds only for the given MEC schedule, the given level of government expenditures, the given level of tax receipts, and the given propensity to save function. If any one or several of these factors change then there occurs a shift in the GES. Thus, for example, an increase in the MEC schedule or $G$, or both, results in an increase in the GES, that is, a shift to the right. Similarly, a cut in taxes will shift the GES to the right, as will an increase in the consumption function— a fall in the saving function. The converse of any of the foregoing changes will result in a decline in the GES, that is, a shift to the left. The student is well advised to satisfy himself on these counts.

## EQUILIBRIUM IN THE SYSTEM

### Equilibrium

Let us review the extent of our progress. The MES relates the associated levels of income and rates of interest *when there exists equilibrium in the money market*. Similarly the GES relates associated levels of income and interest rates *when there is equilibrium in the goods and services market*. These two schedules, the MES and GES, determine interest rates and income levels consistent with equilibrium in their respective markets. But what of equilibrium for the entire economy?

In order for there to be equilibrium for the entire economy both the

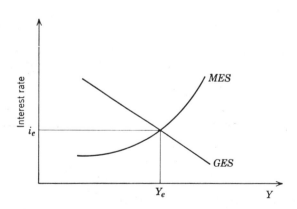

*Figure 18-6* Simultaneous equilibrium in the money and goods markets.

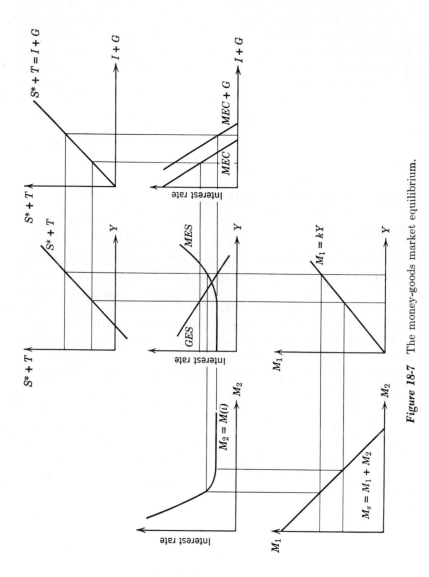

*Figure 18-7* The money-goods market equilibrium.

goods market and the money market must simultaneously be in equilibrium. The question thus arises: Is there an interest rate and level of income at which both the goods market and the money market are simultaneously in equilibrium and, consequently, the entire economy in equilibrium? To answer this question we need only to turn to the MES and GES just derived. Since each of these schedules relates interest rates and levels of income we may plot them on the same diagram. This is done in Figure 18-6. The intersection of the two curves provides the answer to the question. The level of income $Y_e$ and interest rate $i_e$ satisfy both relations, and thus we have an equilibrium for the entire economy.

The situation we are dealing with is one we have seen before. In the discussion of the loanable funds interest rate theory we maintained that for total equilibrium to exist, an interest rate satisfying both sets of equilibrium conditions, both $S = I$ and $M_S = M_D$, was necessary. Until an interest rate satisfying $S = I$ and $M_S = M_D$, as well as $LF_S = LF_D$, is forthcoming, the level of income will change. Here also: *until* there occurs an interest rate satisfying both the money market *and* the goods market simultaneously we do not have equilibrium.

It may be instructive if our charts A–H are brought together in one place. If we do this we shall have seven charts, since Chart D and Chart H have the same axes and, consequently, we may put both the MES and GES functions in one chart. This summary graph may then be used to trace out the path whereby equilibrium is attained for the entire system. The summary graph is presented in Figure 18-7 where the four lower left charts describe the money market and the four charts in the upper right depict the goods market.

### The Multiplier Revisited

Earlier we introduced the concept of the investment multiplier. This previous discussion was carried on with the assumption that the investment expenditures were maintained at a fixed level. It seems clear, however, that the analysis in this chapter indicates this assumption to be somewhat unrealistic.

Assuming, for example, an initial increase in investment spending, caused, let us say, by a decline in the interest rate, what happens? The answer is simple enough: the increased investment spending in the goods market has repercussions on the money market, which in turn induce changes in the goods market, etc. Thus, the increased investment spending brings about a higher income level, but this higher level of income necessitates larger money balances and so drives up the rate of interest.   As the interest rates rises, however, this acts as a brake on investment spending and investment expenditures tend to decrease —or not to rise as much as they otherwise would.   Consequently, income does not rise as far as it would.   Only if the MES curve is perfectly elastic shall we get the "full" multiplier effect, for only then will there be no changes in the interest rate to dampen the investment expenditures.

## EQUILIBRIUM AND ECONOMIC POLICY

The level of income determined by the intersection of the MES and GES curves is an equilibrium level of income.   That is, until some change occurs in one or several of the basic relations determining the MES or GES, the level of income so determined will persist.   There is nothing, however, to guarantee that this income level is a desirable one; it may, for example, be a less than full-employment level of income.

The value of the general model developed is that it makes clear the principal factors that determine the level and growth of income. These factors are both real factors and monetary factors.   Consequently, if we wish to change the level of income, to alter the rate of growth in income, etc., the model sheds light about which variables may be manipulated in order to bring about the desired change.

Indeed, the value of economic theory lies in its providing a firm basis for formulating and carrying out economic policy.   Thus, for example, if a less than full-employment level of income and a lagging growth rate are problems of immediate concern, then the appropriate economic policy is one designed to move the MES and GES to the right.   In order to achieve the desired expansion in income, and to increase its rate of growth, the theory indicates the appropriate variables to manipulate to attain these ends.   On the monetary side there would be the institution of a climate of monetary ease through open market purchases, the lowering of the rediscount rate, and the reduction of reserve ratio requirements.   On the expenditure side, increased expenditures are in order.   These increases may come about by reducing taxes and thus stimulating consumption spending, while maintaining or increasing the level of government spending, and by increased investment expenditure due either to monetary measures that lower the rate of interest, or to changes in the tax laws.

In summary, the point being made is that to formulate effective policy to achieve some desired goal, the policy maker must understand the workings of the economic system.   It is a framework for this understanding of the economic system which economic theory provides.    Economic policy specifies the ends; economic theory, the means to attain the desired ends.

## REVIEW QUESTIONS

1. Write brief essays on the relations underlying the money equilibrium schedule.
2. Write brief essays on the relations underlying the goods equilibrium schedule.
3. If the equilibrium level of income as determined by the MES and GES is too low, what kind of economic policy is indicated?   Discuss briefly the appropriate manipulation of the real and monetary variables in order to achieve a higher income level.
4. Discuss the relationship between economic theory and economic policy.

## SUGGESTED REFERENCES

See the suggestions on the ends of Chapters 15 and 16 for appropriate references to this chapter.

# PART V

# INTERNATIONAL MONEY AND FINANCE

CHAPTER *19*

# International Money and Banking: Theory

Except for passing reference, the discussion thus far has been limited to money matters affecting the United States. Now the scope of our analysis is expanded to admit the other nations of the world. At this juncture we begin an explicit consideration of the role of money in a world comprising numerous countries engaged in trading goods and services with one another.

Although international trade and international finance are topics worthy of intensive study in their own right, we shall provide only a brief introduction to them. Our purpose is to gain sufficient understanding of these subjects in order to assess better their implications for current problems of monetary policy.

For this understanding we shall look briefly to the basis for international trade, and to its effects on the level of employment and income—effects so far ignored. We shall see that money performs as a medium of exchange in international trade, just as in domestic trade, but that difficulties arise because of the different national currencies involved. In order to analyze the trade of nations we shall find it useful to reintroduce the "rest of the world sector" into our income accounting scheme. Upon looking at the "balance of payments" account we shall have the principal factors with which to carry out the necessary analysis.

In this section we shall be concerned with such things as the level of imports and exports, the long-term import and export of capital, and, finally, the short-term import and export of capital and gold. We shall conclude our study of international monetary matters with a consideration of the various international financial institutions and their respective roles.

There are similarities and differences between international trade, on the one hand, and domestic trade, on the other. The basic reason for trade or exchange is that the parties to it find it mutually advantageous. This simple statement—that each trader gains—explains all trade, including international trade. It should be noted that the "standard rules" of international trade may not be applicable in the case of state trading, that is, where a government becomes an important exporter or importer, and where the motives may range from economic warfare, to long-run planning for economic development, to dumping of surpluses.

The gains from international trade from the over-all point of view of an economy are simple and direct; they result from more efficient allocation of resources through specialization. International trade allows the countries of the world to specialize in the production of those particular products they can produce most cheaply, given prevailing exchange rates, and to engage in trade for products other nations produce more cheaply. Thus, nations find themselves exporting some products in order to pay for the import of other products produced more efficiently elsewhere. In this fashion, specialization provides higher living standards than would be attained by nations attempting self-sufficiency. The United States, in effect, "raises" coffee by exporting manufactured goods to Latin America.

Specialization requires trade. This is true for individuals, states, regions, nations. Thus, specialization means producing those things in which the trader is relatively most efficient, trading the excess over its own needs to others in exchange for those goods in which the latter have the relative advantage. Consequently, the gains to a nation from specialization and the trade that specialization necessarily implies are the fundamental reasons for international trade, as well as for domestic trade at any level.

International trade does differ from domestic trade on several scores, even though the *raison d'etre* is the same for each. Specifically, international boundaries serve to spur trade because productive resources do not move across boundaries as easily as they move within them, and secondly, because payments involve the exchange of national currencies concurrent with the exchange of goods. Thus, the immobility of resources tends to preserve, even sharpen, relative efficiencies in the production of various goods and services among the trading nations. By each nation's specializing in the activities having the greatest relative advantages, total production is increased in much the same fashion as though the resources were mobile.   International trade serves, in a sense, as a substitute for resource mobility.

The fact that nations have their own monetary units acts to complicate international trade.   In the normal situation, private traders find it necessary to exchange their goods or services for money, and also to exchange one kind of money into another.   And problems can arise here if the various national currencies fluctuate in relative value, or when governments place restrictions on the conversion of one currency into another.

There is one final difference between domestic trade and international trade.   Unlike domestic trade in which the flow of goods and services between regions goes unnoticed, since the goods do not cross national boundaries where track is kept of them, international trade keeps records of the flow of goods and services.   It is the summary of the value of these flows of goods and services between a nation and the rest of the world which we call the "balance of payments."   As we shall soon see, this will be an important tool for our later analysis.

## NATIONAL INCOME AND INTERNATIONAL TRADE

Gross national income is the value of a nation's output of final goods and services over a year's time.   This gross income can be viewed from both a "sources of income" approach and a "uses of income" standpoint.   However, the income definitions used earlier must now be modified to deal with "open" economies; that is, international trade with exports and imports of goods and services must now be taken explicitly into account.

The definition of income from the "sources" standpoint must be modified by adding export expenditures as a source of income within the nation's income circuit.   Similarly the "uses" definition of income now includes imports, since the purchase of imports certainly constitutes a use of income.   If we use the letter $X$ to represent exports and $M$ to stand for imports, the income definitions for an open economy become:

$$Y = C + I + G + X \quad \text{(Sources definition)}$$

$$Y = C + S + T + M \quad \text{(Uses definition)}$$

Let us now consider a simplified model of an open economy, country $A$, and the rest of the world.   Note carefully in this definition that the rest of the world is identified as country $B$.   In this model $A$'s exports are $B$'s imports and, conversely, $B$'s exports are $A$'s imports.   Since changes in expenditures result in changes in income levels, let us write down the income definitions in terms of expenditure streams for the two countries $A$ and $B$, using the subscripts $a$ and $b$ to denote the respective country. Thus we have $A$'s income

$$Y_a = C_a + I_a + G_a + X_a \quad \text{(with } X_a = M_b)$$

and $B$'s income

$$Y_b = C_b + I_b + G_b + X_b \quad \text{(with } X_b = M_a)$$

By virtue of writing the income definitions in terms of expenditure streams, we shall be able to analyze changes in income arising from changed levels of expenditures and thereby derive the "foreign trade multipliers." That a change in one country may "spill over" and affect the other country is evident from their linkage through trade. In effect, the trade relationship makes the levels of income in the two countries interdependent, since imports by one of the nations are expenditures, or a source of income, to the other.

Our previous discussion of income theory was facilitated by the concept of the propensity to consume, or consumption function. Now we shall find it equally helpful to introduce the "propensity to import," or *import function*. This import function states that the level of imports depends on certain factors, the most important of which for our purposes are the prices of the import goods and the level of income in the importing country. The relationship is that the volume of imports is greater the lower their prices and the higher the level of income in the importing country. Given this import function, it is a simple matter to see that price or income changes in one country can have price and income effects in other countries.

To isolate the effects of trade on national income, let us simplify our model by ignoring government expenditures and taxes. When we do this the income definitions from a sources and uses standpoint, respectively, are $C + I + X = Y = C + S + M$. From these relations the equilibrium conditions follow directly: injections to the expenditure stream (investment plus export expenditures) equal withdrawals (savings and imports) from the income circuit. The equilibrium condition is consequently written $I + X = S + M$.

To illustrate diagrammatically, assume that savings and imports are functions of the level of income; investment and exports may be considered as autonomously determined. The situation is illustrated in Figure 19-1. Here we have an economy with a balanced international position: exports equal imports, and domestic saving and investment are equal. Clearly the equilibrium condition $I + X = S + M$ is satisfied.

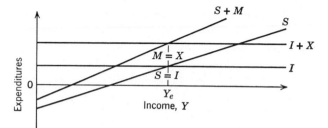

**Figure 19-1**  A "balanced" international equilibrium, $S = I$ and $X = M$.

We can have an equilibrium level of income without, however, having exports equal to imports or saving equal to domestic investment.    For example, if long-term lending is taking place exports may exceed imports provided saving exceeds investment by an equivalent amount.    This is illustrated in Figure 19-2.    Similarly it is possible to have an equilibrium income with imports in excess of exports, provided investment exceeds saving by an equal amount.

The difference between exports and imports is called the *balance of trade*.    Clearly a change in one or several of the schedules depicted in Figures 19-1 and 19-2 will cause income to change.    Thus, in Figure 19-1, for example, an increase in either exports or investment will shift $X + I$ up, resulting in a higher level of income.    It makes no difference to national income whether the increased expenditure comes from export or investment spending.    It does, however, make a considerable difference to the balance of payments.    To demonstrate this, assume there occurs an increase in export spending but no increase in investment spending.    Letting $\Delta$ stand for change, we have initially $X +$

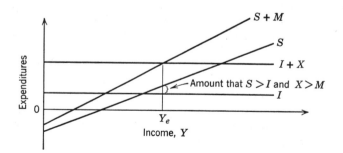

**Figure 19-2**  Equilibrium with $S + M = I + X$, but $S \neq I$ and $X \neq M$.

$I = S + M$.   Given a change in exports of $\Delta X$ we must have a change in savings and imports to balance our equations.   Thus,

(1) $X + I = S + M$

(2) $X + \Delta X + I = S + \Delta S + M + \Delta M$.

On subtracting equation (1) from equation (2) we obtain

(3) $\Delta X = \Delta S + \Delta M$.

This may be written finally as

(4) $\Delta X - \Delta M = \Delta S$

This $(\Delta X - \Delta M)$ is an export surplus.   On the other hand, if the increased expenditures had been due to increased domestic invest-ment spending not accompanied by increased exports we would have obtained in place of (3) $\Delta I = \Delta S + \Delta M$ or $\Delta I - \Delta S = \Delta M$.   With no increase in exports ($\Delta X = 0$ by assumption), the increased imports $\Delta M$ mean the balance of payments becomes adverse by the amount $(\Delta I - \Delta S)$, which is the amount domestic investment exceeds domestic savings.

Thus, in general, taking the equilibrium condition $X + I = S + M$ and recasting it in the form $\Delta X + \Delta I = \Delta S + \Delta M$ or $\Delta X - \Delta M = \Delta S - \Delta I$ provides a useful device for analyzing the effects of changes in one or several of the factors entering into income determination and the balance of payments.

So far we have discussed the income effects of trade on one country alone.   This may be realistic if the country under consideration is small relative to the rest of the world, or if other countries have low marginal propensities to import from the first country.   But, in gen-eral, we may expect some outside repercussions resulting from changes emanating from the first country.   That is, the change of exports or imports in one country affects incomes in other countries, which has a repercussive influence on trade and income in the first country.   Our two-country model defined income for countries $A$ and $B$ as follows:

$$Y_a = C_a + I_a + G_a + X_a \quad (\text{where } X_a = M_b)$$

$$Y_b = C_b + I_b + G_b + X_b \quad (\text{where } X_b = M_a)$$

Given this kind of formulation it is clear that changes in $A$'s imports affect $B$'s income, and reciprocally this will affect $A$ through increased imports by $B$.   The repercussion multipliers sum up all the backwash effects of some given change to determine the magnitude of income changes in the two countries.   Although it is not profitable to pursue this multiplier topic further here, the interested student is referred to the readings at the end of the chapter.

## THE BALANCE OF INTERNATIONAL PAYMENTS

The principal tool for the analysis of the monetary aspects of international trade is the balance of international payments.   This *balance of payments* may be defined as the orderly statistical tabulation of all types of international transactions between one country and the rest of the world, or another country, or some group of countries, during a given year.   The balance of payments account is divided into transactions giving rise to payments and receipts.

The record of international transactions includes items that give rise to receipts (exports) and items that generate payments (imports).   All transactions that result in payments to the United States (receipts to U. S.) increase the stock of, or claims on, foreign currencies, and may be recorded as credit entries in the balance of payments.   Conversely all payments by the United States (receipts to foreigners) deplete the stock of, or claims on, foreign currencies, and may be recorded as debit entries in the balance of payments.   Thus international transactions result in the creation of claims against foreigners or the receipt of funds in the case of exports, and the reduction of claims (on foreigners) or the payment of funds in the case of imports.

Table 19-1 lists the principal factors giving rise to receipts and payments for the four years 1960, 1961, 1962, and 1963.   It shows that the United States had an adverse balance of payments for the four years, meaning that the United States spent or gave away to foreigners more than it received from them.   The deficit on the balance of payments was $3,929 million, $2,360 million, $2,181 million, and $1,958 million for 1960, 1961, 1962, and 1963 respectively.

The table shows that these deficits were covered by sales of gold and by foreigners building up their holdings of short-term dollar liabilities.   For analytical purposes, the Department of Commerce measures the payments deficit by adding United States gold sales to the increase in foreign holdings of short-term United States liabilities,[1] that is, the increase in bank balances owned by foreigners, their purchases of Treasury bills, etc.

---

[1] The Department of Commerce defines the payments deficit as the loss of gold plus the build-up of foreign holdings of short-term dollar liabilities.   This is, of course, an arbitrary definition, and there is considerable debate as to its appropriateness.   A study of other definitions to the measure of the payments deficit is presently underway.

**TABLE 19-1**   United States Balance of Payments, Recent Years (millions of dollars)

|  | 1960 | 1961 | 1962 | 1963 |
|---|---|---|---|---|
| United States Payments | 31,412 | 31,805 | 33,245 | 35,544 |
| Imports: |  |  |  |  |
| Merchandise | 14,722 | 14,514 | 16,193 | 16,962 |
| Military expenditures | 3,048 | 2,947 | 3,006 | 2,880 |
| Income on investments, private | 597 | 604 | 651 | 796 |
| Income on investments, government | 332 | 278 | 338 | 400 |
| Transportation | 1,942 | 1,991 | 2,064 | 2,154 |
| Travel | 1,744 | 1,747 | 1,918 | 2,071 |
| Other services | 942 | 842 | 826 | 855 |
| Remittances and pensions | 848 | 878 | 924 | 812 |
| Government grants and capital outflow | 3,381 | 4,051 | 4,271 | 4,532 |
| U. S. private capital: |  |  |  |  |
| Direct investments | 1,694 | 1,475 | 1,377 | 1,799 |
| Long-term portfolio | 850 | 1,006 | 1,207 | 1,641 |
| Short-term | 1,312 | 1,472 | 467 | 642 |
| United States Receipts | 28,131 | 30,073 | 32,064 | 34,081 |
| Exports: |  |  |  |  |
| Merchandise | 19,409 | 19,915 | 20,566 | 21,902 |
| Military sales | 335 | 406 | 638 | 632 |
| Income on investments, private | 2,856 | 3,303 | 3,711 | 4,067 |
| Income on investments, government | 349 | 379 | 471 | 498 |
| Transportation | 1,816 | 1,685 | 1,842 | 1,848 |
| Travel | 968 | 975 | 1,003 | 941 |
| Miscellaneous services | 1,567 | 1,403 | 1,583 | 1,715 |
| Repayments on U. S. Government loans | 631 | 1,274 | 1,275 | 974 |
| Foreign capital | 200 | 733 | 975 | 1,504 |
| Errors and omissions | −648 | −628 | −1,000 | −495 |
| Net receipts or payments (−) | −3,281 | −1,732 | −1,181 | −1,463 |
| Balance of payments | −3,929 | −2,360 | −2,181 | −1,958 |
| Balanced by: |  |  |  |  |
| Gold sales by United States | 1,702 | 857 | 890 | 461 |
| Increase in liquid dollar liabilities | 2,227 | 1,503 | 1,291 | 1,497 |
| Total to balance | 3,929 | 2,360 | 2,181 | 1,958 |

*Source:* Department of Commerce, *Survey of Current Business*, March, 1962; March, 1963; March, 1964.

Transactions which, for the United States, are import or debit-type transactions are a source of dollar supply for the rest of the world, for it must offer dollars to acquire the foreign exchange to pay for the goods; alternatively, we may view these debit-type transactions as a demand for foreign exchange.   Thus, what is an import or debit-type transaction for the United States is an export or credit-type transaction for the rest of the world, for which the other nations receive payment.   In a similar fashion American export or credit-type transactions reduce the supply of dollars to the rest of the world, since the rest of the world must pay dollars to the United States; or alternatively, we may say these export or credit-type transactions increase the United States supply of foreign exchange.

Let us now take a closer look at the various items which compose the balance of payments, examining the meaning and significance of the data presented in Table 19-1.

## THE BALANCE OF TRADE

Five items comprise what is often termed the balance of trade.   These five categories are the receipts and payments for merchandise, transportation, travel, miscellaneous services, and military purchases.

The importance of merchandise trade in the payments account, and its importance to the supply and demand for dollars and foreign exchange, are apparent.   However, not only are goods traded internationally, but services are also bought and sold across international boundaries.   These sales and purchases of services have effects on the balance of payments exactly similar to those from the movement of merchandise.   Thus, money spent abroad by tourists is the same as an import of goods into this country.   Similarly, shipping and insurance are invisible items in the balance of payments.   If American goods are carried in foreign merchantmen and their cargoes are insured by foreign insurance companies, the United States is importing services.

The item *military purchases* has bulked large in recent years. Indeed, for the seven years 1955–1961 military purchases abroad averaged over three billion dollars annually.   These expenditures by and for United States forces are for construction, logistical support, services, and most personal purchases by servicemen and their families. These expenditures are for goods and services supplied by foreigners, and consequently they affect the balance of payments precisely the same as the import of any other good or service.

These purchases of goods and services—merchandise, transportation, travel, miscellaneous services, and military purchases—constitute what is called the balance of trade. Not so very long ago it was believed that the wealth of nations depended on the maintenance of a *favorable* balance of trade, which is to say that exports must exceed imports. This view is the *mercantilist* doctrine. The mercantilists held that the resulting inflow of precious metals to pay for the excess of exports over imports would lead to an increase in the wealth and power of the country receiving the gold. Although this view still has some adherents, it is easy to show that this doctrine has little relevance for a modern economy with a sophisticated monetary system.

Let us consider the consequences of an export surplus in the balance of trade. This means more goods and services exported than imported. If the imbalance is not covered by unilateral transfers, that is, gifts, how is payment made? The mercantilist answer was by the importation of gold to cover the difference. But what if the importing countries do not have gold to export to us in payment of our favorable—their unfavorable—balance of trade? In this case the United States can extend them credit. This extension of credit is a capital movement which consists of the import of foreign promissory notes, or the American purchase of foreign assets.

By extending credit the United States is lending, and by lending abroad or exporting capital it makes available dollar balances for foreigners' use. These dollars enable payment to be made for American goods and services. What is of principal importance in this capital movement is the movement of real capital (investment goods), which results from the movement of financial capital or credit. Thus it is that countries with expanding or developing economies are often importers of capital. Similarly, underdeveloped economies are borrowers, or importers of capital, from more mature economies.

The United States, for example, was a borrower or a capital importer, from the founding of the first colonies to about the time of the Civil War. The developing nation needed all sorts of tools and equipment, and these had to be imported from abroad. Although it shipped various raw materials, produce, and tobacco abroad, particularly to England, it nevertheless ran an unfavorable balance of trade. This unfavorable trade balance was financed by borrowing. At this stage of its development the United States was what is called an immature debtor nation.

Thus, we imported capital over the years. The interest payments on this accumulating debt grew as the capital import continued. But at the same time, this borrowing was being used to develop the manufacturing capacity of the nation, including the ability to provide the needed capital goods for further development. As this process wore on, the need to import capital declined, and eventually the payment of interest and dividends abroad became greater than the imports of capital. This resulting shift in money flows meant that other countries could now buy more from us than we imported. In this manner, we began to run a favorable balance of trade and became a mature debtor nation during the 1870s. We were beginning to lend abroad ourselves, and this tended to offset any borrowing; the repayment of loans and interest on previous capital imports offset the favorable trade balance.

After the 1870s we began lending more abroad. More importantly, our net foreign debt was decreasing. We were becoming an immature creditor nation, and the First World War ended our net foreign indebtedness. In the 1920s other nations had to pay us interest and dividends, as well as repay earlier loans, larger than our new investments and loans to them. When a country has exported so much capital that interest, dividends, and repayment of loans exceed current capital exports the country is said to be a mature creditor nation. The United States is rapidly reaching this stage of development. Great Britain for years prior to the Second World War was a mature creditor nation.

What has this discussion to do with the mercantilist doctrine of a favorable balance of trade? For a long time British traders exported a great deal more than they imported. Concurrently, British investors were providing funds to pay for the excess over imports. So much capital was eventually exported that for many years England received much more interest and dividend income than was paid out in new investments. The investment income became available to importers through the foreign exchange market and was used to pay for the large import surplus which England maintained for many years prior to the Second World War. Thus, in spite of the import surplus—an *unfavorable* balance of trade—England as a mature creditor nation had a higher standard of living than she would have otherwise had. The English unfavorable balance of trade was, in fact, a very favorable situation for England. Thus it is that import surpluses enable a country to have more goods to use and enjoy than it is able to produce for itself. Certainly it is this result, a higher living standard, which constitutes the "wealth" of nations.

## INVESTMENT INCOME

The item listed under the current account as *investment income* is precisely that. It is the interest and dividend receipts from foreign notes and securities. It also includes the return to the United States of profits of foreign subsidiaries of United States businesses. The receipt of interest, dividends, and profit is the same as an export of goods or services, since it results in payments to the United States. Conversely, payments of interest and dividends by American companies to foreigners is the same as an import of goods or services, since both result in payments being made abroad.

As noted above, the net investment income of a mature creditor nation can support an import surplus in the balance of trade. This was the situation of Great Britain until the Second World War forced her to liquidate her holdings of foreign investments in order to acquire the funds for financing her wartime purchases. It was the loss of this income, together with her rundown and war damaged productive capacity, that led to England's postwar balance of payments difficulties.

## UNILATERAL TRANSFERS

Transactions involve an exchange of values. Unilateral transfers do not involve an exchange of values; rather they involve a one-way flow of value. The party giving up the value does not receive a *quid pro quo*. All gifts are of this character, whether they are private gifts or public gifts.

Unilateral transfers consist of private gifts and United States government foreign aid. In 1960 gifts from the United States abroad totaled $4.2 billion, and amounted to $4.9, $5.2, and $5.3 billion in 1961, 1962, and 1963 respectively.

These unilateral transfers have the same effect as imports generally, on balance of payments. A good deal of foreign aid consists of dollar grants to underdeveloped countries to assist them in their development. These dollar balances are established for them just as though they were receiving payment for goods imported by us. The recipient countries can then draw on these balances to purchase goods and services from us, or, perhaps, convert the dollars into other currencies to buy goods elsewhere. The grants enable the recipient countries to buy the goods and services they need abroad.

## THE BALANCING ITEMS: CAPITAL AND GOLD

The balance of payments by definition balances. Any imbalance on current transactions and transfers must be offset by an opposite imbalance in capital movements, gold movements, or both. Typically it is short-term capital movements and gold flows that keep the balance of payments balanced on a short-run basis; thus gold and short-term capital flows are the temporary balancing items. On the other hand, any prolonged imbalance on the current account must be offset by movements of long-term capital.

Gold purchases and sales have the same effect on the balance of payments statement as exports and imports of goods and services: gold exports are a source of foreign exchange, and gold imports are a source of dollars to the rest of the world. Central banks are the principal shippers of gold. For example, gold may be purchased (imported) by central banks that have acquired foreign balances in excess of foreign exchange requirements. Similarly, gold might be exported by central banks needing to replenish their stocks of foreign exchange. Most of the United States loss of gold since 1958 can be attributed to the decision of foreign central banks to convert part of their holdings of dollars, which they felt were excessively large, into gold. They thus purchased gold with their surplus dollar balances.

Before gold movements take place, however, they are generally preceded by short-term capital movements. A country with an export balance on current account, for example, may simply use the excess of its receipts to increase its foreign demand deposit balances and holdings of other short-term securities. This constitutes a short-term capital export, since the accumulation of these short-term claims on foreigners represents the *import* of promissory notes. Similarly, a country with an import balance on current account will reduce its short-term foreign assets to cover its deficit before it will resort to gold export. The drawing down of short-term assets is the same as a short-term capital import, since the promissory notes are being *exported*, or returned to the other country.

Much of the recent United States difficulty is due to the foreign accumulation of dollar balances adequate to carry on normal trade relations. As the United States trade deficit continues, these dollar balances become excessive and foreign traders swap dollars for their own currencies. Thus foreign commercial banks, and, through them, foreign central banks acquire dollar exchange in excess of normal requirements. These excess dollar balances are convertible into gold at the request of the foreign central bank.

Since gold is available only in finite amounts to any country, it is apparent that gold movements cannot continue indefinitely in one direction only. Thus gold movements are temporary means to cover a payments deficit. If the deficit is persistent it must be covered by long-term capital flows.

Under United States balance of payments accounting, the payments' deficit is measured by the increase in liquid dollar liabilities and the decline in the gold stock. The increase in liquid claims against the United States and gold sales are shown in Table 19-1 below the payments statement. The increase in liquid liabilities is essentially the increase in foreign-owned demand deposits and short-term credit instruments. That is, foreigners are "buying" demand deposit "receipts" and other short-term liabilities from us, "paying" dollars for these liquid claims against us.

For the period 1950–1957 the United States experienced persistent payments deficits, short-term and liquid liabilities rising $8.4 billion and gold losses reaching the amount of $1.7 billion. The payments deficits for this eight-year period thus averaged $1.25 billion annually. The more recent payments deficits have been:

> 1958, $3.477 million
> 1959, $3,826 million
> 1960, $3,929 million
> 1961, $2,360 million
> 1962, $2,181 million
> 1963, $1,958 million

For the six year period, 1958–1963, the average is about $3.0 billion annually. It is this recent rise over the pattern of earlier years which prompts concern over the United States balance of payments deficit. Now gold is being shipped rather than dollar balances simply being accumulated. Over the six-year period nearly $6.9 billion of gold was lost by the United States, an annual rate of nearly $1.2 billion, which is roughly the size of the average payments deficit over the preceding eight years.

## THE BALANCE OF PAYMENTS: RECENT EXPERIENCE[2]

With the single exception of 1957, the balance of payments of the United States has been in deficit since 1950. The payments deficit was, however, moderate from 1950 to 1957, averaging about $1.3 billion a year. It was substantially larger from 1958 to 1960, ranging from about $3.4 billion to $3.9 billion. In 1961, considerable progress was

---

[2] This section draws heavily on the paper, "The Long-Run Prospects for the U. S. Balance of Payments" by Edward M. Bernstein, in *Factors Affecting the United States Balance of Payments*, Joint Economic Committee (Washington, D.C.; Government Printing Office, 1962).

made in reducing the payments deficit and, despite some adverse factors, it declined to roughly $2.4 billion. In 1962 the deficit was slightly reduced to $2.2 billion. Further progress was made in 1963, reducing the payments deficit to about $1.96 billion.

Although the improvement in the United States balance of payments in the past several years is encouraging, particularly as this occurred during a period of cyclical expansion in the United States, the payments deficit is still large and the pressure on United States reserves remains. From 1950 to 1957, net sales of gold by the United States Treasury averaged $260 million a year, and the increase in foreign short-term and liquid dollar assets, official and private, averaged slightly over $1 billion a year. From 1958 to 1963, however, net gold sales averaged $1.2 billion a year, and the increase in foreign short-term and liquid dollar assets averaged nearly $1.8 billion a year.

For most countries, the measures necessary to solve a balance of payments problem, however difficult, are clear cut—that is, to restrain the demand for imports and to encourage an inflow of short-term funds. The United States must be careful in using such measures. This problem is compounded by our attaining a near mature creditor position, where an import surplus is both necessary and desirable. A reduction in aggregate demand to restrain imports will depress the economy and cause difficulties for other countries dependent on exports to the United States to keep their balance of payments in order. Nor can the United States eliminate its payments deficit by attracting a large influx of funds from other financial centers through a sharp rise in interest rates. The high interest rates would tend to hamper the growth of the American economy, and the influx of funds would shift the payments problem to other countries. The solution to the United States payments problem must be found in an environment of expanding world trade, supported by a high level of economic activity in this country.

The United States monetary authorities are, however, attempting to raise the short-term interest rate while leaving the long-term interest rate unchanged. The rationale for this policy is that a high short-term interest rate structure will induce foreign holders of dollar claims to hold them in short-term instruments, instead of converting them to gold. This would ease pressure on the United States gold stock. At the same time, if the long-term interest rate remains relatively low then domestic investment activity will not be slowed down. The monetary authorities have implemented this policy by having the Treasury increase the supply of bills, thus driving up the short-term rate, while at the same time the Federal Reserve has concentrated its open market activities at the intermediate and long-term end of the market.

Other remedies have been discussed, and include fiscal policy, direct controls over imports and capital movements, export subsidies, devaluation, etc. In the summer of 1963, for example, President Kennedy proposed a tax on United States capital exports. This is a form of control over the capital market, and it would make less attractive the raising of funds by selling foreign securities in the United States. Thus it would reduce payments made to foreigners, and so lower the deficit on the balance of payments. We shall examine the attack on the payments problem later in somewhat more detail. It suffices here to say that it involves several methods of approach, and the cooperation of foreign authorities and central banks as well as our own efforts.

The United States payments problem can be better understood only as part of a long postwar adjustment designed to restore a pattern of international payments under which the world economy can prosper and grow. This has involved the rebuilding of the productive capacity of Western Europe and Japan, the strengthening of their competitive position through the depreciation of their currencies in 1949, the resumption of their former important roles in world trade, and the establishment of convertibility of their currencies. The international economic policies of the United States have been directed to the attainment of these objectives since 1946. That these policies have been successful is indicated by the high level of production and trade, the balance of payments surplus, and the greatly increased monetary reserves of Western Europe and Japan.

It is not surprising that the adjustment that has been going on for so many years should have finally resulted in a shift in the pattern of international payments. This has been a necessary and desirable shift, away from excessive dependence on United States exports financed by American aid. The fact that it has resulted in a payments deficit for the United States would not be a matter for concern if the deficit were not so large and apparently so persistent. Within the limits imposed by its economic and political position, the United States has taken measures to strengthen its balance of payments.

Until the postwar adjustment comes to an end, the basic long-run strength of the United States international economic position will continue to assert itself. A study of three important sectors of the United States balance of payments shows that there are forces acting on trade, capital outflow, and United States government expenditures which may be expected to eliminate or greatly close the payments deficit within the next several years.

## United States Exports

The United States provides by far the largest amount of exports in world trade. In 1961, American exports, excluding transfers under military grants, amounted to $19.9 billion. In 1962, United States exports increased slightly to a total of $20.6 billion. A further increase in exports to $21.9 billion occurred in 1963. There is reason to believe that the world's need for United States exports will continue to grow and that the United States will be able to meet this demand at prices competitive with those of other countries.

Although the payments difficulties of the United States are not caused by a lag in exports, an increase in exports certainly will help close the payments gap. It is necessary to increase exports as part of a broad program to strengthen the United States balance of payments. From 1959 to 1963, the United States share of exports of manufactures held almost constant at about 21 per cent of the total for the leading industrial countries. It should be noted that while the United States share of exports of manufactures of the leading industrial countries declined from 1950 to 1963, the dollar value of such exports more than doubled.

Now that the reconstruction of their productive facilities has been completed, the growth in industrial production in Western Europe will tend to be slower. With its efficient economy, the United States will likely be able to match the increase in productivity in Western Europe in the future, as it has since 1958. Also the high level of production and employment in Europe has been accompanied by a much greater rise in wage rates, so that costs of production in manufacturing are apparently rising more in European countries than in the United States. The greatest rise in European costs are not in the export trades, however. Yet the rise in European costs will ultimately be likely to affect the prices of their exports of manufactured goods, too. With the apparent end of inflationary pressures on this country, the United States should be able to strengthen the competitive position of its exports of manufactures during the next few years.

## United States Imports

Since 1951 the ratio of imports to the gross national product has had a downward trend and in 1961, when there was a recession, the ratio was the lowest of the postwar period. In 1962, the ratio of imports to the gross national product rose again, but this was a cyclical phenomenon.

The lower ratio of imports to the gross national product in recent years probably reflects two separate factors.    One is the steady decline in the prices of basic commodities which constitute a large part of United States imports.    The second factor is the continued rise in the proportion of the gross national product in the form of services, whose import content is considerably less than that of commodities.    As a proportion of gross expenditures on *commodities*, imports have tended to be fairly constant in recent years.    The behavior of United States imports in recent years consequently does not support the view, argued by some, that the competitive position of the United States has deteriorated.

In fact, the trade surplus of the United States has increased markedly in recent years.    Merchandise exports, excluding transfers under military grants, exceeded imports by $4.7 billion in 1960, by $5.4 billion in 1961, by about $4.4 billion in 1962, and by $4.9 billion in 1963.    In contrast, the trade surplus averaged less than $2 billion a year from 1950 to 1955.    It is true that a large part of United States exports, over $2.0 billion in 1961, 1962, and 1963 for example, is financed by United States aid.    This was equally true in the early 1950s.    But directly and indirectly, the aid component of United States exports is proportionately lower now than it was ten years ago.

### United States Capital Outflow

One of the principal factors in the balance of payments deficit of recent years has been the large outflow of American private capital.    From 1950 to 1955, the outflow of private long-term and short-term capital averaged about $1.1 billion a year.    In 1960 and 1961, however, recorded American private capital outflow was $3.9 billion a year. In 1962 this declined to $3.0 billion but in 1963 rose to about $4.0 billion.    A considerable amount of unrecorded capital outflow must also have taken place as net payments on unrecorded transactions were some $600 million each year for 1960 and 1961, $1 billion in 1962, and $495 million in 1963.

In the early postwar period, direct American investment was kept down by uncertainties about the strength and stability of the world economy.    The rapid increase in direct investment since 1956 reflects the effort made by American companies to enlarge their role in production and trade to a level commensurate with improved economic prospects abroad.    This has required an unusually large volume of investment in recent years to make good the deficient level of investment in the earlier postwar period.

American companies were slow in resuming direct investment on a large scale in Western Europe. But because of the remarkable growth of their production and trade, direct American investment in the countries of Western Europe has increased considerably since 1958. The establishment of the European Common Market has been another factor inducing United States direct investment in this area. Although the peak of direct investment may not yet have been reached in Western Europe, it is apparently leveling off.

A moderate outflow of American private short-term funds is a normal accompaniment of the financing of United States trade and payments with other countries. The amounts involved in the steady growth of such financing are not large. But the large differentials in short-term interest rates in the United States, Canada, and Europe have recently induced rather large movements of short-term funds. Until a few years ago, American banks and business firms were not willing to transfer funds on any large scale in response to higher interest returns. But, because of the greater confidence in European currencies, such capital flows have now become much larger.

The greater part of the outflow of private short-term funds takes the form of an increase in the foreign claims of American banks. Until mid-1960, the increase in foreign short-term claims held by banks was small. But in the period from July, 1960, to December, 1961, American banks increased their foreign claims by almost $2 billion. This large increase probably represents an attempt by United States banks to make good their past relatively small extension of credit in this form. Although foreign claims of United States banks will likely continue to increase, the increases are not likely to be of the magnitudes reached in 1960 and 1961.

American private foreign investment is a source of large receipts in the current sector of the balance of payments. Earnings from dividends and interest and from the profits of branches abroad brought receipts of $2.8 billion in 1960, $3.3 billion in 1961, $3.7 billion in 1962, and $4.1 billion in 1963. In addition to the earnings from private foreign investment, the United States government received $471 million in 1962 as interest on its foreign loans and $498 million in 1963. On the other hand, foreign investments in the United States result in remittances of their earnings in this country. Such payments to foreigners amounted to $939 million in 1960, $882 million in 1961, $987 million in 1962, and $1,196 million in 1963.

The substantial excess of United States receipts over payments on income from foreign investment is due to several factors. First, American investments abroad are much larger than foreign investments in this country.   Second, about 90 per cent of United States private investments abroad are long-term, and two-thirds of these are direct investments in American enterprises abroad.   Foreign assets and investments in this country, on the other hand, are predominantly liquid assets that yield a low return.   Furthermore, American direct investment abroad is concentrated in the high-risk industries that yield a high return while a considerable part of foreign direct investment in the United States is concentrated in finance, insurance, and trade, where risks and earnings are smaller.

Income from American private foreign investments has been rising steadily.   Remittances of income from foreign investment in this country have also been rising, but the magnitudes are much smaller. Thus, due to the large net receipts from foreign investment, the private capital sector, which has placed a considerable strain on the balance of payments in recent years, is very likely to be a source of great strength in the future.

### Foreign Aid and Military Expenditures Abroad

The United States balance of payments is distinguished by the very large transfers and payments of a political or quasipolitical character. For example, in 1961, American transfers and payments for military expenditures, military grants, economic grants, and government long-term and short-term capital amounted to nearly $8.5 billion.   In one form or another, these have a direct or indirect effect on the United States balance of payments.

Expenditures made in connection with United States forces stationed abroad involve the payment of dollars to foreigners for goods and services provided to the Defense Department or to American personnel.   The principal elements in United States payments arising from defense establishments overseas are expenditures of troops, civilian personnel, etc.; purchases of materials, supplies, and equipment; expenditures for utilities, transportation, communication, and other services.   The balance of payments effect is the full amount of such expenditures, since these expenditures are nothing more nor less than the import of the goods or services involved.

Economic grants and government loans may have a different impact on the balance of payments.   Where the grants or loans are made directly for the purpose of buying surplus American agricultural commodities, there is no adverse effect unless such sales should displace normal sales that would have otherwise been made.   If the grants or loans are used to purchase goods abroad, the balance of payments effect is the same as that of any capital outflow not directly or indirectly related to United States exports.

## THE BALANCE OF PAYMENTS: PROSPECTS

The balance of payments deficit of the United States will most likely continue in the foreseeable future, but at a considerably moderated level below that of the 1958–60 period. A number of steps have been taken to reduce the deficit and these are having some effect, though progress may be slow.

Some of the factors that give rise to the payments deficit are not readily subject to economic considerations, and consequently balance of payments considerations are of secondary importance. These factors are United States military expenditures abroad, and American economic grants and loans in foreign aid. Steps have been taken, nevertheless, to minimize as much as possible the effects of these expenditures on the balance of payments.

Procurements by the military establishment abroad have been restrained. Some items, for example, that were formerly purchased abroad are now shipped from the United States, though this may increase the cost of maintaining the forces abroad. It does, however, reduce the effect on the balance of payments. Within the next several years it is hoped finally to reduce the net impact of military expenditures abroad on the balance of payments to about $1 billion a year.

Many people urge that the United States reduce or eliminate its large payments to the outside world in the form of foreign aid. At first glance this seems to be a principal troublemaker, but the problem, like most economic problems, is not that simple. If the United States were to cut its foreign aid its exports would also decline. This export decline would reduce the current account surplus. Although the United States makes large grants and loans to foreign countries, a major portion of these grants and loans are spent in the United States. The government has already moved to "tie" its loans and grants increasingly to the purchase of American goods. It cannot do so, however, with all of its aid dollars nor can it prevent foreigners from using tied funds to buy American goods they would have bought anyway, and then to use their earned dollars to buy goods from other industrial areas. Consequently foreign aid, while on the surface a promising area for reduction, does not turn out to be as promising a target as originally envisioned. And furthermore, foreign aid and military spending are vital parts of a broader policy shaped to increase the security and prosperity of the non-Communist world.

Despite the headway made, military expenditures abroad and economic grants and loans will probably continue to place some pressure on our payments position. Military expenditures abroad will likely prove to be irreducible below some given level, and foreign aid for underdeveloped areas will continue to be supplied chiefly by the United States, though some other Western nations are beginning to extend such aid in increasing amounts.

Of crucial concern are short-term capital outflows. Monetary policy here at home, and also abroad, must allow for the effects of large differences in interest rates on the movement of short-term funds. As we shall soon see, this factor has been recognized. Cooperation between the Treasury and Federal Reserve in the United States and among the monetary authorities of several Western European nations with respect to monetary policies offers encouragement here.

It appears, then, that measures have been taken that will tend to close the present payments deficit of the United States. Further efforts must be made to increase American exports relative to imports. If this can be accomplished, the balance of payments on current account will provide a surplus sufficiently large to cover continuing military expenditures abroad and foreign aid grants and loans. When this occurs, the payments deficit will have been closed.

On the other hand, perhaps a continuing deficit, but on a reduced scale, may be desirable as the United States dollar continues in its role as the key currency in the world's international payments system. We shall take up this question in Chapter 21, but first we shall examine in the following chapter the mechanics of the international payments system.

## REVIEW QUESTIONS

1. Draw up a balance of payments account for the United States using the latest Department of Commerce figures available. Consult the *Survey of Current Business*.
2. Why does the balance of payments account always balance?
3. What items in the balance of payments seem to be the principal factors in recent United States payments difficulties.
4. What are the reasons for international trade and commerce?
5. Using simple income definitions, show how international trade ties the levels of national income of several countries together.
6. Explain the role of unilateral transfers in our balance of payments.

## SUGGESTED REFERENCES

Department of Commerce, *Survey of Current Business;* the March issue presents the annual balance of payments for the preceding year.

*Economic Report of the President,* Washington, D.C.   This annual report presents a useful collection of data on the economy, including the international aspects.

Board of Governors, *Federal Reserve Bulletin.*   Useful analyses on international finance and payments appear from time to time.

Joint Economic Committee, *Factors Affecting the U. S. Balance of Payments* (Washington, D.C., 1962).

Kindleberger, Charles P., *International Economics,* 3rd ed. (Homewood: Richard D. Irwin, 1963).   Especially useful are Chapters 1–4 and the Appendix E on the trade multiplier.

Ranlett, John G., "The Regional Income Multiplier," *Western Economic Journal,* Vol. I, No. 2, Spring, 1963, pp. 81–95.

# CHAPTER 20

# International Money and Banking: Theory II

Why nations engage in international trade and how this trade may affect income are now both known. How the balance of payments statement summarizes the trading nation's position relative to current transactions, capital outflows, and gold movements is also known. Therefore, the present chapter moves on to mechanics—the process of determining exchange rates, the mechanism for making international payments, and the foreign exchange market. Finally, it will explore the method of achieving equilibrium in international payments.

The discussion of the mechanics of international payments and the two principal types of instruments used in making them—transfers and bills of exchange—is rather brief. Nevertheless, the treatment is sufficient to illustrate the principal concepts involved. The discussion will make evident that trade between nations requires the presence of a foreign exchange market. That is, the need to make payments for imports in terms of the exporting country's monetary unit establishes the necessity for a market whose function is to exchange one currency for another.

The process of supplying and demanding these various currencies results in establishing prices on foreign currencies—in determining, for example, the dollar price of foreign money. The prices so determined are called exchange rates. As with other prices, supply and demand factors are basic to the determination of the exchange rate. Unlike most prices, however, exchange rates are not likely to be left to the vagaries of supply and demand. By and large, exchange rates are regulated prices, administered by some governmental agency. Often

352

the price is not an equilibrium price; thus, at the official rate of exchange the supply of and demand for the particular currency are not equated.   In this situation there is pressure on the exchange rate to rise or fall, as the case may be, and these pressures require active intervention in the exchange market.

## FOREIGN EXCHANGE RATES: BASIC FACTORS

From time to time we have referred to foreign exchange.   By foreign exchange we mean foreign currencies or, more commonly, claims to foreign money balances in the form of bank deposits.   The process of trading, of exporting and importing goods and services, gives rise to the supply of and demand for foreign exchange.   Imports by the United States generate a demand for foreign exchange, since the exporters will desire payment in their own currency.   Similarly, American exports create a demand for dollars by foreign importers to pay American exporters.   Thus, we shall analyze the price of foreign exchange, the exchange rate, in terms of familiar supply and demand considerations.   The balance of payments statement, since it lists all transactions making dollars available to the rest of the world and requiring payment of dollars from the rest of the world, provides a convenient framework for the supply-demand analysis.

We can think of each item in the balance of payments statement as reflecting a separate supply and demand function.   If we take as given the domestic prices of each country, the quantities of goods and services supplied and demanded internationally will depend on the exchange rate.   Exchange rates are important because an importer can determine the attractiveness of goods only by converting their foreign prices into domestic prices through reference to the exchange rate.   Exchange rates are an integral part of the total prices of foreign goods and services and other transactions included in the balance of payments.

The exchange rate is the price of one national currency in terms of another.   For example, the official dollar exchange rate for British pounds sterling is $2.80.   This means the price of one pound in dollars is $2.80.   Conversely, the price of one dollar in terms of pounds is £.357.   These prices are reciprocals of each other.[1]   Because of the reciprocal nature of the exchange rate on dollars and the exchange rate on foreign money a rise in the exchange rate on dollars means a fall in the exchange rate on foreign money.   Thus, since exchange rates are

---

[1] If £1 = $2.80 then clearly £1/2.80 = $1.00 or £.357 = $1.00.

an important part of the price of foreign goods, a fall in the exchange rate on foreign money will lower the import prices of foreign goods; conversely, a rise in the exchange rate on foreign money will raise the import prices of foreign goods and services.  Thus, the 1949 British devaluation of the pound from $4.03 to $2.80 lowered the import prices of British goods to Americans.  It raised the prices of American goods to the British, however, since the price of dollars in pounds rose from £.248 to £.357.

### The Determination of Free Exchange Rates

The determination of free exchange rates follows the same basic principles of supply and demand which determine prices generally. The intersection of an aggregate demand curve and an aggregate supply curve for foreign exchange determines the exchange rate.  In the normal case we should expect a situation similar to that depicted in Figure 20-1.

The supply schedule of pounds slopes upward to the right.  This reflects the fact that at higher exchange rates more pounds are offered for sale—in the New York money market, for instance.  This illustrates the reciprocal relation between pound-dollar exchange rates, for as the exchange rate of pounds in dollars rises, the price of dollars in pounds falls; with cheaper dollars acquired by Britishers, American exports increase.   The increase in American exports may also increase the supply of pounds in New York, since our exports may in part be purchased with pounds.  Because sellers of pounds are buyers of dollars, the supply of pounds is also the demand for dollars to provide payment for American exports.

The demand schedule for pounds slopes downward to the right, indicating that greater quantities of pounds are demanded at lower

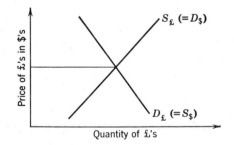

*Figure 20-1*  The basic determinants of the rate of exchange.

prices.   When the pound is cheap in terms of the dollar, Americans will want a larger quantity of pounds because they will spend more on British goods.   But, clearly, this demand for pounds is the supply of dollars.

This exchange rate is a free exchange rate, which is to say that the rate determined by the supply-demand relations is free to fluctuate as the underlying supply-demand determinants change.   Thus, if the demand for pounds were to increase, given the supply schedule for pounds, the exchange rate would necessarily rise.   But should the demand for pounds decline in the face of an unchanged supply schedule for pounds the exchange rate would fall, as it would if the supply of pounds increased with the demand schedule for pounds unchanged.

What are the basic determinants of the supply and demand schedules for foreign exchange?   We might beg the question by replying that import transactions are the source of the demand schedule for foreign exchange, and similarly that export transactions form the basis of the supply side.   It is possible, however, to single out some basic determinants underlying the volume of the various import and export transactions.   The four principal determinants are: levels of income and changes in the levels of income in the trading countries; tastes and preferences for domestic versus imported goods in the various countries; relative prices and changes in relative prices in the trading countries; and relative yield and safety of investments in the various countries.

Since we have seen that the demand for pounds is the supply of dollars, we may summarize the basic supply-demand forces as follows, remembering that country $A$'s exports are country $B$'s imports:

1. The level of income influences the level of imports of goods and services.   The higher the income level the greater is the volume of imports, and so, the greater is the need for foreign currencies to pay for the imports.

2. Tastes and preferences affect the schedules for foreign exchange.   The greater the taste for foreign goods, other things equal, the greater is the demand for foreign exchange.   A change in tastes will result in shifting of the basic schedules.

3. Similarly the relative prices of domestic and imported goods is important in determining the schedules.   The higher domestic prices are relative to foreign prices the more we tend to import, which translates into an increased demand for foreign exchange.

4. Relative interest rates influence capital movements, with relatively high interest rates abroad resulting in the export of capital (the import of notes).   But unless there is the prospect of reasonable

safety, even high rates may not attract lenders' attention. Another factor affecting capital exports is the level of government aid programs, with higher levels of foreign aid commitments showing as an increase in the supply of dollars, with its concurrent significance for the demand for foreign exchange.

After the foregoing discussion of exchange rate determination, it must be repeated, however, that exchange rates are generally not left to fluctuate freely according to the dictates of supply and demand. As a matter of policy, nearly all exchange rates are controlled rates.

## MECHANICS OF INTERNATIONAL PAYMENTS

The basic forces in the supply and demand for foreign exchange can be made clear by investigating the mechanism for making international payments. Just as banks facilitate the payment process in domestic trade by the clearing and collection of checks, so do banks facilitate international payments. Almost every bank in the United States maintains a correspondent relationship with a bank in New York or other financial center, or else has such a relationship with some other bank which does have a New York correspondent bank. In this fashion even the smallest bank can provide its customers who wish to make payments to foreigners with a check drawn on a major New York bank, and since the major New York banks have correspondent relationships with foreign banks the payments can even be made by a check drawn on a foreign bank.

Banking systems in different countries are linked together in two principal ways, through foreign branch offices and through international correspondent relationships. The first instance may be illustrated by banks such as the Bank of America and the Chase Manhattan Bank, which operate a number of overseas branches. Similarly, a number of British, French, Dutch, and Canadian banks have foreign branches in various parts of the world. Typically foreign branches become members of the clearing and collection systems of the country in which the branch is located, and they carry on banking activities to the extent permitted by the laws of the country. These foreign branches perform numerous services for the head office and its correspondents, by drawing and selling drafts, collecting or paying drafts, providing market information, etc.

These same services, however, can also be provided through foreign correspondent banks. In a correspondent relationship a domestic bank and a foreign bank agree to perform or provide certain services for each other. Typically the banks maintain deposit accounts with each other. Each bank acts for the other, and correspondents of the other, in the collection of drafts and other items, in presenting bills of exchange for acceptance, etc. Often the correspondent banks lend to each other up to some given amount. Thus, if for some reason the deposit balance becomes depleted, payment services may still be extended.

In the area of international payments banks perform two basic functions. The first is to facilitate payments, and this we may term the *transfer function*. This transfer function is provided by banks in the clearing and collection of checks internationally through foreign branches or correspondents in a manner similar to the domestic clearing and collection of checks. The second basic function provided by banks is the granting of credit to carry on international trade. This function of banks is termed the *credit function*. But before we take up the transfer and credit functions of banks engaged in international banking we must first discuss the chief instruments used in making international payments.

## Instruments of International Payment: Transfers

The instruments involved in the payments process fall into two principal categories, transfers and bills of exchange. Most transactions in foreign exchange involve the transfer of a deposit held in a foreign bank. In order to effect these transfers the cable transfer is the major instrument used. A cable transfer is simply an order sent by cable to a foreign bank holding an account for the seller of a foreign currency, instructing that bank to charge the seller's account and credit the buyer's account, or the account of someone designated by the buyer, with a specified sum. The cable transfer is, in effect, a check sent by cable line.

For example, assume that a United States export firm owns a deposit balance abroad in excess of what it considers desirable. In this situation the export firm might wire its foreign bank to transfer the excess funds to the account of its United States bank. The firm will receive the dollar equivalent at the going market rate of exchange on the same day the balance changes hands, and the American bank will obtain a supply of foreign exchange from the transaction. Since most American firms, however, do not maintain foreign bank accounts perhaps the following is more typical. Assume our American firm has a foreign business account from whom payment is due. In this case the United States firm might cable the foreign customer directing it to make payment to the American bank purchasing the exchange. The

American bank then credits the firm's account by the amount of the dollar equivalent. Conversely, when an American importer wants to make a payment abroad it arranges for a cable transfer from its bank. The American bank directs its correspondent bank to transfer the specified amount from its account to the account of the firm buying the transfer or to a payee designated by the purchaser, whereupon the American bank collects the equivalent dollar amount from the American importer.

The mail transfer is similar to the cable transfer, except that the order to the foreign bank is sent by mail instead of by cable. Prior to the widespread use of air mail, mail transfers were discounted, since the seller had the use of his funds abroad until the mail transfer arrived. Today, however, there is often no difference in the rates quoted by banks for air-mail transfers and cable transfers.

Sometimes it may be desired to make a payment abroad directly to the firm or individual involved without going through a foreign bank. In this situation the United States bank sells the payer a draft on the bank's foreign balance. This is a written order from the American bank directing its foreign correspondent to make a specified payment to a designated payee on presentation of the draft. The paying individual or firm then mails the draft to the designated payee abroad who cashes it as he would any other check presented him.

### Bills of Exchange

One of the commonest instruments used in international finance is the *bill of exchange*. The bill of exchange may be a commercial bill or a bankers' bill. The commercial bill is drawn on a commercial concern, the importing firm, and the bankers' bill is drawn against a bank. Frequently a bill of exchange is referred to as a draft, and it may be payable on demand (on sight) or payable on some specified future date. A bill payable at some future date becomes an acceptance when the payer *accepts* the bill by signing it; that is, when the payer promises to pay the bill according to its terms, which, in effect, converts the bill into a promissory note. The commonest situation is that of a draft drawn by an export firm on the importer's bank (or its correspondent) under a letter of credit.

To illustrate the principles involved, let us consider an example. Let us suppose that a British exporter, when he ships goods to an American importer also sends along a draft drawn on the importer for the value of the transactions, normally expressed in pounds, ordering the importer to pay the exporter or someone designated by the exporter. As a condition of taking possession of the goods the importer may be required to accept the draft. In accepting the bill the drawer writes "Accepted," the date, and his signature on the face of the bill. This acceptance or endorsement of the bill is a promise to fulfill the conditions of the bill, which converts it into a promissory note on the part of the importer. If the draft is payable on demand the importer must arrange to transfer funds immediately to the exporter before taking possession of the goods. Should the draft be payable at a future date the importer may also be required to have his bank accept the draft, to become a cosigner to the note to guarantee payment. The export firm now has for presentation an instrument with a very high credit standing, a *banker's acceptance*. If the British export firm wants immediate payment it may discount the acceptance to its bank which would hold the note till due and then present it to the American bank for payment.

A bankers' bill works in much the same fashion, with the draft being drawn directly on a bank instead of on a commercial firm. The paying firm, the American import house, must have sufficient funds in its account at the bank on which the draft is drawn, or else must make arrangements for an extension of credit. The commonest form that the extension of credit takes is that of the letter of credit. A letter of credit is a letter that states that the writer of the letter (a commercial bank) will honor for the account of a buyer (the importer) drafts drawn by a seller (the exporter). The purpose of such a letter is to give the seller assurance that he will receive payment from the bank. Thus, for example, an importer may arrange with his bank for the issuance of a letter of credit under which the exporter may draw bills on the bank, or on one of its correspondent banks, rather than on the importer. The letter of credit is assurance to the exporter that the bill will be paid by the bank or its correspondent if it is a sight bill, or that it will be accepted by the bank if it is a time draft. The issuance of a letter of credit gives the seller greater assurance of payment than if he had relied only on the credit standing of the buyer. The exporter can rely on the standing and integrity of the bank rather than the credit standing of the importer alone.

## The Transfer and Credit Functions

The various transactions summarized in the balance of payments statement clearly require payments—payments made by Americans to foreigners and vice versa. The banking system greatly facilitates these payments between nations, often involving the conversion of one currency into another.

Foreign exchange transactions are commonly arranged by a pair of correspondent banks, or else through a bank that has an overseas branch. As an example, suppose we have two correspondent banks, Bank A (the American bank) and Bank B (a British bank). Assume that these two banks maintain deposit balances with each other. For example, since the official exchange rate between dollars and pounds is £1 equals $2.80, the two banks might establish deposit balances with one another by Bank A crediting a $28,000 deposit account to Bank B which in turn credits Bank A with a deposit of £10,000. The balance sheets of the two banks will appear as below:

### Bank A

| A | L |
|---|---|
| Due from B, $28,000 (= £10,000) | Due to B, $28,000 (= £10,000) |

### Bank B

| A | L |
|---|---|
| Due from A, £10,000 (= $28,000) | Due to A, £10,000 (= $28,000) |

Having established these credits with each other, the banks are in a position to provide their customers with checks or drafts drawn in the other country's money. An American importer may want to make a payment to a British exporter who has specified payment in pounds. Let us assume the amount of the payment to be made is £500. The American importer goes to Bank A—let us assume the importer is a customer of A—and exchanges part of his deposit balance, $1,400, for the draft of £500. The importer then sends the draft to the British exporter who deposits it to his account at an English bank, say Bank B. The position of the two banks involved is now as follows:

### Bank A

| A | L |
|---|---|
| Due from B,    $28,000 | Due to B,        $28,000 |
| Due from B, −$ 1,400 | DD Importer, −$ 1,400 |

### Bank B

| A | L |
|---|---|
| Due from A,    £10,000 | Due to A,        £10,000 |
| | Due to A,       −£500 |
| | DD Exporter   +£500 |

At the same time the above transaction was going on suppose British importers were buying dollars to pay for the import of American goods worth $4,200 and, needing this amount of dollars in order to pay, exchanged £1,500 from their demand deposit balance for a draft for $4,200. When the draft is received by the American exporter and deposited in his account at Bank A the final results are:

### Bank A

| A | | L | |
|---|---|---|---|
| Due from B, | $28,000 | Due to B, | $28,000 |
| Due from B, | −$ 1,400 | DD Importer, | −$ 1,400 |
| | | DD Exporter, | +$ 4,200 |
| | | Due to B, | −$ 4,200 |

### Bank B

| A | | L | |
|---|---|---|---|
| Due from A, | £10,000 | Due to A, | £10,000 |
| | | Due to A, | −£500 |
| | | DD Exporter, | +£500 |
| Due from A, | −£1,500 | DD Importer, | −£1,500 |

The preceding example illustrates how banks expedite international payments. The individual firms in Britain and America maintain their deposit accounts in their own banks and they, themselves, generally cannot write a check payable in foreign currencies. They can, however, have their banks write such checks for them, since the banks do maintain deposit balances with each other.

As we know, the drafts involved in the payments process may be *sight* drafts, which are payable on demand, or they may be *time* drafts, which are payable on or after a specified date. In the preceding illustration the drafts were sight drafts payable on demand. Perhaps more common is the use of time drafts to make international payments, and the use of these time drafts means that not only are banks facilitating payments but typically they are also providing credit.

In the typical transaction the exporter wishes to be paid immediately, while the importer prefers delaying payment until he has sold the goods and received the proceeds from their sale. We have here a conflict of interest between the parties to the transactions, between the exporter wanting payment now and the importer wanting to pay later. This difference may be reconciled by the introduction of credit into the exchange.

Let us suppose that the British exporter, when he ships the goods valued at £500 to the American importer, also sends along with the goods a draft ordering the importer to pay £500 to the exporter or to someone designated by the exporter.   As a condition of taking possession of the goods the importer may be required to accept the draft; that is, endorse it or promise to carry out its conditions.   This makes the draft into a promissory note showing the importer's obligation to the exporter.

If this draft is payable on demand, the analysis of the previous illustration holds.   If, however, the draft is payable after some specified time the following is likely to occur.   After accepting the draft, the American importer can ask his bank to *accept* it, to become, in effect, a cosigner to guarantee the carrying out of the terms of the commercial bill.   This makes the bill into a bankers' acceptance.   More typically, however, the bills are drawn initially on a bank under a letter of credit.   But whatever the method, once accepted the bankers' acceptance enjoys high credit standing.

In our example, the British exporter can now sell this acceptance to his bank at a discount in order to receive immediate payment.   The British bank in turn holds the acceptance till its due date when it collects the £500 from the importer's bank.   It goes without saying, of course, that the American importer must provide his bank with the necessary funds to make the payment, or must have made arrangement for credit through a letter of credit or in some other fashion.

## THE FOREIGN EXCHANGE MARKET

The principal United States foreign exchange market is, as might be expected, in New York.   The term market, like the open market in which the Federal Reserve engages, is, however, a bit misleading since there is no centralized meeting place, no fixed hours, and no formal requirements for engaging in trading activities.   It has been suggested that the foreign exchange market can best be thought of not as a place, but as a mechanism for bringing buyers and sellers of foreign exchange together.[2]   The participants in this foreign exchange market are United States commercial banks with overseas deposits, the customers of these commercial banks, who are both demanders and suppliers of foreign exchange, foreign exchange brokers, and finally foreign banks that deal in foreign exchange with domestic banks.

In New York there are approximately twenty-five banks that main-

---

[2] Alan R. Holmes, *The New York Foreign Exchange Market:* 1959, Federal Reserve Bank of New York, p. 10.

tain deposits abroad to facilitate their dealings in foreign exchange. Of these banks fewer than half account for the bulk of the business. These commercial banks, in order to be able to meet the needs of their customers, keep inventories of foreign exchange in the form of working balances in foreign banks.   Thus it was that the American importer in the example of the last section could purchase a sterling draft for £500. These inventories of foreign exchange are acquired by the purchases of foreign balances owned by firms, individuals, or other banks; by the purchases of bills of exchange, traveler's checks, foreign bond coupons, etc.; and by selling dollars to foreign banks that need funds available in New York.

In serving their customers, the banks purchase foreign exchange from some of their business customers and sell foreign exchange to other customers.   Each commercial bank thus acts as a clearing house, where purchases of exchange can be offset by sales of foreign exchange. But since it is most unlikely that any given day's transactions in a particular foreign money will balance out, the bank finds its inventory position altered.   Some banks find that purchases of exchange from exporters are exceeding their sales of exchange to importers.   Other banks find themselves in just the opposite position.   In order to iron out these imbalances, to eliminate excessively large foreign exchange balances of some banks and to replenish and restore exchange positions of other banks so they may serve customers needing exchange, there has grown up in New York an active market in foreign exchange among the banks.

The banks themselves do not deal directly with one another.   They instead use the services of foreign exchange brokers.   These brokers have direct telephone connections with the foreign exchange trading rooms of the principal commercial banks.   They are in almost continual contact with the bank traders.   The brokers have as their chief function the bringing together of the buyers and sellers of exchange among the banks.   In this fashion the selling banks can maintain their exchange balances at a normal level, instead of piling up excessively large balances.   By using a broker the banks save time and effort.   A bank wanting to buy or sell foreign exchange informs the broker of the amount it is interested in and the exchange rate at which it is ready to do business.   With this information the broker then tries to match up the bank's bid or offer in the market.   If successful in carrying out the transaction, the broker receives a commission from the selling bank.

This interbank foreign exchange market serves to smooth excessive purchases or sales made by individual banks.   On occasion, however, the quantity of some exchange offered will exceed the quantity demanded, or vice versa. When one of these situations occurs, an imbalance between the quantity of exchange supplied and demanded, the exchange rate begins to change. If the exchange is in excess supply the rate falls, and if the exchange is in demand the exchange rate rises. The movement in the exchange rate may help to correct the situation by encouraging or discouraging additional buyers and sellers into or from the market.

If the imbalance between the supply and demand for the particular exchange continues, then a very important means of correcting the situation and limiting the movement of the exchange rate is through the purchase of foreign exchange from, or sales to, foreign banks by the New York banks. These foreign banks operate in their own foreign exchange markets abroad, and are active dealers in United States dollars, buying and selling dollars just as the New York banks buy and sell, say, British pounds. Thus, when the New York banks attempt to correct an excess supply of some exchange by selling it to banks in the particular country, the New York banks obtain dollars in exchange for the foreign money balance. Conversely, if New York banks buy exchange from foreign banks to correct an excess demand they pay for it with dollars. In this era of pegged exchange rates, in order to keep the exchange rate stabilized foreign central banks or exchange authorities will enter the market if necessary. They enter the market both as buyers and sellers to prevent excessive swings in the exchange rate. Thus, if there occurs an increased demand for, say, pounds the British Exchange Stabilization Account is prepared to enter the market and sell pounds for dollars to prevent the exchange rate from rising above £1 = $2.82. Similarly, should pounds be in excess supply the Exchange Stabilization Account will enter the market to buy all pounds offered to it for dollars to prevent the exchange rate from declining below £1 = $2.78. Through this or a similar form of intervention in the foreign exchange market by exchange authorities the balance between quantities supplied and demanded of foreign exchange is maintained at the pegged rate of exchange.

### The Foreign Exchange Market: Forward Rates[3]

Not only is there an active foreign exchange market that determines the so-called spot rate of exchange, which is simply the day-to-day

---

[3] The following section draws heavily from the excellent work of Holmes noted earlier. See Alan R. Holmes, *The New York Foreign Exchange Market.*

rate, but there is also a market in forward exchange.  The forward exchange market functions side by side with the spot exchange market. A forward exchange transaction simply involves a purchase or sale of a foreign currency for delivery at some time in the future.  The rate at which the transaction is to take place is determined at the time of sale, but the payment is not made until the exchange is delivered by the seller.  Forward exchange rates are usually quoted on the basis of a discount or premium over or under the spot rate of exchange; thus, forward rates may be expressed as a percentage deviation from the spot rate of exchange.

The value of a forward exchange market to exporters or importers should be obvious.  Exporters and importers or anyone else who antici-pates either the receipt or payment of foreign exchange at some future date may find it advantageous to engage in forward exchange transactions.  Since cost in the case of exporters and selling prices in the case of importers are in terms of dollars, it is important for them to know just what the dollar value of their foreign exchange receipt or payment will be.  The forward exchange market provides a method for hedging against exchange risk by providing to importers or exporters facilities for buying or selling exchange forward.  This forward exchange market is closely associated with the spot foreign exchange market and bears a resemblance to it, just as the futures mar-ket is closely connected with spot trading in the commodity market.

Thus exporters have to cover the risk of exchange depreciation for payments due them at some time in the future, say ninety days hence. Similarly importers have to be on guard against the risk that the cur-rency will appreciate between the time they acquire an obligation to make a payment in a foreign currency, and the time that that obli-gation is discharged.  In general, the process of covering exchange risks in the forward market is simply a way of eliminating uncertainties of the foreign exchange element of international transactions.

The forward exchange rate is quite sensitive to speculative influences and to changes in sentiment with respect to various currencies.  The forward exchange rate is not independent of the spot rate of exchange, however.  The relationship between the spot and forward exchange rates is not a direct one; it works through the relationship of the interest rates prevailing in the two countries.

As borrowers and lenders attempt to take advantage of differences in interest rates the movement of short-term funds between inter-national centers is a major factor which tends to limit the spread between the forward and spot rates of exchange.  Whether it is profit-able to move short-term funds from one financial center to another depends not only on the additional interest that might be obtained, but also on the relationship of the two currencies in the spot and forward exchange markets. For example, an American investor contemplating the temporary investment of funds in British Treasury bills because of higher interest rates in England must first purchase sterling in the spot market in order to buy the British bills. While he is a holder of the British Treasury bills he is exposed to the possibility of a depreciation in sterling, a depreciation that might more than offset his anticipated gain from the higher interest rate in England. Speculative capital flows, by their very nature, are not covered in the forward market, but an arbitrageur seeking a sure gain must always cover his exchange risk by executing a forward sale to coincide with the maturity of his foreign investment.

Forward exchange theory holds that under normal circumstances the forward discount or premium on one currency in terms of another is directly related to the difference in the interest rates prevailing in the two countries. The forward exchange rate is said to be at interest parity whenever the interest differential and the forward discount or premium are equal.

Consider, for example, a situation where the short-term interest rate in some foreign country is 2 per cent higher than at home and the forward discount on the foreign currency is, let us say, 0.5 per cent. In these circumstances, a transfer of funds abroad with exchange risks covered would return an additional yield of 1.5 per cent per annum. In this situation, the actual movement of the funds abroad would tend to restore the interest parity by means of, first, increasing the forward discount on the foreign currency as a result of the demand for spot exchange and the offering of forward exchange by the arbitrageur, and second, lowering the interest rate differential as funds are transferred from one area to another.

The Treasury and Federal Reserve have recently been operating in the forward exchange market. An example of the complexity of these operations is the following. In the spring of 1961 West Germany and the Netherlands appreciated their currencies by 5 per cent. There was a widespread belief in the international money market that this appreciation was not sufficient, and that it would be followed by additional appreciation of those currencies and, perhaps, the currencies of other countries with surplus balance of payments positions. As a result of this, there was a large increase in the flow of short-term capital to continental countries.

Accompanying this activity in short-term speculative capital movement was a substantial premium on the German mark and the Swiss franc in the forward market, that is, a substantial discount on the forward dollar.   Speculators were hoping for an official appreciation of the Swiss franc and additional appreciation of the German mark. These speculative fears led foreigners anticipating dollar receipts to seek a means of hedging against the risk of a depreciation of the dollar in terms of their own currency.   Selling forward dollars did not look attractive because of the low price of forward dollars in terms of marks or francs.   Thus, foreigners, expecting to receive dollars in the future, found it cheaper to cover the exchange risk by borrowing dollars and selling them in the spot market for the desired local currency, investing the proceeds in short-term foreign claims.   This type of transaction increased the outflow of dollars from the United States, as these dollar loans were made, into official holdings abroad, as the borrowers converted the dollars into the local currency.

Faced with these circumstances the Treasury began to operate in the forward exchange market.   The Treasury sold German marks and Swiss francs forward in an effort to reduce the premium, the discount on the dollar.   The Treasury was successful in this effort.   Reduction of the forward premium wiped out the incentive for foreigners who anticipated dollar receipts to borrow dollars and sell them, and also eliminated the potential profit from covered interest arbitrage.   To aid in this kind of forward exchange operation, the Federal Reserve has arranged "swaps" of dollars for other currencies with the central banks of a number of countries.   These swaps give the Federal Reserve a supply of assorted foreign exchange to sell either spot or forward during periods of weakness of the dollar.

## Foreign Exchange Rate: Summary

Exchange rate policy is one part of the broader problem of maintaining equilibrium in the balance of payments.   By definition the balance of payments always balances, but though in balance it is not necessarily in equilibrium.   Equilibrium in the balance of payments is defined as a situation containing no tendencies to produce change in the balance of payments components.   As we saw earlier, the balancing items in the balance of payments statement are presumably gold and short-term capital movements.   Thus, when there are no net movements of gold or short-term capital the balance of payments is said to be in equilibrium.   Any surplus or deficit on current account is financed by long-term capital movements.

An equilibrium in the balance of payments consequently corresponds to a situation of balance in the foreign exchange market.   The quantities of exchange supplied and demanded are in balance.   The exchange demanded to pay for imports of goods and services and to invest abroad will be offset by the supply of exchange from exports of goods and services and sales of long-term securities.   In this situation, there are no dealers in foreign exchange who find themselves with unwanted inventories of exchange, and no international movements of exchange between banks to correct imbalances.

Since, however, equilibrium conditions are generally not satisfied, it is important to examine how equilibrium is attained, or at least, how the equilibrating process operates.

## THE EQUILIBRIUM PROCESS AND EXCHANGE RATES

From the definition of equilibrium as a situation of balance in the supply of and the demand for foreign exchange, it follows that disequilibrium exits when there is imbalance in the foreign exchange market.   When movements of foreign exchange assets occur, pressures to change the exchange rate are generated.   To understand how these pressures originate and how they are brought under control is to understand the equilibrating process.

Since the exchange rate is a price it can be analyzed in terms of supply-demand considerations.   Thus, the pressures on the exchange rate in a disequilibrium situation are due to factors that affect the supply and demand schedules for foreign exchange.   The basic determinants of the supply and demand schedules for foreign exchange, it will be recalled, are four in number: (1) levels of national income; (2) tastes and preferences; (3) relative price levels; and (4) relative interest rates. A change in any one or several of these factors will produce shifts in the supply-demand schedules for exchange, and thus cause the exchange rate to change.

It will be instructive to examine the equilibrating process under three exchange rate situations, namely, (1) the gold standard, (2) a free fluctuating situation, and (3) pegged conditions.

### Equilibrium under the Gold Standard

How given changes in the supply and demand for foreign exchange cause the exchange rate to vary depends on the basis of the currencies involved; that is, it depends on what backs the money.   As we know, in the last century money was almost universally backed by gold. A gold standard requires that the government define its monetary unit in terms of gold and then stand ready to buy and sell gold without limitation internally or externally at the price fixed for it.   When all countries were on a gold standard, the different national currencies, all defined in gold, were automatically related to one another.

Thus, an American with dollars or an Englishman with pounds or a Frenchman with francs could buy gold at a fixed price.   Each could ship the gold to another country and buy another currency at a fixed price.   Under these conditions, as we shall see, the exchange rates could fluctuate only within narrow limits, the gold points, determined by the costs of actually shipping and insuring the gold.   Under these conditions how did the process of equilibration work itself out?

When the gold standard was in fashion the exchange rate was determined by the respective gold equivalents of the currencies involved. Thus, if the dollar was then defined as now as 0.888671 grams of fine gold and the pound sterling as 2.48828 grams of fine gold, the exchange rate would have been automatically determined as $2.80 equals one pound sterling.

Under gold standard conditions the exchange rate tended to stay close to the ratio of gold values, or the *mint parity*.   The exchange rate was free to fluctuate within limits called the *gold points*.   Since gold could be freely bought and sold, these gold points were determined by the costs of insurance, transportation, and handling charges attendant on the physical shipment of gold between countries.   For example, a man buying pounds would be willing to pay a price above the mint parity if necessary, but that price could not be greater than the cost of buying gold in New York and shipping it to London to acquire the pounds.   In similar fashion, a man selling pounds would accept a price below mint parity so long as it did not fall below by an amount equal to the cost of using his pounds in London to buy gold and bring the gold to New York where he could sell the gold for dollars.

Between the gold points, which, for example, were only a few pennies apart in the case of the pound, the price of foreign exchange was determined by the forces of supply and demand.   At the gold points the supply and demand schedule became infinitely elastic.   This situation is illustrated in Figure 20-2.

Thus a change in the supply schedule for pounds within the interval $DD'$ would simply result in a divergence of the exchange rate from mint parity; a shift in the demand for pounds with the range $SS'$ would similarly result in a price different from the mint parity.   Any substantial shifts in the schedules, however, would bring about a gold flow.

Equilibrium was restored conceptually in this situation when the country gaining the gold found its money supply increasing and prices

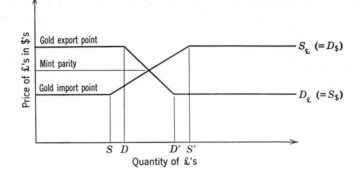

**Figure 20-2**   The exchange rate under gold standard conditions.

and income rising, while the reverse was going on in the country shipping the gold.   The lower prices and higher interest rates in the gold exporting country now made it attractive for the gold receiving country to increase its imports and purchase securities from the deflated area.   This shifted the supply-demand schedules so that the gold flow was halted and equilibrium restored.   This was the classical price-specie-flow mechanism, which depended on internal price adjustments occurring before gold stocks were exhausted, two requirements which are unlikely to be met in modern day circumstances.

Let us consider the following famous example.   Assume England trades woolen cloth to Portugal for wine and that there is equilibrium in the balance of payments with no net movements of gold or short-term capital.   The value of wine shipped to England by Portugal equals the total value of woolens shipped by England to Portugal.   Now assume an increase in English demand for wine, that is English tastes and preferences shift in favor of Portuguese wines.   What are the consequences of this increase in demand for Portuguese wine and, hence, increase in demand for Portuguese escudos to pay for the wine?

The immediate consequence of this increase in English demand for escudos is to drive up the price of escudos in terms of pounds.   But how high will this rise go?   As soon as the price rises above the upper gold point it becomes cheaper for British importers to ship gold.   With gold being shipped, the price of escudos in pounds no longer rises. Thus gold flows from England to Portugal to pay for the increased import of wine.   But how long can this gold flow go on?   Is it possible England will drink herself out of gold?

Clearly as gold moves to Portugal there is more money there.   This raises Portuguese demand for goods, and prices there begin to rise.

Wine now becomes more expensive in escudos and England consumes less of it at the higher prices.   At the same time, as gold flows from England there is less money in England and prices begin to fall.   At these lower prices Portugal imports more woolen cloth.   The effects of these *internal* price changes caused by the flow of gold bring the balance of payments on current account back into balance and gold no longer needs to be shipped.

This argument is based on the quantity theory of money.   In England the money supply was reduced and prices fell, while in Portugal the supply of money increased, accompanied by a rise in prices.   The operation of the gold standard, as described here, depends on the quantity theory of money really working, and in a present day economy things do not seem to work this way.   The gold standard determines fixed exchange rates or *external* prices.   Internal prices must be flexible if the adjustment process is to work, and this does not seem to be the case.   But what if prices do not fall as gold leaves a country, but rather income and employment fall instead?   In this situation, with no price adjustments taking place due to price rigidities, a multiplier effect will reduce income.   In this situation, if income, employment, and prices are all to be maintained, the international trade adjustment process through flexible internal prices cannot be made.

In today's economies the flow of gold out of a country to make international payments does not necessarily reduce the country's money supply.   As we know, the supply of money depends on central bank policy and is largely independent of the amount of gold a country possesses.   Since gold coins and gold certificates are no longer the principal circulating media, the central bank would have to manipulate the nongold money supply for the gold standard to work under these conditions.   If gold flowed into a country, the central bank would have to act to increase the supply of money.   The automatic nature of the gold standard is present only because the central bank is willing to have it that way.   But as the maintenance of income and employment have become the primary objectives of monetary policy, central banks have refused to play the gold-standard game according to its rules.   Indeed, following the rules has become ever more difficult since all the factors that make monetary policy ineffective also make the gold standard less workable.

In all likelihood the gold standard never did work either as well or as neatly as its supporters claim.   The adjustments did not all take place through internal price changes resulting from the gold flow.   Changes in the level of income also contributed to the process of adjustment.

Thus, when exports rise in a country there is a multiplier effect which raises the level of income. But this very rise in income induces an increase in imports, which contributes to the restoration of balance in the balance of payments. With the level of income and employment becoming the principal considerations, countries have given up playing the gold-standard game according to its rules. Instead of worrying about internal price adjustments, they now center attention on the maintenance of income and employment, and put the burden of adjustment on external prices through the exchange rate.

### Equilibrium under Fluctuating Exchange Rates

After the First World War many countries permanently went off the gold standard, which had been suspended during the war period. They halted the unlimited buying and selling of gold at a fixed price, and adopted inconvertible paper standards in the place of the gold standard. Under these conditions, what then determined the exchange rate between nations on inconvertible paper standards?

The answer is that the exchange rate was set free to fluctuate, moving up and down in response to changes in the supply and demand for the various goods and services in international trade. Thus, if England buys more of Portugal's wine, increasing the demand for escudos and driving up their price in terms of the pound, there is no upper gold point to halt the rise in the exchange rate. However, changes in the exchange rate tend to restore the balance of trade to equilibrium. As the price of the escudo rises in terms of pounds, Portuguese goods become increasingly expensive to the British, which curtails England's purchases of them. Internal prices are free to change or not as the case may be, since the international adjustment is brought about by changes in external prices, by the change in exchange rates.

Under flexible exchange rates countries are free to pursue which ever type of domestic price and employment policies they wish without having to consider the exchange rate. An expansionist domestic policy may, however, produce embarassing international money flows and changes in the composition of the balance of payments on current account. In any event, conflicts among policies to maintain domestic income and employment, price rigidities, and fixed exchange rates are resolved by the simple expedient of abandoning the latter. But this solution has shortcomings also. Exchange rates can fluctuate rather widely, and these fluctuations cause uncertainties which discourage international trade and capital movement. For example, under conditions of freely fluctuating exchange rates an exporter may hesitate to ship goods abroad for fear that by the time the shipment is paid for the exchange rate on the importing country's money may have fallen, resulting in losses instead of profit on the transaction.

The factors causing the exchange rate to fluctuate are, of course, changes in the supply of and demand for foreign exchange; that is, changes in the current and capital accounts in the balance of payments. Changes in the trade balance in goods and services are generally not enough to produce large fluctuations in the exchange rate. But movements or changes in the trade balance are not the only ones to affect the price of foreign exchange; capital movements also play a part in determining the exchange rate. Indeed, capital movements may play a major role in explaining sharp changes in the price of foreign exchange.

For example, when Americans lend more abroad this action drives up the price of foreign exchange. The cessation of a period of lending may cause exchange rates to shift, as will the granting of a large loan in a period otherwise free of lending activity. In addition, speculative capital movements may make the situation even more unstable. Thus, for example, if the price of a currency falls, fears of further decline may arise. People may react in such a fashion as to make their fears come true by selling the weakened currency and buying other currencies, and by this process force the exchange rate down still further. Precisely this type of self-justifying behavior was frequently encountered in the period following the First World War. This kind of capital flight can become self-aggravating and can cause rather sharp fluctuations in exchange rates. Under a gold standard such capital flights would, conversely, produce no change in exchange rates, but would result in inflationary and deflationary pressures within the economies of the countries involved in the shift of capital.

This kind of exchange rate instability caused many countries to try to regain stability in exchange rates, but to do so without resumption of the gold standard. The method used was to *peg* the exchange rate, and today the exchange rates of all major trading nations are pegged rates. The last major trading nation finally to adopt a pegged rate was Canada, which ended her experiment with a free rate in June, 1962.

### *Equilibrium with Pegged Exchange Rates*

The method of pegging an exchange rate is similar to the procedure used to peg United States Treasury bond prices during the period 1945–51. The government involved in a pegging operation maintains an exchange stabilization fund which it uses to buy and sell foreign exchange; the process is quite similar to an open market operation except that foreign exchange is bought and sold to maintain its price within narrow limits.  To stabilize the price of a currency it is necessary to buy it whenever it should start to fall, the purchase mopping up the excess supply.  Conversely, when the price of a currency starts to rise the government or exchange authority sells some of the currency, thus increasing its supply and forcing down the price.

To engage in stabilization activities the exchange stabilization authorities need sufficient resources so they will not be drained of all their holdings of gold and foreign exchange.  For example, the British Exchange Stabilization Account undertakes to prevent the exchange rate from rising above $2.82 or falling below $2.78.  To do this it uses sterling to demand dollars whenever the exchange rate on the pound rises to $2.82; that is, it is supplying sterling to prevent its price from rising further.  On the other hand, when the exchange rate drops to $2.78 it now sells dollars in exchange for sterling; that is, it removes sterling from the exchange market thus preventing any further price decline.  But what happens if the exchange rate is fixed too high, if the supply of exchange consistently exceeds the demand for it at the official rate?  This situation is shown in Figure 20-3, using the pound and the dollar as the currencies involved.

At the official rate of £1 = $2.80 the supply of sterling exceeds the demand for it by the amount $AB$.  In the absence of intervention by the Exchange Stabilization Account the rate would drop to $E$, below the official rate of $2.80.  If the Exchange Stabilization Account is to maintain the exchange rate at $2.80 it must be prepared to take off the market sterling in the amount $AB$.  To do this it must use its holdings

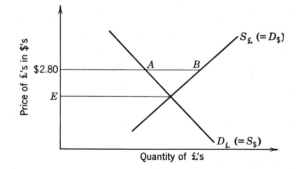

**Figure 20-3**  Disequilibrium with a pegged exchange rate.

of gold, dollars, and other foreign exchange. If this kind of disequilibrium persists for very long, however, the Stabilization Account may be drained of all its resources. If this should happen, what then?

The question of the appropriate policy for a nation to follow when it has a chronic disequilibrium in its balance of payments, and is balancing its payments position only by drawing down its gold stock or by piling up large short-term liabilities to foreigners, is one of the most important policy questions in international finance. One method to equalize its receipts and payments would be to impose import quotas and other direct controls over trade and payments. Another possible solution is to adjust the exchange rate, for example, to devalue in order to equalize the supply of and demand for its money in the exchange market. Devaluation, quotas, or other controls, however, may have adverse effects on other economies and lead them in turn to retaliate. If this competitive retaliation were to occur widely, the action would fail to improve the disequilibrium situation.

If the above solutions to disequilibrium in the payments balance are unsatisfactory to the nation involved, if the nation refuses to impose direct controls or to devalue, how can the drain on its gold and exchange be stopped? If the exchange rate is to be maintained at its pegged level, and direct controls not resorted to, then the drain on international reserves may be stopped only by developments which shift the demand for the nation's exchange up to the right, shift the supply of the exchange up to the left, or shift both sufficiently to equate the demand and supply of exchange at the pegged level.

### United States Payments Equilibrium

The United States payments position since 1958 has placed pressure on the dollar. The United States payments deficit has resulted in a large supply of dollar exchange, but a supply which foreign banking institutions are ever more reluctant to hold. Thus, a large proportion of these surplus dollars has been converted to gold. The problem of the late 1940s and early 1950s of a *dollar shortage* has now become a situation of a *dollar surplus*. The problem for the United States is how to bring the supply of and demand for dollar exchange into balance.

We are familiar with the principal factors determining the supply and demand schedule for foreign exchange. To recapitulate these factors are (1) levels of income in the trading countries, (2) tastes and preferences for domestic versus imported goods in the several countries, (3) relative price levels in the trading countries, and (4) relative rates of interest in the trading countries. The developments leading to shifts in the supply and demand schedules may consequently originate either at home or abroad, or both.  Thus, if incomes abroad were to rise, or income at home to fall, the situation would improve.  Similarly, if prices were to rise abroad and fall domestically, and if interest rates fell abroad and rose at home, the exchange situation would improve.

Should income abroad rise this would translate into an increased import demand for American goods and services, thereby increasing the demand for dollars.  Similarly, a fall in our level of income would reduce American imports and so reduce the supply of dollar exchange.  Either of these situations lessens the pressure on the dollar exchange rate.

Increases in prices abroad will produce a two-pronged effect.  A rise in prices abroad increases the demand for dollars at each exchange rate (price) by increasing the demand for American exports.  At the same time, high prices abroad tend to reduce the supply of dollar exchange by discouraging American imports.  In similar fashion, a decline in American prices will tend to increase the demand for dollars through cheapening United States exports, simultaneously decreasing the supply of dollar exchange by reducing American imports since foreign goods have become relatively more expensive.

Interest rates also figure in the equilibrating process.  A reduction in interest rates abroad may slow down, halt, or even reverse the flow of capital from the United States.  This reduces the supply of dollars or even increases the demand for dollar exchange if capital starts flowing into the United States.  Or if there occurs a rise of interest rates in the United States, the results are similar.  In fact, a rise in the short-term rate is one of the policies being actively pursued by American monetary authorities.

From the foregoing discussion it is clear that if the developments shifting the exchange supply-demand schedules do not originate abroad, the necessary developments in the United States are rather unpleasant, being at best *anti-expansive* if not downright contractive in nature.  It is obvious why countries in this kind of payments disequilibrium hope the bulk of the adjustment may come from price and income increases and interest rate declines abroad.

The forces that must act to restore a payments equilibrium while maintaining both a pegged rate and freedom of trade are essentially those that would produce equilibrium under gold-standard conditions.  For example, if the payments disequilibrium arose because of an increase in imports there would likely be both income and monetary effects, just as developed under the gold-standard workings.  The increase in imports increases the supply of exchange, thus starting the downward pressure on the exchange rate. This has income effects both in the country experiencing the difficulty and in the rest of the world. The shift of expenditures to imports has a downward multiplier effect on domestic income. At the same time, this increase in exports by the rest of the world has positive multiplier effects raising incomes elsewhere. In a somewhat parallel fashion monetary effects will occur also. The loss of gold or exchange or its equivalent serves to tighten credit conditions in the country experiencing the payments difficulties. The acquisition of gold or its equivalent in the rest of the world tends to ease credit conditions there. These monetary effects induce a capital inflow or reduce the capital outflow of the country that is tightening credit and raising interest rates. They also reinforce the income effects, tightened credit conditions tending to reduce income (and, hence, imports) of the country experiencing difficulties. The easing of credit abroad likewise serves to stimulate incomes there, which will lead to increased import demands. These various factors tend to raise the demand for the exchange relative to the supply, and thus hasten the end of the payments disequilibrium and the drain on gold and exchange reserves.

If these adjustments home and abroad do not occur, or cannot be made to occur, then the payments disequilibrium will continue, along with the drain on gold and foreign exchange reserves. There are, furthermore, good reasons for expecting that the necessary changes may be slow in being made, if in fact they ever come about. For example, countries whose payments position show receipts in excess of payments frequently refuse to allow their incomes and prices to rise, or their interest rates to fall. In these circumstances, the burden of adjustment falls on the country with the unfavorable payments position. A second source of difficulty is that many costs and prices seem to be inflexible downward. If this is the case, a policy of deflating domestic demand in order to equate international receipts and payments translates into a policy of reduced employment and income, instead of reduced prices. A final problem connected with a policy of price reductions is the possibility of having inelastic supply-demand schedules for imports and exports. In this situation, unreasonably large price reductions may be needed to effect the adjustment.

## REVIEW QUESTIONS

1. What is the foreign exchange market? Who are its participants and what is its product?

2. What functions are provided by commercial banks in international finance?
3. Trace the steps in the use of an United States bank's letter of credit and acceptance in the financing of an import transaction by an American firm.
4. What are the basic forces underlying the determination of foreign exchange rates?
5. What is meant by *mint parity* and *gold points?*   Why are changes in foreign exchange rates of countries on the gold standard limited by the gold points?
6. With inconvertible paper standards and free exchange markets, what happens to foreign exchange rates of a nation whose imports exceed exports?
7. Discuss the equilibration process in the balance of payments under:
   a) gold standard conditions
   b) flexible exchange rates
   c) pegged exchange rates.
8. Why do nations with a payments deficit and with pressure on their foreign exchange reserves and gold stock hope that a large share of the necessary adjustments can be made externally by rises in foreign prices and incomes and a fall in foreign interest rates?

## SUGGESTED REFERENCES

Board of Governors, *Federal Reserve Bulletin.*   Contains frequent articles on international financial matters and the United States balance of payments.

Henning, Charles N., *International Finance* (New York: Harper and Row, 1958).

Holmes, Alan R., *The New York Foreign Exchange Market* (New York: The Federal Reserve Bank of New York, 1960).

Joint Economic Committee, *Factors Affecting the United States Balance of Payments* (Washington, D.C., 1962).

Kindleberger, Charles P., *International Economics*, 3rd ed. (Homewood: Richard D. Irwin, 1963).

# CHAPTER *21*

# *International Financial Institutions*

The two preceding chapters referred to exchange rate problems and payment difficulties which occurred at various times in the past. The present chapter traces out these happenings in greater detail, and in this fashion provides a better understanding of the need for and the development of present-day international banking institutions.

The present major international financial institutions, the International Bank for Reconstruction and Development (commonly called the "World Bank"), and the International Monetary Fund, are comparatively recent developments, dating from the Bretton Woods Conference of 1944. Long before the establishment of these institutions there had been a long period of trade under conditions of the gold standard extending from the late 1800s to the First World War. The onset of that war forced most countries to suspend operation of the gold standard. After the end of hostilities, some countries went back on gold, whereas others adopted inconvertible paper standards. The inconvertible paper standards were typically associated with fluctuating exchange rates. In an effort to curb undesirable fluctuations in exchange rates or, to put it another way, to recreate the exchange rate stability present under gold-standard conditions, various exchange rate controls were introduced. The difficulties of fluctuating rates under paper standards were compounded by the world-wide depression of the 1930s, which forced off gold those few countries that had previously managed to re-establish some semblance of the gold standard.

The final blows to international monetary stability were the tensions and fears which preceded the hostilities of the Second World War.

Considerable shifts occurred of capital funds, of flight capital, to places such as the United States, Britain, or Switzerland. These rapid shifts of funds made any return to the gold standard even less feasible.

Let us turn now to the major chapters of international monetary standards and institutions.

## THE INTERNATIONAL PAYMENTS SYSTEM: HISTORICAL PRESPECTIVE

The gold standard as an international monetary standard actually operated only briefly, from the 1870s to the onset of the First World War in 1914, and then again briefly after the War to its collapse in the period 1931–33. In spite of this limited history, the gold standard appears to many persons to be a part of the natural order of things. But the late nineteenth century in most regards was considerably different from the present-day situation, and this is particularly true with respect to economic conditions. Thus, it is not surprising to find that the gold standard appropriate in, say, 1900 is not now the appropriate monetary standard. What events led up to the collapse of the gold standard?

As we have seen, when the various monetary units are defined in gold the international gold standard provides the framework for fixing and stabilizing exchange rates. The exchange rates may fluctuate, but only within the narrow limits imposed by the gold import and export points.

To review briefly, in a disequilibrium situation characterized by a surplus or deficit in the current account not offset by an import or export of long-term capital the gold standard operates to correct the situation in the following manner. To rectify a deficit, say, current exports must rise, current imports must fall, or both. Under the gold standard, the loss of gold reduces the money supply in the deficit country and increases the supply of money in the nation with the surplus. In both countries this has both price and income effects which work to restore equilibrium. Provided the nations losing and gaining gold play the game according to the rules, deliberately contracting and expanding money and credit in response to the outflow or inflow of gold, equilibrium will be restored. The deficit country, experiencing the gold outflow, tightens money and credit conditions, which tends to lower domestic prices and incomes while at the same time pushing up the interest rates. The country receiving the gold experiences monetary expansion, with accompanying upward pressure on prices and income and downward pressure on interest rates. As a consequence of these changes, capital moves to the deficit country to take advantage of the higher interest yields available there. Additionally, the price and income declines in the deficit country tend to raise its exports and to reduce its imports. The international gold standard tends automatically to set forces in motion to wipe out deficits and to restore international equilibrium.

This equilibrating process is not without its difficulties, especially to the country running the deficit. The necessary lowering of prices and incomes can easily be accompanied by a loss of business confidence, business failures, and unemployment. On the other hand, in the countries receiving the gold inflow, inflation, or inflationary pressure, becomes a problem. But should a nation have a domestic policy whose objectives are the maintenance of income and employment, the rules of the gold standard game would involve a conflict by imposing internal adjustments in order to adjust to the external imbalance.

Thus, the international gold standard provided stability in the exchange rate at the expense of destabilizing internal prices and income and employment levels. The presumed advantages of a gold standard, the confidence it engendered, the automatic nature of its operation, and price stability, all these plus exchange rate stability, were considered to outweigh any drawbacks it might have. Thus, the gold standard reigned supreme during the period from the 1870s to 1914. With the onset of hostilities, the major powers suspended the gold standard in order to conserve whatever gold stock they might possess so as to be able to purchase supplies and armaments from those countries that would not accept paper promises to pay. Gold continued to be an international means of payment, even though the gold standard as an international monetary institution was abandoned. Internally in the various countries, the large budget deficits necessary to finance their war efforts resulted in increases in the money supplies with accompanying increases in price levels. But all the while it was expected that, after the war ended, the gold standard would be resumed.

The inconvertible paper standards resorted to after the outbreak of the First World War were regarded as only temporary; the suspension of gold was thought to be only a wartime expedient. As things worked out, the economic confusion that followed the end of hostilities made the restoration of the gold standard in its prewar form impossible. Among the major nations, only the United States was able to return promptly to the prewar arrangements. The United States was able to resume the gold standard because of a sufficiently ample gold stock and also because its prices had risen relatively less than other nations' prices during the wartime inflations.  Great Britain, on the other hand, was not able to resume the gold standard until 1925.

Most other countries, attempting to maintain some connection with the gold standard despite their small holdings of gold, adopted a variant of the gold standard, the gold-exchange standard.  This standard allowed some countries to get along with next to no gold at all.  Under the gold-exchange standard, a country's central bank held part of its reserves in currencies which were convertible into gold at fixed prices.  These convertible currencies, such as the dollar, became "key currencies" since they formed part of the base upon which the monetary systems of other countries were built.  The gold stock of some countries thus did double duty, supporting not only the domestic currencies, but also enabling these key currencies to support monetary and credit systems abroad; supporting, in this fashion, a large inverted pyramid of international liquidity.

The base of this inverted pyramid may, however, be precarious.  Under a gold-exchange standard relatively large claims on key currency countries may be held abroad.  Then, if a key currency country should experience a period of balance of payments deficits, these foreign claims against it would grow.  Foreign central banks accumulating the key currency in excess of their reserve needs are likely to convert it into gold, and so the key currency nation loses gold.  Should these gold losses continue for any length of time they may begin to impair confidence in the key currency and touch off a run on the gold backing of the currency.  Indeed, it was precisely this, a run on the British pound in 1931, that collapsed the gold-exchange system that had developed after the First World War.  Thus, Britain in 1931 was forced off the gold standard, only six years after having reinstated it.  What factors led to this situation?

In 1925 when Britain went back on gold she set the price of gold at the prewar level, £1 = $4.87.  This price proved to be too high, making British goods too expensive in the world market.  The pound was overvalued.  The basic reasons for this overvaluation of the pound were twofold: (1) relative to prewar prices, during and after the war prices in Britain had more than doubled; (2) coupled with this price rise, or fall in purchasing power of the pound, was the fact that Britain's ability to sell in the postwar world markets had declined.  Over the years, as other nations, especially the United States, had become more industrialized, England and other northern European nations had faced increasing competition in world markets.  The First World War simply hastened this trend.  After the war, England found many former customers had obtained new suppliers of goods and services. The result of these two factors was the overvaluation of the pound. England immediately began to run a trade deficit at her over-valued rate, that is, at this rate she could not sell all the output of her export industries.

Concurrent with the trade deficit, Britain's gold stock was put under pressure. To prevent gold from leaving the country England responded in the usual fashion; the money market was tightened and interest rates moved up. In response to higher interest rates in England than elsewhere, short-term funds moved to Britain. This movement of short-term capital enabled Britain to cover her trade deficit without the export of gold. According to gold-standard theory, however, reductions in wage rates and prices should have accompanied the tightened money and credit situation in order to stimulate exports abroad and reduce import demand at home. Britain's income did fall some, but the decline was not the result of prices and wages falling but of a high level of unemployment. Owing to an inability to make the necessary internal adjustments, there was chronic and persistent depression in the British export industries throughout the prosperous 1920s. Finally, in September, 1931 after a run on the pound, Britain abandoned the gold standard. With the abandonment of converti-bility of the pound into gold, the death knell to the gold-exchange standard of the period was sounded, for the pound was one of the so-called key currencies.

The years immediately following were disorderly ones for inter-national banking. Other countries followed Britain and abandoned gold. Now neither the gold standard nor gold-exchange standard was functioning. With paper standards the order of the day, exchange rates were subject to wide fluctuations. Fluctuating exchange rates, as we have seen, introduce added risks and complications in making international payments and serve to discourage world trade and invest-ment. In an attempt to reintroduce stability into the exchange rate, various devices were used. One of the principal instruments used to maintain rate stability was the exchange stabilization fund. As we know, this technique entails the setting up of funds to buy and sell foreign exchange for the purpose of maintaining exchange rates within narrow limits. These pegging operations were for the most part car-ried out by the various central banks.

Stabilization funds alone could not long ward off the problems of fundamental disequilibrium. Also used were such approaches as pro-tective tariffs, import quotas, and exchange controls. The latter, exchange controls, were perhaps the most important. Exchange controls essentially involved the pooling of all foreign exchange earned by a nation's citizens and the allocation of this foreign exchange among importers and other persons wanting to make payments abroad. Determination of exchange control policy was no easy task. For example, the exchange control authority had to determine how much exchange to allocate for specific imports and other purposes, whether to favor certain countries over others in its imports, whether to encourage domestic industries by providing exchange to pay for competing imports, etc. In order for exchange controls to be effective, the cooperation of the commercial banking system was required. Because of their close relationship with the commercial banks, the central banks played major roles in the administration of these programs.

The abandonment of the gold standard and its "rules of the game" in favor of inconvertible paper standards, pegged exchange rates, and exchange controls was also accompanied by policies deliberately aimed at maintaining domestic income and employment levels. Indeed, the above package of instruments could and did contribute to the solution of the problem of unemployment. But they did suffer from a serious shortcoming, since all countries could employ them to help themselves at the expense of other countries. In the process of correcting unemployment at home, a nation might well "export" this unemployment to some other country.

By the end of this sad decade of the 1930s, the Second World War had started, which further disrupted the pattern of world trade. Practices that were restrictive to begin with were further tightened. It was clear that the gold standard could not be restored in the postwar period. But it was also recognized that the lack of any mechanism like the gold standard invites instability of exchange rates and discourages international trade and investment. After all, the 1930s provided an eloquent reminder of competitive devaluation, tariffs, and exchange controls. Thus it was that monetary authorities the world over recognized the need for a way to make international trade and payments more stable and efficient. To this end, a meeting of representatives and monetary experts from forty-four countries was held at Bretton Woods, New Hampshire, in July, 1944. The countries represented at this meeting wanted stable exchange rates, but rates that could change to meet changing conditions and provide for making international payments without the need for exchange controls. The result of this meeting was the establishment of the International Monetary Fund and the International Bank for Reconstruction and Development.

## POSTWAR INTERNATIONAL MONETARY INSTITUTIONS: THE IMF

The purpose of the Bretton Woods conference was to devise means for assuring a system of international trade and payments consistent with the dual objectives of high world productivity and the maintenance of high levels of domestic employment and income and economic stability. Further, it was believed that postwar reconstruction and development was a problem requiring international cooperation. To this end, proposals which resulted in the establishment of the International Monetary Fund and the International Bank for Reconstruction and Development were forthcoming.

### The International Monetary Fund

In discussing the establishment of the International Monetary Fund, it is important to keep in mind the international monetary chaos of the period of the 1930s. The principal goal of the IMF was the avoidance of competitive devaluation and exchange controls that had characterized the 1930s. The Fund was set up for the purpose of making short-term loans to member nations experiencing temporary payments deficits, to enable them to weather these payments difficulties without resorting to devaluation or exchange control, while at the same time following internal policies to maintain domestic income and employment at high levels. As secondary objectives, the Fund sought to reduce existing exchange controls and to introduce currency convertibility with stable exchange rates.

In essence, the Fund is an attempt to achieve the external or international advantages of a gold standard without subjecting nations to its internal disadvantages, and at the same time maintain the internal advantages of paper standards while bypassing the external disadvantages of paper standards. These objectives are summarized in the Fund's Articles of Agreement as follows:

1. To promote international monetary cooperation through a permanent institution that provides the machinery for consultation and collaboration on international monetary problems.

2. To facilitate the expansion and balanced growth of international trade, and to contribute thereby to the promotion and maintenance of high levels of employment and real income and to the development of the productive resources of all members as primary objectives of economic policy.

3. To promote exchange stability, to maintain orderly exchange arrangements among members, and to avoid competitive exchange depreciations.

4. To assist in the establishment of a multilateral system of payments in respect to current transactions between members and in the elimination of foreign exchange restrictions which hamper the growth of world trade.

5. To give confidence to members by making the Fund's resources available to them under adequate safeguards, thus providing them with opportunity to correct maladjustments in their balance of payments without resorting to measures destructive of national or international prosperity.

6. In accordance with the above, to shorten the duration and lessen the degree of disequilibrium in the international balances of payments of members.

The basic principle underlying the Fund is found in paragraph 5. This provides that a member nation experiencing a balance of payments difficulty can borrow from the Fund to cover its deficit, thus not having to cover its deficit by shipment of gold or by resort to exchange controls or by devaluation. The borrowing is accomplished by a member nation purchasing the desired exchange from the Fund by giving its own currency in exchange.

The resources of the Fund are subscribed by the various member nations—at present there are over one hundred—according to quotas based on prewar national income and volume of international trade. The original member nations had assigned quotas of about $8 billion. This total grew as additional nations became members of the Fund until in 1959 it amounted to about $10 billion. In this year, member nations agreed to a 50 per cent increase in quotas, to a new total of roughly $15 billion. Of this sum, the United States has contributed over $4 billion, consisting of slightly over $1 billion in gold and over $3 billion in dollars.

Each member nation must pay part of its quota in gold; the balance may be in its own local currency. Specifically, a member nation must contribute gold equal to 25 per cent of its quota, or 10 per cent of its gold stock and United States dollar holdings, whichever of these alternatives is smaller. The portion of the subscription paid in a nation's own local currency is generally paid in the form of a deposit balance in favor of the IMF held in the nation's central bank. Thus, the Fund has a pool of foreign currencies to lend, together with gold which it may use to acquire additional amounts of currencies should its initial supply of some currencies become depleted.

The lending operations of the Fund technically take the form of sales of currency. The member nation experiencing the payments deficit on current account purchases the desired exchange from the Fund, paying for it with its own currency. Since the Fund's resources are limited, especially before the increase in quotas in 1959, the Fund's resources were intended to be used only to cover a *temporary* deficit in a nation's balance of payments. Because of the limited resources of the Fund, the right of access to the Fund's resources are subject to certain conditions. These conditions are:

1. The member nation desiring to purchase currency must affirm that the currency to be purchased is necessary for making payments consistent with the Fund's Articles of Agreement (i.e., are to cover a temporary imbalance in current account transactions).

2. The Fund must not have given previous notice that its holdings of the desired currency have become scarce.

3. The proposed purchase must not cause the Fund's holdings of the purchasing country's currency to increase by more than 25 per cent of its quota over the preceding year, nor to cause it to exceed 200 per cent of its quota.

4. The Fund must not have declared the member nation ineligible to use the Fund's resources.

The above conditions on a member nation's drawing rights emphasize the concept of the Fund as providing short-term assistance in covering deficits that are moderate in amount and temporary in nature. The Fund is not set up for long-term lending. The Fund is not required to lend more than 25 per cent of a member nation's quota in any one year, nor to lend more than twice its quota at any one time. The Fund expects repayment within three to five years. As a condition of borrowing, the borrowing nation must agree to buy back for gold or convertible currencies one-half of any increase in the Fund's holdings of its currency that occurs during the year, plus one-half of any increase (or less one-half of any decreases) in the member's monetary reserves of gold or convertible currencies. These various conditions were established to prevent the Fund's getting all its resources tied up in long-term commitments. In this fashion, the Fund's resources will be available to cope with temporary balance of payments deficits of modest size.

The first decade of the Fund's operation was characterized by persistent, rather than temporary, deficits in international payments. Such persistence of payments difficulties is a sign of fundamental disequilibrium in the balance of payments. The questions are, how did this fundamental disequilibrium arise, and what is its cure? To answer the questions in reverse order, the cure for a fundamental disequilibrium in the balance of payments is, as we saw in the previous chapters, a change in the exchange rate. This brings us to the first question, why were exchange rates too high?

In order to get the Fund's operations started as early as possible, member nations were asked to set par values on their currencies in terms of gold or dollars. These par values were announced by the IMF in December, 1946. Unfortunately, the postwar world had not settled down enough so that *equilibrium* exchange values for the various currencies could be determined. The hope was, of course, that the par values selected would balance current transactions yielding neither deficit or surplus. But for whatever reason, many of the initial parities selected proved overvalued. Or, if originally appropriate, subsequent inflation often resulted in overvaluing the currency.

The question soon arose as to what circumstances might justify a change in the established par value, since according to the Fund's Articles of Agreement, member nations were pledged to maintain exchange stability and to avoid competitive devaluation. The Board of Governors of the Fund interpreted the Articles of Agreement as permitting changes in par value only to correct "fundamental disequilibrium" in the balance of payments. Thus, if balance of payments difficulties turned out to be prolonged, the concept of exchange stability with flexibility would come into play. IMF rules provide that, after consultation with the Fund, a member nation may depreciate its currency up to 10 per cent of the original parity whether the Fund approves or not. If the proposed change exceeds 10 per cent, the Fund's approval is necessary. The exchange rates are to be stabilized at the official par values through the operation of exchange stabilization funds, the fluctuations in currency prices not to exceed 1 per cent of the established official prices.

As noted above, a member nation may depreciate its currency as much as 10 per cent of its original parity whether the Fund approves or not. Further depreciation, or a proposed depreciation in excess of 10 per cent of the original par value, requires explicit consent. If a member nation in this situation depreciates over the objections of the Fund it may be deprived of the right to use the resources of the Fund and may even be forced to withdraw from membership. Under the Articles of Agreement, the only mechanism sanctioned for the adjustment of fundamental disequilibrium in payments problems is this limited, Fund-approved devaluation of currency. Hopefully, the principle of international consultation in adjustments of exchange rates has been established so that such adjustments will be orderly and will not lead to competitive devaluation.

In the immediate postwar years it turned out that most currencies were overvalued in relation to gold and dollars. In 1947, for example, in markets where free currency exchanges could take place, currencies sold at discounts running from 10 to 60 per cent of their par values in terms of gold and dollars.[1] But whereas the Fund had been so eager to get par values established so it could begin operations, it now proceeded to drag its feet with respect to the requests for currency depreciation and gave its approval only reluctantly. This reluctance to approve depreciation coupled with timidity in its lending operations, due to its lack of resources and the difficulty in separating legitimate requests for temporary accommodation from illegitimate ones, made the Fund's early years of operation rather unsuccessful. Although the massive foreign aid program of the United States reduced the need of many member nations to borrow from the Fund, it is nevertheless true that many nations were forced to practice exchange control and use multiple exchange rates and other devices to balance their payments—all this in violation of the Fund's Articles of Agreement. Faced with this situation, the Fund simply looked the other way.

For example, several devaluations occurred which were presented to the Fund as a *fait accompli* without any prior consultation and in excess of the 10 per cent adjustment. In 1948 France, for instance, devalued by nearly one-half. Similarly in 1949, Great Britain served notice on the Fund of a devaluation of the pound from $4.03 to $2.80, a 30 per cent change. The devaluation was presented to the Fund on a take it or leave it basis. The Fund took it.

Although the early years of the Fund's operations were disappointing, in more recent years the situation has improved considerably. Until the mid-1950s, balance of payments deficits were so widespread and so persistent that the Fund's limited resources could not have reasonably been expected to cope with them. But as some semblance of order was restored to the economic scene, and as postwar reconstruction and development programs began to come into their own, payments problems began to ease. For example, the balance of payments situation of Western Europe with respect to the United States began to improve in the early 1950s. European dependence on the United States for imports lessened, while at the same time increasing production and productivity enabled Europe to compete vigorously in world export markets and to recover her former share of world trade. This rapid growth of European economies encouraged the export of long-term, private American capital to Europe. The effect of these

---

[1] Robert Triffin, *Europe and the Money Muddle* (Yale University Press, New Haven, Connecticut, 1957), p. 87.

developments was to reverse the so-called dollar shortage to a dollar surplus, to change the European balance of payments deficits to surpluses, and in turn to shift the United States into balance of payments deficits. Although the United States has run a balance of payments deficit since the early 1950s, it is only since 1958 that this has caused any real concern to United States monetary authorities.

The payments deficit of the United States means that foreigners are accumulating liquid dollar claims against the United States. Starting in 1958 many of these dollar claims were converted into gold and withdrawn from the United States. In 1958, Western Europe used most of its trade surplus to acquire gold—$2.3 billions in gold, to be exact. Since that time there have been continuing losses of gold by the United States. We shall return to this point later, but for now let us consider the effects of the flow of gold to Europe.

With the elimination of the balance of payments problems for Western Europe, the situation shifted from one of a chronic shortage of gold and dollar reserves to one in which these nations now possessed gold and dollar reserves sufficient to weather all but the severest international financial disturbance. In particular, it meant that member nations of the IMF could pay more than lip service to the principles embodied in the Articles of Agreement of the Fund. Member nations of the Fund practicing exchange controls have been able to abandon or reduce their restrictive practices. Thus, late in December, 1958, Great Britain, France, Germany, Austria, Italy, Holland, Sweden, Denmark, Norway, Belgium, and Luxembourg adopted policies allowing foreigners to convert money earned in *current* transactions into dollars or any other currency at official rates of exchange. Furthermore, all agreed to maintain their respective currencies stable in terms of gold and dollars.

It will also be recalled that one of the primary goals of the IMF is the achievement not only of free convertibility but also of a multilateral system of payments. On February 10, 1961, ten member nations accepted the obligations of convertibility as set forth in Article 8 of the Fund's Articles of Agreement. These nations were Belgium, France, Germany, Ireland, Italy, Luxembourg, the Netherlands, Peru, Sweden, and the United Kingdom.[2] Under the provisions of Article 8, these nations agree to avoid restrictions of payments and transfers on current transactions, to forego multiple exchange rate practices, and to refrain from discriminatory currency arrangements. With the acceptance by these nations of the principle set forth in Article 8, the number

---

[2] *Annual Report*, 1961, International Monetary Fund, Washington, D.C., p. 12.

of nations so committed rose to twenty-one. As a consequence of this action, almost all the currencies used to finance international trade are now convertible. These developments plus the increase in member quotas agreed to in 1959 place the Fund in a much more viable position than it formerly occupied. The probability is now good that the Fund will be able to operate in the fashion originally contemplated for it, and to achieve the limited but important functions for which it was established.

Throughout the discussion of the IMF it has been abundantly clear that one of its principal functions is to augment international liquidity. Before concluding this discussion of the IMF it is important that we explicitly consider this problem of international liquidity and determine the Fund's role in this problem.

In some certain aspects the IMF fulfills some of the roles assigned to a central bank. For instance, just as the Federal Reserve may make an advance to a member bank needing additional reserves, so does the Fund lend to central banks short of desired foreign exchange. Thus, both a central bank and the Fund provide their respective member institutions with a source of additional liquidity should this be necessary. But this does not make the IMF an international central bank. Far from it.

Indeed, the basic characteristic of the institution that we call "bank" is its ability to create funds. This is true of central banks just as it is true for private commercial banks. But it is not true for the Fund. The IMF cannot create purchasing power. When the Fund lends it is lending out subscribed capital, it is not expanding its liabilities (creating funds) but is giving the borrowing nation some other country's currency in exchange for the borrowing country's money. Instead of obtaining a deposit with the IMF, the borrowing country obtains a deposit in the central bank of the nation whose currency was borrowed. The Fund does not increase its own liabilities, does not create the funds it lends, and so is not an international central bank.

Although we denied that the Fund is a bank, since it does not possess the basic money creating ability true banks have, we cannot argue that the Fund has failed to increase the world's international liquidity. The usual concept of international liquidity, or international monetary reserves, includes the gold holdings of official institutions (central banks, treasuries, and stabilization funds) as well as their holdings of foreign convertible currencies. Drawing rights to the resources of the IMF in gold and convertible currencies, although not counted as national monetary reserves by most nations, may thus be regarded as part of international monetary reserves insofar as the

Fund is prepared to make them immediately available to its members.[3]
Since 1944 the volume of international liquidity so defined has
increased substantially. The question has been raised as to whether
this increase in international liquidity will continue to be adequate to
match the increasing demands placed upon it. The adequacy of gold
and other international payments reserves relative to the volume
world payments is the basis of this increasing concern. The present
payments system is essentially a gold-exchange standard, and one with
a rather high ratio of exchange to gold in official monetary reserves.
The gold base on which this payments system is based cannot increase
by more than about 2 per cent per year. This rate of increase of gold
reserves is considerably less than the rate of increase in the volume of
international payments.

The increases in international monetary reserves since about 1940
have resulted from the accumulation of large foreign holdings of
sterling balances in the 1940s, and the large increase of foreign holdings
of dollars in the 1950s. For example, in the fifties the increase in the
monetary gold reserves of the non-Soviet bloc rose by roughly $6
billion, but this was only about one-third of the increase of total
monetary reserves during this period. The remaining two-thirds of
the increase of monetary reserves took the form of increases of foreign
holdings of convertible currencies, in particular holdings of United
States dollar balances. The build-up of these dollar balances was the
natural consequence of the payments deficits incurred by the United
States during the 1950s. Thus, the major increase in international
monetary reserves has been the direct result of the creation of dollar
balances occasioned by the United States balance of payments deficits.

How long can the United States afford to run payments deficits
comparable to those of the late fifties? And even if the United States
were to incur such deficits, would other countries be willing to continue
to acquire further dollar holdings? It appears unlikely they would
do so, as witnessed by the continuing pressure on the United States
gold stock.

Since it is unlikely that further significant increases in foreign-held
dollar balances will be forthcoming, much attention has been given to
the problem of finding ways to keep international liquidity adequate
in relation to growing world payments needs. Back in the gold-
standard days of the nineteenth century there were two reserve media,

---

[3] Pieter Lieftnick, "Recent Trends in International Monetary Policies," Essays in
International Finance, No. 39, September, 1962, International Finance Section,
Princeton University, p. 6.

gold and sterling balances. Later in the gold-exchange era of the 1930s the sources of monetary reserves increased to three: gold, sterling, and the United States dollar. The gold-exchange standard of the present day uses these same three media for monetary reserves. But it now seems that new reserve media may emerge, currencies which will be held as reserves along with gold, sterling, and dollars. The German mark seems eminently eligible for this purpose, and there are several other candidates. But to create these international reserves requires a strong and reliable country to have a payments deficit covered by short-term credit. It may be, however, that there are no, or few, countries that can provide this function in the necessary magnitude. One authority, Professor Brian Tew, suggests as candidates the major European currencies, the two North American dollars, and the yen.[4]

With an increase in the number of reserve media, however, there may arise other problems, particularly the likelihood of switches or flights from one reserve medium to another. Thus Professor Tew concluded that the present form of the gold-exchange standard would become increasingly unstable, unless propped up by the IMF.[5] The question is thus raised, what support can be offered by the IMF?

The amount of support the Fund can render to a member nation in difficulty depends on (1) the size of the member's quota (recall the Fund's holding of any member's currency may not exceed 200 per cent of its quota), and (2) on the size and composition of the Fund's resources. The latter consideration means that a drawing nation can gain access only to currencies the Fund possesses, or which it can obtain by gold sales.

The composition of the Fund's resources is an important consideration in determining the extent to which the Fund can support a currency. Although the increase in quotas in 1959 raised the resources of the Fund to roughly $15 billion, only approximately $9.7 billion are in gold and convertible currencies. Of this $9.7 billion nearly half, $4.6 billion, are in dollars and sterling, with the remaining $5.1 billion in gold and other convertible currencies. But until members purchasing currency from the Fund are willing to acquire *any* one of the key currencies mentioned earlier instead of only United States dollars, far less than half of the Fund's convertible resources are being effectively utilized.

---

[4] Brian Tew, "The International Monetary Fund: Its Present Role and Future Prospects," Essays in International Finance, No. 36, March, 1961, International Finance Section, Princeton University, p. 10.
[5] *Ibid.*, p. 9.

Even assuming that the Fund's resources are more effectively marshaled there is the possibility that they might still prove inadequate. For example, should the United States ever exercise its rights to the fullest extent it would essentially deplete the Fund of usable resources. The recognition of this kind of possibility led to an agreement in October, 1962 between the Fund and the major industrial nations (Belgium, Canada, France, Germany, Italy, Japan, the Netherlands, Sweden, the United Kingdom, and the United States) whereby standby arrangements would give the Fund access to an additional $6 billion of resources ($2 billion in United States dollars, $1 billion in sterling, and $3 billion in other convertible currencies). These arrangements will make possible the rapid mobilization of additional resources by the Fund for the preservation and defense of the international monetary system.

That these arrangements can strengthen national monetary reserves has been amply demonstrated. Even before the standby arrangements for the supplemental resources for the Fund were completed, two events illustrated the size and flexibility of the kind of aid possible. For example, during 1961 the United Kingdom was experiencing some temporary payments difficulties. In August, England exercised her drawing rights to the extent of $1.5 billion to ease the pressure on the pound. This borrowing was completely repaid by July, 1962. Assistance of this magnitude is indeed significant. Similarly in 1962 the Fund, the United Kingdom, and the United States multilaterally came to Canada's assistance. In June, 1962, the Canadian dollar came under heavy pressure. To ease this pressure the Fund participated on short notice in the more than $1 billion of support given to Canada. By the end of December, 1962, the Bank of Canada had repaid the $100 million assistance extended by the Bank of England and the $250 million assistance extended by the Federal Reserve System.

The fact that an efficient payments system benefits all trading nations is clearly recognized. It is also becoming recognized that the responsibility for adjustments to correct payments imbalances and for defending the payments system is the common responsibility of the trading nations. Thus, the increase in quotas, the IMF standby borrowing arrangements, and increasing international cooperation raise expectations that the Fund may soon be operating in the fashion envisaged in its Articles of Agreement.

### International Liquidity and Proposals for Reform

There has been a great deal of recent discussion about the problem of international liquidity. It is both difficult to measure international liquidity and to assess its adequacy. The adequacy depends on gold and the foreign exchange holdings of a country, and also on the country's ability to borrow from other countries and from international organizations. And there is no exact relationship between the volume of international transactions and the amount of necessary reserves. Reserves are necessary to finance imbalances between international receipts and payments, not only the transactions as such. Thus, international liquidity serves the same purpose as domestic liquidity, to provide a medium of exchange and a store of value.

The most important components of reserves are the gold and foreign exchange held by countries. Gold, of course, is the major reserve instrument because of its universal acceptability. The United States dollar and the pound sterling are the principal reserve currencies because of their role as the major trading currencies for carrying out a large share of international trade and investment transactions.

There has been considerable debate over whether there is presently a shortage of international liquidity. The consensus is that there is not, but that a shortage may occur in the future. There is a fear of no guarantee that the present international monetary system will automatically provide an increase in the supply of international liquidity over the years to finance the expanding volume of world trade and payments.

Certainly it appears that the growth of gold reserves is too small in relation to the rate of increase in international transactions to permit gold to be the answer to the world's future needs for international liquidity. Thus, national currency holdings must form an ever increasing proportion of total international reserves. For example, during the 1950s until 1958, United States balance of payments deficits were moderate and the resulting increase in dollar reserves of other countries was a welcome addition to international reserves. Starting with 1958, however, other countries declined to build up their dollar reserves at the earlier rate, and chose to convert into gold excess dollar balances over those needed as normal working balances.

If international reserves are to consist increasingly of foreign currency holdings, a rather serious problem emerges. If currencies form an increasing part of international reserves, this implies an increase in relation to their gold stocks of the liquid liabilities of the countries whose currencies are held as reserves by other countries. But should these liquid liabilities grow beyond the reserve-currency countries' own gold reserves, confidence may be seriously weakened in their continued ability to maintain the par values of their currencies. Stability of the international payments system may thus be undermined. This is the precise situation which confronts the United States dollar today.

There is no exact relation between the magnitude of liquid claims against a country's gold reserve and the degree of confidence in its currency. But there may be limits to the volume of international liquid liabilities a given amount of gold reserves can support without a serious erosion of confidence in the currency involved.

To remedy the dangers and defects of the present international payments system a number of proposals have been made. We shall examine a few of them here, but these by no means exhaust the list. The four proposals we shall review are: (1) a premium price on gold; (2) flexible exchange rates; (3) multiple key currencies; (4) an international central bank.

DOLLAR DEVALUATION. This plan proposes to devalue the dollar relative to other currencies or with other countries. Advocates urge raising the price of gold. It seems likely, however, that the United States would not gain any advantage since other countries would probably devalue along with the dollar to maintain existing exchange relationships. A chief argument against United States devaluation is that it would result in an international monetary crisis. Other countries have accumulated over $23 billion of liquid dollar assets, over $12 billion of which they hold as official monetary reserves. They have been willing to acquire these assets on the official assurance that the United States would not devalue. Should we devalue other countries might never again trust the dollar as an international store of value, and correspondingly reduce international liquidity.

Some proponents of devaluation argue that a drastic increase in the price of gold to, say, $105 per ounce by all countries would sufficiently increase the value of gold stocks to more than offset any decline in international liquidity resulting from the conversion of liquid dollar assets into gold. Total international liquidity would therefore increase due to the increased value of existing gold holdings.

Unfortunately, after a time lag the same old problems would arise. Even with the increased price of gold it is doubtful that gold production would be greatly increased, and the principal benefactors would be South Africa and Russia. But even more crucial, once gold speculators and hoarders have been rewarded, they would probably divert larger proportions of new production away from reserves, setting the stage for a future liquidity crisis. And finally, the scheme would reward most countries that have not cooperated with the United States by holding large proportions of their reserves in dollars but in gold, and would tend to penalize cooperative countries that held large dollar balances relative to gold.

FLEXIBLE EXCHANGE RATES. The need for international reserves could be greatly reduced by allowing flexible exchange rates to equilibrate the demand for and the supply of foreign exchange. Paradoxically, the banking community, which generally advocates pricing through a free-market mechanism, does not favor the determination of the price of foreign money through the free interplay of supply-demand forces. The present system, although allowing for limited exchange rate adjustment under the terms of IMF Articles of Agreement, is nonetheless characterized by the fixity of exchange rates, rather than by their flexibility. That fixity of rates is apparently to be a central element of the international payments system is emphasized by the statement of Frank A. Southard, Jr., deputy managing director of the IMF, who in a speech dealing with international monetary arrangements stated, "No consideration is being given to a policy of fluctuating rates of exchange."[6]

Nevertheless, as has been pointed out,[7] although fixed exchange rates may tend to increase international transactions it is the *optimizing* of world trade rather than the maximizing of international transactions which should be the objective. Optimization implies that the international sector as well as the domestic sector should share the burden of adjustment to international imbalance, but with fixed exchange rates the burden of adjustment falls disproportionately on the domestic sector. It appears likely, however, that for the forseeable future the international payments system is committed to fixed exchange rates.

MULTIPLE KEY CURRENCY SYSTEM. The proposal to add additional currencies to the status of reserve currencies would at first glance seem to increase considerably international reserves. Such a result, however, may not be the case.

For continuing growth in total international reserves under a multiple currency reserve system, the reserve-currency countries would have to run perennial deficits in their international payments. If countries were willing to accumulate additional reserves in the form of other national currencies, some additional reserves could be generated. But the countries whose currencies seem candidates for reserve-currency status may not be willing to incur the regular deficits required of them.

---

[6] Quoted from a speech reprinted in supplement to *International Financial News Survey*, IMF, XVI, No. 3, April 3, 1964.
[7] Gerald A. Pollack, "Perspectives on the United States International Financial Position," p. 56 in *The United States Balance of Payments—Perspectives and Policies*, Joint Economic Committee, 88th Congress, 1st Session, Washington, 1963.

Furthermore, whose currencies would be held? The plan requires the accumulation of other countries' currencies when they are in deficit, that is, when their currencies are weak. Is it reasonable that these currencies would be attractive as international stores of value?

Professor Machlup has summarized the key currency proposal thus:

"What has been the trouble with the dollar-reserve standard is likely to remain the trouble with the multiple-currency-reserve standard—and it represents a real paradox: The supply of reserve currencies to other nations depends on payments deficits incurred by the reserve countries; but the demand for these currencies will not endure if the reserve countries incur continual deficits. In a nutshell, the truth about reserve currencies is this: the more easily available, the less wanted."[8]

In any event, the international monetary system seems to be evolving toward a multiple key currency system, whatever its difficulties.

**AN INTERNATIONAL CENTRAL BANK.** The leading advocate of thoroughgoing reform is Professor Robert Triffin of Yale University who has proposed what amounts to an international central bank. In this so-called *Triffin Plan* there is to be created an international monetary institution which would have the ability to create international credit. These credits would be the reserves of national central banks, and this new international monetary institution would be a central banker's bank. It would do for central banks what the Federal Reserve, for example, does for member commercial banks in the United States.

This international central bank could be established by modifying the present IMF. National central banks would pool their gold reserves with the IMF, and the credits received in exchange would in turn be counted as part of individual central bank's reserves—for example, in place of gold certificates as is the present situation in the United States. This international central bank would also be authorized to create "international reserve credit," analogous to Federal Reserve credit, by open market purchase of the domestic financial assets of deficit countries.

The Triffin Plan has basically two objectives. First, it aims at replacing the present international reserves of gold and certain key currencies with a new international currency, namely, deposits at the international central bank. The second objective of the plan is to introduce elasticity into international reserves. This element would

---

[8] Fritz Machlup, *Outlook for United States Balance of Payments*, p. 201, Joint Economic Committee, 87th Congress, 2nd Session, Washington, 1963.

be provided by the ability of the new institution to engage in open market operations in member nations' domestic financial assets.

Triffin's plan offers the most comprehensive reform discussed in recent years.  Certainly it will not be implemented in the immediate future, if, indeed, ever.  It does, however, merit careful study and consideration.  There are certain apparent difficulties; for example, how much credit should be created?  Triffin would limit the growth to perhaps 3 or 4 per cent per year.  What about the likelihood of conflict between an international monetary policy and a domestic monetary policy, etc.?  The mechanics of such a system must be worked out and evaluated.  But the very least that can be said for Triffin's proposal is that it has evoked an examination of the international payments system and courses for its reform which were sorely needed, however unlikely the prospects for the implementation of the specific proposal itself.

## POSTWAR INTERNATIONAL MONETARY INSTITUTIONS: THE WORLD BANK

The second major postwar financial institution in the area of international finance is the so-called *world bank*.  This institution, the International Bank for Reconstruction and Development (IBRD),[9] is also an outgrowth of the Bretton Woods Conference.  Initially, only nations that were members of the IMF could be members of the IBRD; this restriction to membership was subsequently relaxed.

Since the Fund was established to provide for temporary assistance in correcting payments difficulties the possibility was evident that many member nations of the Fund might need long-term funds so desperately that they might be sorely tempted to use the Fund's resources for long-term investment purposes.  Thus, in an attempt to prevent the Fund from becoming illiquid through tying up its resources in long-term undertakings, the IBRD was established, its function being the promotion of long-term foreign investment loans on reasonable terms.  The purposes of the IBRD are set forth in Article I of the Articles of Agreement as follows:

---

[9] The IBRD is only one of a number of international lending institutions.  Other organizations, for example, are the International Finance Corporation (IFC), associated with the IBRD, and the International Development Agency (IDA), also associated with the world bank.  In addition to these international lending institutions, the United States has several agencies that lend as an adjunct to U. S. foreign policy.  These include the Export-Import Bank, the International Cooperation Administration (ICA), and the Development Loan Fund (DLF).

1. To assist in the reconstruction and development of territories of members by facilitating the investment of capital for productive purposes including the restoration of economies destroyed or disrupted by war, the reconversion of productive facilities to peacetime needs, and the encouragement of the development of productive facilities and resources in less developed countries.

2. To promote private foreign investment by means of guarantee or participation in loans and other investments made by private investors; and when private capital is not available on reasonable terms, to supplement private investment by providing, on suitable conditions, finance for productive purposes out of its own capital, funds raised by it, and its other resources.

3. To promote the long-range balanced growth of international trade and the maintenance of equilibrium in balances of payments by encouraging international investment for the development of the productive resources of members, thereby assisting in raising productivity, the standard of living, and conditions of labor in their territories.

4. To arrange the loans made or guaranteed by it in relation to international loans through other channels so that the more useful and urgent projects, large and small alike, will be dealt with first.

5. To conduct its operations with due regard to the effect of international investment on business conditions in the territories of members and, in the immediate postwar years, to assist in bringing about a smooth transition from a wartime to a peacetime economy.

The IBRD was created to promote private foreign investment (paragraph 2 above) and not to replace private foreign investment. The Bank considers its role to be a marginal one, to supplement and assist private foreign investment in the member nations.

As with the IMF, the International Bank has its capital subscribed on a quota basis by the participating nations. And like the Fund, in 1959 the member nations voted to increase the Bank's capital. In deciding to increase quotas in the Bank, the consensus was to double member quotas, a 100 per cent increase, whereas Fund quotas were increased by 50 per cent. As of June 30, 1963 the Bank's total subscriptions to capital stock were nearly $20.7 billions. Of the total capital subscriptions, only 10 per cent has actually been paid in, and of this, 1 per cent has been payable in gold and 9 per cent payable in the member nations' own currencies.[10] The remaining 90 per cent

---

[10] Actually 20 per cent of the quota was initially paid in. When the quotas were doubled in 1959 none of the increase in subscription was called and so, in effect, paid in capital amounts to 10 per cent of the total subscribed capital.

is callable if and when funds are needed to meet obligations to lenders from whom the Bank has borrowed, or to private investors whose loans the Bank has guaranteed. Member subscriptions are shown in Table 21-1.

The funds the Bank lends are composed of its paid up capital and surplus plus money that it has itself borrowed.[11] Furthermore, if the Bank can sell loans which it has made, then to this extent it reduces its needs to go to the money market for additional funds. The amount of lending activity that the Bank can engage in is limited. The Bank may lend up to 20 per cent of its capital and surplus, can lend funds which it has borrowed, and may guarantee loans made by private investors. But its total outstanding loans and guarantees may not exceed its total subscribed capital, though it does exceed its paid in capital. Specifically the limitation reads: "The total amount of outstanding guarantees, participations in loans and direct loans made by the Bank shall not be increased at any time if by such increase the total would exceed 100 per cent of the unimpaired subscribed capital, reserves and surplus of the Bank" (Article III-3).

Since its beginning of operations in 1946 through June 30, 1963 the IBRD has generated total credits of more than $6,983 million. As Table 21-2 shows, less than 10 per cent of the loans in value terms went for reconstruction purposes, with more than 90 per cent utilized for developmental projects throughout the world. Although the Bank did make reconstruction loans in its first years, it was early recognized that this was an undertaking beyond the Bank's capabilities. With the launching of the European Recovery Program (the Marshall Plan) to aid the recovery of war-devastated Europe, the Bank was free to turn its attention to a more permanent purpose, the assistance of the economic development of its member nations.

Before the Bank may participate in a lending operation, either directly or indirectly through guarantees, certain conditions must be fulfilled. These conditions are spelled out in Article III of the Articles of Agreement and include such requirements as lending only to governments, or requiring the guarantee of the government in whose territory the borrower is located as to repayment of the principal and the payment of interest and other charges. They further include that a competent committee of the Bank has reported favorably on the project, that the Bank is satisfied that the borrower is unable to obtain the loan elsewhere on reasonable terms, that in the opinion

---

[11] Thus, like the Fund, the Bank is not a "bank" since it does not create the funds it lends.

**TABLE 21-1** Statement of Subscriptions to Capital Stock and Voting Power—June 30, 1963 (expressed in United States currency in thousands)

| Member | Subscriptions | | | Amounts Paid in | | Subject to call to meet obligations of Bank | Voting Power | |
|---|---|---|---|---|---|---|---|---|
| | Shares | Per cent of total | Amount | In United States dollars | In currency of member other than United States dollars | | Number of votes | Per cent of total |
| Afghanistan[a] | 300 | .14 | $ 30,000 | $ 300 | $ 1,200 | $ 27,000 | 550 | .24 |
| Argentina | 3,733 | 1.80 | 373,300 | 3,733 | 27,000 | 335,970 | 3,983 | 1.74 |
| Australia | 5,330 | 2.57 | 533,000 | 5,330 | 41,985 | 479,700 | 5,580 | 2.44 |
| Austria | 1,000 | .48 | 100,000 | 1,000 | 9,000 | 90,000 | 1,250 | .55 |
| Belgium | 4,500 | 2.17 | 450,000 | 4,500 | 40,500 | 405,000 | 4,750 | 2.08 |
| Bolivia[a] | 210 | .10 | 21,000 | 210 | 13 | 18,900 | 460 | .20 |
| Brazil | 3,733 | 1.80 | 373,300 | 3,733 | 33,597 | 335,970 | 3,983 | 1.74 |
| Burma | 400 | .19 | 40,000 | 400 | 1,207 | 36,000 | 650 | .28 |
| Canada | 7,500 | 3.62 | 750,000 | 7,500 | 67,500 | 675,000 | 7,750 | 3.39 |
| Ceylon | 600 | .29 | 60,000 | 600 | 1,136 | 54,000 | 850 | .37 |
| Chile | 933 | .45 | 93,300 | 933 | 8,397 | 83,970 | 1,183 | .52 |
| China | 7,500 | 3.62 | 750,000 | 7,500 | 681 | 675,000 | 7,750 | 3.39 |
| Colombia | 933 | .45 | 93,300 | 2,613 | 6,717 | 83,970 | 1,183 | .52 |
| Costa Rica | 80 | .04 | 8,000 | 440 | 360 | 7,200 | 330 | .14 |
| Cyprus | 150 | .07 | 15,000 | 150 | 14 | 13,500 | 400 | .18 |
| Denmark | 1,733 | .84 | 173,300 | 1,733 | 14,128 | 155,970 | 1,983 | .87 |
| Dominican Republic | 80 | .04 | 8,000 | 80 | 5 | 7,200 | 330 | .14 |
| Ecuador | 128 | .06 | 12,800 | 1,280 | — | 11,520 | 378 | .16 |

| | | | | | | | | |
|---|---|---|---|---|---|---|---|---|
| El Salvador | 60 | .03 | 6,000 | 240 | 360 | 5,400 | 310 | .14 |
| Ethiopia | 100 | .05 | 10,000 | 885 | 115 | 9,000 | 350 | .15 |
| Finland | 760 | .37 | 76,000 | 760 | 6,840 | 68,400 | 1,010 | .44 |
| France | 10,500 | 5.07 | 1,050,000 | 10,500 | 94,500 | 945,000 | 10,750 | 4.70 |
| Germany | 10,500 | 5.07 | 1,050,000 | 10,500 | 86,700 | 945,000 | 10,750 | 4.70 |
| Ghana | 467 | .23 | 46,700 | 467 | 2,273 | 42,030 | 717 | .31 |
| Greece | 500 | .24 | 50,000 | 500 | 4,500 | 45,000 | 750 | .33 |
| Guatemala | 80 | .04 | 8,000 | 440 | 360 | 7,200 | 330 | .14 |
| Haiti | 150 | .07 | 15,000 | 150 | 35 | 13,500 | 400 | .18 |
| Honduras | 60 | .03 | 6,000 | 546 | 54 | 5,400 | 310 | .14 |
| Iceland | 150 | .07 | 15,000 | 330 | 124 | 13,500 | 400 | .18 |
| India | 8,000 | 3.86 | 800,000 | 8,000 | 21,932 | 720,000 | 8,250 | 3.61 |
| Indonesia | 2,200 | 1.06 | 220,000 | 2,200 | 198 | 198,000 | 2,450 | 1.07 |
| Iran | 900 | .43 | 90,000 | 900 | 6,048 | 81,000 | 1,150 | .50 |
| Iraq | 150 | .07 | 15,000 | 150 | 1,080 | 13,500 | 400 | .18 |
| Ireland | 600 | .29 | 60,000 | 600 | 4,149 | 54,000 | 850 | .37 |
| Israel | 333 | .16 | 33,300 | 333 | 2,997 | 29,970 | 583 | .25 |
| Italy | 3,600 | 1.74 | 360,000 | 3,600 | 32,400 | 324,000 | 3,850 | 1.69 |
| Ivory Coast | 200 | .10 | 20,000 | 200 | 18 | 18,000 | 450 | .20 |
| Jamaica | 267 | .13 | 26,700 | 267 | 24 | 24,030 | 517 | .23 |
| Japan | 6,660 | 3.21 | 666,000 | 6,660 | 59,940 | 599,400 | 6,910 | 3.02 |
| Jordan | 150 | .07 | 15,000 | 150 | 30 | 13,500 | 400 | .18 |
| Korea | 250 | .12 | 25,000 | 250 | 2,250 | 22,500 | 500 | .22 |
| Kuwait | 667 | .32 | 66,700 | 667 | 60 | 60,030 | 917 | .40 |
| Laos | 100 | .05 | 10,000 | 100 | 900 | 9,000 | 350 | .15 |
| Lebanon | 90 | .04 | 9,000 | 900 | — | 8,100 | 340 | .15 |
| Liberia | 150 | .07 | 15,000 | 150 | 14 | 13,500 | 400 | .18 |
| Libya | 200 | .10 | 20,000 | 200 | 15 | 18,000 | 450 | .20 |
| Luxembourg | 200 | .10 | 20,000 | 200 | 1,800 | 18,000 | 450 | .20 |

TABLE 21-1   (Continued)

| Member | Subscriptions | | | Amounts Paid in | | | Voting Power | |
|---|---|---|---|---|---|---|---|---|
| | Shares | Per cent of total | Amount | In United States dollars | In currency of member other than United States dollars | Subject to call to meet obligations of Bank | Number of votes | Per cent of total |
| Malaya | 500 | .24 | $ 50,000 | $ 500 | $ 4,500 | $ 45,000 | 750 | .33 |
| Mexico | 1,733 | .84 | 173,300 | 1,733 | 15,597 | 155,970 | 1,983 | .87 |
| Morocco | 700 | .34 | 70,000 | 700 | 75 | 63,000 | 950 | .42 |
| Nepal | 100 | .05 | 10,000 | 100 | 9 | 9,000 | 350 | .15 |
| Netherlands[a] | 5,500 | 2.65 | 550,000 | 5,500 | 49,500 | 495,000 | 5,750 | 2.52 |
| New Zealand | 1,667 | .80 | 166,700 | 1,667 | 150 | 150,030 | 1,917 | .84 |
| Nicaragua | 60 | .03 | 6,000 | 60 | 540 | 5,400 | 310 | .14 |
| Niger | 100 | .05 | 10,000 | 100 | 9 | 9,000 | 350 | .15 |
| Nigeria | 667 | .32 | 66,700 | 667 | 60 | 60,030 | 917 | .40 |
| Norway | 1,333 | .64 | 133,300 | 1,333 | 11,997 | 119,970 | 1,583 | .69 |
| Pakistan | 2,000 | .97 | 200,000 | 2,000 | 2,049 | 180,000 | 2,250 | .98 |
| Panama | 4 | b | 400 | 40 | — | 360 | 254 | .11 |
| Paraguay | 60 | .03 | 6,000 | 60 | 540 | 5,400 | 310 | .14 |
| Peru | 350 | .17 | 35,000 | 3,500 | — | 31,500 | 600 | .26 |
| Philippines | 1,000 | .48 | 100,000 | 3,700 | 6,300 | 90,000 | 1,250 | .55 |
| Portugal | 800 | .39 | 80,000 | 800 | 7,200 | 72,000 | 1,050 | .46 |
| Saudi Arabia | 733 | .35 | 73,300 | 733 | 22 | 65,970 | 983 | .43 |
| Senegal | 333 | .16 | 33,300 | 333 | 2,997 | 29,970 | 583 | .25 |
| Sierra Leone | 150 | .07 | 15,000 | 150 | 13 | 13,500 | 400 | .18 |

| | | | | | | | | |
|---|---|---|---|---|---|---|---|---|
| Somalia | 150 | .07 | 15,000 | 150 | 1,350 | 13,500 | 400 | .18 |
| South Africa | 2,000 | .97 | 200,000 | 2,000 | 18,000 | 180,000 | 2,250 | .98 |
| Spain | 2,000 | .97 | 200,000 | 2,000 | 3,780 | 180,000 | 2,250 | .98 |
| Sudan | 200 | .10 | 20,000 | 200 | 1,800 | 18,000 | 450 | .20 |
| Sweden | 2,000 | .97 | 200,000 | 2,000 | 18,000 | 180,000 | 2,250 | .98 |
| Syrian Arab Republic | 200 | .10 | 20,000 | 200 | 44 | 18,000 | 450 | .20 |
| Tanganyika | 333 | .16 | 33,300 | 333 | 30 | 29,970 | 583 | .25 |
| Thailand | 600 | .29 | 60,000 | 2,850 | 84 | 54,000 | 850 | .37 |
| Togo | 150 | .07 | 15,000 | 150 | 13 | 13,500 | 400 | .18 |
| Tunisia | 300 | .14 | 30,000 | 300 | 22 | 27,000 | 550 | .24 |
| Turkey | 1,150 | .55 | 115,000 | 1,150 | 271 | 103,500 | 1,400 | .61 |
| United Arab Republic[c] | 1,066 | .51 | 106,600 | 1,066 | 96 | 95,940 | 1,316 | .58 |
| United Kingdom | 26,000 | 12.54 | 2,600,000 | 26,000 | 234,000 | 2,340,000 | 26,250 | 11.49 |
| United States | 63,500 | 30.63 | 6,350,000 | 635,000 | — | 5,715,000 | 63,750 | 27.89 |
| Upper Volta | 100 | .05 | 10,000 | 100 | 9 | 9,000 | 350 | .15 |
| Uruguay[a] | 105 | .05 | 10,500 | 210 | 438 | 8,400 | 355 | .15 |
| Venezuela | 1,400 | .68 | 140,000 | 1,400 | 1,997 | 126,000 | 1,650 | .72 |
| Viet-Nam | 300 | .14 | 30,000 | 300 | 2,700 | 27,000 | 550 | .24 |
| Yugoslavia | 1,067 | .51 | 106,700 | 1,067 | 9,603 | 96,030 | 1,317 | .58 |
| Totals | 207,298 | 100.00 | $20,729,800 | $793,032 | $976,951 | $18,655,770 | 228,548 | 100.00 |

*Source: Annual Report 1962–1963*, International Bank for Reconstruction and Development, Washington, D.C., 1963.

[a] Amounts aggregating the equivalent of $2,990,536 receivable and of $1,265,627 payable as a result of revaluation of these currencies are not included in the "Amounts Paid in" columns.

[b] Less than .005 per cent.

[c] Additional subscription in the amount of $35,500,000 is in process of completion.

TABLE **21-2** Bank Loans Classified by Purpose and Area—June 30, 1963 (millions of U. S. dollars, initial commitments net of cancellations and refundings)

| | | | Areas | | | |
|---|---|---|---|---|---|---|
| Purpose | Total | Africa | Asia and Middle East | Australia | Europe | Western Hemisphere |
| **Grand Total**. . . . . | 6,983.2 | 917.6 | 2,354.6 | 417.7 | 1,554.5 | 1,738.8 |
| **Development Loans:** Total | 6,486.5 | 917.6 | 2,354.6 | 417.7 | 1,057.7 | 1,738.8 |
| ELECTRIC POWER | | | | | | |
| Generation and Distribution. . . . | 2,336.0 | 251.6 | 516.3 | 129.3 | 464.0 | 974.9 |
| TRANSPORTATION. . . | 2,260.9 | 442.5 | 1,022.6 | 132.3 | 103.4 | 560.1 |
| Railroads . . . . | 1,089.8 | 274.1 | 600.5 | 37.3 | 2.3 | 175.6 |
| Roads . . . . . | 741.5 | 87.7 | 209.0 | 50.9 | 35.0 | 358.9 |
| Shipping . . . . | 12.0 | — | — | — | 12.0 | — |
| Ports and Waterways | 296.7 | 30.7 | 193.5 | — | 46.9 | 25.6 |
| Airlines and Airports. | 56.9 | — | 5.6 | 44.1 | 7.2 | — |
| Pipelines . . . . | 64.0 | 50.0 | 14.0 | — | — | — |
| COMMUNICATIONS | | | | | | |
| Telephone, Telegraph, etc. . . . . . | 26.9 | 4.4 | — | — | 0.3 | 22.2 |
| AGRICULTURE AND FORESTRY . . . | 528.8 | 59.1 | 178.5 | 103.4 | 87.8 | 100.0 |
| Farm Mechanization | 121.1 | — | — | 89.4 | 2.0 | 29.7 |
| Irrigation and Flood Control . . . . | 330.6 | 35.0 | 163.9 | 6.0 | 73.3 | 52.4 |
| Land Clearance, etc. . | 49.3 | 22.1 | 13.6 | 6.0 | 2.1 | 5.5 |
| Crop Processing and Storage . . . . | 7.0 | 1.0 | — | — | 4.2 | 1.8 |
| Livestock Improvement | 12.6 | 1.0 | 1.0 | — | — | 10.6 |
| Forestry . . . . | 8.2 | — | — | 2.0 | 6.2 | — |
| INDUSTRY . . . . . | 1,128.9 | 120.0 | 562.3 | 52.7 | 312.2 | 81.6 |
| Iron and Steel. . . | 380.3 | — | 314.2 | 13.4 | 22.7 | 30.0 |
| Paper and Pulp . . | 138.7 | — | 4.2 | 1.1 | 113.4 | 20.0 |
| Fertilizer and Other Chemicals . . . | 82.0 | — | 25.0 | 0.3 | 56.7 | — |
| Other Industries . . | 97.0 | — | 5.2 | 23.7 | 58.8 | 9.3 |
| Mining . . . . . | 203.5 | 101.0 | 54.5 | 14.2 | 11.9 | 21.8 |
| Water Supply . . . | 2.0 | — | — | — | 2.0 | — |
| Development Banks . | 225.4 | 19.0 | 159.2 | — | 46.7 | 0.5 |
| GENERAL DEVELOPMENT. | 205.0 | 40.0 | 75.0 | — | 90.0 | — |
| **Reconstruction Loans:** | | | | | | |
| Total . . . . . . | 496.7 | — | — | — | 496.7 | — |

*Source: Annual Report 1962–1963*, International Bank for Reconstruction and Development, Washington, D.C., 1963.

of the Bank the rate of interest and other charges are reasonable and such rate, charges, and the schedule for repayment of principal are appropriate to the project, and that in guaranteeing a loan made by other investors, the Bank receive suitable compensation for its risk.

As mentioned earlier, the Bank borrows funds for lending through the sale of its own bonds.   In the New York money market the Bank has been able to borrow at long term at less than 1 per cent more than the United States Treasury for comparable maturity.   In addition to New York, the Bank has sold its securities in Canada, Great Britain, France, Germany, the Netherlands, and Switzerland.   When the Bank lends the funds it has borrowed, borrowers are charged what the money costs the Bank itself plus 1 per cent as a loss reserve, and an additional $\frac{1}{4}$ of 1 per cent for administrative expenses.

An appraisal of the Bank's usefulness is likely to be misleading. Since beginning its operations in 1946 it has generated total credits only about double what the United States appropriates for foreign aid in a single year.   Even so, the IBRD has demonstrated its usefulness. It has enabled member nations to obtain needed capital funds from abroad which would otherwise not have been obtained.   But the Bank does more than just provide capital, it also provides the kinds of technical advice and assistance that are invaluable to developing nations. This provision of technical assistance may turn out to be the most important service offered by the Bank, since one of the problems of developing areas is the slow rate at which they can usefully absorb capital.

Another important aspect of the Bank's operations is that its lending activities have often created additional investment opportunities for private foreign funds.   This aspect, together with the fact that the Bank participates only in supplying the foreign exchange needed to import capital equipment, means that rather substantial additional expenditures in terms of both foreign and domestic currencies are generated.   The total impact of the Bank's operations thus exceeds rather substantially what the figures of Table 21-2 would at first seem to indicate.

## A PREVIEW TO INTERNATIONAL MONETARY POLICY

Since the end of the Second World War, as we have seen, a new international payments system has emerged.   This system has been created by the efforts of international organizations like the IMF and the cooperation of many trading nations.   The new system is a gold-exchange standard.   It differs, however, from its predecessor of

1925–31 in that it is considered as a permanent system and not as a temporary expedient. Also the present system has seen the dollar added to gold and sterling as the basis for monetary reserves, and other key currencies are emerging.

The present gold-exchange standard has seen a higher pyramiding on the available gold base than was the case in the 1920s. The greater pyramiding, however, carries with it the possibility of greater instability. The stability of the present payments system depends on cooperation among the world's monetary authorities. This cooperation has been forthcoming, if only from a recognition that national economic self-interest demands it. Specifically, the stability of the present structure rests in maintaining confidence in the key currencies to prevent flights from one currency to another or to gold. This requires the key currency countries to manage their external affairs and internal finances with prudence so as to engender this kind of confidence.

Balance of payments developments are of special significance to the central bank of a key currency country. As we have seen, the key currency holdings have resulted from payments deficits. A payments surplus would tend to mop up other countries' holdings of this key currency and deprive them of part of their monetary reserves. On the other hand, continuing deficits place increasing amounts of the key currency in the hands of foreign central banks. If these central bank holdings of a key currency become excessively large they may result in large-scale conversion into gold. This is the situation in which the United States now finds itself in the 1960s, a situation that Great Britain knows well from long years as the world's banker, but a brand new and still uncomfortable role for the United States.

From 1950 to 1957 the United States ran a small but persistent payments deficit averaging about $1 billion a year. Over these years foreigners and foreign central banks were willing to hold dollars. But since 1958 United States deficits have been much larger, averaging around $3 billion per year. These increased deficits have led to increased dollar holdings by foreigners, and foreign central banks have shown a tendency to convert their additional dollar holdings into gold. Over the last six years about $7 billion has been converted.

The kind of dangers to which the dollar has become exposed by these gold losses was illustrated by the sharp rise in the price of gold in the London market in the fall of 1960, and the shift of short-term funds to Europe. These short-term capital movements, possibly inspired by speculation concerning United States devaluation, meant the conversion of dollars to local currencies in large amounts, and left the foreign central banks with increased dollar balances.   Many of these central banks already had larger dollar balances than they customarily held for their reserve needs.   The stage was set for massive demands on the United States gold stock.

In this situation the Treasury's Exchange Stabilization Fund began buying dollars with foreign currencies in the foreign exchange market. If excess dollars could be purchased this would reduce the purchase of gold by foreign central banks.   Early in 1962, the Federal Reserve System began operating in foreign exchange.   Operations for both the Fed and the Treasury are conducted by the Federal Reserve Bank of New York, thus insuring coordination of the two agencies.   Through interest-rate policy—the short-term rate has been kept high by means of the Treasury maintaining an ample supply of short-term bills in the market and the Fed concentrating its open market operations in intermediate and long-term issues—and foreign exchange operations, the Treasury and the Fed have moderated the pressure on the dollar and the gold stock.

But the achievement of this degree of success has required the cooperation of foreign central banks and monetary authorities.   Thus, for example, in the last half of 1960 several European countries took action to limit flights of short-term capital from the United States. Switzerland tried to discourage the inflow of foreign funds by changing the regulations governing time deposits.   England and Germany loosened credit there, lowering the short-term rate and thereby making themselves less attractive to short-term capital inflows.

But cooperation is a two-way street.   In the example of the previous paragraph the United States received the cooperation of the English, German, and Swiss monetary authorities.   In June, 1962, however, the Federal Reserve joined with the Bank of England, the Export-Import Bank, and the IMF to extend to Canada over $1 billion of support when Canada was experiencing payments problems.

The essential element of international cooperation to maintain a viable, functioning international payments system seems finally to be arriving.   Problems still remain, however, and we shall return to this area in our later discussion of international monetary policy.


## REVIEW QUESTIONS

1. Explain the equilibrating mechanism of the international gold standard.
2. Explain the working of a gold exchange standard.   How does pyramiding occur under this standard?
3. What is the purpose of the International Monetary Fund?

4. What is the purpose of the International Bank? Have its operations been more significant than the rather small size of its operations would suggest?
5. Why was it wise, indeed, necessary, that, when the Fund was established, the World Bank was also organized?
6. What is the problem of international liquidity?
7. What progress is being made toward increasing world liquidity?

## SUGGESTED REFERENCES

*Economic Report of the President,* Washington, D.C., Government Printing Office.
*Factors Affecting the U. S. Balance of Payments,* Joint Economic Committee (Washington, D.C.: Government Printing Office, 1962).
Harris, Seymour E., ed., *The Dollar in Crisis* (New York: Harcourt, Brace and World, 1961).
Triffin, Robert, *Gold and the Dollar Crisis* (New Haven: Yale University Press, 1960).
See also the annual reports of the IMF and the IBRD.

# PART VI

# ECONOMIC POLICY

# CHAPTER 22

# Economic Policy and Economic Goals

Economic theory, as we have said, is much like a road map—the principal landmarks and features are included, but most of the details are left out. The landmarks in our theory consist of those particular economic magnitudes believed to be most relevant in determining the level and growth of national income. To put it in a somewhat different fashion, an economic theory singles out those independent variables that determine the values of the dependent variables. The kinds of economic variables we deal with are such things as the rate of interest, the supply of money, the level of prices, the level of employment and income, etc.

Having studied the theory, we may put the map to work. Perhaps the following discussion will be helpful. Science is concerned with means rather than with ends. The test is the ability to predict. Thus, the scientist is looking for regularities in whatever field he happens to be studying. So is the economist. If economics is a science, the economist must search for these regularities. He must formulate statements that are valid oftener than not, and that coincide with the realities of the economic world. Given the set of statements, or assumptions, certain conclusions follow as a consequence. Every theory rests on certain assumptions. Through deduction, the assumptions determine the conclusions, or theorems. Should the assumptions be altered or changed, the conclusions would likewise change. If the theory is valid, certain outcomes can be predicted, provided other certain actions or conditions are observed to be occurring or are caused to occur.   Thus "science" may perhaps be defined as a set of rules about *what is*.

On the other hand, we may be interested in manipulating the means in order to attain certain ends, or objectives.   Policy may be defined, perhaps, as the set of rules which may bring about some desired end. Policy is thus not necessarily concerned with what is, but with *what may be*.   The end or objective is specified, the appropriate variables or conditions are manipulated to bring about the desired goal.   Thus it is that economic theory and economic policy are intimately connected. But even though the theory is perfectly sound, it is possible that the conclusions or policy recommendations that emerge may lead some persons to reject the theory itself.

In order to carry out economic policy, it is necessary to have the desired economic objectives established.   These objectives may be single goals or multiple goals.   Examples of economic objectives are stability of prices, rapid economic growth, full employment, stability in the balance of payments, etc.—or a combination of these.

In 1946 Congress enacted the so-called "Full Employment Act," which put forth the goals of maximum employment, production, and purchasing power.   More recently, Congress has determined the following national economic objectives of ". . . a high and stable rate of employment, a high rate of growth in our national output and productive capacity, and a high degree of stability in the general level of prices."   Notwithstanding these objectives, there remains the knotty problem of determining what constitutes "full" employment, what is a "high degree of price stability," and what is a "high" growth rate. There can be wide differences of opinion here—to paraphrase the familiar old saw, one man's relative price stability may be another man's poison.   There is thus a serious definitional problem which needs consideration.

In addition to the need for clarifying the meaning of *full* employment, a *high* rate of economic growth, and a *high degree* of price stability, there is also the necessity of ordering these goals in the event that they may not be simultaneously attainable.   That is, should full employment be incompatible with stable prices, which is given priority?   Or if price stability is inconsistent with a high rate of economic growth, which goal is ranked the higher?   It is quite likely, as we shall see, that at least one goal may have to be sacrificed if we are to attain the others.   Let us turn to the meaning of these goals, and some possible orderings of them.

## ECONOMIC GOALS: SOME PROBLEMS AND DEFINITIONS

### Full-Employment Goal

It is generally recognized that *full employment* is a goal toward which the various monetary and fiscal policy measures should be directed. Indeed, Congress itself has deemed this one of the nation's goals.   But Congress has left unanswered what full employment is.   Let us at least indicate the minimum considerations necessary to answer this question.

Full employment, for most observers, is generally defined in terms of the availability of jobs for those who want them.   To this definition is usually appended the statement, "jobs readily available on reasonable terms for those persons able and willing to work."   This means that hours, wages, and other conditions are in keeping with normal standards in the various occupations and areas of the country.

But this still has not answered the question.   There remains the problem of measurement.   Who is in the labor force or out of it?   Of those in the labor force, who are employed?   That is, are part-time workers who want full-time work employed or not?   Or how about those workers, supposedly full-time, who work a shortened week, say thirty hours, because of a lack of orders?   Who, in the labor force, is unemployed?   Those who have lost their job and are *not* seeking a new one, or only those actively seeking new ones?   These are the kinds of measurement questions which must be answered if the monetary and fiscal authorities are to make intelligent decisions.   The data must be both accurate and complete if reasonable judgments are to be made.

Assuming that the problems posed have been satisfactorily answered, that we have a workable concept of full employment and that reliable data thereto are available, an additional qualification enters.   Full employment in the sense of 100 per cent employment is not what is meant.   There will always be those, for example, changing from one job to another, etc.   This kind of *frictional* unemployment is a necessary by-product of a free economy.   Thus we have to allow for *tolerable* unemployment, for a certain percentage of the labor force to be unemployed at all times.

But when does tolerable unemployment become intolerable?   There is no general agreement on this question, with figures ranging from 3 to 6 per cent of the labor force given by various scholars and statesmen. Although we shall not here stump for any specific figure, by now the concept involved should be understood by the student. Until the level of unemployment rises above the tolerable level, the authorities need not undertake massive action. But as this critical level is approached, the monetary and fiscal authorities will undoubtedly begin to formulate their policies to deal with and to correct the situation.

### Price-Stability Goal

Price stability is considerably easier to define than full employment. An acceptable definition is:[1] "Price level stability means the absence of any marked trend or sharp short-run movements in the general level of prices." It must be clearly understood at the outset that price stability means stability of an average, an index of prices, and not the keeping of all prices constant. Individual prices are free to fluctuate according to the vagaries of supply and demand, to rise or to fall. Only the average of all prices as measured by, say, the consumer's price index, is stabilized.

One of the principal justifications for price-level stability as a goal is the certainty and confidence which accompany it. This element of price stability eliminates doubt about future price levels, and makes economic calculations more efficient. However, if it were known that prices in general would change no more than $x$ per cent a year the same efficiency would result.

Given the past instability of prices, a stabilized price level does perhaps seem desirable. Money would be as neutral as possible, allowing economic decisions to be made on the basis of the real underlying determinants. And finally, price-level stability is a straightforward, easily understood kind of proposition, one which is likely to command wide public support.

After saying all this, it is generally agreed that a stable price level does not assure a full level of employment. Certainly with widespread unemployment we would expect stable prices. But the stable prices then existing probably do little to generate a movement to a higher level of employment. As a matter of fact, in such a situation it is conceivable that the monetary and fiscal authorities would take what action they could to raise prices in order to widen profit margins so as to stimulate business activity.

By the same token, the maintenance of full employment in the face

---

[1] "The Problem of Economic Instability," *American Economic Review*, September, 1950, p. 506.

of declining prices does not appear likely. Price declines translate into narrowed profit margins, and they may lead to a reduction in the level of productive economic activity. On the other hand, rising prices do not, at least initially, seem to be harmful. The rising prices expand profit margins, thus stimulating business activity. But how long can this bloom continue? The probability is that continued price rises will lead to widespread maladjustments, culminating in economic collapse.

Since it is clear that the paramount goal of economic policy is the maintenance of full employment, price stability becomes a secondary goal. The level of prices that is consistent with full employment will become the appropriate price-level policy, since it yields the greatest price stability *relative* to the principal goal of full employment. This policy appears most likely to be one of permitting the price level to drift up gently, if the simultaneous goal of full employment and absolute price-level stability prove to be incompatible. Thus, price-level stability is desirable only as long as full-employment conditions exist, but should unemployment rise above the tolerable level, policies to reduce unemployment, regardless of the price-level effect, are to be employed. Price-level stability is thus downgraded into a position of secondary importance, residually determined by the requirements of the full-employment goal.

### Economic-Growth Goal

With the consideration of the triumvirate of economic goals—full employment, price stability, and rapid economic growth—it is likely that price stability will be even further lowered in priority to third position.

Proponents of the growth thesis put forth two basic arguments in favor of their position: (1) a domestic welfare argument; and (2) an international argument. Under the domestic welfare argument it is suggested that growth will enable the United States to achieve higher consumption standards (a higher standard of living) and also that desirable public services can be expanded without curtailing private consumption. On the international level, the increased growth will enable the United States to provide additional economic aid to the underdeveloped areas, to expand world trade, and to shoulder more easily the responsibility for protecting the free world from the peril and threat of international Communism.

How high a rate of growth is envisioned in this growth objective? The record of economic growth in the United States does not suggest that the average realized growth rate is the ceiling. Rather, the rate of growth of output has varied considerably from one period to another, depending on specific economic circumstances. The decade of the 1930s, for example, was a period of stagnation, when output grew much less slowly than the nation's historic average long-term rate of growth. Conversely, the years immediately following the Second World War were a period of growth exceeding the average.

Since fluctuations in business activity are an inherent characteristic of our economy, it is too much to expect a high rate of growth year in and year out. But the swings in business activity are legitimate targets for stabilization policies, and the attempt to iron out some of the cyclical fluctuations implies that the growth objective should be an *average annual rate of growth* and should be judged over the length of the average business cycle, say 42 to 48 months. Saving and investment to increase capacity and raise productivity wax in prosperous times and wane in recession times. Therefore, reduction of business fluctuation lowers the risks associated with investment and innovation, and reduces resistance to technological improvements. A fully employed economy can achieve a more rapid growth rate than one alternating between boom and recession. For that reason, effective stabilization policy is the first step toward a policy of more rapid economic growth.

Rapid economic growth requires a continual increase in capital facilities. In order to increase the amount of capital goods, net saving is necessary. The mere creation of money cannot perform the job of saving—it must be real saving. Thus, our ability and willingness to save set limits on our capacity to grow.

It is evident that the full-employment objective and the growth objective are compatible, and to some extent overlapping. Clearly, a high rate of economic growth requires intensive use of all productive resources, including labor. Conversely, a high level of employment supports and maintains a high level of aggregate demand, which is vital to the achievement of a high rate of growth in output. On the other hand, the price-level objective may not harmonize with the employment and growth objectives.

If we were to order our national goals as: (1) Full employment; (2) Price stability; (3) Economic growth, we would essentially be saying that after achieving full employment and obtaining whatever price stability possible given the employment goal, the rate of growth that emerged would be the appropriate rate. This was the ordering of the objectives from 1946 through 1960. But, because the growth rate was declining from 4.6 per cent per year for the period 1947–1953 to about 2.4 per cent per year for 1953–1959 period, the order of the growth and price-level goals has been interchanged. The ordering of the national economic objectives is now generally accepted as:

(1) Full employment; (2) High rate of growth; (3) Price stability.

There do not appear to be any serious conflicts between the goals of full employment and a higher rate of economic growth. These two goals are consistent with each other and mutually reinforcing. High-level employment is a stimulus to business concerns to invest in labor-saving equipment to improve productivity, and maximum growth is certainly not being achieved if unemployment is high.

On the other hand, the relationship of price stability to rapid economic growth and full employment is likelier to be somewhat incompatible. For example, if unemployment is running at a high level monetary ease is appropriate for stimulating demand. But this increased demand may have an inflationary effect as employment moves toward the full-employment level.

The principal problem connected with the achievement of all three economic objectives is that the policy designed to achieve one of them may conflict with the action to attain some other goal. Nevertheless, the Commission on Money and Credit, a study group sponsored by the Committee for Economic Development, concluded that the three goals may be simultaneously achieved. In its words:

The Commission concludes that all three goals—an adequate rate of economic growth, low levels of unemployment, and reasonable price stability — can be achieved simultaneously, and that they are fundamentally compatible if we do not expect the *impossible* for each. While conflicts may arise under certain conditions between reasonable price stability and low levels of unemployment, there are no conflicts between low levels of unemployment and economic growth, and between reasonable price stability and an adequate rate of economic growth.[2]

But even this optimistic statement implies that conflict is likely, for if one does order the goals and give priority to high-level employment and rapid economic growth then price stability becomes a residually determined goal. Reasonable price stability is then that degree of price stability consistent with growth and full employment.

## ECONOMIC POLICY AND THE ECONOMIC GOALS

The Federal Reserve System is the principal channel for the exercise of monetary policy in the pursuit of the economic goals, although as we

---

[2] *Money and Credit*, Report of the Commission on Money and Credit (Englewood Cliffs: Prentice-Hall, 1961), pp. 44–45. Italics are added.

saw earlier the Treasury does have some discretionary monetary powers. Whereas we have discussed a trinity of economic objectives, the Federal Reserve until 1929 historically had only two goals, one domestic and the other international. The domestic goal was to prevent the occurrence of financial panics by promoting the orderly flow of credit for productive purposes. Internationally, the goal was to protect the gold reserve, something that needed very little doing until 1958. Since 1958 there has been emerging a fourth goal, that of stability in the balance of payments.

The 1930s saw a shift of objectives to helping overcome depression and to promoting and restoring domestic economic recovery. Then, with the onset of the Second World War, the aim became to facilitate the successful financing of the war effort. Subsequent to the end of the war, the Federal Reserve to 1949 followed policies aimed at curbing inflationary pressures. This was followed by alternate easy and tight money policies aimed respectively at easing unemployment in recession, and at restraining inflation and moderating boom conditions. Now the promotion of economic growth has been added as a third objective and balance of payments stability has drawn increasing attention since 1958.

The attempt to achieve the economic goals of high-level employment, rapid economic growth, stable prices, and, more recently, stability in the balance of payments is made through the use of various economic policies. The types of economic policy which are most significant to our study of money and banking are monetary policy, fiscal policy, and debt management policy.

Although in many cases it will be somewhat difficult to separate one policy from another, since fiscal actions have monetary consequences, for example, it will be helpful to indicate the general nature of monetary, fiscal, and debt management policies.

### Monetary Policy and Economic Goals

Monetary policy may be defined as the regulation of the quantity of money for the achieving of some objective or set of objectives. Thus, the central bank regulates the cost and availability of credit as it seeks to promote a high level of employment, growth, stability in the balance of payments, and stable prices.

The principal tools used by the Federal Reserve in regulating the money supply are its open market powers, its authority to vary reserve ratio requirements, and manipulation of the discount rate. These quantitative controls aim at influencing the cost and availability of credit in general. They operate on the commercial bank's reserve position by changing the volume of reserves (open market operations), by altering the disposition of a given amount of reserves relative to required reserves and excess reserves (reserve ratio requirements), and by changing the cost of borrowed reserves (discount rate policy).

We may illustrate monetary policy by the following examples. In order to promote a higher level of employment or to increase economic growth, greater aggregate spending is needed. To stimulate this spending, an easing of credit conditions and an increase in the money supply would be appropriate monetary policy. On the other hand, in periods of vigorous spending the central bank will tighten up on credit to prevent inflationary price rises which often accompany these periods, and to attempt to stretch out the prosperous boom period over a longer time span.

## Fiscal Policy and Economic Goals

Fiscal policy deals with the receipts and expenditures by government. Government affects spending, employment, and prices through its revenue absorptions and its expenditures. Government expenditures are part of final demand, and so are part of the gross national income stream.

Government revenues include funds collected through taxation and also money raised by borrowing. As we saw in the theory chapters, taxation reduces disposable income and consequently reduces final demand for output. Borrowing, on the other hand, depending on the sector that lends, has various effects on the money supply. Thus, the effect here depends on the source of the funds.

Because fiscal policy includes government expenditures it is clear that fiscal policy provides a powerful tool for offsetting declines in economic activity, the area in which monetary policy is weakest. Total expenditures on final output can be stepped up in a recession by expanding government expenditures financed by newly created money. Conversely, in a period of rising aggregate demand and expenditures, by reducing governmental expenditures inflationary pressures can be reduced. Thus fiscal policy, by allowing for changes in both government expenditures and revenues, provides an important tool for pursuing the policy objectives of full employment, growth, and price stability.

## Debt Management and Economic Goals

The difference between government tax receipts and expenditures provides a surplus or a deficit. If it is a deficit it means that tax collections fell short of expenditures, and the difference was financed by borrowing.   The sources of the borrowed funds have a direct bearing on the money supply, as we have already seen.   Similarly, a surplus used to retire debt has monetary consequences.   Thus, one aspect of debt management is determining how a deficit is to be financed or a surplus to be utilized.

But debt management is important even if government tax revenues and expenditures are in balance.   This is so because, owing to the large size of the debt, a sizable portion of it matures each year.   This necessitates a decision as to what kind of debt should be issued to replace the maturing debt.   The average maturity of all issues outstanding is less than five years, so this implies that about one-fifth of the debt is subject to refunding and refinancing each year.

As maturing debt is paid, the Treasury sells new debt to get the dollars needed for repayment.   Or if old debt is exchanged for new debt, the new debt may not be of the same type as is being retired. Thus, by its choice of new debt forms, and possibly by a choice of what to repay, the Treasury can influence the supplies of securities and the pattern of interest rates.   Even if the amount of debt out-standing is not changing, how it is managed can influence the economy. How the debt is managed can reinforce Federal Reserve policies, or it can conflict with them—but the debt must be managed.

## THE COORDINATION OF ECONOMIC POLICY

It is generally agreed that the various policy instruments are com-plementary in nature, and should be used in a coordinated fashion. For example, monetary policy, most effective in choking off excessive spending in boom periods, should nevertheless be utilized in combatting recession, even though in this situation major reliance may have to be on fiscal instruments.   Thus, a minimum condition to expect of economic policy is the use of the tools available—monetary, fiscal, and debt management—in a consistent and coordinated fashion.

That economic policies should be consistent seems obvious.   There have been, however, many instances of contradictory policies being simultaneously pursued, especially in the years following the Second World War.   Thus, for example, it would be unfortunate, to say the least, if in an inflationary situation an expansive monetary policy negated restrictive fiscal measures, or vice versa.

Each of the various packages of policy tools have their advantages and disadvantages, strengths and weaknesses.   Proper coordination sees to it that the various instruments reinforce one another, rather than work at cross-purposes.

An advantage of monetary policy is its flexibility.   It can be altered quickly and sharply if need be.   This advantage can be used to offset the inflexibility of fiscal policy.   It takes time to formulate major changes in government revenues and expenditure patterns, except insofar as fiscal policy has built-in automatic stabilizers.   But these advantages and disadvantages of the various policy instruments can be combined in order to obtain optimal results at any given time for the situation at hand.

Thus, if recovery from a recession is the problem at hand, monetary policy by itself is rather weak.   But at least the appropriate monetary climate of easy credit should be set.   This, when combined with direct fiscal expenditures and reduced tax collections, will help restore vigor into the economy.   And appropriate debt management can be useful also, even assuming no change in total debt outstanding.   For example, by refunding into shorter term issues held by commercial banks, greater liquidity is introduced into the system.   All of these measures reinforce one another, and there are no policies working at cross-purposes.   Is this kind of policy coordination too much to ask of the nation's monetary and fiscal authorities?

In the following chapters we shall study in much more detail the general problems involved in the application of economic policy.   In particular, we shall examine monetary policy and its instruments; fiscal policy and its tools; and debt-management policy.   The operation of the various instruments and their influence on the level of employment, rate of growth, and prices will be pursued.


## REVIEW QUESTIONS

1. Discuss the relationship of economic theory to economic policy.
2. What is meant by "full employment" as a goal of economic policy?   Discuss some of the problems of definition and measurement.
3. What is meant by stabilizing the price level?
4. What is the basis for a more rapid rate of economic growth?
5. What is the likely relationship between high-level employment and rapid economic growth; between high-level employment and stability of prices?
6. What is the nature of monetary policy?   Give an example of its use.
7. What is fiscal policy?   Give an example of the use of fiscal policy to combat inflationary pressures.
8. What constitutes the area of debt management policy?   Give an example of debt management.
9. What is the minimum to ask of our economic policy makers?

## SUGGESTED REFERENCES

Boulding, Kenneth, *Principles of Economic Policy* (Englewood Cliffs: Prentice-Hall, 1958).

*Money and Credit,* The Report of the Commission on Money and Credit (Englewood Cliffs: Prentice-Hall, 1961).

*Economic Report of the President,* Washington, D.C.: Government Printing Office. The annual reports data on principal national economic goals and policies designed to attain them.

# CHAPTER 23

# The Role of Monetary Policy

What is meant by monetary policy? Monetary policy is the deliberate management of the money supply for the explicit purpose of attaining a specific objective or set of objectives. In this sense, monetary policy involves the conscious, planned manipulation of the volume of money in circulation to achieve the specific objectives of employment, growth, balance of payments stability, and price stability.

The instruments used in monetary policy are of two types, quantitative and qualitative. We shall begin this study of monetary policy by first discussing the development of the quantitative instruments, and then how monetary policy operates. Later, we shall examine in detail the principal quantitative policy weapons and their operation, concluding with a consideration of the qualitative instruments.

## THE DEVELOPMENT OF QUANTITATIVE CONTROLS

The quantitative instruments for carrying out monetary policy are (1) reserve requirement variations, (2) discount rate policy, and (3) open market operations. All of these instruments have been discussed previously, but now a brief historical note on their development is in order.

### Reserve Requirement History

In early American banking, there were no requirements for the holding of reserves against either deposits or bank notes. The first legal

425

reserve requirements were made in 1837 in Virginia, and 1838 in New York, to provide specie reserves against bank note issue. At about the same time, 1838, banks in New Orleans voluntarily began to maintain a specie reserve requirement equal to one third of their combined note and deposit liabilities. This requirement was later made compulsory (1843) by the Louisiana legislature.

Some years later, in 1858, the New York Clearing House banks agreed to maintain reserves equal to 20 per cent of their net deposits. The same year Massachusetts passed legislation requiring a specie reserve against note and deposit liabilities. These actions influenced the provisions of the National Bank Act of 1863.

The National Bank Act established the National Banking System. The Act required member national banks in New York, Chicago, and St. Louis to maintain a reserve in their own vaults equal to 25 per cent of their notes and deposits. Banks in sixteen other cities were designated "city banks" and were required to hold reserves equal to 25 per cent, but only half needed to be held in their own vaults, with the remainder on deposit with New York City banks. The other national banks, "country banks, had to hold reserves of 15 per cent, but three-fifths could be held as deposits with "city" banks or New York City banks. The large city banks typically paid interest on these deposits of reserves, on the order of 2 per cent.

With the establishment of the Federal Reserve System in 1913, there was a revision of the legal reserve requirements. After a transition period, the Federal Reserve Act provided that member bank reserves had to be held as deposits with the Federal Reserve Banks. The reserve ratios established were 13 per cent for banks in central reserve cities, 10 per cent on city banks, and 7 per cent on the deposits of country banks. Time deposits were subject to a 3 per cent reserve requirement.

These requirements went unchanged for about 20 years. The Banking Act of 1935, among other things, provided the Board of Governors with authority to establish reserve ratios anywhere from the old 13-10-7 per cent levels to twice these amounts—26-20-14 per cent—for banks in reserve cities, city banks, and country banks respectively.

Again these requirements went unchanged for nearly two-and-a-half decades until, in 1959, there was another change in legislation governing reserve requirements of member banks. The 1959 legislation authorized the Board of Governors to allow member banks to count vault cash as well as deposits at the Federal Reserve Banks as reserves. The classification of central reserve city was to terminate on July 28, 1962, and reserve requirements of the remaining two bank classifications, "city" banks and "country" banks, were to range from 10 to 22 per cent and 7 to 14 per cent respectively. Time deposit requirements, regardless of class, were to range from 3 to 6 per cent. These were the regulations in effect at the time this book was written.

### Discount Rate History

The Federal Reserve Banks extend credit directly to member banks in the form of discounts and advances. The distinction between the two kinds of borrowing is that in the discount the member bank submits some instrument of one of its own borrowers (eligible paper), while in the advance the member bank borrows on its own note. Banks typically are reluctant to borrow except for good and compelling reasons. One observer put it thus: "Member banks are generally unwilling to remain in debt to a Reserve Bank for long periods. This tradition against continued borrowing, inherited from pre-Federal Reserve practices, is a powerful restraint."[1]

When the Federal Reserve System was launched, it was believed the desired elasticity of the money supply was built in by providing for the member banks' discounting of business paper at the Reserve Banks. But during the depression of the 1930s, member banks had so little eligible paper, or were so reluctant to discount what they had, that new types of collateral were required. One provision of the 1935 Banking Act provided for advances secured "to the satisfaction" of the Reserve Banks. Typically this collateral is United States government securities.

Through the late 1930s, the vast excess reserves of member banks precluded effective use of the discount rate as a monetary control device. But in 1951, after being freed from the commitment to support Treasury debt operations, the Federal Reserve began to make use of the discount rate as a tool of monetary control. Effectiveness of discount rate policy depends on (1) the cost of borrowing by discounting relative to other sources of reserves, (2) demands by borrowers for bank accommodation, and thus the banks' needs to borrow from Reserve Banks, and (3) the particular bank's attitude toward borrowing from the central bank.

Over the first fifteen years or so of the Federal Reserve System's existence, member banks did borrow in substantial magnitude. But after 1933, for nearly 20 years, the member banks seldom, if ever,

---

[1] W. Randolph Burgess, *The Federal Reserve Banks and the Money Market*, rev. ed. (New York: Harper and Bros., 1946), p. 231.

borrowed.   The large inflow of gold into the United States during the 1930s created such large excess reserves that banks did not need to borrow.   The banks also acquired large holdings of government securities during this period and during the Second World War.   If additional reserves were needed they could be obtained by selling some of these securities, and thus the banks did not need to borrow.   Since 1951, member banks have resumed borrowing from the Federal Reserve Banks.

The discount rate has more effectiveness as a control device in normal or boom situations; in a recession it is of little significance. The present situation may be summarized as follows:

Discount rate increases will have no immediate effect in tightening credit, apart from . . . psychological significance, if banks are in possession of excess reserves or acquire reserves as a result of open-market purchases of government securities by the Reserve System.   Similarly, rate decreases will have no immediate effect in easing credit if member banks are out of debt and have no need for additional reserves.

If Federal Reserve credit is not being supplied through the open market, individual member banks needing reserves will be forced to obtain them by borrowing or through the sale of government securities . . . To discourage excessive borrowing, the discount rate must be higher than the rates for securities used in the adjustment of reserve positions.[2]

## Open Market History

The Federal Reserve Act granted the Reserve Banks the authority to engage in open market operations.   Specifically, the Banks were empowered to buy or sell (1) cable transfers and bankers' acceptances, and bills of exchange eligible for discount, (2) United States government securities, and (3) municipal warrants maturing within six months.

The use of open market operations as an instrument of monetary policy began in 1922 on a coordinated basis.   The previous year had seen the Federal Reserve Banks, in the wake of a drop in discounting, purchase government securities as a means to bolster their earnings. These purchases were made on an individual Bank basis.

Before long it was realized that purchases of securities by the Reserve Banks were not adding to the total assets of the System.   Rather, the reserves created by the purchases were being used to reduce total discounts at the Reserve Banks.   In May, 1922, a committee was estab-

[2] *The Federal Reserve Re-Examined* (New York: New York Clearing House Association, 1953), p. 88.

lished to execute open market transactions in an orderly manner. Further refinements in techniques and procedures were made through the 1920s and 1930s until the 1935 Banking Act defined its present form.  This Act provides for a Federal Open Market Committee, composed of the Board of Governors and five representatives from the Federal Reserve Banks.  Each Reserve Bank is required to participate in the operations undertaken by the Committee.

Purchases of securities by the Federal Reserve supply reserve balances to member banks; open market sales, on the other hand, absorb reserves.  Open market operations are *defensive* if they simply offset factors that would otherwise change member bank reserves; they are *dynamic* if they more than offset these factors and deliberately cause reserves to expand or contract.

Although open market operations had not been used prior to 1922, from this time through 1929 they were continuously used to vary the ease or tightness of the money market.  But after about 1933, for nearly twenty years, the Federal Reserve did not use open market operations for the purpose of controlling member bank reserves.  During the 1930s and the war and postwar years, open market operations were used only to maintain orderly conditions in the government securities market, and also to support the government bond market in order to facilitate Treasury war finance operations and to minimize the Treasury's debt management problems.

Thus, during the Second World War, the primary objective of Federal Reserve policy was to supply the banking system with sufficient reserves to finance the war.  During the war, the Federal Reserve increased its holdings of United States government securities tenfold, from about $2.5 billion to $25 billion.  The war was financed, and at low interest rates.  But at war's end the size of the debt and its management presented problems.  Until 1951 the Federal Reserve undertook to support the government securities market by pegging the market at high prices, or, in other words, at low interest rates. Thus, holders of government debt were assured of a ready market should they wish to sell, and the Federal Reserve could not engage in open market operations without disturbing the interest rate patterns it had agreed to support.

In March, 1951, the so-called Treasury-Federal Reserve "Accord" was reached.  This provided for the cessation of direct Federal Reserve support of government securities prices.  The effect of the Accord was to take away from the money market the immediate and unlimited access to reserves, which had been the case when the Federal Reserve had been obligated to purchase all Treasury securities presented to it at a set price.   After the Accord, Federal Reserve credit was available at the initiative of the market only through discounting, and at a cost determined by the Federal Reserve.   Thus, open market operations finally became anticyclical instruments of monetary policy, instead of a mechanism for supplying Reserve credit to the banking system without limit.

### Summary

The purpose of these historical notes is to sketch out the basic development of the quantitative monetary policy instruments.   It is not intended to be comprehensive in detail or to study exhaustively the application of the basic tools.   It is designed to present a synopsis of the instruments and their development to the present time.   Following a brief preview of the channels through which monetary policy operates, we shall study each instrument in some detail.

### THE PATH OF MONETARY POLICY

Let us review briefly the operation of monetary controls, and the paths along which monetary policy operates.   The monetary instruments available to the Federal Reserve for carrying out monetary policy are the quantitative instruments—variation of the legal reserve ratio requirements, discount rate policy, and open market operations—and the qualitative instruments; that is, the stock market margin requirement control and moral suasion.   Now let us sketch out the nature of credit expansion and credit contraction, and the channels through which monetary policy operates.

### Credit Expansion: Review

By loosening credit and permitting mild inflationary pressure to develop, the Federal Reserve will attempt to stimulate employment in order to help ward off recessionary pressures and stimulate economic growth.   To do this the Federal Reserve can do one or more of three things: lower reserve ratio requirements, engage in open market buying operations, and lower the discount rate.   These actions all lead to increasing the reserve positions of the commercial banks and to improving the terms on which they can acquire reserves.

When their reserve positions are eased by the Federal Reserve, commercial banks are encouraged to expand their loans and deposits. Since excess reserves as such earn no return, the banks in attempting to maximize profit search for ways of committing these idle reserves. The first impact of excess reserves might be simply to increase secondary reserves—principally the banks' holdings of short-term government obligations.   But if many banks attempt this, the increase in demand for short-term instruments relative to the supply may drive the price up, and, hence, the rate of return down.   This lowered rate may then induce banks, on the one hand, to try to drum up suitable borrowers in order to increase their loans.   On the other hand, the downward pressure on interest rates may induce business borrowers to increase their borrowing from the commercial banks.   Thus, it is likely that easing of credit by the Federal Reserve will be followed by an increase in the loans and deposits of commercial banks.   Likely, but by no means certain.   In order to expand loans and deposits there must be three conditions satisfied: (1) banks must have excess reserves; (2) the banks must be willing to lend; and (3) someone must be willing to borrow.   If any one of the above is lacking, no credit expansion ensues.

Thus, easing of credit conditions by the Federal Reserve is likely to induce an increase in bank loans and deposits.   The downward pressure on interest rates raises the over-all liquidity position of banks by raising the market value of their existing portfolio.   This enhanced liquidity position in itself may be enough to make banks more eager to accommodate potential borrowers, while the lowered interest rates may stimulate borrowers' willingness to incur new debt.

### Credit Contraction: Review

When the Federal Reserve undertakes to tighten credit, the reverse occurs.   As their reserve position is tightened or brought under pressure, banks are forced to curtail their lending and investment activities.   In order to moderate inflationary pressures on the price level by restraining aggregate expenditures, the Federal Reserve will either singly or in combination (1) increase the required reserve ratio, (2) raise discount rates, and (3) engage in open market selling operations.

When the Federal Reserve tightens the reserve positions of the commercial banks, banks are forced to reduce their lending activities.   As a consequence of tightened credit, interest rates rise.   Perhaps discount rates have risen, signaling a general rise in short-term rates, or perhaps the Fed has sold bonds on the open market at bargain prices, thus driving rates up.   Whatever the cause, the effect of the interest rate rise is to lower the market value of existing portfolio.   Thus banks are less likely to liquidate their investment holdings to secure additional reserves for new loans. Then also, the reduction in over-all liquidity, through the fall in asset values, will make banks more cautious in their lending activities, causing them to screen loan applicants more closely and perhaps to ration their loans among their best customers.

### How Monetary Policy Operates

Monetary policy impinges on employment and output (and, hence, on income), economic growth, and prices in a somewhat involved and indirect manner. Recall from Chapter 14 the accounting relation between gross national product (GNP) and gross national income (GNI). We saw that GNP = GNI. Furthermore we found that GNP is the sum total of *expenditures* on current output. Thus, GNP = expenditures = GNI.

Now expenditures are the product of two factors, the volume of output times a price index, or $E = T \cdot P = PT$. The equation of exchange may be helpful here in supplying the other side of our relation. The expenditures, equal to $PT$ (or to the level of income, $Y$), must be equal also to the money supply $(M)$ times its rate of turnover, or velocity $(V)$. Thus $MV = PT$, where $T$ is restricted to transactions in new, currently produced final products. We then have finally, GNP $= E =$ GNI $= MV = PT$.

Thus, the channel of Federal Reserve monetary policy becomes evident. The Federal Reserve attempts to affect output $(T)$, prices $(P)$, and income $(PT)$ by influencing the level of expenditures $(MV)$ for output. The Federal Reserve attempts to affect expenditures $(MV)$ but its actions influence $(M)$, the size of the money supply, and not $(V)$, the rate of turnover or velocity.

That the Federal Reserve can affect $M$ is a result of the fact that the bulk of the nation's money supply is in the form of demand deposits at commercial banks. By influencing the banks' willingness to expand deposits, the Federal Reserve exerts influence over $(M)$, the money supply.

Those transactions $T$ that are financed on borrowed money can thus also be affected by Federal Reserve policies. Similarly, given $T$ and $V$, the Federal Reserve can influence to some extent prices, $P$.

Monetary policy can control the size of the money supply $M$, but not the *effective* money supply, $MV$. Thus, a significant limitation of monetary policy is this lack of control over velocity. This is particularly so when monetary policy is being eased to cushion a decline in economic activity or to promote the recovery from a recession. Even if the money supply $M$ gets increased, if it is not spent, if its velocity is zero, then the effective money supply has not changed at all.

The extent to which monetary policy will succeed in cushioning a downturn or promoting recovery from recession depends on whether expenditures increase with the lowered cost and greater availability of credit. If investment is stimulated by a fall in interest rates and if easy money encourages other expenditures, then monetary policy will be successful. If these increased expenditures fail to materialize, then monetary policy fails in stimulating recovery or in cushioning a downturn in economic activity.

A policy of monetary ease will likely stimulate expenditures and facilitate recovery or cushion a decline if there are a number of marginal borrowers who have previously been restrained by the cost and availability of credit. With the relaxation of credit conditions and lower interest rates, these marginal borrowers may now enter the market and so increase expenditures.

On the other hand, monetary policy can be quite effective in curbing inflationary excesses. Because the Federal Reserve has control over the money supply $(M)$ it does have some considerable control over $(MV)$, the effective money supply. This recognizes that $(MV)$ is the product of motivation to spend on the one hand, and the money wherewithal on the other. As recognized, if the motivation to spend is lacking $(V = 0)$ the Federal Reserve can do little. But if the motivation to spend is present, the Federal Reserve by reducing the money supply $(M)$ can curb expenditures $(MV)$.

The above chain of reasoning suggests rather precise ability to temper economic fluctuations. Such, however, is not the case. As noted, ability to temper downswings is limited because of no control over velocity. Similarly on the upswings, the necessary monetary contraction to stabilize prices might easily violate the full-employment and growth objectives. Thus monetary policy, although effective in curbing expenditures, will be supplemented by fiscal policy on the upswing as well as on the downward cycle phase.

## THE METHODS OF MONETARY POLICY

The reserve equation developed in Chapter 10 shows how member bank reserves depend on Federal Reserve credit. This reserve equation derived member bank reserves as the difference between the sources of member bank reserve funds and the competing uses for member bank reserve funds, thus:

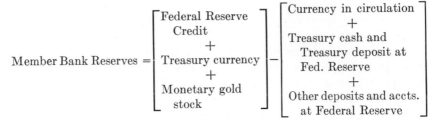

$$\text{Member Bank Reserves} = \begin{bmatrix} \text{Federal Reserve} \\ \text{Credit} \\ + \\ \text{Treasury currency} \\ + \\ \text{Monetary gold} \\ \text{stock} \end{bmatrix} - \begin{bmatrix} \text{Currency in circulation} \\ + \\ \text{Treasury cash and} \\ \text{Treasury deposit at} \\ \text{Fed. Reserve} \\ + \\ \text{Other deposits and accts.} \\ \text{at Federal Reserve} \end{bmatrix}$$

The only factor in this reserve equation susceptible to any degree of deliberate control, as we saw, is Federal Reserve credit. Federal Reserve credit is composed of four elements: United States government bonds held by the Federal Reserve; discounts and advances to member banks; other discounts and advances to nonmember banks (this item is negligible); and float. Not all of these items are subject to direct Federal Reserve control.

One item in Federal Reserve credit, the amount of United States government securities held, is subject to the sole and direct control of the Reserve authorities. They can vary the holdings of United States government securities on their own initiative by buying and selling in the open market. And as we have earlier seen, this part of Federal Reserve credit provides the bulk of the sources of member bank reserve funds.

With regard to open market operations in government securities we must look to the sales as well as the purchases of these securities. With something over $35 billion of government securities in their portfolio the Reserve authorities are well equipped for carrying out open market sales should this be necessary. But suppose open market purchases become necessary, then what? The Federal Reserve must maintain a 25 per cent gold-certificate reserve against its note and deposit liabilities. When the Federal Reserve purchases securities on the open market its deposit liabilities increase. The ratio of gold certificates to note and deposit liabilities as of July 31, 1964 was 29.5 per cent. Thus, while the Reserve authorities have some elbow room, their position becomes ever more restricted as the gold drain persists. If the situation, however, grows too critical, Congress will undoubtedly reduce or even abolish the reserve requirement on Federal Reserve note and deposit liabilities.

Another limitation to Federal Reserve control over bank reserves can arise if the central bank must support the government securities market. For example, during the Second World War and until 1951 the Federal Reserve did support government bond prices. This meant that the Reserve authorities bought and sold bonds, not to control bank reserves, but to stabilize bond prices. Control over bank reserves was lost.

The principal tool used for influencing the banks' reserve position is the open market operation. These operations are, of course, the purchases and sales by the Federal Reserve of securities in the open market. The securities traded are primarily United States government obligations, but they sometimes include small amounts of bankers' acceptances. Since banker's acceptances constitute a negligible fraction of total transactions we shall assume that the securities traded are government obligations.

There is an active market in government securities maintained by dealers who specialize in buying and selling these securities, both for their own accounts and for others. Competitive bidding among these dealers determines the terms of trade in any given instance. The Federal Reserve System conducts open market operations, as we have learned, through the open market trading desk in the Federal Reserve Bank of New York, and all purchases and sales are made here. The total purchases or sales made for the open market account are allocated among the twelve Reserve Banks in proportion to their total assets. The traders at the trading desk are continually in contact with the credit market and with the reserve position of the banks.

Whereas Federal Reserve open market sales are made outright, open market purchases may be outright or they may be made under a repurchase agreement. In the latter case, the dealers sell securities to the Federal Reserve and agree to buy them back within a specified time period of 15 days or less. The purpose of such arrangements is the provision of Federal Reserve credit on a temporary basis. But regardless of who sells or who buys the securities from the Federal Reserve, the transactions have a direct impact on the volume of member bank reserves. The distinguishing feature of open market operations is that they are undertaken solely on the initiative of the Federal Reserve.

Open market purchases by the Federal Reserve build up bank reserves and open market sales reduce bank reserves.

### Open Market Purchases

When the Federal Reserve goes into the market to purchase securities there is no coercion used to force holders of government securities to sell.   When the Federal Reserve engages in an open market purchasing operation the prices of the securities are bid up, and the owners of securities can sell their holdings at a profit.

Although the Federal Reserve's open market trading desk deals with only a limited number of security dealers or financial institutions, bond-holders in general can engage in the trade of these securities through their own banks and security dealers.   Should the Federal Reserve purchase securities from a member bank the transaction, it will be recalled, is as follows: The bank takes the government securities from its portfolio and exchanges them for an increase in its reserve account at the Federal Reserve.   The commercial bank exchanges one kind of asset for another.   The Federal Reserve gains assets, the government securities, and pays for them by increasing its liabilities, the member bank reserve balance.   What should be clearly understood is that by this open market purchase of Treasury securities additional reserves have been channeled into the commercial bank system.

If the seller of the securities is other than a commercial bank the end result is still the same because all other individuals and institutions maintain their bank accounts with commercial banks.   Thus, when they sell securities to the Federal Reserve they take the check received in exchange and deposit it to their account at a commercial bank. When the commercial bank credits its customer's account it then sends the check to the Federal Reserve for payment, receiving payment as a credit to its reserve balance.   Consequently, what has occurred is an exchange of assets by the nonbank public, trading securities for a bank deposit; the commercial bank increases both liabilities, the customer's deposit, and assets, its reserve balances; and the Federal Reserve increases both assets, government securities, and liabilities, commercial bank reserve balances.   Again we see the creation of bank reserves by this open market purchase by the Federal Reserve.

## Open Market Sales

The effect of open market sales by the Federal Reserve is the reverse of that caused by open market purchases.   When the Federal Reserve sells securities on the open market, as we have seen, it reduces the level of bank reserves.   The manner by which buyers are induced to buy is simply by offering securities at attractive prices; that is, the offering price is lowered with a concurrent increase in the yield.

When commercial banks buy securities from the Federal Reserve they pay for them by having the Reserve Banks charge their reserve balances the amount of the purchase.   The commercial banks exchange assets, part of their reserve balance for government securities. The Federal Reserve loses an asset, the securities, but reduces its liabilities, member bank reserves. Note the destruction of bank reserves due to this open market sale by the Federal Reserve.

If the purchaser of the securities is the nonbank public the securities are paid for by checks drawn on commercial banks. The end result is as before: the public owns government securities instead of bank deposits; the commercial bank reduces its assets, reserve balances, and liabilities, deposits due the public; and the Federal Reserve reduces its assets, securities, and its liabilities, member bank reserve balances. As before, the open market sale has reduced member bank reserves.

The direct impact of open market operations is clearly on bank reserves. But there are indirect effects to be accounted for, as well. In the case of open market purchases, if the member banks are in debt to the Reserve Banks they are likely to use the new reserves to reduce their indebtedness, otherwise they will use the reserves to expand their loans and investments since idle funds earn them no income. But, in order to put these reserves to work, it may be necessary for the banks to lower the interest rate they charge. On the other hand, open market sales tend to have the reverse effect. Open market sales deplete member bank reserves and this may cause the banks to borrow from the Reserve Banks in order to meet temporarily reserve requirements. Banks, however, will either have to obtain additional permanent reserves or run off some of their loans and investments, that is, reduce their deposit liabilities. And reduced reserves may cause the banks to increase the interest rate on the loans they do make during this period.

Another effect of open market operations is the effect on security prices and, hence, on interest rates. Federal Reserve purchases of securities tend to bid up their prices and to lower the effective rate of return; conversely, open market sales lower the securities' prices and increases their yield. Because government securities are such a large part of the securities market, changes in their effective rate of return tend to spread to the rest of the market causing similar changes in the general pattern of rates on private securities.

The foregoing discussion of the impact of open market sales and purchases forms the basis for analyzing their effect on the level of income and employment. The impact of these open market operations can be traced by finding the effect on the money equilibrium schedule, which we developed earlier. The MES, it will be recalled, was determined by the supply of and demand for money balances; open market operations clearly affect the supply side of this schedule.

### Money-Market Consequences

The impact of open market operations may affect the money supply
directly if the purchases or sales are conducted with the nonbank
public.   If, however, the operations are conducted with commercial
banks the impact is on their reserve position, not directly on their
loans and deposits, and does not impinge on the money supply except
indirectly.   The effect of open market sales to banks, however, uses
reserves; thus, even if the money supply is not directly affected the
impact is basically contractive in nature.   On the other hand, open
market purchases from bank portfolios increase bank reserves; thus,
even though not of themselves expansive the stage is set for later bank
expansion of loans and deposits.

The impact of the open market purchases of government securities
can be diagrammed as below.   Assume an open market purchase from
the nonbank public.   The money supply increases because of the
increased demand deposits owned by the public.   In the framework
of the money-market analysis of Chapter 15, the effects of this open
market purchase of securities shows as an increased money supply,
indicated by the dotted line.   The result is to shift the MES to the
right, to MES*, as shown in Figure 23-1.

Open market purchases from the nonbank public thus increase the
money supply, and shift the money equilibrium schedule to the right.
Although open market purchases from banks do not directly increase
the money supply, the potential in the form of increased reserves exists
for an expansion in loans and deposits.

Open market sales reverse the process.   Open market sales destroy
money if made to the public, and in any event, whether sold to the
public or to banks, use up reserves.   Hence the stage is set for a shift
of the MES to the left.

### Some Complications

This analysis is subject to some qualifications.   There have been
periods when open market operations were ineffective.

In the years 1933–51 the Federal Reserve did not use open market
operations for the purpose of affecting member bank reserves.   The
first part of this period 1933–37 saw banks with excess reserves.   Since
this was during the Great Depression, monetary policy called for ease.
With excess reserves already present, there was no reason for the Federal Reserve to purchase securities to provide more reserves.   And

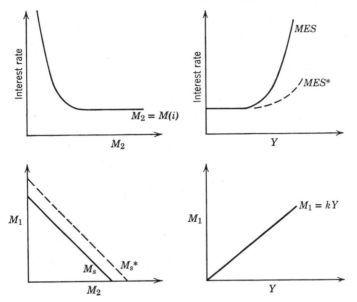

*Figure 23-1*  Shift in MES due to increase in money supply.

had the System wished to mop up the excess reserves through open market sales, its own holdings of securities were not large enough to permit it to do so.

After the entry of the United States into the Second World War, the Federal Reserve's objective was to supply the banking system with reserves for financing the war.   To do so, the Federal Reserve undertook to support the price, and thus the rates, on government securities. The yield was put low and held there by an unlimited offer of the Federal Reserve Banks to buy or sell at the pegged rate.   This assured the commercial banks that any additional reserves necessary to accommodate the Treasury would be forthcoming in the necessary volume. It also had the effect of converting government securities into interest-bearing excess reserves for the commercial banks.   By the pegging operation, the Federal Reserve lost all control over the bank reserves through open market operations.

After the cessation of hostilities, the Federal Reserve continued its wartime policy of government securities price support.   It did so to keep down the interest cost of servicing the debt, and also to maintain a stable market for government securities in order to make the debt more easily manageable.

This was an unhappy predicament for the Federal Reserve, for it could not make it easy for the Treasury to borrow without also making it easy and cheap for everyone else.  The wartime direct controls over prices, wages, and consumer credit had been removed by 1947. The resulting rise in the velocity of money, together with the expansion in the money supply, which occurred as the banks and other financial institutions sold their government bonds to the Federal Reserve and used the funds to support new credit expansion, led to sharp inflationary rises in prices.  This combined expansion in the money supply and increase in the velocity resulted in a sharp increase in the money equilibrium schedule.  The increase in the money supply is shown by the dotted line in Figure 23-2, as is the new transactions demand schedule (recall $k = 1/V$ so increased velocity shows as a lowered $k$).  The increased money equilibrium is MES*.

The question was how to deal with this inflation.  One view was to impose monetary restraint and have the Federal Reserve cease its sup-

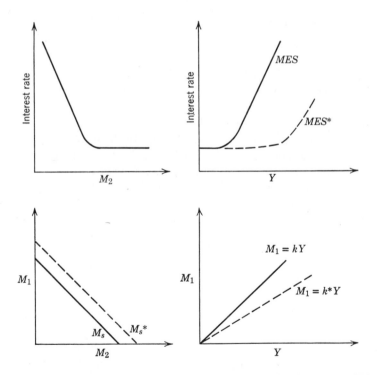

**Figure 23-2**  The effect of increased money supply and velocity on MES.

port of the government securities market.   This view lost to adherents of the easy money, government securities price support policy.   These persons argued for a continuation of easy money while curbing inflation through fiscal means and selective credit controls—that is, to manipulate the goods equilibrium schedule.

Those wanting a continuation of easy money based their desire on two grounds: (1) they were concerned about the effects of higher interest rates on the cost of servicing and managing the debt; (2) they also feared that tight money might lead to economic stagnation.

In an effort to control inflationary pressures while having their principal weapon of open market operations denied them, Federal Reserve officials proposed various new regulations.   One would have required banks to hold compulsory secondary reserves of government bonds, and would have "locked in" a large amount of bank held, short-term government debt.   This "security reserve requirement" was, however, turned down by Congress.   The System requested and was given temporary authority to raise reserve requirements above the statutory maximums.   These expired after one year on June 30, 1949.

But at this time the first postwar recession appeared.   Thus, the expiration of the reserve requirement legislation was of little importance.   However, the next year saw the resumption of inflationary pressure as recovery set in and then these pressures were intensified by the start of the Korean War.

Because of lack of support and in order to win followers to its cause, the Federal Reserve was developing the doctrine of "lender reluctance"—of decreased credit availability arising from a "lock-in" effect exerted on portfolios by rising interest rates.   According to this doctrine, the monetary authority could restrain credit expansion either by selling government securities or by limiting purchases of them and permitting the prices to adjust downward to demands for securities.   A rise in yield accompanies the fall in price.   This price decline inhibits banks and also nonbank financial institutions—which are inclined to sell government bonds—from doing so.   They become reluctant sellers of securities because of the capital losses involved.   They also, therefore, become reluctant lenders because of the cost of obtaining added reserves.

On the one hand, because of uncertainty about future securities prices, financial institutions become more cautious about disposing of their holdings of "governments."   Thus, as a result of these reactions by lending institutions, there is a reduction in the amount of lending done even if borrowers' demands for credit do not lessen because of higher interest rates.   Thus, it was concluded, open market policy could succeed in limiting the availability of credit even without causing interest rates to rise sharply in the process.

The debate became academic in 1951.   In the spring of 1951 the so-called Treasury-Federal Reserve Accord was achieved.   The Treasury agreed to the withdrawal of Federal Reserve support of the government securities markets and the Federal Reserve was left free to engage in open market operations to control bank reserves and the money supply.

### "Bills Only" Doctrine

Finally the Federal Reserve was free to pursue open market policies to manage bank reserves.   Open market operations were freed, the requirement of supporting government securities price was lifted, and sales and purchases were to be conducted at the discretion of the Federal Reserve authorities, not at someone else's initiative.   But now the question was raised, would open market operations to influence bank reserves be conducted in short-, medium-, or long-term securities?

In 1952 an *ad hoc* Federal Reserve committee recommended the following principles to guide open market procedures: the Federal Reserve in the future should (1) act to correct "disorderly situations" in the money market, rather than maintaining "orderly" conditions, (2) discontinue support operations during Treasury refinancing operations, and (3) confine open market operations to the short end of the market.   These principles were adopted by the Federal Open Market Committee and adhered to, with only three exceptions, until 1961. Since the principal short-term instrument is the Treasury bill, this procedure came to be known as the "bills only" doctrine.

As far as influencing bank reserves go, the particular kind of security, whether short- or long-term, is a matter of indifference.   Whenever the Federal Reserve makes a payment, reserves go up; whenever the Federal Reserve makes a sale, they do down.   The reasons given for selecting the short-term bills were that at the short end of the market the System's intervention would cause the least disturbance.   At the short end of the market dollar prices react least in response to a given change in yield, and thus asset values of portfolios are least affected. For example, if the rate on three-month Treasury bills doubles from 2 to 4 per cent, the price falls only from $995 to $990; but on a long-term instrument the price may fall by nearly one half.   Second, it was argued that interest-rate effects in the short end of the market would spread out and influence interest rates generally, short and long rates alike.

Consequently, when we analyze the effects of open market operations we see that there are essentially two effects to this operation. There is the effect on bank reserves and the effect on interest rates. The position of the Federal Reserve was that this latter effect, interest rates, was not important and furthermore, it was improper for the Federal Reserve to attempt to influence the structure of interest rates directly.   The Federal Reserve held that it should simply control the level of bank reserves and let the free market then allocate the available reserves among the different uses and maturities of securities.   If the Federal Reserve *does* operate in all maturities of government securities, it *is* going to affect and very likely determine the maturity structure of interest rates.   In this light the "bills only" debate is really only part of a broader question of whether the Federal Reserve should be concerned solely with the total supply of money and should not attempt to control the uses to which the money supply is to be put.

The Federal Reserve's opponents argued, on the other hand, that affecting the structure of interest rates was an important weapon and concern of the Federal Reserve and that it should not abandon this consideration without very good reason.   One critic of "bills only" put it this way:

The hamstringing of the open market weapon which has been developed after a long evolution is rather like the case of a higher ape who, having come down from the trees and having learned over the eons to use his thumb and brain then appoints an *ad hoc* committee which negates the evolutionary development by a decision to limit the use of thumb and brain.[3]

Although "bills only" was not as rigid in application as its critics have implied, it was nevertheless breached on only a very few occasions until 1961.   In 1955 the system bought a few certificates as well as bills to support a Treasury finance operation.   In 1957 the Federal Reserve sold certificates, probably because it was nearly out of bills. In July, 1958, the system bought some longer-term securities to prevent the development of disorderly conditions in the bond market.   But more important was the change of policy in 1961 from "bills only" to the present policy of operating in whatever maturity range is deemed most appropriate.

---

[3] Paul A. Samuelson, "Recent American Monetary Controversy," *Three Banks Review*, March, 1956, p. 12.

In 1961 the Federal Reserve purchased long-term securities in substantial amounts. There were some excellent economic reasons for the abandonment of "bills only" at this time. In 1961 the economy was in a recession. This situation would normally call for open market purchases. At the same time the United States balance of payments position was under pressure. Because of the higher short-term rates abroad it was undesirable to lower short-term interest rates any further, which would have happened should Treasury bills be purchased. At the same time long-term rates were too high and had not responded to monetary ease.

In an attempt to slow down the loss of gold, in February, 1961 the Federal Reserve reversed its "bills only" position and began to deal in securities of all maturities. The logic of this is simple: by selling short-term government securities, increasing the supply relative to demand, the prices of these securities can be lowered, thus raising the short-term rate. By raising the short-term rate it is hoped to keep short-term funds from being converted into gold and leaving the country.

At the same time the short-term rate was being kept high, the intermediate and long-term rate was lowered through open-market purchases. This was done in the hope of stimulating domestic income and employment.

The result of all this is that at long last the Federal Reserve is acting like a central bank in pursuing monetary policy. Remember we defined monetary policy as the deliberate control of the volume of money in the pursuit of some economic objective. Here the objectives are quite clear: on the one hand, to manipulate the short-term rate in the interest of protecting the monetary gold stock, and on the other hand, to stimulate the domestic economy through a reduction in the long-term rate of interest—to stimulate investment given the marginal efficiency of capital by lowering the rate of interest, and thus increase the level of income and employment.


## APPENDIX

In this appendix we summarize in T-account form the various open market operations discussed in the body of the chapter. The key to understanding the effect of the various operations is in the final status of the commercial bank balance sheet, where the impact on reserves and the money supply is clearly displayed.

## OPEN MARKET PURCHASES

### *From Commercial Bank System*

Commercial Bank

| Assets | Liabilities |
|---|---|
| Government securities — | |
| Reserve balance at Federal Reserve + | |

Federal Reserve

| Assets | Liabilities |
|---|---|
| Government securities + | Reserve balance of Commercial Bank + |

The effect of this open market purchase of securities from the commercial bank system is to increase total reserves and set the stage for expansion of the money supply.

### *From the Public*

Public

| Assets | Liabilities |
|---|---|
| Government securities — | |
| Demand Deposit at Commercial Bank + | |

Commercial Banks

| Assets | Liabilities |
|---|---|
| Reserve at Federal Reserve + | Demand Deposit of Public + |

Federal Reserve

| Assets | Liabilities |
|---|---|
| Government securities + | Reserve balance of Commercial Bank + |

The effect of open market purchases from the public is to increase both the money supply and commercial bank reserves by the same amount. Excess reserves are also created so further expansion of loans and deposits is possible.

## OPEN MARKET SALES

### To the Commercial Bank System

|  | Commercial Banks | |
| --- | --- | --- |
| Assets | | Liabilities |
| Government securities | + | |
| Reserve Balance at Federal Reserve | − | |

|  | Federal Reserve | |
| --- | --- | --- |
| Assets | | Liabilities |
| Government securities | − Reserve balance of Commercial Bank | − |

The effect of open market sales to the commercial bank system is to reduce reserves by the amount of the sale.

### To the Public

|  | Public | |
| --- | --- | --- |
| Assets | | Liabilities |
| Government securities | + | |
| Demand Deposit at Commercial Bank | − | |

|  | Commercial Bank | |
| --- | --- | --- |
| Assets | | Liabilities |
| Reserve at Federal Reserve | − Demand Deposit of Public | − |

|  | Federal Reserve | |
| --- | --- | --- |
| Assets | | Liabilities |
| Government securities | − Commercial Bank Reserve Account | − |

The effect of open market sales to the public is simultaneously to contract the money supply and the level of bank reserves by an amount equal to the sale of securities.

## REVIEW QUESTIONS

1. Monetary policy influences the levels of income and employment, the rate of economic growth, the balance of payments, and the level of prices through certain quantitative instruments. Briefly review the development of the use of these instruments.
2. Trace the path along which monetary policy acts in order to influence, say, the level of income.
3. In order for the money supply to expand, what three conditions must be satisfied?
4. Given the three conditions necessary for expanding the money supply, does it follow that monetary policy is likelier to be effective in choking off expenditures and moderating a boom than in stimulating recovery from a recession period?
5. What is meant by defensive open market operations; dynamic open market operations?
6. Given the items which enter into the member bank reserve equation, why are open market operations so important in executing monetary policy?
7. Assume the banking system is fully loaned up. Show the effect on the level of income and the interest rate of an open market selling operation. Use the money equilibrium-goods equilibrium schedules.
8. Prior to the Treasury-Federal Reserve Accord, commercial bank holdings of government securities amounted to being interest earning reserves. Explain.
9. What is the doctrine of "lender reluctance?"
10. What was the so-called "bills only" doctrine?
11. Recent Treasury debt offerings have included large amounts of short-term Treasury bills, while simultaneously the Federal Reserve has stopped making open market purchases of these bills. Is this an example of coordinated policy between these two agencies, and why were these actions undertaken?

## SUGGESTED REFERENCES

Consult the references listed at the end of Chapter 24.

CHAPTER 24

# Monetary Policy: Other Measures

In addition to the principal quantitative monetary control instrument at the disposal of the Federal Reserve authorities, the open market operation, there are additional controls. The latter instruments for executing monetary policy, which will be examined in this chapter, are discounting policy and manipulation of the legal reserve requirement.

Although not presently of significant import, the role of qualitative controls is also discussed in this chapter. The only currently operative qualitative control is the stock market margin requirement. It will be argued, however, that the general area of installment credit offers a fruitful area for qualitative credit regulation in order to increase the efficacy of monetary policy.

## MEMBER BANK BORROWING: DISCOUNTING POLICY

From the point of view of the borrowing member bank, the decision to discount is the result of a shortage of required reserves. The bank that finds itself in this situation may choose to restrict its lending activities, may sell securities out of its portfolio in the open market to obtain reserves, may borrow reserves from another bank that has excess reserves (Federal Funds), or may borrow from its district Reserve Bank. Because commercial banks attempt to maintain customer good will, recourse is usually had to one of the last three methods, that is, the liquidation of secondary reserves, borrowing in the Federal Funds market, or borrowing from its Reserve Bank. The choice of method depends on the relative convenience and costs

448

involved.   Discounting is used when it is cheapest or appears otherwise most advantageous to the borrowing bank.

The borrowing process is a simple one.   Whether the member banks are discounting some of their customer's notes or borrowing on their own notes, the proceeds are credited to the member banks' reserve balances.   The balance sheet of the commercial bank has an increase in its notes payable in the case of an advance and in contingent liabilities in the case of a discount.   Thus, in T-accounts:


Commercial Bank

| Assets | Liabilities | |
| --- | --- | --- |
| Reserve balance at Federal Reserve    + | Notes payable (advance) or Bills payable (discount) | + + |


Federal Reserve

| Assets | Liabilities | |
| --- | --- | --- |
| Discounts or advances    + | Reserve balance of Commercial bank | + |


By raising or lowering the discount rate, the Reserve Banks can make it more or less costly for member banks to obtain additional reserves by borrowing.

When the Federal Reserve System was set up, it was expected that the discount rate would be the principal tool for making Federal Reserve monetary policy effective.   If commercial banks were to obtain additional reserves, they would obtain them by discounting with the Reserve Banks.   But events did not work out that way. During the 1920s the discount rate frequently could be made effective only by coupling it with the then emerging open market operation technique, and during the thirties and forties the discount rate became almost ineffective.   For how could discount rate changes affect member bank borrowing when member banks had no reason for borrowing? The large gold inflows during the thirties had built up reserves far in excess of required levels.   During this period and during the Second World War there occurred an enormous expansion in government security holdings by the banking system.   Thus, reserve positions could be increased by the simple expedient of selling government securities instead of borrowing.   The policy of supporting the government bond market, which was followed by the Federal Reserve until the Federal Reserve-Treasury Accord in March, 1951, meant that whenever banks found it necessary to acquire additional reserves they had a ready market for their government securities and did not have to borrow.   They merely sold some of their "governments" to the Federal Reserve for additional reserves.   Since the Accord, the discount rate has become a more important instrument of monetary policy.   But this is a result of the Federal Reserve actively engaging in open market operations to manipulate the reserve position of the banking system, not for the support and stabilization of government bond prices.

If discount rate changes are to serve effectively as a monetary policy tool, the money and credit situation should be tight.   The commercial banks' reserve position must be under pressure with the result that many banks find themselves needing additional reserves, and have no more advantageous method of obtaining them than by borrowing from the Federal Reserve.   Thus, as the Federal Reserve operates on member bank reserves through open market operations the more effective discount rate changes become.   Indeed, the maximum degree of discount rate effectiveness is attained when open market operations force member banks into having to borrow to meet their legal reserve requirements.   But this degree of effectiveness is reached as a result of open market policy, and not through discount rate changes alone.

The question may naturally arise that if banks can borrow to obtain the necessary additional reserves to fulfill their legal reserve requirements, does not this borrowing destroy the effectiveness of a policy of credit restraint?   The answer to this question is "no."   The reasons that borrowing fail to nullify restrictive measures are: (1) borrowing is a privilege, not a right, of member banks and this is continually emphasized by the Reserve authorities; and (2) bankers typically are reluctant to borrow.   The initiative in borrowing lies with the member banks.   The Federal Reserve has not encouraged such borrowing, and the tradition has become established that borrowing is a privilege to be used only as a temporary source of reserves.   Thus, a bank that attempts to keep continuously in debt to its Reserve Bank will have the right to borrow refused.   As a result of these factors, member banks try to manage their affairs so that they do not need to resort to borrowing except for such contingencies as unforeseen currency withdrawals, unfavorable clearing balances, etc.   But, once in debt, it is expected that they will repay such debt promptly.   Many banks, perhaps as many as one-half or more, never borrow, preferring to make necessary adjustments in other ways.

### Assessment of Discount Policy

When the Federal Reserve Act was set into law it was expected that the discount mechanism would be the most important monetary policy tool. Discounting was indeed important in the early years of the System, but after 1930 and through the 1940s the large volume of excess reserves held by the commercial banks tended to reduce the importance of the discount rate. It was not until the 1950s, with the increase in use of restrictive monetary policy, that the discount rate regained its earlier importance.

From time to time there have been proposals for change in the discount mechanism, and some criticisms regarding its use. For example, some critics have pointed out that the discount rate is not effective in combating a recession period. On the other hand, it has also been argued that in an inflationary period allowing banks access to the discount mechanism effectively permits them to escape from the effects of restrictive monetary policy. It is true that the volume of borrowing from the Federal Reserve System is larger during periods of tight money than during periods when money is easy. However, it does not seem that this is too serious a problem. The Federal Reserve can take whatever steps might be necessary to negate the increase in the reserves accomplished through the discount mechanism.

One suggestion that has been made is that the discounting privilege be eliminated. The reason for this suggestion is to avoid the potential reserve expansion that may result from access to discounting facilities during periods of credit restraint. To eliminate completely the discount privilege would be to eliminate the safety valve which may be very necessary at some future time. A modification of this proposal may have merit; namely, to retain the discounting mechanism but to keep the discount rate at a high level; perhaps at a level of 6 or 8 or 10 per cent. A discount rate that high would discourage borrowing. It would, however, provide a safety valve, the "lender of last resort" feature for the banking system in an emergency situation.

It appears that discount rate policy when used in conjunction with open market operations provides the monetary authority with another flexible instrument of monetary control. Since member banks are not all alike, the borrowing privilege provides the member bank with a temporary refuge, should it need one, from the undiscriminating impact of restrictive open market operations. Those banks needing time to adjust to the loss of reserves can buy temporary reserves as they adjust permanently to the loss of reserves. A final significant feature of the member bank borrowing privilege is that should the public desire for cash ever become very large the Reserve Banks would, of course, lend on almost any type of commercial or business paper presented to them in order to provide the liquidity demanded. Thus, the Reserve Banks would be lenders of last resort in an emergency.

## MEMBER BANK RESERVE REQUIREMENTS

The last principal quantitative tool available to the Federal Reserve authorities for influencing the money supply is the authority to change the legal reserve requirements of the member banks. The Board of Governors may set the required reserve ratios for the various member bank classes anywhere within their specified limits. For the class "reserve city banks," the limits are 10 to 22 per cent on demand deposits and 3 to 6 per cent for time deposits; for "country" banks the limits are 7 to 14 per cent and 3 to 6 per cent. Changes in reserve requirements may be applied to one or both classifications at the same time, but they must be kept within the limits set for each class.

In contrast to open market operations and discounting which directly affect the volume of member bank reserves, alterations in the required reserve ratio do not change the level of total reserves. Changes in the reserve ratio change the amount of deposits any given volume of reserves can support. That is, open market operations and member bank borrowing affect available reserves; changes in reserve ratios alter the composition of available reserves as to required reserves and excess reserves.

When the legal reserve ratios are changed two things happen. There is, first of all, an immediate impact on the secondary reserve position of the member banks. That is, if the reserve ratio requirements are raised, any member banks not having excess reserves will either have to sell some of their secondary reserves, generally short-term government securities, or else borrow either from banks having excess reserves or borrow from the Reserve Banks. For the whole system of banks, however, additional reserves needed can be obtained only if they are provided by Federal Reserve open market operations or by borrowing from the Federal Reserve Banks.

On the other hand, if reserve requirements are reduced the member banks find themselves with excess reserves. After retiring any indebtedness the banks are likely to increase their holdings of secondary reserves, at least temporarily.

The second major effect of a change in the reserve ratio is the change in the volume of deposits any given amount of reserves can support. Neglecting currency and time deposit complications, if the required reserve ratio is 20 per cent then $1 of reserves, as we have noted before, can support $5 of deposits. Increase the required ratio to 25 per cent and this same $1 in reserves can support only $4 in deposits; lower the required reserve ratio to 10 per cent and this same dollar in reserves can support $10 in deposits.

As an instrument of monetary control changes in required reserve ratios are blunt and inflexible, less flexible than open market operations and discounting. Indeed, it is probably not amiss to say that the bluntest and strongest control measure available to the Reserve authorities is that of manipulating legal reserve ratios. But this is not a tool to use frequently, however, or to use to produce small changes in the money and credit situation. For example, to show the effect of changing the reserve ratio assume banks hold $20 billion in reserves. If the legal reserve ratio were, say, 20 per cent, what would be the effect of lowering the required reserve ratio 1 per cent from 20 per cent to 19 per cent? Neglecting currency and time deposit complications, the system expansion potential would increase, as we have previously seen, from 5 to about 5.26. On the reserve base of $20 billions this represents a potential increase in demand deposits of 0.26 of $20 billion, or about $5.2 billions. This is equivalent to an open market purchase of about $1.04 billion with the reserve ratio held at 20 per cent. Of course, the lowering of the reserve ratio and thereby the making available of excess reserves by no means assures an expansion in deposits, but at the very least it provides the basis for potential deposit expansion.

On the other hand, if the $20 billion in reserves were all required reserves (no excess reserves) then an increase in the reserve ratio by 1 per cent from 20 per cent to 21 per cent forces a contraction in deposits unless additional reserves are made available by the Federal Reserve. With an increase in the reserve ratio from 20 per cent to 21 per cent the expansion potential, again neglecting currency and time deposit complications, falls, as we saw earlier, from 5 to about 4.76. This means the $20 billion reserve base can support 0.24 times $20 billion less than before, or about $4.8 billion less demand deposits. That is, the demand deposits shrink from $100 billion to roughly $95 billion if the $20 billion reserves are all required reserves. The increase in reserve ratio of 1 per cent is equivalent to an open market sale of about $1 billion with the reserve ratio left at 20 per cent.

Unless the banks are permitted to obtain additional reserves by borrowing from Reserve Banks or by an open market purchase operation, the increase in reserve requirements will force a contraction in deposits.  Thus, the restraining effects of an increase in the reserve ratio are determined, in part, by the terms on which member banks are permitted to obtain additional reserves from the Federal Reserve. An increase in required reserves will be more effective if accompanied by an increase in the discount rate and a reduction in the Reserve System's buying price for government securities.

### Perspective on Reserve Requirements Policy

For member banks of the Federal Reserve System, reserves are computed at the end of the day, while reserve requirements are assessed at the beginning of the day.   Given this procedure, a bank that finds itself short of reserves has an entire day in which to make the necessary adjustments.   But, as a matter of fact, a member bank does not have to meet its reserve requirements on a daily basis.   The Federal Reserve, although computing reserve requirements and actual reserves of each member bank daily, allows reserve city banks to average their reserve position over a one-week period, and country banks may average out over a two-week period.

This means that a bank may have a substantial deficit in its reserve position for a few days, so long as this deficit is made up for by a period of excess reserves.   Even if a bank occasionally fails to maintain its average reserve at the required level, the bank is charged only a penalty for its deficiency, which is 2 percentage points over the discount rate for the period it is deficient.   No bank wants to be forced to pay such a penalty, but the possibility of running a temporary reserve deficiency does a great deal to offset the pressure that a large and unexpected loss of reserves might otherwise put on a bank.

The changes in reserve requirements over the last few years seem to indicate certain attitudes about reserve requirements on the part of the Board of Governors.   The Board of Governors apparently feels, first of all, that the level of reserve requirements that prevailed during the late 1940s is too high for 1960 situations.   Behind this feeling is the notion that bank earnings are a function of the level of reserve requirements.   The Board of Governors apparently agrees with the position of many bankers that, unless bank earnings are at some satisfactory level, banks will not be able to obtain the necessary capital funds to provide for sound banking growth.   As a corollary, reserve requirements of member banks are considerably higher than the requirements of nonmember banks.   The Board thus fears that the level of member bank reserve requirements may well be a serious deterrent to membership in the System.   Since membership is purely voluntary, except for national banks, the Board must consider the effects of its actions upon the relative attractiveness of membership as opposed to nonmembership.

The following testimony by George W. Mitchell, a member of the Board of Governors of the Federal Reserve System to the House Committee on Banking and Currency on March 4, 1964, is pertinent to this point with respect to membership and reserve requirements. Governor Mitchell stated:

The main reason that more banks do not belong to the Federal Reserve System is that it is more profitable to stay out.  The non members usually benefit from having lower reserve requirements, or none at all . . . Among the member banks there are many that would become non members if the advantages of membership were to become slightly less . . . I believe it would be unwise to make membership in the System any more costly from a competitive standpoint than it is now.[1]

A second change in attitude concerning reserve requirements on the part of the Board of Governors is a reflection of the desire to make requirements more uniform among banks.  Many authorities argue that the differences between reserve classifications, which are an inheritance of the National Banking System, are both illogical and inequitable.  The differences in reserve requirements for different reserve classifications are, as we have seen, becoming less than they were previously, but there is still the distinction between reserve city banks and the so-called country banks.

As we have seen, the principal advantage of a change in reserve requirements as a policy weapon rests in the magnitude of the effects that can be brought about by a rather small change in reserve requirements.  For example, when faced by a serious inflationary situation an increase in the legal reserve requirement may well be the only practical way of reducing reserves.  Contrarywise, in a recession situation a reduction in reserve requirements will tend to encourage the banking system to expand its loans and investment portfolio.

This characteristic of changes in reserve requirements, which makes the use of this policy instrument desirable in certain but infrequent situations, also makes it unsuitable for the day-to-day control of the monetary system.  Although it is possible that changes in reserve requirements might be made in smaller steps than the usual one-half of one percentage point or one percentage point that is customary, it is quite clear that reserve requirements are not as conducive to fine

---

[1] *Federal Reserve Bulletin*, March, 1964, p. 311.

adjustments as are the other policy weapons.   It is possible, though, that the reserve requirement might be varied by a 32nd of a percentage point or a 16th of a percentage point, and that this would give added flexibility and reduce the bluntness of the use of this instrument.

However, adjustments to changes in reserve requirements are difficult, and this difficulty would be present whether the adjustments were in full percentage points or in small fractions of a percentage point.   The adjustment process is more difficult for small banks, and if changes become more frequent the effects would likely be more disruptive to bank management.   Because of this rather blunt impact it is likely that the power to alter reserve requirements will be an infrequently used but powerful means of control by the Federal Reserve.

As indicated earlier, there are several inequities in the structure of reserve requirements needing correction.   Chief among these is the fact that there is no real justification for some commercial banks avoiding the imposition of higher reserve requirements by remaining outside the System.   One way of correcting this situation, of course, is to make System membership compulsory for all commercial banks, not just national banks, as is now the case.   This suggestion, although having much to recommend it, is not likely to be implemented.   Another suggestion, this one with the backing of the Federal Reserve itself, is to make all banks, member and nonmember banks alike, subject to the same reserve requirements.   This would go a long ways toward eliminating the inequity of the present system.   It would also allow the Board of Governors to determine reserve requirements on the basis of the financial situation of the nation without having to be concerned about the possible effects of a reserve requirement change on the attractiveness of membership in the Federal Reserve System.   This is the point made by Governor Mitchell in his comments to the House Banking and Currency Committee on March 4, 1964.

We have also discussed the inequity involved in having member banks in different cities subject to different reserve requirements. As we have observed, progress has been made toward reducing this inequity.   It is very likely that further progress will be made in the future.   And it is quite conceivable that eventually a uniform set of reserve requirements will be imposed on all member banks.   This view is buttressed by the fact that all member banks may now count their vault cash as part of their required reserves.   This change in the computing of reserve requirements has eliminated a great amount of inequity which was previously present between country and city banks. The inequity arose because country banks had to hold larger amounts of currency on hand in view of their difficulty of getting cash when they needed it; they are often long distances away from their Reserve

Bank or from a large correspondent bank.  As a consequence it was considered unfair to require a country bank to maintain the same reserves as a city bank.  The country bank might very likely have had to hold vault cash over and above required reserves equal to perhaps as much as 5 per cent of its deposits.  Now, this 4 or 5 per cent of vault cash held to meet customer demands also counts as legal reserves.  Given this situation, it seems reasonable to subject the country banks to the same reserve requirements as reserve city banks.

## SELECTIVE OR QUALITATIVE CONTROLS

The foregoing tools of monetary control are often referred to as *quantitative* controls.  They operate primarily through influencing the cost, volume, and availability of bank reserves.  They lead to the regulation of the supply of credit.  They cannot be used effectively to regulate the use of credit in particular areas or sectors of the credit market.  In contrast to these "impartial" quantitative controls, the Federal Reserve authorities at various times have had authority to regulate the terms on which credit is granted in specific sectors.  These latter powers are called *qualitative* or *selective* controls.  Qualitative controls typically seek to regulate the *demand* for credit for specific uses by two principal means: (1) determining minimum down payments, and (2) regulating the period of time over which the loan is to be repaid.  Quantitative instruments, on the other hand, seek to influence the *supply* of credit.

The stock market margin requirement in use at present is a product of the stock market crash of 1929.  Previous to the crash large amounts of borrowed funds were being used in stock market transactions.  Lacking specific means for curbing credit used here without also curbing other uses of bank credit, Reserve officials hesitated to restrict credit until too late.  This selective control of margin requirements was granted to the Board of Governors in the Securities and Exchange Act of 1934.

Other selective controls have been available at times in the past.  One of these was the regulation of consumer credit during the Second World War and the early postwar years.  This regulated the terms on which credit was granted to consumers for the purchase of autos, refrigerators, radios, and other consumer durables.  By increasing the down payment and shortening the payment period the controls denied credit to many persons who purchase by looking only at the size of the monthly payments and the down payment rather than at the total cost.  In this fashion, credit may be denied even though the banking system may have ample reserves to extend it.

The other selective control concerned the regulation of real estate credit. In specifying loan periods, maximum loan values (minimum down payment), etc., it was similar in general to consumer credit regulation. The consumer credit control, regulation W, expired in 1949 and was renewed in 1950. Regulation X, real estate credit, was imposed in 1950. Both regulations expired in 1952.

Thus, the only selective control currently in use, as noted previously, is the margin requirement for regulating the flow of credit into the stock market. There is, however, debate among the students of monetary affairs as to the wisdom of this state of affairs. There is a rather considerable sentiment in favor of permanent controls over consumer credit.

The qualitative methods of monetary policy affect the demand for credit. Indeed, qualitative or selective controls are so called because they regulate the terms on which credit for *specific* selected users is to be had. Thus, selective controls affect the *demand* for credit, and intrude into each lender-borrower operation by regulating the terms under which the transaction may occur.

This kind of direct regulation of private transactions is contrary to our long standing free-enterprise tradition. For this reason qualitative controls are unpopular with many persons. Indeed, with the exception of the stock-market margin requirement, Congress and the Federal Reserve have consistently refused to consider selective controls except during periods of national emergency. Quantitative methods of monetary policy, due both to greater use and lower costs of administration and to their impersonal operation, are preferable to selective controls. Nevertheless, we are about to argue for the extension of one area of qualitative control, namely consumer installment credit. This is because quantitative methods are not capable of performing all the jobs of monetary restraint they are so often called upon to service. There are areas of credit expansion, and consumer installment credit is one, which are not sufficiently responsive to pressure from the existing quantitative instruments.

The reason that areas such as consumer installment lending are immune from pressure exerted by quantitative instruments is that these quantitative methods are themselves quite selective in their impact. Consider, for example, a period of inflation being resisted by the Federal Reserve using quantitative measures. In these circumstances, when bankers ration credit they ration it according to a ranking of loan priorities that they have well in mind. The lending is distributed according to old established customer relations and credit worthiness. In allocating their limited funds among the various competing loan types, commercial bankers will naturally be influenced by the relative profitability of the various types of loans. Thus, ordinarily the last kind of loan expansion to be slowed down by pressure on bank reserves is consumer installment lending, since it is roughly twice as profitable on the average as the other kinds of lending they do.[2] In this situation, even after reserve pressure has stopped over-all expansion of the *total* loans, consumer installment loans may keep on rising.

This kind of credit extension—consumer installment credit—tends to be inflationary even though the total money supply is not increasing in the aggregate. This is so because installment loans get spent, and this tends to increase the velocity of circulation. Therefore, because monetary policy instruments are essential to the control of inflationary pressure, and because the quantitative instruments are hardly adequate to cope with the problem, it is necessary to introduce some new techniques of monetary control, namely, standby controls over consumer installment lending. This qualitative control is necessary because in practice the quantitative controls are themselves selective, making consumer installment lending unresponsive to the usual quantitative restraints. And the problem becomes further aggravated by the increases generated in money velocity.

## SUMMARY AND EVALUATION OF MONETARY POLICY MEANS

The principal tools of monetary control are open market operations, discounting, and control over reserve requirements. Supplementing these major quantitative instruments is one qualitative control, the stock-market margin requirement. The quantitative controls influence the supply side of the credit market, affecting the volume, cost, and availability of credit. Qualitative controls affect the demand for credit.

When the Federal Reserve authorities settle on the use of one or several of the general quantitative tools, their purpose is to influence, either directly or indirectly, the volume of member bank reserves, in particular the amount of excess reserves available for a further expansion of deposits. An important feature of the various monetary instruments is the nature of their direct and indirect effects. Open market operations affect directly both the volume of member bank

---

[2] Since installment loans are repaid monthly, the borrower, on the average, has the use of only one half of the amount borrowed. Thus, $500 borrowed at 6 per cent for one year means the $30 interest charge is actually 12 per cent of the $250 average balance available for use.

reserves and deposits, with open market purchases increasing them and sales decreasing them. This direct effect on member bank deposits is unique to this particular instrument. The amount of excess reserves is modified by changes in the total volume of member bank reserves. A further consequence of open market purchases and sales is the tendency to raise or depress government security prices. In contrast, the discount rate does not directly affect either the total amount of reserves or the amount of excess reserves. Changes in the discount rate merely lower or raise the price of obtaining reserves from Reserve Banks through borrowing. Changes in reserve requirements alter the amount of required reserves, but do not directly affect the total volume of member bank reserves. Control over reserve requirements also affects all member banks of the class to which it is applied.

The indirect effects of the various instruments must also be taken into account in determining the certainty and degree of impact on the member banks. Open market operations may have rather significant indirect effects. By affecting the pattern of interest rates, open market operations may influence the investment policies of institutions other than commercial banks. Similarly, changes in the discount rate or reserve requirements can have indirect side effects. For instance, raising the discount rate may be interpreted as a signal of tighter credit to come, and banks may raise their interest rates and screen loan applications more carefully. The nature and extent of such side effects depend to a large extent on the general business conditions and the market psychology at the time. Changes in reserve requirements may also indirectly influence interest rates by changing the excess reserve position of member banks. An increase in reserve requirements, for example, may force some member banks to borrow or to sell securities to obtain reserves to meet the new requirements. Security prices tend to fall and the effective yield rises.

The excess reserve position of the member banks is changed by both open market operations and by changes in reserve requirements. With either of these tools, the degree of restraint obtained is dependent on how easy and expensive it is to obtain additional reserves. If the banks can acquire fresh reserves at low cost, either by discounting or by selling securities, the restrictive effects of these instruments are seriously reduced.

A second important feature of the various monetary control instruments is the extent to which their impact can be directed into certain channels. For example, it is next to impossible to say how the effects of open market operations are going to be distributed among the banks. The initial impact is mostly in New York, simply because the open market transactions are made there.   But which banks gain or lose reserves is not a decision of the banks themselves, but depends on the extent of the participation of nonbank investors who are buying or selling the securities the Federal Reserve is offering or buying.   The impact of open market operations is, therefore, determined by the market forces prevailing.   Similarly, the impact of changing the discount rate, by changing the cost of borrowed reserves, affects only those member banks needing additional reserves.   Changes in reserve requirements hit all banks in the affected classification.   The impact of reserve requirement changes is felt by all the member banks to which it applies, though not necessarily distributed according to the degree of effect needed.   Banks with excess reserves will not feel the effects of an increase in requirements as much as banks without excess reserves.

Flexibility of the various monetary controls is a third important consideration.   The point at issue here is whether they can be applied so that the effects will be appropriate, mild or drastic, as the situation warrants.   On this count open market operations and discount rate changes have the edge over changes in reserve requirements.   Open market operations are flexible in that the volume of purchases or sales can be made in any amount according to the needs of a given situation. And even in pursuing some given type of action the open market instrument is so adaptable that occasional reversals of operation may be taken to offset temporary fluctuations in factors affecting reserves, such as a change in float due to a severe storm disrupting ordinary transportation patterns, unexpected demand for currency by the public, etc.   The limitations to the use of this open market instrument lie in the System's holdings of securities, which seem more than adequate for any foreseeable selling operation, and on the System's ability to create credit with which to purchase securities.   This is limited by the requirement to hold a 25 per cent gold certificate reserve in back of the Federal Reserve's note and deposit liabilities.   This may become a more serious problem in the future should the present gold drain continue.

Changes in the discount rate are flexible in that they can be small and frequent, and can impinge on only those banks needing additional reserves.   Changes in reserve requirements are less flexible.   This is an awkward tool to use if changes are made in full percentages, since relatively large amounts of reserve funds are involved.   It is more flexible on this score if changes are made in fractions of 1 per cent, since the impact of reserves can be better gauged to the needs of a particular situation.   It is blunt, however, in that any given change affects all banks in the particular class, and may cause some banks considerably more adjustment difficulties than others in the same classification. Frequent changes in reserve requirements are ruled out because of the difficulties in adjustment.

Qualitative or selective instruments similarly have both advantages and disadvantages. Qualitative controls influence the demand for credit rather than its supply, and their impact is on a particular segment of the credit market. On the other hand, selective controls are distasteful to many persons because they intrude upon the setting of the terms of a contract between two private parties. They also tend to be discriminatory, since restrictions are placed on some uses of credit and not on other uses. At the present time, as we have seen, only one selective control is in use, the regulation of margin requirements in the stock market. Nevertheless, there is some support for control over consumer credit as a supplement to the quantitative instruments now in use.

### Evaluation of Monetary Policy

As a general proposition it may be said that monetary policy is more effective in contracting the economy than in getting it to expand. In other words, monetary policy is more effective in choking off boom conditions than in generating recovery from recession conditions. If commercial bank reserves are under pressure from open market selling operations coupled with a high discount rate, and if business spending is largely financed by the extension of bank credit, then further contractive action by the Federal Reserve will cut deeply into the expenditure circuit and slow down or stop the expansion of the economy.

On the other hand, in a period of slack business activity central bank actions to stimulate the economy are likely to have little effect. If interest rates are already low and the banking system is in possession of excess reserves—this situation certainly describes the 1930s, for instance—then monetary policy is powerless with respect to expanding or contracting the economy.

If, however, the economic climate is relatively buoyant with interest rates high and credit reasonably tight, then monetary policy is sufficiently powerful to contract or expand the economy from its previous level. Thus, it appears that monetary policy is at its best in curbing expansive situations, and has only rather limited efficacy as a stimulative device.

Open market policy, discount rate policy, and reserve requirement policy are the three principal instruments of monetary control used to regulate the total supply of money and bank credit toward the achievement of the basic objectives of a high level of employment, rapid economic growth, stability of prices, and stability in the balance of payments. These instruments all affect the supply of money and credit. The open market instrument is powerful and effective, and is administratively flexible; open market operations are the primary instrument of monetary control. Discount rate policy is a weaker instrument of control; the initiative lies in the hands of the borrowing bank, and it affects only those banks that have need to borrow reserves. Reserve requirements policy is an extremely powerful instrument of control, but as typically used in steps of a half or full percentage point it is too cumbersome for frequent use.

Although monetary policy appears to be of limited effectiveness in promoting the high level of employment and high growth rate objectives, it does seem admirably suited to situations requiring the restraint of inflationary pressures or requiring high, short-term interest rates to lessen the flow of capital and these reduce a payments deficit.

If United States balance of payments deficits are likeliest to appear during periods of rising incomes and increasing prices, then clearly tight money policies are appropriate for both the internal and external situations. If the payments deficit occurs during recession an easy money, low interest-rate policy is called for domestically, while high rates are desirable to reduce capital outflows. In this latter situation, net selling of short-term securities by the Federal Reserve in the open market would drive up the short-term rate, thus tending to attract short-term funds and minimize capital outflows. At the same time, the Federal Reserve could make net purchases of intermediate and long-term securities in order to lower or prevent a rise in the long-term interest rate, thus stimulating investment expenditures domestically and helping to overcome the recession. Monetary policy thus seems to be a powerful instrument for helping to achieve balance of payments stability.

Monetary policy has certain advantages despite its limited area of applicability. Perhaps the chief of these is its flexibility. Given the reliance on open market operations as the principal instrument of control, decisions relative to monetary policy can be quickly made and put into operation, and the decisions can be quickly reversed if mistakes are made or if the economic conditions change.

The economic goals of a high level of employment and a high rate of economic growth can be best approached through the use of fiscal policy. These two objectives are mutually reinforcing—rapid growth requires a high level of employment and full employment encourages the introduction of labor-saving capital goods. Fiscal policy contributes directly to both employment and growth by increasing total expenditures to maintain aggregate output and, hence, employment, and by also channeling expenditures in ways to stimulate growth—research and education, for example—as well as by altering spending decisions through tax changes.

But after saying that fiscal policy is most appropriate for achieving the employment and growth objectives, this does not mean that monetary policy has no role to play. The appropriate climate of monetary ease should accompany the expansionist fiscal policy. For example, a low interest-rate, easy money policy will tend to stimulate investment spending, which is necessary for achieving both the high level employment and rapid growth objectives.

There does arise the potential conflict between an easy money, low interest-rate policy to stimulate investment, growth, and employment, and the curbing of inflationary pressures, which may thereby be generated. Perhaps the most appropriate economic policy for resolving the potential conflict between the objectives of employment and growth, and relative price stability may be a policy of using fiscal restraint and monetary ease.

In the next chapter we shall examine the nature of fiscal policy and debt management policy.

## REVIEW QUESTIONS

1. Under what type of monetary conditions is discount policy likely to be of significant aid as a monetary control device? What type of accompanying action by the Federal Reserve authorities is necessary to make discount policy effective?
2. What prevents member banks from borrowing from the Federal Reserve on a permanent basis?
3. Consult the current *Federal Reserve Bulletin* to determine the present legal reserve requirements. Why is the authority to vary reserve ratios characterized as a blunt instrument of monetary control? Does it necessarily have to be blunt?
4. In what fashion may it be argued that the present quantitative instruments are, in fact, selective in their impact?
5. Develop the arguments for and against granting the Federal Reserve permanent standby controls over consumer installment credit.
6. What is the appropriate type of monetary action to pursue when a lapse from full employment occurs?
7. What role can monetary policy play in promoting high level employment and rapid economic growth?
8. Why is monetary policy generally considered more effective in curbing inflationary pressure than stimulating recovery from recession?

## SUGGESTED REFERENCES

Coleman, George W., "Legal Reserve Requirements," in *The Federal Reserve System*, Herbert V. Prochnow, ed. (New York: Harper and Row, 1960).

Commission on Money and Credit, *Money and Credit, Their Influence on Jobs, Prices, and Growth* (Englewood Cliffs: Prentice-Hall, 1961).

Ellis, Howard S., "Limitations of Monetary Policy," in *United States Monetary Policy* (The American Assembly, Columbia University, 1958).

Federal Reserve Bank of Philadelphia, *Monetary Policy-Decision Making, Tools, and Objectives*, 1961.

Federal Reserve Bank of Philadelphia, *The Quest for Stability*, 1954.

Grove, David L., "Selective Credit Controls," in *The Federal Reserve System*, Herbert V. Prochnow, ed. (New York: Harper and Row, 1960).

Hart, Albert G., "Making Monetary Policy More Effective," in *United States Monetary Policy* (The American Assembly, Columbia University, 1958).

McKinley, George W., Jr., "The Discount Rate and Rediscount Policy," in *The Federal Reserve System*, Herbert V. Prochnow, ed. (New York: Harper and Row, 1960).

Meek, Paul, "Open Market Operations," Federal Reserve Bank of New York, 1963.

Smithies, Arthur, "Uses of Selective Credit Controls," in *United States Monetary Policy* (The American Assembly, Columbia University, 1958).

Young, Ralph A., "Tools and Processes of Monetary Policy," in *United States Monetary Policy* (The American Assembly, Columbia University, 1958).

Youngdahl, C. Richard, "Open Market Operations," in *The Federal Reserve System*, Herbert V. Prochnow, ed. (New York: Harper and Row, 1960).

CHAPTER *25*

# *Fiscal Policy and Debt Management Procedures*

Fiscal policy is concerned with the receipts and expenditures by government. We may define fiscal policy as the deliberate manipulation of government receipts and expenditures in the pursuit of some economic objective or set of objectives. This kind of fiscal policy is often called *functional finance,*[1] in that it calls for deliberate changes in the flow of tax revenues and expenditure programs to offset or compensate for shortages or excesses in the private sectors of the economy. Whether or not one believes in fiscal policy, given the large size of the government sector relative to all transactions in the economy, the government must have a fiscal policy.

Since the government sector's receipts and spending are certain to affect the economy, most economists will argue that the government must see to it that its revenue absorbing and disbursing operations do not contribute to instability, but lead instead to the achievement and maintenance of a high level of employment, growth, and price stability. This kind of government finance, functional finance, signifies government willingness to incur budgetary deficits in recession periods and budgetary surpluses in boom periods to provide stabilizing offsets to deficits or surpluses in the private sectors.

The instruments of functional finance are the combinations of changes in tax revenues and government expenditure patterns. To combat unemployment, for instance, four opposing courses to inade-

---

[1] A term developed by Professor Abba P. Lerner, *The Economics of Control* (New York, Macmillan Co., 1944).

quate private spending are possible: (1) a reduction in tax revenues with government expenditures unchanged; (2) a policy of leaving taxes unchanged, while concurrently increasing government expenditures; (3) a policy of concurrently reducing taxes and increasing government expenditures; and (4) a policy of increasing both tax revenues and government expenditures. To combat inflationary pressures, the reverse of these four programs are in order.

Increased levels of government expenditures raise national income both directly and indirectly. The increase in spending itself draws forth an initial rise in production and employment, and then, through a multiplier process, sets off additional expenditures on production. Taxes also produce changes in expenditure streams. For example, an increase in taxes removes purchasing power from the hands of the public, keeping people from spending what has been taxed away. Government borrowing *per se* leads to tighter credit through reducing loanable funds otherwise available; but then the expenditure of these borrowed funds by the government can easily eliminate this tightening effect.

Thus, it is important to treat each fiscal act separately in order to see its effects. By themselves, borrowing and taxing have deflationary effects on the economy by removing purchasing power or potential purchasing power. Government expenditures, on the other hand, are inherently expansive in effect.

Functional finance has a great deal of appeal, but there are inherent difficulties in the method. The greatest difficulty is the gearing of spending and tax changes to compensate for changes in private spending; that is, to make fiscal instruments flexible enough for prompt and effective use. There are lags and delays in changing tax programs and expenditure programs. Once started, programs often cannot be stopped, even though the situation which prompted their inauguration has passed. Then, too, there is the difficulty in forecasting, which compounds the problem of timing. Fortunately, our fiscal machinery has considerable "built-in flexibility" which operates automatically to counteract fluctuations in economic activity.

Built-in fiscal stabilizers may be defined as those Federal receipts and expenditures that, in response to an economic contraction, operate in the direction of increasing the Federal deficit, or decreasing the surplus, *without the need for policy decision or action.* The major built-in stabilizers are individual and corporation income taxes, excise taxes, employment taxes, and unemployment compensation benefit payments.

The built-in fiscal stabilizers help to support the economy in recession.   Mainly they reduce the rate at which an initial decrease in aggregate demand tends to have a magnified or "multiplier" effect on the economy by inducing further declines in expenditures for personal consumption.   For example, because a drop in income reduces tax liability, after-tax incomes—and private expenditures based on after-tax incomes—fall by less than if there were no decline in tax liability. Similarly, the rise in unemployment compensation in recession helps cushion the decline in consumption by keeping the drop in disposable personal incomes less than the drop in incomes earned in current production.   In addition to these effects on consumption, the built-in stabilizers also cushion potential declines in private investment.   This is done to the extent that inventory or fixed investment is influenced by private consumption expenditures which, as a result of the stabilizers, are higher than otherwise.

Thus, the built-in fiscal stabilizers are those factors that automatically cause government expenditures to rise and tax receipts to fall as income falls, and to do the reverse as income rises.   The tax system closely relates revenues to changes in income.   Declines in national income not only reduce tax receipts, but also induce a reverse effect through an increase in unemployment benefits.   The effect of these automatic or built-in stabilizers is to decrease disposable income during upswings and rising income, and to reduce the fall in disposable income during periods of economic decline.

## THE EFFECTS OF FISCAL POLICY

Fiscal policy as we have defined it includes the acquisition of revenues by the government, as well as government expenditures.   Since this is the case, to discuss the operation of fiscal policy for the achievement of the several policy objectives it is necessary for us to examine the consequences of government expenditures, tax collecting, and borrowing operations.   In this section we shall take up first the effect of expenditures, then the effect of taxes, and finally the act of government borrowing *and* spending.   In the latter case we shall see that the fiscal actions of borrowing and spending by the government may very likely have associated monetary consequences.   We shall find our theoretical constructs of the money and goods equilibrium schedules of rather considerable assistance in determining the consequences of various policy proposals.

## Government Expenditures

The analysis of the income effects of government expenditures is a simple procedure to outline.    Recall our earlier derivation of the goods equilibrium schedule (GES).

Starting in Chart A of Figure 25-1, interest rate $r_1$ and the marginal efficiency of capital schedule determine investment level $I_1$.    In Chart B, the equilibrium chart, investment $I_1$ is equated to savings $S_1$. This equilibrium level of saving $S_1$ is transferred to Chart C to determine the equilibrium level of income $Y_1$.    In Chart D, income $Y_1$ and the associated rate of interest $r_1$ are plotted.    A similar procedure is followed for the second interest rate, $r_2$, and in this fashion the GES is generated.

Government expenditures, $G$, are introduced into the picture by adding them to the MEC schedule; this is the MEC $+$ $G$ schedule

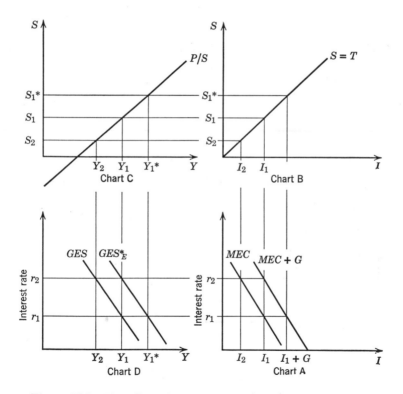

*Figure 25-1*    The effect of government expenditures on the GES.

and the repetition of the foregoing procedure now yields $GES_E{}^*$—the schedule has shifted to the right due to the addition of government expenditures.   At every rate of interest, the equilibrium income in the goods market is higher with the addition of government expenditure.

Thus, the basic rule is that an increase in government expenditures shifts the GES to the right (increases it).   Conversely, a decrease in government expenditures shifts the GES to the left (decreases or lowers it.)

### Government Taxes

In a similar fashion it is a simple matter to illustrate the effects of taxes on the goods equilibrium schedule.   This is shown in Figure 25-2. Taxes enter into the analysis through their effect on consumption, and hence, through their impact on the saving function.   Since taxes shift the consumption function down, they shift the saving plus taxes

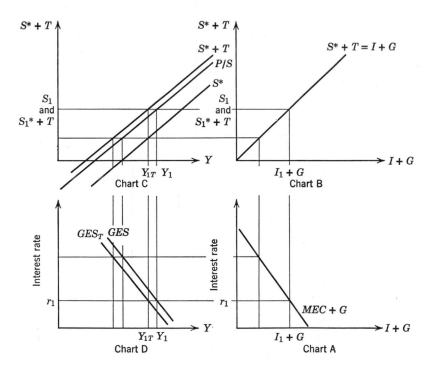

**Figure 25-2**   The effect of introduction of taxes on the GES.

function up and to the left.    Thus Charts A and B are identical with
their counterparts in Figure 25-1.    But Chart C shows the shifted
propensity to save through the imposition of increased taxes.    Tracing
the effects of interest rates $r_1$ and $r_2$ we generate the two goods equilibrium schedules GES and $GES_T$.    The point to be noted here is the
shift to the left, that is, the fall in the goods equilibrium schedule due
to the imposition of taxes into the model.

Therefore, the basic rule is that an increase in taxes shifts the GES
to the left (lowers it).    Conversely, a reduction in taxes shifts the
GES to the right (increases it).

## Government Borrowing and Spending

Taxes are not the only source of revenues to finance government
expenditures.    Governments also borrow funds to finance expenditures
in excess of current tax revenues.    Indeed, our national debt today
exceeds $300 billion because at times in the past the government
decided it was economically infeasible or politically inexpedient to
cover expenditures by tax collections.    Borrowing was resorted to,
and the debt has grown to its present size.

The government has three areas from which it can borrow.    It can
borrow from the public, from the commercial banks, or from the
Federal Reserve.    It can, of course, and typically does, borrow from
several of these sources of funds in any given borrowing operation.
Borrowing by itself tends to be deflationary, since it removes actual or
potential purchasing power from the public.

But when the Treasury spends its borrowed funds the contractive
effects are removed.    Not only removed, but in two instances completely replaced by increases in the money supply.    Thus, when the
Treasury borrows from the public and then spends with the public, no
new money is created.    However, if the funds are borrowed from the
banks or central bank new money equal to the expenditure is lodged
in the public's hands.    Furthermore, if the central bank provides the
borrowed funds, not only is new money created but the banking system
also comes into the possession of additional reserves, which makes for
a potential further expansion in the money supply.    Thus the money
equilibrium schedule, as well as the goods equilibrium schedule, can be
affected by government finance and expenditures.

To review, when the Treasury borrows from the public the public
exchanges part of its demand deposits for Treasury bonds.    The
Treasury increases its liabilities outstanding (bonds), and when it
arranges to switch the proceeds of the borrowing operation into its

deposit balance at the Federal Reserve the commercial banks lose part of their reserve balances.

The effect of the Treasury borrowing operation has been to reduce the public's money supply and commercial bank reserves. The Treasury has a deposit balance at the Federal Reserve which it can spend. When the Treasury does spend this deposit balance, the contractive effects of the borrowing are removed. The effect of government expenditures is basically expansive in nature. The consequences of the Treasury borrowing from the public and spending the proceeds may be summarized in T-accounts as follows, where the borrowing effects are indicated by "1" and the expenditure effects by "2."

Commercial Banks

| Assets | | Liabilities | |
|---|---|---|---|
| 1 Reserve balance at Federal Reserve | — | 1 Demand deposits, Public | — |
| 2 Reserve balance at Federal Reserve | + | 2 Demand deposits, Public | + |

Treasury

| Assets | | Liabilities | |
|---|---|---|---|
| 1 Deposit balance at Federal Reserve | + | 1 Bonds | + |
| 2 Deposit balance at Federal Reserve | — | | |

Federal Reserve

| Assets | Liabilities | |
|---|---|---|
| | 1 Member bank reserve balances | — |
| | 1 Treasury deposit | + |
| | 2 Member bank reserve balances | + |
| | 2 Treasury deposit | — |

Government expenditures financed by borrowing from the public produce no change in the money supply or bank reserves. The increased holdings of government bonds by the public may tend to increase the velocity of circulation, however, through the public's increased stock of liquid assets. Thus, even though the money supply $M$ may not have increased, the effective money supply $MV$ may be increased through this borrowing-expenditure operation.[2]

When the Treasury borrows from the commercial banks or the Federal Reserve and then spends the sums obtained, the money supply of the public increases.   The reserve position of the commercial banks is unchanged when the banks lend to the Treasury, but when the Federal Reserve lends to the Treasury commercial bank reserves are increased. In this latter case, there is the potential for further monetary expansion.   These resulted are summarized in the T-accounts below.

The effect of government expenditures financed by Treasury bank borrowing is presented here.   As before, the initial borrowing effects are labeled "1" and the second-step expenditure effects are numbered "2."

### Commercial Banks

| Assets | | Liabilities | |
| --- | --- | --- | --- |
| 1 Bonds | + | | |
| 1 Reserve balance at | | | |
| Federal Reserve | − | | |
| 2 Reserve balance at | | 2 Demand deposits, Public | + |
| Federal Reserve | + | | |

### Treasury

| Assets | | Liabilities | |
| --- | --- | --- | --- |
| 1 Deposit balance at | | 1 Bonds | + |
| Federal Reserve | + | | |
| 2 Deposit balance at | | | |
| Federal Reserve | − | | |

### Federal Reserve

| Assets | | Liabilities | |
| --- | --- | --- | --- |
| | | 1 Member bank reserve | |
| | | balances | − |
| | | 1 Treasury deposit | + |
| | | 2 Member bank reserve | |
| | | balances | + |
| | | 2 Treasury deposit | − |

---

[2] There is also the question of the spending propensities of the lenders and the recipients of the government expenditures.   If, as is likely, the recipients of the expenditures have higher propensities to spend than the lenders, then velocity increases and so the effective money supply has increased.   Thus, the question of the distribution of ownership of the money supply is also important.

In this government expenditure operation financed by Treasury borrowing from the commercial bank system, the net effect has been to increase the public's money supply leaving bank reserves unchanged. Since commercial bank reserves are unchanged, the banks could have purchased the Treasury securities only if they had excess reserves to begin with. But if they did initially have excess reserves, then they could have increased the money supply directly without buying Treasury bonds by the simple process of expanding their loans and deposits, that is, by monetizing private debt instead of public debt.

The sale of Treasury bonds directly to the Federal Reserve and spending the proceeds results in increasing the public's money supply and also increasing commercial bank reserves. The net effects are summarized in the following T-accounts for the various sectors where, as before, the initial borrowing stage is labeled "1" and the subsequent expenditure is called "2."

Commercial Banks

| Assets | | Liabilities | |
|---|---|---|---|
| 2 Reserve balance at Federal Reserve | + | 2 Demand deposits, Public | + |

Treasury

| Assets | | Liabilities | |
|---|---|---|---|
| 1 Deposit balance at Federal Reserve | + | 1 Bonds | + |
| 2 Deposit balance at Federal Reserve | − | | |

Federal Reserve

| Assets | | Liabilities | |
|---|---|---|---|
| 1 Bonds | + | 1 Treasury deposit | + |
| | | 2 Treasury deposit | − |
| | | 2 Member bank reserve balances | + |

It is evident that this last borrowing-expenditure transaction leads to not only an increased money supply, but also to an increase in bank reserves. The banking system now possesses excess reserves, which may be used for further expansion of the money supply. By comparing the effects of these three sets of deficit financed transactions, it is apparent that it makes a rather considerable difference who finances the deficit.

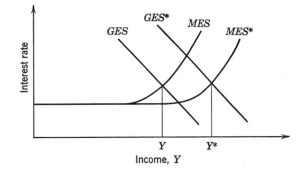

*Figure 25-3*   The income effect of bank financed government spending.

Although we have indicated that the above processes occur in two steps, as a matter of practice the stages are closely coordinated.   In this fashion, the impact on bank reserves is minimized.   The funds are switched to the Treasury's account at the Federal Reserve out of Tax and Loan Accounts at commercial banks only as needed.   Thus, when the Treasury borrows from the public or commercial banks, the commercial banks' reserve positions are insulated from pressure.

The additional money created when expenditures are financed by funds borrowed from either the commercial bank system or the central bank affects the MES by shifting it to the right.   This is shown in Figure 25-3.   Not only do the government expenditures shift the GES to the right, but being financed by the banking system or by the central bank the MES shifts to the right as well, to MES*, with the new equilibrium income occurring at a higher level, $Y^*$.

We now have the necessary tools for an adequate assessment of various policy proposals.   As we have seen, taxes and expenditures, as such, affect the GES, shifting it out or back depending on the policy. Additionally, when financed by borrowing expenditures may have an impact on the MES, thus shifting it.   We can now analyze the four programs to combat unemployment or a lowered growth rate mentioned earlier: (1) lower taxes, leaving government spending unchanged; (2) leave taxes alone, increasing expenditures; (3) reduce taxes and increase expenditures; (4) increase both taxes and spending.

### Case I: Lower Taxes, Unchanged Government Spending

In this situation, with lower taxes and with government spending maintained, borrowing must be resorted to to cover the expenditures.

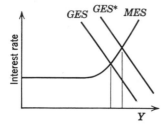

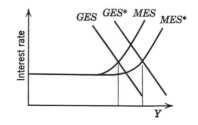

**Figure 25-4a** Deficit financed by the public (reduced taxes, constant expenditures).

**Figure 25-4b** Deficit financed by banks (reduced taxes, constant expenditures).

The reduced taxes serve to stimulate consumption, hence the GES increases to GES\*. If the funds are borrowed from the public the MES may not be affected (Figure 25-4a); if the funds are borrowed from the banking system the MES increases to MES\* (Figure 25-4b) with a higher level of income than when public borrowing was employed.

### Case II: Taxes Unchanged, Spending Increased

This situation is similar to Case I. There is again a deficit incurred to cover the increased expenditures with taxes unchanged. This shifts the GES to the right to GES\* as before; however, the increase is more than before since the tax cut shifted the GES horizontally only by the marginal propensity to consume times the tax change. Here the shift is the full dollar of increased expenditure. As before, borrowing from the public may not affect the MES, whereas borrowing from the banks does. These results are shown in Figure 25-5.

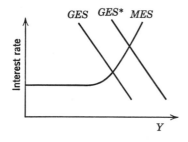

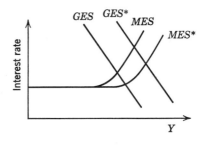

**Figure 25-5a** Deficit financed by public (taxes constant, expenditures increased).

**Figure 25-5b** Deficit financed by banks (taxes constant, expenditures increased).

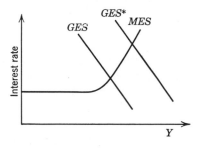

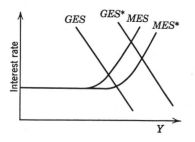

**Figure 25-6a** Deficit financed by public (taxes reduced, expenditures increased).

**Figure 25-6b** Deficit financed by banks (taxes reduced, expenditures increased).

## Case III: Reduce Taxes, Increased Expenditures

This policy will produce the largest deficit, and hence the greatest impact on the MES if covered by borrowing from the banks. At the same time, the two fiscal operations reinforce each other and shift the GES to the right more than either one singly will do. This policy of reduced taxes and increased government expenditures is therefore the most stimulative proposal to spur a lagging economy. The effects are shown in Figure 25-6.

## Case IV: Increased Expenditures Offset by Increased Taxes

This approach produces no deficit, and thus no effect on the MES. The effect on the GES, however, is modest. This is due to increased taxes lowering the GES and the increased expenditures shifting it back out. The net effect is to shift the GES to the right by the marginal propensity to save times expenditures (or taxes). Figure 25-7 shows the modest change from any given level of changed expenditures and taxes.

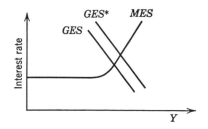

**Figure 25-7**   Balanced budget with increased expenditures and taxes.

### Fighting Inflationary Pressures

Although the foregoing analyses were for the stimulation of growth and employment, quite clearly they can be reversed should this be desirable. Any policy which serves to shift the GES and MES to the right (to increase them) if reversed will shift them down and be appropriate for combating inflationary pressures.

Instead of running a deficit, the generation of a budgetary surplus is the appropriate policy. This can be done by raising taxes, lowering expenditures or both. Given the possibility of a budgetary surplus, what is done with it to retire debt becomes of great significance. For, depending on which debt is retired—that held by the public, the commercial banks, or the Federal Reserve—different monetary effects are generated.

### THE PROBLEM OF DEBT MANAGEMENT[3]

Debt management policy is more closely akin to monetary policy than to fiscal policy, although fiscal operations gave the debt its being. Whereas the purposes of monetary policy and fiscal policy are to promote and maintain employment, growth, balance of payments stability, and price stability, the primary purpose of debt management is to maintain the credit of the government by successfully maintaining the debt. Any contracyclical policy advantage of debt management is secondary in importance. The primary problem is to maintain the debt.

Even when the size of the Federal debt is not growing, borrowings are quite large. When issues of securities mature they must be paid, either from surplus tax revenues or by borrowing through the issue of new securities. Since the average maturity of the debt in recent years has grown steadily shorter, given the size of the debt, refundings— that is, sales of new issues to retire maturing issues—of necessity have grown larger. If these refundings can be accomplished without interfering with the objectives of monetary and fiscal policy, a rather considerable operation in its own right will have taken place.

### Routine Debt Management

If the debt can be brought into a situation where a given maturity distribution can be maintained this will simplify debt management

---

[3] This section draws heavily on the recent work by Tilford Gaines, *Techniques of Treasury Debt Management* (New York: Free Press of Glencoe, 1962).

operations.   This would allow for refunding operations on a predictable schedule, and would remove a considerable element of uncertainty from the money market.

This uncertainty exists because of an uneven maturity distribution requiring occasional huge refunding operations, and also because the Treasury permits holders of maturing issues a choice of debt instruments to replace the matured issues in the refunding operations.   This choice leaves the maturity distribution in investors hands rather than in the Treasury's hands where it properly belongs.   Given the frequency and size of the Treasury financing operations, the money market is kept off balance a good share of the time.[4]

The Treasury's natural proclivity is to finance at short-term, to minimize the interest cost burden of carrying the debt.   This tends to shorten the maturity distribution of the debt.   A positive contracylical debt management policy would call for lengthening the debt during boom periods and shortening it during recession.   The idea here is that long-term instruments sold during booms soak up liquidity. Indeed, one can even argue for selling long-term instruments to the public and using the proceeds to retire Federal Reserve held debt. This would be quite contractive in that it destroys an equal amount of money and bank reserves, with a further money contraction if the banks are loaned up in this boom period.   In T-accounts:

Public

| Assets | | Liabilities |
|---|---|---|
| (1) Government bonds | + | |
| Demand deposit at | | |
| Commercial Bank | − | |

Commercial Banks

| Assets | | Liabilities | |
|---|---|---|---|
| (2) Reserve balance at | | Demand deposits, Public | − |
| Federal Reserve | − | | |

Treasury

| Assets | | Liabilities | |
|---|---|---|---|
| (3) Balance at Federal Reserve | + | Bonds to Public | + |
| (4) Balance at Federal Reserve | − | Bonds to Federal Reserve | − |

[4] *Ibid.*, p. 265.

Entries 1 through 3 simply show the exchange of assets by the public through swapping demand deposits for bonds (1).   The Treasury deposits the checks drawn on commercial banks to the Federal Reserve and receives credit (3), and the commercial banks lose reserves and deposits (2).   When the Treasury uses the proceeds to retire Federal Reserve held debt (4), the effect is "permanently" to retire money and bank reserves as well.

Whereas the foregoing shows how extending the maturity of the debt during the boom (and with contractive effects) can be accomplished, the sale of long-term debt places the Treasury in competition with other demanders of long-term funds precisely at the time interest rates are highest.   Thus, for two reasons, the Treasury does not typically take the long-term course in boom periods: (1) it would be committed to high interest costs for a lengthy period; and (2), it is fearful that it might choke off the boom by crowding out other private demanders of long-term funds.

During recession periods one would ask the Treasury to issue short-term securities—near monies—in order to increase the liquidity of the economy and stimulate spending, hence promoting recovery.   But this is just the time the Treasury can sell long-term securities on favorable interest terms.   Thus the Treasury has a built-in predisposition to finance at low rates, and this moves perversely or contrary to a positive program of contracyclical debt management.

But as our T-account clearly showed, debt management maneuverings are essentially like monetary policy.   That is, the debt management maneuver in the example had the same effect on the money supply and bank reserves as a Federal Reserve open market sale to the public.

Thus it is that the first efforts toward improving debt management procedures should be directed to putting the maturity structure on a systematic basis.   One authority suggests 30 to 35 per cent of the debt maturing within one year, 45 to 50 per cent within one to ten years, and 15 to 20 per cent beyond ten years.   He recognizes that this appears to constitute the abandonment of debt management as an instrument of economic policy.[5]   He argues that a more ambitious objective is not technically feasible at present.

But if a manageable maturity distribution is obtained where refundings are predictable, then more sophisticated management techniques could be employed.   Thus, as the example showed, debt management policies could be employed to reinforce monetary policies to obtain the goals of economic policy.

---

[5] *Ibid.*, p. 274.

## Monetary Aspects

A budgetary surplus can be used to retire debt, and, as might be expected, it has various monetary consequences.   It will be recalled that Treasury borrowing and spending operations have various monetary consequences, as have debt retirement operations, depending on which debt is retired—that belonging to the public, the banks, or the Federal Reserve.   Assume that a tax surplus is available to be applied to debt reduction.   What results if the funds are applied to public held debt?

### Public

| Assets | | Liabilities | |
|---|---|---|---|
| Demand deposit at Commercial Bank | − | | |
| Demand deposit at Commercial Bank | + | | |
| Bonds | − | | |

### Commercial Banks

| Assets | | Liabilities | |
|---|---|---|---|
| Reserve balance at Federal Reserve | − | Demand deposit, Public | − |
| Reserve balance at Federal Reserve | + | Demand deposit, Public | + |

### Treasury

| Assets | | Liabilities | |
|---|---|---|---|
| Surplus balance at Federal Reserve | + | | |
| Balance at Federal Reserve | − | Bonds, Public | − |

### Federal Reserve

| Assets | | Liabilities | |
|---|---|---|---|
| | | Reserve balance at Commercial Bank | − |
| | | Treasury balance | + |
| | | Treasury balance | − |
| | | Reserve balance of Commercial Bank | + |

The items above the dotted line show the transfer of money from the public to the Treasury—the surplus is nothing more nor less than taxes paid to the government in excess of those taxes disbursed to the public. The entries below the dotted line show the effects of "spending" the surplus to retire debt held by the public. The money supply and bank reserves are restored. This is the opposite of borrowing from the public and spending the proceeds. The operation is monetarily neutral except for possible redistribution effects.

As might be expected, since borrowing from the banks and spending the proceeds creates money and uses reserves, retiring debt held by banks does the reverse—initially, at least, it destroys money and creates reserves. Again the items above the dotted line show the transfer of funds from the taxpaying public to the Treasury.

### Public

| Assets | | Liabilities | |
|---|---|---|---|
| Demand deposit at Commercial Bank | − | | |

### Commercial Banks

| Assets | | Liabilities | |
|---|---|---|---|
| Reserve balance at Federal Reserve | − | Demand deposit, Public | − |
| Bonds | − | | |
| Reserve balance at Federal Reserve | + | | |

### Treasury

| Assets | | Liabilities | |
|---|---|---|---|
| Surplus balance at Federal Reserve | + | | |
| Balance at Federal Reserve | − | Bonds, Commercial Bank | − |

### Federal Reserve

| Assets | | Liabilities | |
|---|---|---|---|
| | | Reserve balance of Commercial Bank | − |
| | | Treasury balance | + |
| | | Treasury balance | − |
| | | Reserve balance of Commercial Bank | + |

The entries below the dotted line show the impact on bank reserves, and the reduced demand deposits of the public. This gives the banks excess reserves; thus it is likely that they will quickly act to expand their loans and deposits.

The final case to be considered is the retirement of central bank held debt. This is quite contractive, as it destroys both money and reserves. Again the entries above the dotted line show the transfer of money from the public to the Treasury's account. Notice the loss of both reserves and deposits of the commercial banks as the surplus is used to retire the Federal Reserve held debt. This is very contractive, especially if the banks are anywhere near loaned up.

|  | Public | |
| --- | --- | --- |
| Assets | | Liabilities |
| Demand deposit at Commercial Bank | − | |

|  | Commercial Banks | |
| --- | --- | --- |
| Assets | | Liabilities |
| Reserve balance at Federal Reserve | − | Demand deposit, Public — |

|  | Treasury | |
| --- | --- | --- |
| Assets | | Liabilities |
| Surplus balance at Federal Reserve | + | |
| Balance at Federal Reserve | − | Bonds, Federal Reserve — |

|  | Federal Reserve | |
| --- | --- | --- |
| Assets | | Liabilities |
| | | Reserve balance of Commercial Bank — |
| | | Treasury balance + |
| Bonds | − | Treasury balance — |

Thus debt retirement operations have monetary effects ranging from essentially neutral to extremely contractive, unless offset by the central bank. Clearly the Treasury does have some monetary power. The effects on the money equilibrium schedule of debt retirement will be either to leave it unchanged, in the case of public held debt, or to

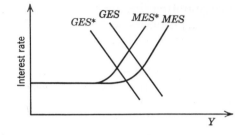

*Figure 25-8* Contractive debt retirement.

shift it to the left, when central bank held debt is retired. Furthermore, if the surplus is achieved by raising taxes leaving government
expenditures unchanged this shifts back the GES. Similar shifts in
the GES occur if expenditures are reduced with taxes unchanged, or if
taxes are raised and expenditures reduced. Thus, the general effect
of debt retirement can be illustrated as in Figure 25-8, showing shifts
to the left in both the MES and GES. The MES is unchanged or
shifted back as MES*; the GES must shift back to GES*.

### Summary on Debt Management Policy

The debt management problem as we know it began about 1951.
Until 1951, the Federal Reserve had been committed to supporting and
stabilizing the government bond market. This was because the
Treasury wanted easy money conditions to facilitate low interest cost
debt management policies. In the late 1940s the Federal Reserve
became restive about its support of the government securities market,
and in March, 1951, the Treasury-Federal Reserve Accord was
reached.

Subsequent to the Accord the Treasury was, by and large, content to
finance on a short-term basis to avoid high interest costs, though some
long-term bonds were placed during the recession years of 1953–1954.
Generally, financing was done short term and the average maturity of
the debt steadily shortened.

In recent years, starting late in the Eisenhower administration, more
imagination and willingness to experiment with debt management
procedures have been evidenced. The auctioning of long-term bonds
is an example. For years, only Treasury bills had been auctioned,
that is, sold at a discount to the highest bidder. Recently, the tech-

nique has been successfully applied to long-term bonds in modest amounts, obtaining the best possible price for the Treasury, that is, the lowest long-term interest cost consistent with money market conditions.

Another technique used successfully is *advanced refunding*. This is the offering of a new bond for one which will mature in, say, another two years. In this fashion the Treasury can keep more debt in permanent investment portfolios than otherwise. By stretching out the debt maturity it also helps minimize churning around in the money market and eliminates some of the all too frequent trips of the Treasury to the money market.

Through these and other techniques the maturity distribution of the debt can be stabilized.[6] After the maturity distribution is brought under control, then perhaps a positive contracyclical debt management program can be implemented. This would be a debt management program that would marginally lengthen the debt in boom periods and marginally shorten it in recession periods. As we have seen, debt management policy has the effect of open market operations. Thus the rule for debt management is this: debt management policy, for maximum effectiveness, should always be coordinated with monetary policy.

## SUMMARY: FISCAL POLICY AND DEBT MANAGEMENT OPERATIONS

The instruments of fiscal policy are controls over government expenditures and revenues. The revenues include funds raised both by taxation and also by borrowing. These expenditures and revenues by the government affect both the goods equilibrium schedule, the GES, and the money equilibrium schedule, the MES.

It is apparent that the government spending will affect the GES, since government expenditures are one of the sources of income. Thus increases in government expenditures, other things given, will shift the GES to the right, that is, will increase it. Conversely a decline in government spending will, other things equal, cause the GES to fall, to shift back to the left.

Similarly, taxes also affect the GES by virtue of affecting the consumption function and hence, also the saving function. An increase in taxes serves to reduce consumption spending, and thus to increase the saving function. This rise in the saving propensity serves to shift the

---

[6] *Ibid.*, pp. 260–299.

GES to the left.   A fall in taxes operates in reverse fashion, raising the consumption function and lowering the propensity to save, thus shifting the GES to the right.

Quite clearly, government expenditures and tax receipts have an effect upon the GES.   Increases in government spending and reductions in taxes each increase the GES.   Conversely, reduced spending and increased taxes each serve to shift the GES to the left.   It is possible to arrive at various combinations of government expenditure and tax policies to reinforce or partially offset one another, in order to shift the GES in the desired fashion.

Unfortunately, fiscal policy is not the most flexible of instruments. It takes time to gear up an expenditure program or for Congress to change tax legislation.   Added to this is another difficulty, the difficulty of accurately forecasting the desired magnitude of change, let alone its timing.   Fortunately, the American economy has certain built-in automatic fiscal stabilizers.   These automatic fiscal stabilizers can help to temper changes in economic activity, but discretionary fiscal policy measures will be necessary to offset fully the changes in business activity.

If government expenditures are covered by borrowing, not only is the GES affected but also the MES may be shifted.   Thus, should the spending operation be financed by borrowing from the commercial banks or central bank the MES would be increased to the right. Additionally, if the funds were borrowed from the central bank the commercial banks would come into the possession of excess reserves, with the potential for further increase of the MES.   Thus, increased expenditures, coupled with reduced taxes and borrowing from the central bank, provide a triple-barreled stimulus to a lagging level of income by shifting both the GES and MES to the right.

For the foreseeable future, government expenditures will be massive. This, together with Congressional reluctance to impose higher taxes, means deficits over time—an increasing level to the national debt. But this prospect of an ever-increasing debt is not altogether a bleak one.   After all, a growing economy needs a growing money supply; and a growth in the money supply requires a growth in debt, both private and public.   This increase in total debt need not be inflationary.   In fact, unless the rate of increase of total debt outstrips the rate of growth the effect can be neutral or deflationary.   Given the significance of government expenditures in the over-all economy, it is reasonable to expect the growth in public debt over time to help finance the growing economy.   Otherwise, to finance the expanding economy, a stable public debt will require a considerably more rapid increase in private debt than the rate of growth of output.

Thus, for the long run it appears that as the government maneuvers its fiscal policies to promote the economic objectives of employment, growth and price stability, the consequences will be a long-run deficit bias.

Debt management is at present the weakest element of the monetary policy-fiscal policy-debt management policy triad. The most crucial problem of debt management is to maintain the debt in existence to preserve the integrity of the government's credit. The first order of business in a debt management program is to stabilize the maturity structure of the debt, to halt the shrinking of its term structure. If this can be accomplished, then a positive contracyclical debt management program of marginal lengthening of the debt in boom periods and a marginal shortening of it during recession could be undertaken. Since contracyclical debt management operations are essentially open market operations engaged in by the Treasury, instead of by the Federal Reserve, the primary rule for a positive debt management program is to coordinate it with the monetary policy operations of the central bank.

## REVIEW QUESTIONS

1. What is meant by the term "automatic" or "built-in" fiscal stabilizers?
2. What is functional finance? How is it supposed to work? What are the practical difficulties in this approach?
3. Why is fiscal policy more effective in promoting high levels of employment and a high rate of economic growth than monetary policy?
4. Government spending financed by borrowing has different monetary consequences depending on the source of the borrowed funds. Trace these different monetary consequences.
5. Outline possible fiscal measures which might be appropriate for curbing inflationary pressures.
6. If less than full employment and slow economic growth are problems, what are appropriate fiscal measures? Discuss.
7. Debt management policy has one overriding consideration: what is this consideration?
8. Why may debt management policy be likened to monetary policy? What is the basic rule for debt management policy?
9. Why is it difficult in many instances to speak of monetary policy or fiscal policy separately? Does the descriptive term "monetary-fiscal policy" make sense?
10. What is the monetary significance of an expanding debt?

## SUGGESTED REFERENCES

Gaines, Tilford C., *Techniques of Treasury Debt Management* (New York: The Free Press of Glencoe, 1962).

Smith, Warren L., *Debt Management in the United States* (Study Paper No. 19, Joint Economic Committee) (Washington, D.C.: Government Printing Office, 1960).

Also consult the references given at the end of Chapters 16 and 18.

CHAPTER *26*

# *The Prospects for Monetary Policy*

In this final chapter the time has come to survey the prospects for monetary policy. The generally accepted goals of economic policy are full employment, growth, price stability, and the continued convertibility of the dollar in international finance. That these are the objectives of monetary policy can be seen from the statement by the Chairman of the Board of Governors to the Joint Economic Committee regarding the goals of monetary policy:[1]

1. Bringing about a maximum rate of sustained economic growth . . .
2. Keeping down unemployment.
3. Maintaining the value of the dollar. Reasonable stability of the general price level is important . . .
4. Developing and maintaining balance in international payments.

These are the objectives of monetary policy, but can they be reached simultaneously with the same set of policies? There is indeed serious question as to their compatibility. Excluded from consideration here is fiscal policy. Fiscal policy will be the chief instrument for the promotion of employment and growth, with price level stability and balance of payments problems primarily engaging monetary policy's attention. This is not to suggest, however, that the proper monetary climate should not pertain to the problems concerning employment and growth.

---

[1] Joint Economic Committee, *Employment, Growth and Price Levels*, Hearings, 86th Congress 1st Session, Part 10, 1960, pp. 3383–84.

## MONETARY POLICY AND EMPLOYMENT

The contribution of monetary policy toward the achievement of a high level of employment lies in its ability to increase aggregate spending. If monetary policy can influence total spending then it is possible to affect the level of employment.

Monetary policy works principally through the supply side, though some influence on the demand side is possible.   Principally, however, the impact of the changes in monetary policy falls on lenders who become more or less willing to lend as the cost and availability of credit changes.   It will be recalled that lending requires that three conditions be met: (1) commercial banks must possess excess reserves; (2) the banks must be willing to lend; and (3) someone must be willing to borrow.   As credit conditions tighten, lenders are less eager or less able to lend, and, even though willing borrowers may be present, credit is choked off through unwillingness or inability to lend.

Conversely, if lenders are willing and able to lend, but borrowers do not wish to incur new indebtedness, no extension of credit can take place.   Thus, even though credit may loosen, its cost decline and availability increase, borrowing will not increase unless borrowers believe it profitable to borrow.

Monetary policy, however, can be expected to be marginally useful even in circumstances with the most adverse expectations.   There will usually be some marginal borrowers willing to borrow if they can gain access to credit.   A general easing of the cost and availability of credit will cause these borrowers to borrow, with a favorable effect on employment, since borrowing is undertaken only with a view to spending. The borrowers likeliest to be affected in any decline in economic activity are the intermediate and long-term ones.   They are the borrowers most sensitive to small shifts in the interest rate, and if monetary policy in the preceding boom was restrictive they most likely had been frozen out of the market by the higher cost of credit.

The principal contribution monetary policy can make to full employment, however, lies in its use to prevent inflationary excesses from occurring in periods of rising economic activity.   Here, as elsewhere, an ounce of prevention is worth a pound of cure.   Such preventive monetary restraint can stretch out the period of prosperity, and, through preventing inflation by moderating aggregate expenditure, can temper and moderate any subsequent economic decline.

Monetary policy can thus contribute to the maintenance of continuous full employment by influencing the aggregate volume of spending.

It operates through curbing monetary excesses on the upswing, and tempers and moderates reductions in spending on the downswing.

## MONETARY POLICY AND ECONOMIC GROWTH

The area of economic growth, of secular or long-run expansion, is another area where fiscal policy will play the predominant role. But here, too, as in the case for high-level employment, monetary policy can and should make positive and useful contributions.

Economic growth requires investment. But monetary policy is, by its nature, unable to help promote growth through direct encouragement of investment. What monetary policy can do, however, is to help achieve and maintain the economic conditions most favorable for economic growth; namely, full employment and stable—or slightly rising—prices. Another thing monetary policy can do is to assure an increase in the money supply over time to accommodate the rise in GNP due to growth. But this may be no easy job, making sure that the money supply increases appropriately. Too little increase and growth is stifled; too large an increase and rising prices negate the goal of relatively stable prices. That there will be an expansion in the money supply, however, seems assured, since the likeliest long-run fiscal policy is one of secular deficit. The problem is thus one of properly monetizing the growing volume of debt, public and private.

## MONETARY POLICY AND PRICE STABILITY

### The Question of Price Stability

The promotion and maintenance of relative price stability is monetary policy's area of maximum effectiveness. Monetary policy thus has as its principal assigned task the preservation of price stability. Even here there is some question of whether monetary policy can do the job of preserving and maintaining price stability without, at the same time, endangering the goals of full employment and growth. Indeed, there is even the question as to monetary policy's ability to maintain price stability at all.

The last question has gained prominence in recent years (1955–1957 and 1958–1960) as prices drifted upward in the face of extremely tight credit conditions. This inability to restrain and control prices is apparently due to monetary policy's inability to influence completely effective purchasing power, or $MV$. Thus, rising prices are ascribed to an increase in the velocity of money, which more than offset restraints imposed on the money supply. In addition to the velocity aspect, there is also a school of thought which holds that price increases result from *cost-push* causes and are not controllable by monetary measures. Let us examine these arguments.

The basis of the *cost-push* theory of inflation is that organized groups, both business and labor, establish higher prices for their products or services than would prevail in impersonal competitive markets. The process is sometimes referred to as *administered price* inflation, since the sellers are able to administer their prices. Cost-push inflation is most clearly indicated when there occur rises in the prices of goods and services in spite of excess capacity, and when wage rates increase despite unemployment.

This type of inflation cannot take place without an increase in available purchasing power. The increase in prices must be accommodated by an increase in aggregate demand, or else output and employment will fall. An increase in the aggregate demand may be the result of an enlargement in the supply of money, or it may be the result of an increase in the income velocity of money. Thus, when the central bank is restraining the growth of the money supply, as it did over most of the last half of the 1950s, the alternatives under the cost-push inflation theory are either: (1) an increase in velocity must occur; or (2) there will occur a decline in the level of employment and output.

There is still another version of inflation. According to this theory, the theory of *sector inflation*, the rise in prices is attributable to "an initial upward thrust of wages and prices . . . [which] occur in particular sectors of the economy because of substantial and rapid shifts in demand in these sectors, though aggregate demand in the economy is not excessive."[2] The rapid shifts in sector demands generate the price increases. Assuming competitive markets, prices might rise in those areas in which demand has increased and fall in those areas in which demand has declined. But according to the sector inflation theory, the situation does not work that way. Prices do rise in the areas experiencing the increase in demand, but, because of institutional rigidities, prices and costs in those areas suffering from a slackening in demand do not fall, or else they fall less slowly than the other prices rise.

As in the case above, unless aggregate demand increases, unemployment will result. As before, the accommodation may occur either through an enlarged money supply or through an increase in velocity. The consequences of a restrictive monetary policy under this theory

---

[2] U. S. Joint Economic Committee, *Employment, Growth and Price Levels*, Staff Report, 86th Congress, 1st Session, Washington, D.C., 1960, p. 116.

are unemployment and a decline in output, unless velocity increases to offset the monetary restraint.

Thus the question of efficacy of monetary policy for combatting inflation arose. Despite the extreme monetary restraint employed by the Federal Reserve throughout most of the late 1950s, prices rose but output and employment lagged. Apparently this was a "new" kind of inflation, not the classic *demand-pull* variety where, at *full employment*, pressures of increasing aggregate demand raise prices. Regardless of the reasons advanced to explain the inflationary process, the rise in prices had to be accommodated. As we know, this required accommodation can be either an increased money supply, which was not the case, or an increased velocity of circulation. Since the Federal Reserve was employing monetary restraint, increases in velocity did the accommodating. Can this rise in velocity be explained? One possible explanation of this velocity increase is given in the following section.

### Monetary Policy and Financial Intermediaries

The rise in velocity is usually explained by the rapid postwar growth of nonbank financial intermediaries, and the liquid claims upon them, relative to the commercial banks. One investigator has found that the postwar expansion in liquidity has been predominantly in the form of growth in nonmonetary liquid claims against nonbank financial intermediaries. He found that these claims grew about four times faster than demand deposits against commercial banks during this period.[3]

The growth of these nonbank financial intermediaries[4] has created a market for various debt instruments and for the provision of liquid assets, chiefly in the form of time deposits, to depositors. Thus these institutions hold various debt instruments, including government debt. Now short-term government debt is a good substitute for money balances. When the Federal Reserve tightens credit, interest rates rise and security prices fall. This rise in yield induces holders of *idle* demand deposits to switch into short-term government obligations or other short-term assets. Out of any given money stock, idle funds are released for lending and spending. Active balances have grown at the expense of idle balances. The spectacular growth of the nonbank

---

[3] John G. Gurley, *Liquidity and Financial Institutions in the Postwar Period*, Study Paper No. 14, U. S. Joint Economic Committee, Washington, D.C., 1960.

[4] A review of Chapter 13, "Nonbank Financial Institutions," may be in order here.

financial institutions has made this sort of activation of idle funds much easier.

Consequently, critics of monetary policy argue that when monetary policy is seeking to restrain the growth of the money supply, the non-bank financial intermediaries increase money's velocity by raising the proportion of active money and reducing the amount held idle. The financial intermediaries take up idle balances by issuing attractive liquid claims against themselves, and transfer the idle balances to active spenders. Since the aim of the Federal Reserve is to curb spending when interest rates are rising, the increase in velocity has been considered evidence of the ineffectiveness of monetary policy. The increased velocity enables spending to continue, even though growth in the money supply has ceased.

Does the increase in velocity when interest rates rise pose a significant limitation on monetary policy? The first thing to note is that a stepping up of velocity signifies that the credit restriction is working, or people would not be economizing on their money balances. Second, during the period that rising interest rates and increased velocity were observed, the Federal Reserve's open market sales were concentrated in short-term bills, a consequence of the "bills only" doctrine. Thus, short-term rates rose and prices fell. Commercial banks, holding predominantly short-term "governments" were "locked in" to some extent, that is, the capital losses that would have been forthcoming on selling any of these short-term issues precluded the banks from liquidating them in large volumes. Nonbank financial intermediaries holding more long-term assets were not so effectively "locked in," and they continued their switching operation with its impact on velocity. These institutions did this because the impact on short-term rates was slow to spread to the long-term rates.

With the abandonment of "bills only," it now seems that restrictive monetary pressure can be more effectively applied. Open market operations can be carried out in all maturities, and not just in short-term instruments. Thus we may lock these nonbank financial intermediaries into long-term portfolios just as effectively as commercial banks are "locked in." In this fashion velocity increases may be curtailed, and rising prices, whatever the brand of inflation they may represent, may be more effectively curbed. All is not lost for the cause of monetary policy as an approach to price stability.

### Monetary Policy: Rules vs. Authority

There is a long-lived, continuing debate over the administration of monetary policy: should monetary policy be determined by some monetary authority exercising discretionary judgment and power, as the Board of Governors now does, or should monetary policy actions be taken only in accord with some set of predetermined rules?  The latter position is the point of view of the so-called "Chicago" school of monetary reform.

The principal spokesman for the Chicago position is Professor Milton Friedman of the University of Chicago.  Under the rules proposal, the monetary authority could not exercise discretionary judgment.  Rather monetary policy actions would follow from a previously established set of rules.  A major difficulty, of course, is finding a good rule: a rule good enough to be appropriate for all circumstances which might arise.  The rule first proposed by the late Professor Henry Simons of Chicago was the stabilizing of a price index. Proponents of the rules approach today advocate a stable growth in the money supply, arguing that the " . . . supply of money should increase by the *average* rate of growth in demand for nominal money at a stable level of commodity prices. . . . the appropriate annual growth rate would be on the order of 3–4 per cent."[5]

To implement this rule the Federal Reserve could engage in open market operations but could not lend through discounting or vary the reserve requirements.  Indeed, to give the Federal Reserve absolute control over the money supply, reserve requirements would be raised to 100 per cent of demand deposits, eliminating the present fractional reserve requirement.  The open market power would be used only for feeding new money into circulation at the predetermined rate.

The major advantage claimed for this proposal is that it would remove the uncertainty attendant to the exercise of discretionary monetary policy.  The establishment of a definite rule or rules would eliminate much uncertainty and make for more efficient economic calculations.  Along the same lines it is argued that the monetary authorities have made, and will doubtless continue to make, errors in judgment and in timing.  Finally, the concentration of so much power in the hands of any single public body, however well intentioned, is incompatible with economic freedom and *laissez faire*.

It may be argued that this "rules approach" to monetary policy differs from the discretionary approach only in degree, not in kind. For after all, someone must exercise judgment about what the rule is to be, when it should be interferred with, and when it should be abandoned, if need be, and a new rule established.

Under a thoroughgoing rules approach, the money supply would

---

[5] Edward S. Shaw, "Money Supply and Stable Economic Growth," in *United States Monetary Policy* (New York: The American Assembly), 1958, p. 60.

increase at a steady rate regardless of economic conditions. If inflation were a problem the money supply would nevertheless be increased; if unemployment were widespread the money supply would still increase by the predetermined rate, no more or no less. The Federal Reserve would have no discretion whatsoever in the matter. To illustrate:

In a serious economic recession, should not the monetary authorities be required to augment the money supply even *more* than this rule would call for? The answer is "no." . . . If the door is opened even slightly to discretionary monetary management, there is no point at which it can be closed.[6]

The viewpoint expressed by the rules proponents seems to be unduly pessimistic. Mistakes have been made and will be made by the monetary authorities. But we are continually learning more about how money affects the economy. It seems reasonable to believe that money management will improve along with an increase in knowledge. And the record, while not perfect, is good enough to hold out hope for the future. The arguments for abandoning discretionary monetary policy in favor of a rigid formula are a surrender of the intellect because the complexities of the modern economic world seem too great for the human mind to cope with. Nevertheless, monetary policy must be employed using thought, judgment, discretion, and concern for the world as it is.

### INTERNATIONAL MONETARY POLICY AND THE DOLLAR

International monetary pressures have recently affected the United States, but until 1958 the United States conducted its monetary policy without regard for international happenings. Since 1958, because of the sizable losses of gold reserves, the United States, through the Treasury and Federal Reserve, has kept an eye focused on international monetary developments. Indeed, during this period the United States has engaged actively in open market operations in the foreign exchange market to stabilize the dollar, an undertaking unheard of since the 1930s.

As we know, member nations of the IMF have par values for their currencies expressed in terms of gold, the United States dollar, or both. They have also agreed to limit fluctuations in their exchange rate to no more than 1 per cent above or below the established par value. In order to keep their country's exchange rates from rising above the

---

[6] *Ibid.*, p. 62.

1 per cent "ceiling" or falling below the 1 per cent "floor," many foreign governments, since 1945, have maintained both gold and dollar reserves in their exchange stabilization fund. They have done so by buying dollars on the open market with their national currency during upward movements in their exchange rate and selling dollars to buy their own currency during a downward movement in their exchange rate.

Until recently, the role of the United States in such matters has been an extremely important, though passive, one. Since the willingness of foreign treasuries and central banks to hold dollars in their stabilization funds depends on the ready conversion of the dollar into gold, the United States government, as a part of the Bretton Woods agreements, has given repeated assurances that it stands ready to buy or sell gold in unlimited quantities at $35 per ounce to any foreign monetary authority subject to the IMF Agreement. Thus, the United States has defined and has guaranteed to maintain the parity of the dollar in terms of gold, while other nations have maintained the parities of their currencies by buying and selling dollars.

Since the United States accepted the role of banker, so to speak, for the international currency system, it found little cause to deal in the foreign exchange market. For years after the end of the Second World War the United States dollar remained in a strong position. When it did come under pressure from time to time in world exchange markets, foreign central banks fulfilled their obligation to the IMF by taking the surplus dollars off the market, thus preventing the dollar rate from falling below the acceptable floor. Rates for the dollar against foreign currencies and the accumulation of dollar reserves by foreign central banks were therefore left entirely to market forces and to the decisions of foreign monetary authorities.

By 1960, however, successive United States balance of payments deficits had brought about both heavy losses of gold and increased dollar liabilities to foreigners. Increasingly, the dollar became the subject of speculative questioning over whether the United States could and would maintain the $35 per ounce price of gold. These early speculative attacks against the dollar were partially assuaged by a Presidential pledge in early 1961 to maintain the gold price and defend the dollar against speculative attack, even if the United States might eventually be forced into borrowing funds from the IMF in the process.

Meanwhile, confidence in the dollar remained vulnerable to sudden shocks, and these were not long in coming. On March 4, 1961, the German government announced a 5 per cent revaluation in the mark.   Almost immediately thereafter, the Netherlands government announced a similar change in the guilder parity.   These revaluations touched off the greatest wave of speculation against exchange rates since the advent of the IMF.   In the words of one observer: "All major currencies immediately became labeled as candidates for either revaluation or devaluation, and an unparalleled flood of speculative funds swept across the exchange."[7]   The speculation on a revaluation of the Swiss franc, for example, became so intense that over $300 million flowed into Switzerland in four days.

The United States dollar emerged from the first speculative attacks relatively unaffected.   But the massive reshuffling of foreign-owned funds, coupled with a continued flow of funds to West Germany in the anticipation of another revaluation of the mark, had the effect of bidding up the price of foreign currencies, particularly the German mark and the Swiss franc, relative to the dollar.   This had the potential consequence of significant drains upon the United States' gold reserves.   To meet this problem, the United States Treasury decided to enter into foreign exchange operations.   During the next few months the Treasury initiated exchange operations in German marks, Swiss francs, Netherlands guilders, and Italian lire.   Perhaps the most interesting, certainly the most extensive and complex, of these operations were those concerned with the German mark and the Swiss franc.   Our examination, though incomplete, illustrates the basic processes involved, not only in the mark operations, but in the others as well.   Let us therefore turn to an examination of the German mark operations, after which we shall conclude with a brief examination of the Canadian experience, which is also interesting and illustrative of the Treasury's and the Federal Reserve System's new approach toward foreign exchange operations.

### Operations in German Marks

The heavy inflow of dollars into West Germany had disruptive effects upon that nation's trade.   Non-Germans with contractual liabilities in marks hurried to pay off their mark liabilities before they were due, and Germans sought to hedge against contracts payable to them in foreign currencies.   As a result, the premium on the forward mark rose to nearly 4 per cent.   This situation became the subject of conversations between the German Federal Bank, the Federal Reserve

---

[7] Charles A. Coombs, "Treasury and Federal Reserve Foreign Exchange Operations," *Federal Reserve Bulletin*, Vol. 48, No. 9 (September, 1962), p. 1140.

Bank of New York, and the United States Treasury in March, 1961. As a result of these talks, the Treasury decided to undertake forward sales of marks through its agent, the Federal Reserve Bank of New York, in an effort to drive the high, speculative-induced price of the mark down toward more normal levels. Or, viewed the other way, the Treasury sought to raise the price of the dollar relative to the price of the mark. The Treasury was insured against any risk of loss in these operations because the German Federal Bank offered to supply it with marks in any quantity desired, at the rate at which the marks had been sold by the Treasury.

Between March 13 and the end of that month, the Treasury sold over $118 million equivalent of marks, payable in three months, in an effort to keep the speculative premium on the forward mark from rising any higher, or the speculative discount on the dollar from sinking any lower. As a result, market demand for the forward mark began to decline in April, but by the middle of June the Treasury had accumulated $340 million in forward mark commitments. By this time, the market demand for dollars to pay off the forward contracts now maturing brought about the first improvement in the dollar rate since the advent of the speculative crisis.

The improvement in the dollar rate convinced the Treasury that the speculative crisis had been successfully weathered. It therefore allowed the forward premium on the mark to rise again.

As the normal flow of marks from private sources began to reappear, the Treasury was able to discontinue sale of forward marks entirely in September. The last of the Treasury's forward mark commitments were liquidated in early December.

The results of this initial venture into the exchange market was satisfying to the Treasury. According to one official:

By thus offsetting a large-scale flow of speculative funds that proved to be reversible within 9 months, the U. S. Treasury operations in forward marks clearly helped both the United States and Germany. The short-term capital outflow from the United States was held down, and the U. S. payments deficit thereby reduced, while the German Federal Bank could restrain its dollar accumulations from becoming too large and also prevent the German money market from being flooded with a heavy volume of liquid funds.[8]

Indeed, Treasury officials were so encouraged by the German mark operation that they decided to undertake operations in other currencies as well. More or less immediate operations were taken in Swiss francs, Netherlands guilders, and Italian lire.

---

[8] *Ibid.*, p. 1842.

When the mark temporarily weakened late in 1961, the Treasury purchased approximately $55 million equivalent of them. They were employed in several minor financial operations in which the dollar rate, relative to the mark, came under temporary pressure. Generally speaking, however, the exchange rate between the dollar and the mark remained fairly constant until the devaluation of the Canadian dollar in May, 1962, and the widespread United States stock-market decline in late May and early June of 1962 prompted a renewed flow of speculative funds to West Germany and other European financial centers.

In combatting this new threat, the Treasury acquired the aid of a powerful ally—the Federal Reserve System. Officials of the Federal Reserve had observed the Treasury's encouraging operations in German marks and other European currencies and had begun to consider whether the Fed should reactivate foreign exchange operations. After study, the Federal Reserve Open Market Committee authorized the resumption of open market transactions in foreign currencies on February 13, 1962—less than a year after the Treasury had begun its initial operations in German marks.

The way in which the Federal Reserve Bank of New York, acting as the agent for the system as a whole, has subsequently consummated its foreign exchange transaction is through the use of the *swap* mechanism. Swaps are reciprocal credits negotiated between central banks, whereby one bank agrees to exchange its currency for the other's for a limited period, say three or six months.

Swap arrangements were rapidly concluded with the central banks of France, England, the Netherlands, Germany, Switzerland, and the Bank for International Settlements. Thus, the Federal Reserve System had a swap agreement with the German Federal Bank in existence at the time of the renewed flows of funds to Germany in late May and early June of 1962, and was therefore prepared to aid the Treasury in protecting the dollar and the gold stock. Accordingly it drew upon its account established by the swap agreement with the German Federal Bank, and sold sizable quantities of the marks thus obtained in an effort to keep the premium on the mark within prescribed limits. This policy was successful. Upward pressure on the mark began to slowly subside, then ceased entirely when the Berlin crisis of August 1962, prompted a reversal of the previous trend. With the rapid calming of speculative fears, the market quickly returned to normal, and it has since remained quiet to the time of this writing.

Past experience with extremely heavy flows of funds to West Germany indicated to Federal Reserve officials the desirability of increasing the size of its swap facility with the German Federal Bank, and in January 1963, the Federal Reserve increased to $150 million (from $50 million) its swap agreement with the German Federal Bank. The Treasury followed suit shortly after, increasing the scope of its operations with the German Federal Bank by issuing to that organization four medium-term bonds denominated in marks. These bonds, totaling $200 million equivalent in amount and having maturities up to two years, "provided the German Federal Bank with a mark investment medium for some of the excess exchange reserves it had accumulated while Germany had very substantial surpluses in international payments."[9]

This type of bond had been used previously by the Treasury in its dealings with Italy and has since come to be recognized as a constituent part of the Treasury's foreign exchange operations. These bonds provide the foreign nations concerned with a profitable investment media for balance of payments surpluses. Moreover, they need not reflect a foreign country's surplus with the United States, but may, instead, reflect its over-all balance of payments with the world. Furthermore, "Issue of foreign currency certificates by the United States provides this country with an additional source of liquidity which may be particularly useful during periods of U. S. balance of payments deficits."[10]

## Operations in Canadian Dollars: An
## Example of International Cooperation

Between January 1 and June 25, 1962, about $900 million, or 44 per cent of Canada's gold and dollar reserves, was swept away by a mounting balance of payments deficit that threatened to force the Canadian dollar off its newly established parity. If that had happened, it might easily have set off a major speculative crisis against other currencies as well. To prevent it from happening, a combined program of $1,050 million was put together in four days. This included a $300 million Canadian drawing from the IMF, a $250 million swap between the Federal Reserve and the Bank of Canada, a $100 million credit facility from the Bank of England, and a $400 million credit facility from the United States Export-Import Bank.

The announcement by the Canadian government of financial assistance on such a large scale, coupled with its pledge to initiate fiscal

[9] *Federal Reserve Bulletin*, Vol. 49, No. 3 (March, 1963), p. 320.
[10] *Ibid.*, p. 312.

and other measures of restraint, immediately broke the speculative attack upon the Canadian dollar. As the historically heavy flow of American funds to Canada began to resume, the Bank of Canada's dollar reserves began to register heavy gains. After renewing the Federal Reserve swap once on September 26, the Bank of Canada began to liquidate its swap drawing. This was completed in late December, 1962.

The speed and effectiveness of international financial cooperation to defend Canada's new exchange rate was highly pleasing to United States monetary authorities. To quote one official, "The potentialities of central bank and intergovernmental financial cooperation in defending currency parities against essentially reversible flows of speculative funds was demonstrated."[11]

## CONCLUSION

During the past two years, the Treasury and the Federal Reserve System have cooperated in initiating a policy of active intervention in the foreign exchange market, not only to protect the United States dollar parity and gold reserve, but also to promote international financial cooperation in general. Through acquisitions of foreign exchange and interventions in the exchange market, coupled with Treasury issuance of certificates and bonds denominated in foreign currencies, United States monetary authorities have helped to offset and restrain large-scale speculation in the free-world exchange markets. Those who might be tempted to speculate against any major currency are now confronted not only by foreign central banks and the IMF, but by the United States Treasury and Federal Reserve System as well.

Furthermore the Treasury and Federal Reserve have coordinated domestic monetary policy with the international situation. In an effort to keep short-term funds at home, the Treasury and Federal Reserve have allowed the short-term rate to rise. The Federal Reserve has confined its open market purchasing operations to intermediate and long-term issues and has been a net seller of short-term issues. The Treasury has also increased the supply of short-term bills. These actions have resulted in lowering their price and raising the short-term rate.

The Federal Reserve's purchases of intermediate and long-term issues have served to lower these rates and to provide the possible stimulus to domestic growth and employment through the availability of credit and low, long-term rates.

---

[11] Coombs, *op. cit.*, p. 1149.

This kind of coordinated policy speaks well for monetary policy's future in the days ahead. Fiscal policy and debt management have important roles to play. Indeed, in promoting employment and growth, fiscal policy is the key variable. Nevertheless, monetary policy offers important assistance here and is of primary importance in the achievement of price stability and protecting the dollar.

## REVIEW QUESTIONS

1. What role can monetary policy take toward achieving and maintaining the objectives of high-level employment and rapid economic growth?
2. What is monetary policy's role in attempting to achieve price stability? Why has this goal apparently been assigned to monetary policy?
3. Define cost-push inflation, sector inflation, and demand-pull inflation.
4. If inflation is of the cost-push variety, why is it fortunate for income and employment if the velocity can increase in spite of restrictive monetary policy?
5. What is the argument that the growth of nonbank financial intermediaries has weakened the Federal Reserve's anti-inflationary power?
6. How may the abandonment of "bills only" increase the Federal Reserve's ability to influence nonbank financial intermediaries?
7. How have the Treasury and Federal Reserve coordinated debt management and monetary policy to protect the international integrity of the dollar?

## SUGGESTED REFERENCES

Coombs, Charles A., "Treasury and Federal Reserve Foreign Exchange Operations," *Federal Reserve Bulletin*, September, 1962; March, 1963; September, 1963.

Gurley, John S. and Edward S. Shaw, *Money in a Theory of Finance* (Washington, D.C.: Brookings Institution, 1960).

Schultze, Charles L., *Recent Inflation in the United States* (Study Paper No. 1, Joint Economic Committee), Washington, D.C.: Government Printing Office, 1959.

Selden, Richard T., "Cost-Push Versus Demand-Pull Inflation," *Journal of Political Economy*, LXVII (September, 1956), pp. 1–20.